DYNAMICS OF CHINA'S ECONOMY

Studies in Critical Social Sciences Book Series

Haymarket Books is proud to be working with Brill Academic Publishers (www.brill.nl) to republish the *Studies in Critical Social Sciences* book series in paperback editions. This peer-reviewed book series offers insights into our current reality by exploring the content and consequences of power relationships under capitalism, and by considering the spaces of opposition and resistance to these changes that have been defining our new age. Our full catalog of *SCSS* volumes can be viewed at https://www.haymarketbooks.org/series_collections/4-studies-in-critical-social-sciences.

DYNAMICS OF CHINA'S ECONOMY

Growth, Cycles and Crises from 1949 to the Present Day

ZHIMING LONG
RÉMY HERRERA

Haymarket Books
Chicago, IL

First published in 2022 by Brill Academic Publishers, The Netherlands
© 2022 Koninklijke Brill NV, Leiden, The Netherlands

Published in paperback in 2023 by
Haymarket Books
P.O. Box 180165
Chicago, IL 60618
773-583-7884
www.haymarketbooks.org

ISBN: 979-8-88890-019-2

Distributed to the trade in the US through Consortium Book Sales and
Distribution (www.cbsd.com) and internationally through Ingram Publisher
Services International (www.ingramcontent.com).

This book was published with the generous support of Lannan Foundation,
Wallace Action Fund, and the Marguerite Casey Foundation.

Special discounts are available for bulk purchases by organizations and
institutions. Please call 773-583-7884 or email info@haymarketbooks.org for more
information.

Cover design by Jamie Kerry and Ragina Johnson.

Printed in the United States.

Library of Congress Cataloging-in-Publication data is available.

Contents

PART 2
Empirical Analyses of the Dynamics of China's Economy: From the Criticism of Neoclassical Mainstream (or Assimilated Currents) to the Marxist Perspective

Appendices

Illustrations

Tables

Graphs

Chart

Box

Introduction

In this book, the fruit of several years of joint work, the authors pursue – not a single, but – a double objective. They provide, on the one hand, an in-depth analysis of the dynamics of the Chinese economy from 1949 to the present day, centered on the domestic productive sphere, and, on the other hand, a practicable pathway, applied to this country, guiding those who seek to find the energy and the courage to tear themselves away from the crushing weight of the mainstream or hegemonic current in economics – namely, the neoclassical "orthodoxy" – or its satellites presented as "heterodox." The reader will therefore be invited to explore the subject at hand, using some of the instruments that the Marxist approach has at his or her disposal. Among these, the study of the role of the rate of profit will offer us, as we will see, a possibility of broadening the issues of growth to those of cycles, much more illuminating, and even of "crises," in terminological circumstances that we will have to delimit.

Throughout the reasoning, the arguments will be conducted by mobilizing various methodologies, essentially statistical and econometric, which are always located as close as possible to what is called the "technological frontier" of the discipline, that is to say the latest techniques, tools, and innovations. As a matter of fact, our opinion is that so-called "formalized" language is not the exclusive monopoly of the economic mainstream and that it cannot in any way constitute its reserved domain – particularly since, in the framework of neoclassical analysis, its grip on socio-economic reality is dangerously slackening as discourse becomes more technical and models become more sophisticated. However, it is elsewhere, in either previous or parallel publications, that the reader will find the foundations and demonstrations of the attacks that we direct against neoclassical macrodynamic theories,[1] as well as the properly mathematical examination upstream of some of the empirical apparatus we choose to use here – especially in the field of statistical and econometric analysis, as we have already said.[2] It should therefore be borne in mind that we consider these theoretical presuppositions (including their conceptual or

---

1 For a technical and radical critique of neoclassical theories in macrodynamics, see: Herrera (2000, 2010b, 2011). A mathematical proof of the compatibility between Solowian model and endogenous growth model is provided by Herrera (1998a). For a more accessible approach to these questions, readable by a wider audience: Herrera (2006a, 2010a). Read also, especially on monetary and financial macrodynamics: Long (2013a, 2013b, 2017).

2 For example, concerning spurious estimators derived from linear trend addition detrending methods in stationary differential processes, see: Long and Herrera (2020c).

mathematical components and extensions) as the inseparable background of the reflections that we deliver here.[3]

This book consists of two main parts. Essentially statistical in nature, the first Part comprises four chapters, which are respectively devoted to detailed presentations of the methods for constructing long-term time series of physical capital, of so-called "human" capital, of research-and-development (R&D), as well as of Gini income inequality indicator. The first two databases relating to capital stocks were by far the most difficult to elaborate, but they had to be developed with the required rigor, insofar as they will serve as a foundation and cement to all the empirical studies that will follow – as diverse as they may be. Indeed, to date there are no official Chinese statistical data relating to physical capital stocks. This lack very concretely hinders the quantitative analyses dedicated to the economic growth of this country. Several well-known works certainly provide data on physical capital stocks, but, as we will see, most of them suffer very serious shortcomings.

The purpose of Chapter 1 is therefore to construct series of various stocks of physical capital for China which are as reliable and as long as possible. The values of the initial capital stocks that we build are calculated on the basis of capital-output coefficients that are less approximate than those generally put forward in the literature. Likewise, the investment flows that we use remain exactly consistent with the statistical perimeters of these initial stocks. Furthermore, the price indices that we apply to investments are recalculated in order to strictly adapt to the contents of the stocks, and the unit root tests carried out show that all the series of these indices are non-stationary and integrated of order 2 – which means that they cannot be substituted for each other, as many authors do. Added to this, our physical capital stock depreciation rates are estimated by type of capital goods, with a compatibility between age-efficiency and retirement assumptions, and the respective shares of investment flows used to approximate an overall capital structure and thereby achieve a total depreciation rate. In this way, we provide the research community – and not just econometricians – with several original and quality series allowing new empirical studies to be performed over a long period (precisely between 1952 and 2014) or, possibly, to improve the old ones.

In Chapter 2, starting from the clear contrast between the accelerated pace of China's economic growth and the moderation of the demographic evolution in this country, we move the center of gravity of our analyzes in order to stress

---

3   In general, the curious reader can visit the site: remyherrera.com. He or she will also find a "China" dossier.

the importance of the qualification of population. So a survey of the literature about Chinese "human capital" is first presented to highlight its advances and limitations. It is once the latter have been identified that our own methodology is proposed for constructing two distinct stocks of human capital, one of total human capital and the other of productive human capital. We detail the methods for determining the depreciation rates of these stocks; then their increment processes; and finally how the values of stocks are defined for different reference years. In many aspects more solid and complete than other currently existing bases, our series of Chinese "human capital," built from 1949 to 2014, are finally made available to scientific researchers – and to all readers – to equip them with new indicators, this time representative of China's educational resource levels.

In continuation, Chapter 3 presents a method chosen to elaborate time series related to R&D expenditure, logically expressed in flows. The study of economic growth indeed requires that special attention be paid to R&D, in particular to understand the acceleration in factor productivity that has been observed there in recent decades, but also the gradual upgrade move of Chinese productions and the growing proportion of high value-added goods in the country's exports. We will see that, although it is only relatively recently (around the mid-1980s) that China has incorporated international regulatory mechanisms for accounting for R&D activities, these have been very powerfully driven by the public authorities, and very soon after the formation of the People's Republic in 1949.

In Chapter 4, we propose this time a Gini income inequality indicator covering the whole country, that is to say which includes both urban and rural areas, in order to have an additional instrument of analyze and find one's bearings in debates on social inequalities in contemporary China. Nevertheless, the extent and timeliness of this question are such that we will have to come back to it two chapters later, to show in particular that Thomas Piketty's conception of these social inequalities in the Chinese case, centered on transmission of inheritance, is far too narrow, since the problem is actually multidimensional, and much more complex.

The second Part of the book brings together four chapters of empirical studies which will use, in quite distinct – and in fact opposed on purpose – axiomatic and methodological frameworks, the statistical series whose construction we have explained in detail previously. Under these conditions, this common base will help to ensure the consolidation and the consistency of our overall demonstration; a set that we will gradually advance from the critique of neoclassical orthodoxy – and some of its dependencies, including

Thomas Piketty's contribution, which is very "Keyneso-neoclassical" in fact – until entering the Marxist perspective. By the same token, the methodologies to which we will have recourse will be deployed successively in conceptual and theoretical frameworks which are resolutely and deliberately antagonistic, finally leading us to adherence to the Marxist project.

We first propose, in Chapter 5, an exercise of econometric estimates carried out on the basis of these original series of physical capital stocks, of human capital stocks and of R&D expenditure, to which we also add a qualitative (or dummy) variable capturing the political-institutional changes characterizing Chinese society since 1949; all this in an attempt to explain the growth of China's gross domestic product (GDP) over the long period (that is, more than six decades). The limits inherent in this neoclassical econometric work are revealed through the use of empirical regression specifications directly derived from a fairly wide spectrum of theoretical models, ranging from standard Solowian formizations to growth modelizations with endogenous technical progress, using various indicators of "human capital" and/or R&D. A mathematical reminder of these typically mainstream theoretical models is presented in the appendices (see Appendix A.5.1).

This approach is continued in Chapter 6 by an evaluation in the Chinese case of the "laws" mentioned by T. Piketty. To do this, we suggest a method of building a general capital stock "*à la* Piketty" for China over the long period (from 1952 to 2012). The elasticities associated with this capital are estimated econometrically thanks to specifications which include, alongside it, human capital, R&D and the variable of political-institutional change determined previously. These regressions are carried out within the framework of modern neoclassical macrodynamic models – a theoretical framework which Piketty lays claim to, although not exclusively. On this basis, we calculate an implicit rate of return on this capital in order to test the validity of what Piketty states to be a "fundamental inequality," comparing the rate of return on capital and the growth rate of income in the long term. Then, it is Piketty's "economic law," connecting the coefficient of capital and the ratio between the rate of savings and the growth rate of income that is examined. The results obtained are then confronted to new estimates made this time over the sub-period 1978–2012 only, corresponding to what many observers call a "capitalism with Chinese characteristics" – this, although we question, for our part, the relevance of this expression.[4]

---

4   For the details of our arguments, read: Herrera and Long (2017c, 2018a, 2018g). See also: Long, Herrera and Andréani (2018c, 2021a).

The last two chapters of the book finally provide the reader with the opportunity to use some of the tools made available to him or her by the Marxist current to enable him or her to enter into intellectual resistance and to broaden the field of reflection by linking the analysis of growth to that of cycles and crises.

Indeed, in Chapter 7, on the basis of a definition as rigorous as possible of the statistical perimeters of the industrial sector, and the construction of stocks of fixed assets of enterprises in addition to those of directly productive physical capital already defined, we make the choice to calculate various indicators of profit rates at the micro- and macroeconomic levels for China in the long period (from 1952 to 2014). The results highlighted thanks to these two approaches (micro- and macro-) are quite similar and can be summarized as follows: i) a downward trend in the rate of profit is observable over the long term, for both levels of analysis. ii) The fluctuations in the rate of profit in the short term reveal, at the macroeconomic level, a succession of cycles (rarely complete), the amplitude of which decreases notably over time. iii) More than a third of the period covered is affected by recessive years for the cyclical component of the rate of profit; the strongest falls being recorded, in decreasing order, after the break between China and the Soviet Union (1961–1963), during the Cultural Revolution (1968), during the 1950s, during the post-Mao transition (1976–1977), when a "neoliberal" type experiment was attempted (1989–1991), and finally with the spread of the crises of globalization (which affected China in 1998, 2001, 2009, and again since 2012). iv) It is essentially the increase in the organic composition of capital – more than the respective changes in the share of profits or in the productivity of the unit of labour cost – which tends to push the macroeconomic rate of profit downwards.

Finally, in Chapter 8, we use SVAR (structural autoregressive vectors) models in order to examine more closely the changes in the structure of the economy studied. Once again, our reflections will focus on the role of the rate of profit, relying on the preliminary calculations of this fundamental variable, the characteristics and behaviors of which have just been indicated. The effects of the Chinese rate of profit on the growth rates of both investment, capital accumulation and the product itself are brought to light through the use of impulse response functions. Based on the *a priori* constraints involved in inspecting this structure, we then test whether or not such hypotheses of restrictions are verified in the context of the profound transformations that China has experienced over the six decades that we cover. According to this same methodology, the impulse response functions are also evaluated in Bayesian analysis to try to further improve the results obtained. Finally, we endeavor to predict for the year 2015 (i.e., one year beyond the end of the period considered) the growth rate of Chinese GDP – which was, as we know, affected by the financial crisis that shook the Shanghai and Shenzhen stock exchanges during the summer of 2015 –, based on data from our sample spanning 1952 to 2014. We conclude that it would be appropriate to divide the global period into several sub-periods, with distinct structural characteristics.

PART 1

Concepts and Methods of Building New Statistical Databases for China: Problems Encountered in the Literature and Proposals of Solutions

∵

Building Time Series of Physical Capital Stocks: 1952–2014

As of today, there are still no official statistical data issued by the People's Republic of China for physical capital stocks, even though this is a fundamental variable for understanding the accumulation and growth dynamics of this economy. Although China is working with the Organisation for Economic Cooperation and Development (OECD), especially in the context of a "*resolution of enhanced engagement*," there is no plan in the near future for the National Bureau of Statistics (NBS) of China[1] to publish such series, in line with the harmonized standards of the OECD.[2] This lack of referential data greatly hinders the possibilities of performing econometric estimates of growth models using time-series, as well as panel-data, for this country. Nevertheless, many empirical analyses of the current extraordinary expansion of China exist in the academic literature, but a vast majority of them does not use capital stocks. Of course, some attempts of building China's capital stock series have been made, beginning with those by the Penn World Tables (PWT).[3] However, it must be observed that most of these works face difficulties and reveal multiple deficiencies. The purpose of this Chapter 1 is precisely to identify these different methodological problems and to suggest some proposals for solutions in order to build original series of China's physical capital stocks which are as reliable and long as possible.

1 Problematics, General Issues and Construction Method of Physical Capital Stocks

In the area that concerns us here, problems stem primarily from the scarcity of historical data prior to the year 1949 – that is, the date of the People's Republic of China's independence. But there are also problems with the recent period, coming from the existence of statistical breaks; the most significant of which

---

1 See: www.stats.gov.cn/english/.

2 Read, for example: OECD (2001). Also: Ward (1976).

3 *Cf.* https://ptw-sas.upenn.edu and, for the most recent version (8.1): www.rug.nl/research /ggdc/data/ptw.

occurred in 1993 with the transition from the Chinese national accounting system established according to balances in the Material Product System (MPS) to the implementation of the modernized System of National Accounts (SNA).[4] This change has made comparisons involving both chronological (vertically) and transversal (horizontally) Chinese series quite risky. In addition, it is an understatement to say that for people who do not read Chinese, the task is difficult to find the information needed for the construction of new statistics from the abundant but scattered yearbooks and directories published by the Chinese authorities.

Several economists, be they foreigners or Chinese – sometimes world famous, like Gregory C. Chow, the creator of the econometric test of the same name – have used capital stocks they had built themselves (with varying success), at the national, provincial or sectorial levels. The series that can be considered as the most credible and seriously conceived are those of Chow (1993) and his co-authors.[5] Nevertheless, the transformation of the statistical regime in 1993 led to the suspension of the issuing of the documents used as a basis for elaborating these series, which are now unavailable. The PWT certainly include China. However, for many critical points, the explanatory notes provided by their compilers and statisticians are strangely blurred, by not distinguishing the methodology employed for the economy studied here from those applied to the numerous other countries covered by this famous inter-university program. Some other databases are available in the literature (Table 1.1), but their calculation modalities, which are almost always inspired by the perpetual inventory method (PIM),[6] are frequently tarnished by estimation biases, due to an approximate application of this approach. Our criticisms mainly focus on the questionable parameterization of capital stock in initial year and of the depreciation rate. But they also relate to the uncertain content of investment series and, above all, to inappropriate choices of price indices.

One of the major problems encountered in the current specialized literature is the vagueness of the outlines of the aggregated capital stocks. It is often unclear whether these stocks contain or not built-up lands and other developed real property for residential use (T),[7] and/or inventories (V). To avoid such a confusion and provide several series enabling the reader to focus the

---

4 The last revision (2008) of the SNA is available on: unstats.un.org/unsd/nationalaccount/sna 2008.asp.

5 For example: Chow and Li (2003).

6 Read here: Goldsmith (1951), Harberger (1978) and OECD (1993, 2009).

7 Let us note that the component "built-up lands" is unproductive and does not contain agricultural lands – which are considered to be productive, and valuated by land improvement investments.

TABLE 1.1   Some examples of series of physical capital stocks for China

Authors	Level of analysis	Period
Zhang Junk. (1991)	National	1952–1990
He J.H. (1992)	National	1952–1992
Chow (1993)	National	1952–1993
Jefferson, Rawski and Zheng (1996)	National	1952–1992
Hu and Khan (1997)	National	1952–1994
Wu F.W. (1999)	Agricultural sector	1980–1999
Wang X. and Fan (2000)	National	1952–1998
Young (2000)	National	1978–1998
Huang, Ren and Liu (2002)	13 manufacturing industries	1978–1995
Li and Tang (2003)	National	1978–2000
Zhang Jun and Zhang Y. (2003)	National	1952–2001
He F., Chen and He L. (2003)	National	1952–2001
Sun and Ren (2003)	33 industrial sectors	1980–1999
Wang Y.X. and Wu Y. (2003)	16 industrial sectors	1980–1998
Zhang Jun, Wu G. and Zhang Ji (2004)	Provincial	1952–2000
Mao (2005)	National	1978–2002
Holz (2006)	National	1953–2003
Ge (2012)	Infrastructural sector	1953–2008
Wang L. and Szirmai (2012)	National, industrial, manufacturing	1953–(1985)–2007
Wu (2014)	National and 5 sectors	1949–2007

researches according to the conception of capital he or she uses, we distinguish here four categories of physical capital stock K: (1) a *stricto sensu* or narrowly-defined productive capital stock, K_{Pe}, excluding the residential buildings and built-up lands (that is, housing and the value of their lands), as well as the inventories; (2) a lato sensu or broadly-defined productive capital stock, K_{Pl}, including the inventories, but not the built-up lands as defined above; (3) a fixed capital stock, K_F, including built-up lands, but not the inventories; and (4) a total capital stock, K_T, including built-up lands and inventories.

Thus, we have:

$$\text{Stock of physical capital} \begin{cases} \text{productive narrowly defined} \left(\text{no built.up lands, no inventories} \right) & K_{Pe} \\ \text{productive broadly defined} \left(\text{no built.up lands, with inventories} \right) & K_{Pe} + V = K_{Pl} \\ \text{fixed} \left(\text{with built.up lands, without inventories} \right) & K_{Pe} + B = K_F \\ \text{total} \left(\text{with built.up lands, with inventories} \right) & K_{Pe} + B + V = K_T \end{cases}$$

In addition to all equipment, machines and tools, the stocks of productive physical capital K_{Pe} and K_{Pl} (and therefore also K_F and K_T), include buildings and business assets for commercial purposes,[8] but also agricultural lands.[9] However, the residential built-up land component is not incorporated into the two productive "cores" K_{Pe} and K_{Pl}, but rather into the extended aggregates K_F and K_T. Built lands, which correspond to dwellings for residential use generating housing services, are treated separately because of their singularity.

To build these series according to the PIM, we use the standard formula of accumulation:

$$K_t = (1 - \sigma) K_{t-1} + I_t \,/\, P_t \qquad (1.1)$$

where K_t is the level of capital stock at the end of year t, I_t the flow of investment in the same year t, P_t the corresponding price index, and σ the depreciation rate of capital stock.

Let us examine in turn the four components needed to build our original capital stock series, that is to say: the level of initial capital stock; the investment flow; the price index; and finally the depreciation rate. As usual in the Chinese accounting systems, and most often employed in the best-known contributions to the academic literature on China (Chow [1993], for example), the monetary unit of measurement of great writing we will use hereafter is hundreds of millions (10^8, or $y\hat{\imath}$ [in Chinese: {亿}]) of yuans (RMB).

2   Initial Levels of Physical Capital Stocks

To estimate the initial levels of physical capital stocks, we go back to the earliest possible base year, namely 1952. It was indeed then (and not in 1949) that mainland China's continental territory was completely unified, and that the NBS was founded with a modern statistical system in order to help prepare calculations of the first five-year Plan (1953–1957). The lack of data prior to the

---

8   Here we are following the suggestions of the Advisory Expert Group of the Intersecretariat Working Group on National Accounts (ISWGNA), adopted by the NBS. Read: http://unstats .un.org/unsd/nationalaccount/aeg.asp. For details of the composition of the various fixed assets, see: Xu (1999).

9   The value of agricultural lands is assessed by the cumulative and depreciated investments in the development of these lands, themselves conceived by the NBS as productive constituents of gross capital formation (Xu [2004]). It is only once improved (by clearing, leveling, fertilizer spreading, equipment start-up for cultivation, irrigation infrastructure, etc.) that the land becomes directly productive capital.

TABLE 1.2   Some estimates of initial physical capital stocks for China

Authors	Year	Level (*yuans expressed in yi or hundreds of millions*)		Content
He J.H. (1992)	1952	946.000	(*at 1990 prices*)	Unspecified
Chow (1993)	1952	1,030.000	(*at 1952 prices*)	No land
Hu and Khan (1997)	1978	235.200	(*at 1978 prices*)	No land
Wang and Fan (2000)	1952	1,600.000	(*at 1952 prices*)	Unspecified
Young (2000)	1952	815.000	(*at 1952 prices*)	Probably with land
Huang, Ren and Liu (2002)	1978	5,821.660	(*at 1978 prices*)	No land
Zhang Jun and Zhang Y. (2003)	1952	800.000	(*at 1952 prices*)	No land
He F., Chen and He L. (2003)	1952	5,428.260	(*at 1990 prices*)	Probably with land and inventories
Li and Tang (2003)	1978	14,112.000	(*at 1978 prices*)	Probably without land
Sun and Ren (2003)	1980	6,959.350	(*at 1980 prices*)	No land
Hao (2006)	1952	1,607.121	(*at 1952 prices*)	Probably with land
Shan (2008)	1952	342.000	(*at 1952 prices*)	No land

year 1952 prevents the direct recourse to capital stocks derived from reliable historical series. In the matter, empirical studies using initial capital stocks for 1952 exhibit significant divergences, due to the different methodologies used by the authors (Table 1.2). However, even when their assumptions are the same, some discrepancies are found. This is the case, among many other examples, between Hao (2006) and Shan (2008). Although they both retain the assumption of a steady state (according to which the growth rates of capital and product are equal), they obtain clearly different stocks of capital for 1952. The differences generally observed can also be explained, as we have said, by the content of these stocks which is often left in limbo. Even the most cited study on the subject does not exhaustively expose the details of calculations performed, namely that of Chow (1993) whose 1952 initial capital stock was built on the basis of the net value of fixed assets of the State-owned enterprises (SOEs). Here are some of the reasons why we consider it useful to offer the reader our own original series of physical capital stocks.

One of the methods to estimate the level of capital stock for 1952 consists in writing it as the sum of investments during several preceding years, weighted by the age-efficiency of the various capital goods according to their seniority. Some authors have ventured down this path, despite the scarcity of the available data.[10] In doing so, they had to accept assumptions which we believe are quite exaggerated. In particular, they have assumed that very old macroeconomic statistical data is reliable, such as those disseminated or established by Maddison (1995) or, before him, by H.X. Wu (1993), for China's gross domestic product in the 1920–1940s – a period of extreme upheaval, marked by wars and the total absence of data collection (including population censuses). These old series seem questionable to say the least, and even indefensible to us, for several reasons related to their spatial-temporal incomparability,[11] as well as to inconsistencies in the evaluation of the cost of wars – which is admittedly difficult.[12] Yet it is in general on the basis of such approximative values that the investment series are constructed, which are subsequently used to estimate the capital stocks of these authors. In addition, such series assume, in a usual but quite unjustified manner, that proportions of investment in the GDP are invariable.[13]

A second method is to rebuild, by retropolation, a complete series of stock of capital thanks to one of its recent, one-off estimates, and to the investment flows. This is what was done, for example, by Wang and Wu (2003), who used a value of the SOEs' fixed capital in 1997, provided by the Ministry of Finance, and by going back in time to 1980. Here, however, the risk lies in seeing whether any calculation errors contained in this initial value – and linked to the choice of the price index, we will come back to this later –, are then conserved throughout the retropolated series of the capital stock.

Consequently, we prefer to move towards a third alternative: that of deriving our capital stock from an evaluation of a capital-output ratio. A large majority of the authors who have preceded us in this way (like Zhang [1991] or He *et al.* [2003], among others), based their estimates for China in 1952 on a hypothesis of a rather high coefficient of capital, most frequently equal to 3, as proposed by Perkins (1988). The PWT suggest a somewhat lower coefficient of 2.6. But these values seem too strong, for several reasons. It is not likely that China

---

10   Some examples are: Huang, Ren and Liu (2002) or Sun and Ren (2003).

11   They cover a China whose territorial space very significantly changed with historical events.

12   Estimates of initial stocks by the sum of past investments should be relativized and put into perspective due to the lack of data prior to 1952, because of the successive wars suffered by China. In addition, the production losses resulting from these conflicts are underestimated – since these are an approximation (at –25.7 percent) of those having affected Japan according to the calculations of Maddison (1994) which is generally retained (Huang *et al.* [2002], Sun and Ren [2003]). Therefore, they are largely underestimated when applied to China.

13   Liu and Yeh (1965, 1973) estimated this ratio to be 5.1 percent for the year 1933; a value also supported by Feuerwerker (1977).

in the early 1950s had a capital-output ratio comparable to India, a country that at the time was relatively more industrialized and for which various official reports[14] give parameters of around 2.5. Moreover, it seems illogical that the coefficient of capital for China taken as a whole exceeds that of Shanghai, which was (and is still) the most developed region, and for which statistics of quality also exist.

In these conditions, our approach will consist here, in a first step, of approximating a value of the capital coefficient in 1952 for the Shanghai region, endowed with both abundant and high-quality statistics, then, in a second step, of calculating, thanks to this point of comparison – and assuming that the coefficient of capital for all of China should be significantly lower than that of Shanghai – a capital-output ratio at the national level.

Table 20.18 of the *Shanghai Statistical Yearbook 2001* provides, for the Shanghai region in 1952, an amount of fixed assets, without building land for residential use nor inventories, which satisfactorily approximates the initial value of our similar concept of productive physical capital to narrow sense ($K_{Pe\ S,1952}$), in this case: 33.65 × 100 million yuan. The inventories, noted $V_{S,1952}$ for 1952 are also known, according to the same source (Table 20.19): 25.10 × 10^8 yuan. Here we assume that inventories were zero one year before base year 1952, so that inventories and inventory change are exceptionally equal for our base year – and for it alone. The Shanghai *lato sensu* productive capital to broad sense ($K_{Pl\ S,1952}$) is then worth 58.75 × 10^8 yuan. But, to obtain the total capital, we still need to have the value of built-up lands for residential use ($T_{S,1952}$).

We were able to calculate an "implicit price" of Shanghai built-up land capital from information provided by the *Shanghai Statistical Yearbook 2001* (in Table 20.56 and Table 20.57) relating to the areas of built-up lands for residential use between 1952 (4.89 × 10,000 m^2) and 1953 (5.02 × 10,000 m^2), as well as to the value of the built-up land investment (0.28 × 10^8 yuan) corresponding to these additional 0.129 × 10,000 m^2 over the year; that is: 10.61 × 10^8 yuan. Consequently, we can deduce the total capital stock for Shanghai in 1952: 69.36 × 100 million yuan. So, as the GDP of the Shanghai region was worth 36.66 hundreds of millions of yuan, then it comes in 1952, that same year, the capital-output ratio for the Shanghai region would be $K_{T\ S,1952}/Y_{S,1952}$ = 69.36 / 36.66 = 1.89.

Even if the influence of the level of initial capital on that of current capital decreases over time, setting an initial stock that is too high risks leading to an artificially low growth rate of this stock. It is therefore preferable to calculate very cautiously – and having this benchmark for Shanghai found at 1.89 – the

---

14 Among others: Government of India (various years) or The World Bank (1995).

capital coefficient for China as a whole. Since the Shanghai region was (and still is today) the most developed, it is reasonable to expect that China's capital-output ratio in 1952 will be below the one we have just estimated for Shanghai and its region on the same date.

Under these circumstances, the use of a procedure by successive iterations to determine the initial level of total capital stock at the national scale leads us to a capital coefficient of 1.50 for the whole country in 1952. This iterative procedure consists in setting any value (if positive non-zero) of the base-year capital stock $K_0^{(0)}$ and to estimate the series of stocks $\left\{ K_0^{(0)}, \ldots, K_T^{(0)} \right\}$ according to the PIM.

We thus obtain the average share I_t / K_t, such that we have, at constant prices:

$$\alpha_0 = \frac{1}{T} \sum_{t=0}^{T} I_t / K_t^{(0)} \qquad (1.2)$$

This share α_0 is then used in order to recalculate a second value of the initial capital $K_0^{(1)}$ and find the series of stocks $\left\{ K_0^{(1)}, \ldots, K_T^{(1)} \right\}$, as well as a new average share α_1, that is to say:

$$\alpha_1 = \frac{1}{T} \sum_{t=0}^{T} I_t / K_t^{(1)} \qquad (1.3)$$

The operation is repeated in this way until finally we obtain a capital value $K_0^{(N)}$ which is unchanged, i.e., when we arrive at:

$$\alpha_N = \frac{1}{T} \sum_{t=0}^{T} I_t / K_t^{(N)} = \alpha_{N-1} = \frac{1}{T} \sum_{t=0}^{T} I_t / K_t^{(N-1)} \qquad (1.4)$$

It is possible for us to resort to such a method insofar as the proportion I_t / K_t is mathematically convergent when t tends towards $+ \infty$. Our procedure thus converges to a value of K_0 equal to 1,018.5 hundreds of millions of yuan in 1952; which is equivalent to a capital coefficient of 1.50 for China as a whole. The main advantage of this approach is that it avoids having to mobilize the unrealistic assumption of a steady state reached from and as soon as the base year. The details of the calculations, as well as their methodological originality with regard to the literature on the subject,[15] are presented in the appendices (Appendix A.1.1).

We can represent this iterative procedure by the following chart:

---

15   On this point, see, in particular: Harberger (1978), Nehru and Dhareshwar (1993), or Caselli (2005).

$$K_0^{(0)} \longrightarrow \left\{ K_0^{(0)}, K_2^{(0)} ..., K_T^{(0)} \right\} \longrightarrow \alpha_0 = \frac{1}{T}\sum_{t=0}^{T} I_t / K_t^{(0)}$$

If $\alpha_N = \alpha_{N-1}$, then α_N

$$K_0^{(N)} = I_0 / a_N$$

Otherwise, return
and new calculation

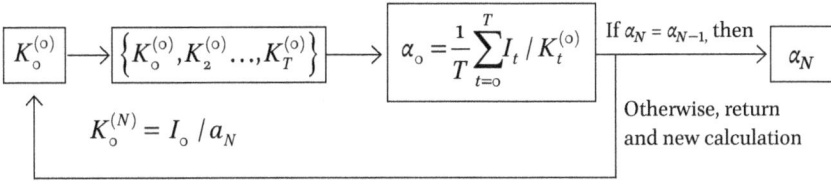

CHART 1.1   Calculation procedure by iterations of the initial physical capital stock

On the basis of the assessments previously carried out for Shanghai, we calculate the narrowly-defined productive physical capital stock (K_{Pe}) for the whole country, assuming that Inada's second condition is satisfied:

$$Y = \lambda f(K,M) = f(\lambda K, \lambda M) \qquad (1.5)$$

where Y is the product, K physical capital, M the aggregate of other inputs, and λ a constant.

It is assumed here that the selected production function is homogeneous of degree 1 (at constant returns to scale)[16] and that Shanghai's GDP (Y_S) is a proportion λ of China's GDP. Therefore the capital of Shanghai (K_S) is also proportional (by the constant λ) to the capital of China (K_C), which is written:

$$Y_s = f(K_s, M_s) = \lambda Y_c = \lambda f(K_c, M_c) = f(\lambda K_c, \lambda M_c) \qquad (1.6)$$

M_s and M_c being the aggregates of non-capital inputs in Shanghai and in the entire China respectively.

We pose, as other authors[17] have also chosen to do:

$$K_s / K_c = Y_s / Y_c \qquad (1.7)$$

In other words, the proportion of Shanghai's capital stock in national capital is equal to that of Shanghai's GDP in national GDP. The capital coefficient in Shanghai is thus assumed to be the same as that at the national level.

---

16   A Wald test carried out within the framework of a Cobb-Douglas production function of Solowian type allowed us to confirm the validity of such an assumption of homogeneity of degree 1.

17   For example: Zhang and Zhang (2003).

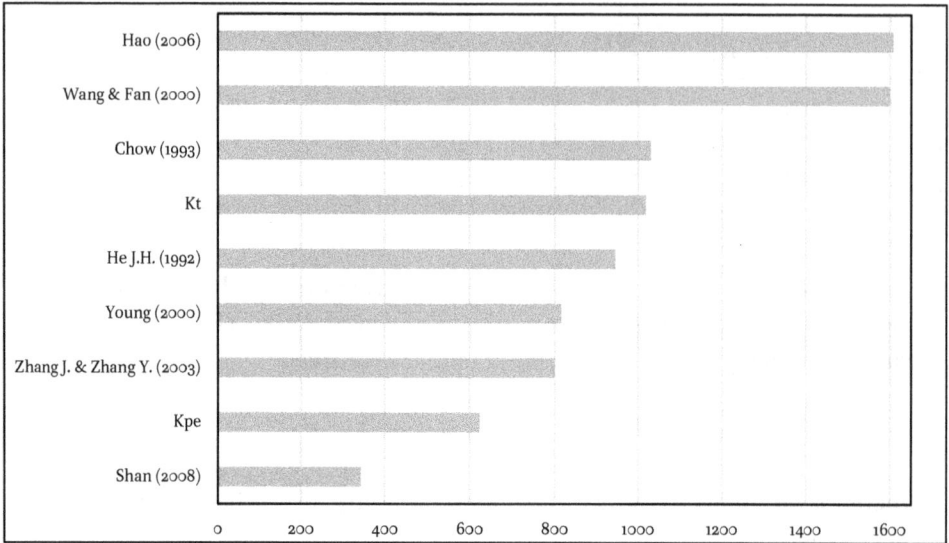

GRAPH 1.1   Comparison of initial physical capital stocks for China in 1952
Note: Estimates of initial capital stocks are all expressed at 1952 prices – except in He (1992), at 1990 prices. The unit of account is one hundred million yuan.

Knowing that in the year 1952, Shanghai's productive capital defined *stricto sensu* was worth 33.65×10^8 yuan and that, from NBS source,[18] also expressed in hundreds of millions of yuan, the GDPs of Shanghai and China were 36.66 and 679.00 respectively, then we find that the narrowly-defined productive capital stock for China ($K_{Pe\ 1952}$) should have been worth $33{,}65 \times (679{,}00\ /\ 36{,}66) = 623{,}25$. It is 18.5 times more than Shanghai's capital; that is to say, a lower proportion than that given, for example (Graph 1.1), by Zhang and Zhang (2003) – who, we believe, overestimate initial stock levels.

By considering the variations in stocks at the national level (73,10) as they appear in the series of GDP calculated according to the extended approach by the NBS in its *China Statistical Yearbook* of the same year,[19] we deduce the largely defined productive capital (K_{Pl}) for whole China: 696.25×10^8 yuan. Total capital (K_T), with built-up lands for residential use, is estimated by

18   Data from NBS sources, found respectively on the NBS online database (http://www
.stats.gov.cn/english/) and in the directory entitled *Data of Gross Domestic Product of China 1952–1995* (p. 35 and p. 367).

19   Source: NBS online database with annual statistics of GDP calculated according to the approach by expenditure. Let us precise that the inventories are considered to be a stock (incremented by changes in the stocks) and equivalent to the difference between K_{Pl} and K_e, with an implicit assumption that their stock was zero in 1951.

TABLE 1.3   Estimated initial levels of four capital stocks in China for the year 1952

Productive capital stock (narrowly defined) K_{Pe} (no built-up lands, no inventories)	Productive capital stock (broadly defined) K_{Pl} (no built-up lands, with inventories)	Fixed capital stock K_F (with built-up lands, no inventories)	Total capital stock K_T (with built-up lands and inventories)
623.250	696.250	945.500	1,018.500

accepting the Kaldorian stylized fact of constant capital-output ratio for the whole country: $K_{T\,1952}$ = 679.00 × 1.50 = 1,018.50 hundreds of million yuan. Hence it comes, once the built-up lands for residential use ($T_{1952} = K_{T\,1952} - K_{Pe\,1952} - V$ = 322.25), are removed, the fixed capital of $K_{F\,1952}$ = 1,018.50 − 73.00 = 945.50 × 10^8 yuans (Table 1.3). In the end, we arrive at results quite similar to those of Chow (1993). Our productive capital of 623.25 is close to what he estimates under the heading of "fixed capital" (582.76). However, it could be that this author might have overstated the value of land (720.00) and agricultural capital (450.00) in the total stock for a China of the 1950s when agricultural production was little capitalistic and where lands were allocated (almost) for free.

3   Investment Flows

As we have seen it, in the literature, the content of initial capital stock is rarely explained with the rigor required by this issue – on which also depends the question of the productive (or not) character of the various components of this stock. Relatedly, the investment series selected to properly perform the accretion of the various capital stocks must be strictly compatible with the statistical scopes of the stocks to be accreted. A capital stock cannot be incremented by a series of investment that does not correspond to it – built-up land for residential use and inventories in particular (Table 1.4). For example, Zhang and Zhang (2003) use an initial capital that excludes land, but investments containing certain land transactions, that is to say, which do not match it. For our part, we have ensured that investment flows coincide as closely as possible with our four original capital stocks. As to us, in order to avoid such inconsistencies, we have to ensure that the investment flows coincide with our four initial capital stocks as closely as possible.

TABLE 1.4   Examples of China's series of investment in capital used in the literature

Investment series	Content of the series	Length	Authors
Gross capital formation	with land and inventories	1952–present	Zhang (2004), Shan (2008), Hao *et al.* (2009)
Gross fixed capital formation	with land, no inventories	1952–present	He F., R. Chen and He L. (2003)
Total investment in fixed assets (national level)	with land	1980–present	Wang X. and Fan (2000), Li and Tang (2003)
Total investment in fixed assets (SOEs)	with land	1952–present	Chen K., Wang H., Zheng, Jefferson and Rawski (1988)
New increase in fixed assets (national level)	with land (excluding real estate), no inventories	1952–1995	Jefferson, Rawski and Zheng (1996)
Productive accumulation investment	with land, with inventories	1952–1993	Zhang (1991), He J.H. (1992), Chow (1993), Zhang and Zhang (2003)

Among the various series available, that of "productive accumulation investment" – already amortized, and in fact preferred by many authors, including Chow (1993) –, has no longer been published since the transition from the MPS to the SNA. Other series, complete, have however existed since 1952 for gross capital formation and gross fixed capital formation. These flow indicators come from a breakdown of GDP according to the expenditure approach, adapted to the investment definitions of the MIP and the SNA. The first of these concepts (gross capital formation) encompasses the second one (gross fixed capital formation), plus changes in inventories. Nevertheless, part of gross fixed capital formation – spending on land acquisition and housing construction, that is, not directly productive or unproductive elements, unlike spending related to building factories and buying equipment – concerns flows which are linked to investments that do not fall under what we have previously called "productive cores." The gross fixed capital formation series do indeed include expenses relating to the acquisition of residential dwellings and their land – elements to be distinguished from those linked to the purchase of equipment or machinery. The fixed asset series provided by the NBS (series called in Chinese "固定资产投资") refer to an investment, as it is interpreted by the MPS, greater than that of the SNA.[20]

Consequently, and logically, we will mobilize, over the period from 1952 to the present day, the series of gross capital formation (F_{BC} or I_T) to construct that of total capital stock (K_T), since both of them integrate built-up lands for residential use and inventories; and the series of gross fixed capital formation (F_{BCF} or I_F), which contains these residential buildings and their lands but not the inventories, for the stock of fixed capital (K_F). In order to obtain the profiles of productive investment necessary for elaborating our two other stocks of productive capital (K_{Pe} and K_{Pl}), investments in residential housing still have to be deducted from these flows. We will therefore have to subtract the investments of residential dwellings, respectively, from the gross capital formation to get the series K_{Pl} and from the gross fixed capital formation for that of K_{Pe}. We were able to find a series of investments in housing construction, with land value, which corresponds to this category of flows, in the *Finance Yearbooks of China* (Ministry of Finance [various years], in Chinese: 中国财政年鉴). However, since these data have only been available since 1982 (see: NBS [1983] *China Statistical Yearbook*, p. 339), we had to resort for the previous years (before 1982) to a very similar series, namely that of investments in non-productive basic constructions of real estate, including dwellings used for residential purposes (or in Chinese: 非生产性基本建设). Its perimeter, however, only covers investments by the State-owned production units and does not incorporate those of the various collective institutions nor those of the private sector. We will therefore have to estimate the investment in construction and non-productive buildings made for the entire national economy.

So we write as a preliminary approximation the investment in productive capital destined to be incremented K_{Pe}, as follows:

$$I_{Pe} = \begin{cases} F_{BCF} - C_{NP} & [1952\text{--}1981] \\ F_{BCF} - C_{HR} & [1982\text{--present}] \end{cases} \qquad (1.8)$$

where I_{Pe} is the investment in productive capital, F_{BCF} gross fixed capital formation, C_{NP} the investment in non-productive buildings, and C_{HR} that in residential housing.

---

20 MPS' "investment in fixed assets" is different from "gross capital formation" of the SNA. To calculate gross capital formation, the NBS uses the following formula (Xu [2002]): "gross capital formation = investment in fixed assets − land use right expenditures − expenditures on purchasing old machines and houses + some other investments (such as sporadic ones in fixed assets under 500,000 RMB)." According to NBS online data, the total amount of investment in fixed assets is higher than gross capital formation.

Nevertheless, this formula tends to underestimate non directly productive building investments from 1952 to 1981, because C_{NP} only concerns State-owned enterprises. So, to correct this bias, we will consider the relative weight of these SOEs (α_j) in the economy during the successive plans (j) until 1981:

$$
I_{Pe} = \begin{cases}
F_{BCF} - \alpha_1 . C_{NP} & [1952-1957] \\
F_{BCF} - \alpha_2 . C_{NP} & [1958-1962] \\
F_{BCF} - \alpha_3 . C_{NP} & [1963-1965] \\
F_{BCF} - \alpha_4 . C_{NP} & [1966-1970] \\
F_{BCF} - \alpha_5 . C_{NP} & [1971-1975] \\
F_{BCF} - \alpha_6 . C_{NP} & [1976-1980] \\
F_{BCF} - \alpha_7 . C_{NP} & [1981] \\
F_{BCF} - C_{HR} & [1981-present]
\end{cases}
\tag{1.9}
$$

To calculate these relative weights, we use the respective proportions of investment in SOEs' fixed assets in that corresponding to the national level and assume them to be equal to those given by the non-productive investment series, for a five-year average (Table 1.5). To do this, we accept the hypothesis – defended by He [1992], among others – of the stability of the economic institutions and policies over each sub-period of the planning system.

The relevance of our estimates is confirmed by comparing them to the actual proportions after 1980 (Table 1.6), as issued by the *China Statistical Yearbook on Investment in Fixed Assets: 1950–1995* (NBS [1997b], p. 22). The differences observed between actual and calculated data from 1981 to 1995 are quite small. They are negligible in the 1980s, and exceed 10 percent only during the 8th Plan (1991), a period when the change of China's accounting system occurred. Our method is valid for the period before 1993, and thus also *a fortiori* over that before 1980, for which we use the relative weights, as follows:

$$
\begin{cases}
\alpha_1 = 1 / 0.8395 & [1952-1957] \\
\alpha_2 = 1 / 0.9900 & [1958-1962] \\
\alpha_3 = 1 / 0.8182 & [1963-1965] \\
\alpha_4 = 1 / 0.7957 & [1966-1970] \\
\alpha_5 = 1 / 0.8962 & [1971-1975] \\
\alpha_6 = 1 / 0.8709 & [1976-1980] \\
\alpha_7 = 1 / 0.6950 & [1981]
\end{cases}
\tag{1.10}
$$

TABLE 1.5   Proportions of the investment in fixed assets of the State-owned enterprises as compared to the national investment in fixed assets in five-year average: China, 1953–1980

Period	Years	Calculated average proportion (*percent*)
First Plan	1953–1957	83.95
Second Plan	1958–1962	99.00
Period of recovery	1963–1965	81.82
Third Plan	1966–1970	79.57
Fourth Plan	1971–1975	89.62
Fifth Plan	1976–1980	87.09

TABLE 1.6   Comparison of the actual and calculated average proportions of the investment in fixed assets by the State-owned enterprises in national investment in fixed assets: China, 1981–1995

Period	Years	Calculated proportion (*percent*)	Actual proportion (*percent*)	Differences (*percent*)
Sixth Plan	1981–1985	66.98	66.70	0.42
Seventh Plan	1986–1990	64.48	64.80	−0.49
Eighth Plan	1991–1995	65.58	59.00	11.15
15-year average	1981–1995	65.68	61.20	7.30

We thus obtain the new formulas for calculating I_{Pe}:

$$I_{Pe} = \begin{cases} F_{BCF} - \alpha_j \cdot C_{NP} & [1952\text{–}1981] \\ F_{BCF} - C_{HR} & [1982\text{–present}] \end{cases} \quad (1.11)$$

with α_j the relative weight of the public enterprises in the Chinese economy during plans (j) from 1952 to 1981.

Then, we deduce the second series of investment in productive capital with inventories, I_{Pl}, according to:

$$I_{Pl} = I_{Pe} + F_{BC} - F_{BCF} \quad (1.12)$$

TABLE 1.7   Investment series corresponding to the four types of capital stocks

Productive capital stock (narrowly defined)	Productive capital stock (broadly defined)	Fixed capital stock	Total capital stock
K_{Pe} (*no built-up lands, no inventories*)	K_{Pl} (*no built-up lands, with inventories*)	K_F (*with built-up lands, no inventories*)	K_T (*with built-up lands and inventories*)
Narrowly-defined productive investment I_{Pe}	Broadly-defined productive investment I_{Pl}	Gross fixed capital formation F_{BCF}	Gross capital formation F_{BC}

4   Price Indices

The passage from current prices to constant prices is particularly delicate. Indeed, it requires the availability of price indices for our investment series. A basic problem comes from the absence of continuous and homogeneous series provided by the NBS's statistical yearbooks of *Data of Gross Domestic Products of China* (in Chinese: [中国国内生产总值核算历史资料, 1952–1995], [中国国内生产总值核算历史资料, 1996–2002], [中国国内生产总值核算历史资料, 1952–2004]). In this section, we propose a new method based on advanced cointegration techniques to get price index series for investment in China over the period 1952–2012, rigorously predicting the missing data (2005–2014), thanks to Shanghai's surveys. Such a method, carefully defining cointegration relationships between price indices, is original – to our knowledge –, and needed, because, as we shall see, this difficulty is treated unsatisfactorily by many econometricians in their works, where, very frequently, the price indices of capital investment have been wrongly selected.

Since the PIM uses constant prices, we must have price indices for our investment flows, which have been expressed so far in current prices. The conversion to constant prices should receive the attention it deserves, as this is really the component of the PIM with the most decisive impact on the construction of capital stock series. This price question is made all the more difficult because the official price index for investments in fixed assets at the national level, for all of China, has only been available since the year 1990. It must nevertheless be recognized that this problem is treated in a way which is not always very satisfactory in the empirical literature on the subject. As a matter of fact, a majority of the authors who were interested in it, faced with this lack of statistical data for the period prior to 1991, thus decided to extend their partially incomplete price series by using instead segments of distinct price indices, or to substitute a missing index by another one, which is available but may be quite different, without having beforehand examined the question of stationarity. The risk is that these econometric estimates will lead to distorted regressions, spurious in the sense of Granger and Newbold (1974).

In this context, the missing segment of the series of price indexes for investments in fixed assets before 1991 has been replaced, in whole or in part, sometimes by the producer price index, sometimes by that of consumer prices (Huang, Ren and Liu [2002], by way of example). According to Jefferson, Rawski and Zheng (1996), this would be justified by the argument that price variations would have been negligible before the 1980s. Wu (1999) regresses the price index of investment in fixed capital on that of production after 1990; Li and Tang (2003), the price indices of investments in Shanghai and national fixed assets one on the other, but for a very small sample (10 points), and without studying the stationarity of their time series of indices of prices, yet deemed to be non-stationary, or even non-linear. Shan (2008) replaces the missing data with points drawn from series of other indices. As to them, Zhang and Zhang (2003) use a Shanghai fixed asset investment price index to replace the national index. Nevertheless, this forgets that the substitution of one price index by another assumes that there is a linear relationship between them, with a unitary coefficient and a zero constant in their regression. That is why He (1992) and Chow (1993), very cautious about their price indexes, rightly so, are somewhat of exceptions – Chow (1993) using an "accumulation index" to calculate the implicit price of fixed assets. In short, it can only be remarked that almost all empirical studies in our subject involving price indices are incorrectly carried out.

Faced with this problem, we must first clarify the nature of the relationship which exists between the price indices of capital investment in Shanghai (P_S) and China (P_C). Bi-univocal or one-to-one Granger causality tests do not yield clear-cut results – it is true, on a small sample (of 25 points, over the sub-period 1990–2014), with low p-values against the null hypothesis "no Granger-causality" suggesting that a relation very probably operates between P_S and P_C. And a glance at the graphical representation of the series allows us to think that the latter look as if they are non-stationary. Furthermore, the associated correlograms reveal slowly decreasing autocorrelation functions, which are characteristic of non-stationary processes. To verify such an intuition, and shed light on the question of the stationarity of the series, and therefore also

TABLE 1.8   Selection criteria for truncation parameter setting of the number of lags (for T = 25)

	Lardic and Mignon (2002)	Newey and West (1994)	Schwert (1989)
Formula(s)	$L = T^{1/4}$	$L = int[4(\dfrac{T}{100})^{2/9}]$	$l_4 = int[4(\dfrac{T}{100})^{1/4}]$, $l_{12} = int[12(\dfrac{T}{100})^{1/4}]$
Lag(s)	2.2	2	2 and/or 8

on that of the possibility of using the price index P_S to reconstruct the series of P_C, we will perform unit root tests on these variables, expressed in level. Their results will depend on the size of the sample T (25 observations), but above all on the – delicate – choice of the truncation parameter for the number of lags of the autocorrelation function. The values obtained according to various formulas of criteria are presented in Table 1.8.

Most criteria lead to a number of lags of 2. To fix the optimal lag of the unit root tests, we select as the maximum lag the estimated value. Four main types of tests are carried out on P_C and P_S: i) an Augmented Dickey-Fuller (ADF) test; ii) an Elliott-Rothenberg-Stock (ERS) test, in the event of a price index non-linearity; iii) an Kwaitkowski-Phillips-Schmidt-Shin (KPSS) test; and finally iv) an Phillips-Perron (PP) test.[21] Out of 24 tests performed, 19 indicate that both price indices are non-stationary (Table A.1.2). Ng-Perron (NG) test improves the PP test through a GLS detrending procedure.[22] For ADF and PP, the information criteria give significant lags (up to 8). As these tests are problematic in the case of a high autoregressive root, because of a risk of loss in their explanatory power,[23] and as too many lags restrict the degrees of freedom and so the credibility of our statistical tests, it appears reasonable to set our truncation parameter or number of lags in unit root tests, at 2.

The test statistics, (almost) all superior to the critical values, indicate that the null hypothesis H_0 "the P_C series has a unit root" cannot be rejected. In addition, the NP tests confirm that P_C is not stationary. This result shows that the authors who do not examine the stationarity of their time series are wrong, as, among many other examples, Li and Tang (2003). However, we

---

21   See: Dickey and Fuller (1979), Elliott *et al.* (1996), Kwaitkowski *et al.* (1992), Phillips and Perron (1988).

22   Ng and Perron (2001).

23   DeJong *et al.* (1992). Also: Ng and Perron (1995).

need to determine the degree of integration of P_C in order to stationarize our series, and thus be allowed to perform linear regressions. All our unit root tests consistency exhibit the fact that the first difference of P_C (denoted by DP_C) is non-stationary, but that its second difference ($D2P_C$) is stationary. Therefore, P_C is integrated to the order 2: $P_c \sim I(2)$.

Turning to P_S, the same method is applied to the first differences (noted DP_S) and, if necessary, to the second differences ($D2P_S$) of P_S. Here, the results of the unit root tests are somewhat less unanimous than in the case of P_C, but allow us to conclude that the variable P_S expressed in level is non-stationary (for all tests, except one [NP]), as DP_S (for all tests, except two [ADF and NP]), but that, on the contrary, $D2P_S$ is stationary (for all tests, except two [ERS (PO)[24] and NP]). Given the consistency of a majority of tests, we conclude that the P_S series is also integrated to the order 2: $P_S \sim I(2)$. As a result, there cannot be any linear relationship ($P_C \equiv P_S$) nor any relationship of cointegration of order 1 between P_C and P_S – and this in contrast to what presupposed (though usually without explanation) many authors, like Zhang and Zhang (2003), who use P_S instead of P_C.

Avoiding any risk of spurious regressions, and being surer and fixed on the relevance of using the P_S series to – partially – reconstruct that of P_C requires in these conditions to know much more about the cointegration relationship likely to exist between the series of P_S and P_C – probably of order 2, given their fairly similar fluctuations, despite a certain divergence of their curves. We reject beforehand, after having applied a multivariate approach to test a second-order cointegration relationship à la Johansen (1988), the use of a Vector Error Correction Model (VECM), which is more suited to studying long-term links and whose explanatory power is reduced by the size of the sample. We prefer the univariate approach à la Engle-Granger (1987), consisting in testing a first-order cointegration relationship between DP_S and DP_C to use such a link – if it exists – in order to estimate the relationship between P_S and P_C. If DP_S and DP_C are found to be integrated into order 1, we can thus use, following Stock (1987), the ordinary least squares (OLS) estimators, which are super-convergent and efficient, as a cointegration relationship allowing us to estimate the relation between P_S and P_C, because, if the series of residuals of the OLS regression is stationary, then the relationship between the stationary explanatory and explained variables will be linear.

---

24   Phillips and Ouliaris (1990).

As a consequence, the estimators describe a cointegration relationship, such as:

$$Y_t = \alpha + \beta X_t + z_t \qquad (1.13)$$

where X_t is the vector of explanatory variables.

TABLE 1.9   OLS Estimates of the relationship between DP_C and DP_S over the period 1990–2014 (with DP_C as the dependent variable and $T = 24$)

		Coefficient		Std. Error	t-Statistic
C		1,995699		0,560579	3,560068
DP_S		0,883542		0,049292	17,92482
R^2	0,938650	R^2 adjusted	0,935729	Mean dependent variable	7,609882
Log likelihood	–50,03208	Sum squared resid	104,4003	s.D. dependent variable	8,794940
F-statistic	321,2992	S.E. of regression	2,229674	Akaike info criterion	4,524529
Prob(F-statistic)	0,000000	Schwarz criterion	4,623267	Schwarz criterion	4,522367
				Hannan-Quinn criterion	4,549361
				Durbin-Watson statistic	2,265485

Therefore, the cointegration test will become a test for stationarity of the residuals z_t. If $\hat{z}_t$ is the estimator of z_t, their distribution functions are different, and the ADF critical values cannot be used to describe the stationarity of z_t. By defining a simulation critical value *à la* MacKinnon (1991), we thus get the series of residuals $\hat{z}_t$ thanks to the estimation:

$$DP_{C_t} = C_1 + C_2 \cdot DP_{S_t} \qquad (1.14)$$

By using the values of the parameters $\hat{C}_1 = 1.995699$ and $\hat{C}_2 = 0.883542$, given in Table 1.9, it comes that the equation allowing $\hat{z}_t$ to be estimated is:

$$\hat{z}_t = DP_{C_t} - 1,995699 - 0,883542 \cdot DP_{S_t} \qquad (1.15)$$

The optimal lags are determined from information criteria which all propose a lag equal to zero. Here, our unit root tests reveal an ADF of $-5.314350 < -4.41$ à la Mackinnon, leading to reject the null hypothesis H_0 "$\hat{z}_t$ has a unit root": $\hat{z}_t$ is therefore stationary; and DP_S and DP_C are cointegrated. Since $\hat{C}_1$ and $\hat{C}_2$ are super-convergent, the equation of $\hat{z}_t$ can be considered as a cointegration relationship.

We can thus set the following new relationship between P_S and P_C, which is recursively related to the previous one:

$$P_{Ct} = P_{C\,0} + 1{,}995699\,t + 0{,}883542 \cdot (P_{S\,t} - P_{S\,0}) \qquad (1.16)$$

This non-linear relationship confirms that the series of P_S and P_C are not substitutable. And the cointegration relationship between price indexes in growth rate is going to allow us to rebuild the Chinese price levels from the base year. However, the price indices of investments in fixed assets P_S and P_C do not exactly coincide with the definitions of the capital stocks selected.

In addition, as the P_C series does not go back below 1991, it is completely inconceivable to use the trajectory of price indices after this date to "forecast" that of the previous sub-period (1952–1990). The price fluctuations observed over the last decades, subsequent to the so-called "opening" reforms, are moreover much stronger than those recorded during the period of planned economy.

We calculate the price indices that we will use at the national level in order to reconstruct the corresponding capital investment series depending on whether or not they include changes in inventories: a price index for gross capital formation F_{BC} ($P_{FBC\,C}$, with changes in inventories) and another one for gross fixed capital formation F_{BCF} ($P_{FBCF\,C}$, without these changes in inventories). This is possible at the national level over the sub-period 1952–2004. From 2005 to 2014, we had to first construct the Shanghai price indices over the complete period (1952–2014), namely: $P_{FBC\,S}$ for the first price index and $P_{FBCF\,S}$ for the second one – both being strictly consistent with the contours of our stocks.

Price indices are calculated using the method presented on historical data from the *Yearbooks of Shanghai* and *Gross Domestic Products of China* respectivement (Table 1.10). The size of our sample now drops from 24 to 53 and 63 observations, and reaches the minimum threshold required by MacKinnon (1991), thereby increasing the relevance of the tests. We therefore estimate the relationship between the indexes of Shanghai and of the whole of China from 1952 to 2004, in order to use it, thanks to the Shanghai data from 2005 to 2014 – i.e., ten years, which is reasonable – to estimate the missing portion of the price index over the sub-period 2005–2014 at the national level.

We therefore complement the series P_{St} with that of the capital formation price index ($Index_t$, with $Index_{1952} = 100$), as it appears in Table 20.17 of the *2001 Shanghai Statistical Yearbook* (Shanghai Municipal Bureau of Statistics [2001], that is to say, in Chinese: 上海统计年鉴):

$$\frac{I_{st} / P_{st}}{I_{s\ 1952} / 100} = \frac{Index_t}{100} \qquad (1.17)$$

Thus:

$$P_{st} = \frac{10\,000 \cdot I_{st}}{I_{s\ 1952} \cdot Index_t} \qquad (1.18)$$

As the four price indices are integrated of order 2 (Appendix A.1.2 to Appendix A.1.10), it is in fact two distinct cointegration relations which are examined, that between $P_{FBC\ St}$ and $P_{FBC\ Ct}$, and that between $P_{FBCF\ St}$ and $P_{FBCF\ Ct}$, respectively.

For indices expressed in first differences, we then obtain:

$$DP_{FBC\ Ct} = 2{,}602348 + 0{,}709832 \cdot DP_{FBC\ St} \qquad (1.19)$$

with an ADF test exiting at –6.051569 < –4.41;
and:

$$DP_{FBCF\ Ct} = 3{,}486494 + 0{,}652279 \cdot DP_{FBCF\ St} \qquad (1.20)$$

with an ADF at –5.648787 < –4.41.

Thus, we deduce the equations which allow us to calculate the variables $P_{FBC\ c}$ and $P_{FBCF\ c}$ between 2005 and 2014:

$$P_{FBC\ Ct} = 381.7975 + 2.6023 \cdot (t - 2004) + 0.7098 \cdot (P_{FBC\ St} - 306.3523) \qquad (1.21)$$

and:

$$P_{FBCF\ Ct} = 388.1796 + 3.4864 \cdot (t - 2004) + 0.6523 \cdot (P_{FBCF\ St} - 263.8592) \qquad (1.22)$$

where $t = 2005, ..., 2014$.

Hence it comes, for the Shanghai region and China taken as a whole, the following four price index series (Table 1.10):

TABLE 1.10 Construction of the four Chinese price indices from 1952 to 2014

Price indices	Length	Sources	Order	Size	Lag
$P_{FBC\,St}$	1952–2014	Data for the periods 1952–2000 and 1978–2014 respectively taken from the 2001 and 2014 *Shanghai Statistical Yearbooks*	$I(2)$	63	3
$P_{FBCF\,St}$			$I(2)$		
$P_{FBC\,Ct}$	1952–2004 and 2005–2014	Data for 1952–1995 and 1978–2004 respectively taken from *Gross Domestic Product of China* (1952–1995) and (1952–2004) + Data for 2005–2014 calculated with cointegration relationships	$I(2)$	53 + 10	3
$P_{FBCF\,Ct}$			$I(2)$		

5 Depreciation Rates

It would have been possible, as some authors argue (Ye [2010]), to dynamically calculate one (or several) depreciation rate(s) of capital stocks, influencing the amortization of capital goods in a structure that is itself variable with time. Nevertheless, to remain consistent with the PIM, which does not use dynamic rates, we will select a constant total depreciation rate of capital. Mathematically, assuming a hypothesis of a constant depreciation rate of capital stock is equivalent to being within an axiomatic configuration where four assumptions are to be satisfied simultaneously, including: (1) the age-efficiency of the different constituent goods of capital geometrically declines, and (2) is proportional to the price index (at constant prices); but also (3) the rate of replacement of capital equals the chosen depreciation rate; and (4) the profile of mortality of the various categories of assets is such that the retirements of capital goods that reach the end of life are done at the same time.

A mistake would be not to take into account the equivalence of these assumptions, and this would lead to confuse the concepts of age-efficiency and replacement rate (Sun and Ren [2005]), and even those of patrimony or "wealth" and capital stock (Shan [2006]). Following the PIM, the capital stock K is written as a sum at infinity of past investments weighted by age-efficiency (at constant prices):

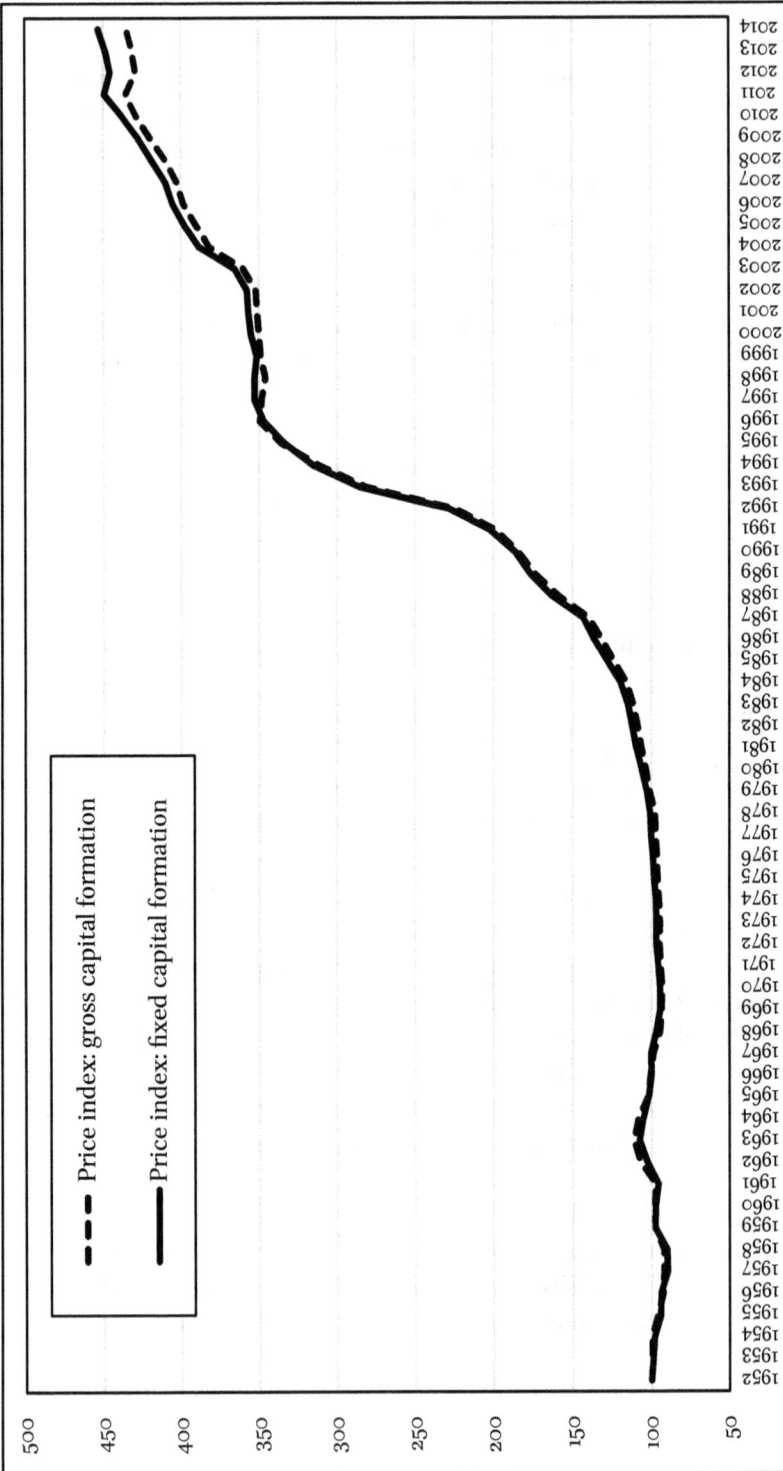

GRAPH 1.2   Price indices of capital investments: China, 1952–2014
Note: Price index of gross capital formation F_{BC} with changes in inventories ($P_{FBC\ c}$) and price
index of gross fixed capital formation F_{BCF} without changes in inventories ($P_{FBCF\ c}$).

$$K_t = \sum_{\tau=0}^{\infty} d_\tau I_{t-\tau} \qquad (1.23)$$

$I_{t-\tau}$ being the investment made τ years ago, and d_τ the age-efficiency of capital goods of τ years. Without new investment, we have $I_t = K_0$ if $t = 0$, and $I_t = 0$ otherwise.

If we assume, reasonably, and with others,[25] that the age-efficiency of capital goods will decline geometrically, then the rate of depreciation is:

$$\sigma_i = 1 - d_i^{1/\tau} \qquad (1.24)$$

with σ_i the depreciation rate for the category of capital goods indexed i, τ the "seniority" of the investment at date t, and d_i the age-efficiency at the moment of the retirement of the residual assets of the same type.

Distinguishing amortization by type of capital goods, we use the total depreciation rate for the calculation of the trajectories of our four capital stocks, taking into consideration the share of these different goods in the structure of total capital and the price index (with inventories):

$$\sigma = \sum_i a_i \sigma_i = \sum_i \frac{\sum_j^t \frac{I_{ij}}{P_j}}{\sum_j^t \frac{I_j}{P_j}} \sigma_i \qquad (1.25)$$

where α_i denotes the part of capital goods of type i in the total capital structure, and P_j the price index for the jth category of fixed assets.

Capital goods are classified by the NBS *Yearbooks* in three categories: buildings and facilities, equipment and materials, and others. We have their respective lifetimes and residual values. For developing countries, China included, the Organisation of Economic Cooperation and Development (OECD) recommends using the following depreciation rates: 80 years for housing and 40 for other buildings; 15 years for machinery; and 20 for the rest. In China, nevertheless, the lifetimes of such goods are regulated, as follows: 70 years for houses and 40 for commercial buildings – the latter remaining a minority building stock compared to the former.

---

25   This is the opinion expressed by Hulten and Wycoff (1995), Jorgenson (1996) or Fraumeni (1997), among others.

Finally, we choose the following values: 55 years for buildings and facilities; 16 years for equipment and materials; and 25 for the rest. And unlike the usually-accepted 5 percent for China, we assume a 10 percent value for residual goods – a higher depreciation rate in order to reflect the running competition existing between local governments to obtain a "good ranking" at the national scale according to the provincial production growth rates, which leads to many public works plans. Such competition results in frequent demolitions of properties and withdrawals of capital goods with use values still often high.

For the three types of capital goods considered, the proportions of which in the capital structure are respectively found at 62.7 percent, 22.5 percent and 14.9 percent, the lifetimes at 55 years, 16 years and 25 years, and the residual values at 10 percent, with rates of amortization for the respective categories calculated at 3.8 percent, 13.4 percent and 8.8 percent, our calculations lead us to a total depreciation rate of: $\sigma = 6.68$ percent; or: $\sigma = (0.627 \times 0.038) + (0.225 \times 0.134) + (0.149 \times 0.088) = 0.068$. For these proportions, we were only able to use data from 1981 to 2014, since those available before the year 1981 only concerned State-owned enterprises – a limitation that would have involved a problematic bias. The weightings by category of capital goods being rather stable over time, the depreciation rate also remains very stable over the period – in fact, almost constant between 1981 and 2014. Thus, our assumption of a constant average depreciation rate for the entire period studied (1952–2014) is quite acceptable.

In comparison, a depreciation of around 3.6 percent is proposed for fixed assets by the NBS (Xu [1999]), but this rate only takes into account physical wear and tear, and not retirement and decommissioning, which leads to underestimate the depreciation rate. The latter is calculated at 3.1 percent by the PWT, which is based on the data of the United States. However, it is a rate of 4 to 5 percent that is most often used in academic work (for example, Wang and Fan [2000]). Others assume a depreciation equal to the Chinese "official" rate (3.6 percent) plus economic growth, assuming a "golden rule" positioning China on a growth trajectory deemed optimal, but resulting in amortization this time too high (Song et al. [2001]).

Still others, using methods of calculation which are nevertheless quite similar to ours, obtain amortization rates of the order of 10 percent (Shan [2008]) – therefore very high –, because of different choices of lifetimes, residual values and weightings of capital goods, but above all price indices. However, it turns out that the rate of depreciation cannot exceed a certain threshold, at the risk of seeing the investment insufficiently high to compensate for too strong amortization of capital, making the growth of the stock of capital artificially low – and even negative in the first years.

On the basis of a separate methodology, using a Leontief-style input–output table on post-1990 data, Xue and Zheng (2007) arrive for their part at a

TABLE 1.11   Amortization rates of capital goods by category and total depreciation rate

	Constructions and installations	Equipment and materials	Other goods
Proportion α_i	62.67 percent	22.47 percent	14.85 percent
Lifetime τ	55 years	16 years	25 years
Depreciation rate σ_i	3.76 percent	13.40 percent	8.80 percent
Total depreciation rate σ	6.68 percent		

depreciation rate of 7.17 percent, quite close to ours. Insofar as our estimate contains information relating to the period of the beginnings of socialist planning, during which infrastructure investments were considerable (infrastructure investments at longer amortization and lower depreciation), it seems logical to us, and reasonable, to propose a depreciation rate of 6.68 percent (Table 1.11).

Furthermore, this value found at 6.68 percent is very close to the average (which is around 6.50 percent) of the depreciation rates calculated for the fixed assets of industrial State-owned enterprises registered in each Chinese province, provided for the period 1991–1998 in the *China Finance Yearbook 1999* by the experts of the Ministry of Finance of the People's Republic of China (1999).[26]

The appropriateness of such a parameter setting is validated by an error analysis, from which several lessons can be drawn. Thus, from an assumption of a positive average capital growth rate $\overline{\dot{K}_t} > 0$, it comes:

$$\sigma < \frac{1}{T}\sum_{t=0}^{T}\frac{I_t / P_t}{K_{t-1}} \qquad (1.26)$$

The depreciation rate should therefore not exceed the average investment rate, calculated at 9.22 percent, using our data. Our estimate is well below this threshold, but those of the authors using a higher rate introduce a bias: among them, the growth rate of the capital stock is indeed excessively low (or even negative) during the first years of accretion.

---

26   See here: Ministry of Finance – P.R. of China (1999), in Chinese: 中国财政年鉴 1999; and more precisely, p. 219, Table 5-4 which is entitled: "*Fixed Assets Depreciation Rate of State-Owned Industrial Enterprises by Region.*"

If σ_1 and σ_2 are two depreciation rates, and $\sigma_2 - \sigma_1 > 0$, then $K_{1T}/K_{2T} \to +\infty$ when $T \to +\infty$. So, a slight difference in the rate of depreciation σ causes the levels of capital stocks to diverge.

Furthermore, the rate of depreciation will influence the level of the growth rate of capital, but not its fluctuations. The higher the value of σ, while remaining below the required threshold, the lower the variance of the capital stock in T will be, and the more will be reduced the possible errors in the econometric regressions carried out (with high expected t-values).

In the end, the new series of physical capital stocks for China from 1952 to the present day are therefore presented to the reader (Table 1.12), according to various more or less broad definitions of it (Graph 1.3 and Graph 1.4).

TABLE 1.12   Time series of physical capital stocks: China, 1952–2014 (*in hundreds of millions of 1952 constant yuans*)

Years	Productive capital K_{Pe}	Productive capital K_{Pl}	Fixed capital K_F	Total capital K_T
1952	623.3	696.3	945.5	1,018.5
1953	645.8	797.2	999.0	1,150.1
1954	698.6	924.6	1,075.8	1,300.8
1955	768.9	1,056.6	1,158.7	1,444.7
1956	897.0	1,208.9	1,315.6	1,626.6
1957	994.7	1,382.9	1,436.1	1,822.2
1958	1,260.1	1,722.9	1,709.9	2,169.9
1959	1,570.7	2,192.8	2,042.1	2,661.6
1960	1,893.6	2,575.7	2,391.9	3,071.2
1961	1,982.0	2,663.2	2,470.4	3,148.6
1962	2,008.0	2,640.0	2,476.2	3,104.9
1963	2,051.3	2,680.3	2,511.1	3,136.3
1964	2,153.0	2,788.7	2,619.1	3,250.2
1965	2,311.3	3,013.6	2,788.1	3,486.0
1966	2,518.2	3,333.5	3,009.4	3,820.3
1967	2,640.6	3,509.4	3,131.5	3,996.7
1968	2,746.2	3,704.1	3,232.7	4,187.9
1969	2,944.3	3,928.1	3,447.4	4,429.4
1970	3,276.8	4,415.9	3,794.9	4,933.0
1971	3,628.6	4,932.3	4,172.9	5,476.8

TABLE 1.12 Time series of physical capital stocks: China, 1952–2014 (*cont.*)

Years	Productive capital K_{Pe}	Productive capital K_{Pl}	Fixed capital K_F	Total capital K_T
1972	3,965.9	5,373.8	4,537.5	5,946.9
1973	4,315.8	5,897.4	4,920.9	6,505.7
1974	4,723.4	6,412.6	5,364.1	7,057.9
1975	5,221.7	7,005.2	5,903.1	7,692.7
1976	5,666.7	7,483.0	6,384.7	8,209.0
1977	6,106.8	8,018.1	6,867.2	8,788.6
1978	6,645.1	8,770.6	7,474.1	9,612.8
1979	7,144.5	9,468.3	8,094.7	10,434.2
1980	7,697.9	10,162.1	8,800.7	11,285.3
1981	8,156.6	10,760.6	9,436.1	12,066.9
1982	8,634.6	11,354.6	10,147.3	12,902.2
1983	9,196.7	12,049.6	10,970.8	13,866.5
1984	9,990.1	13,014.6	12,035.6	15,112.2
1985	10,909.0	14,416.4	13,319.0	16,891.3
1986	11,949.7	15,896.3	14,734.1	18,760.6
1987	13,193.1	17,402.8	16,400.0	20,699.6
1988	14,545.0	19,156.2	18,193.2	22,904.4
1989	15,399.0	20,834.2	19,479.8	25,019.7
1990	16,337.5	22,473.8	20,771.1	27,012.0
1991	17,549.4	24,225.0	22,388.5	29,174.7
1992	19,354.5	26,326.0	24,622.4	31,708.0
1993	21,768.7	29,186.9	27,639.5	35,178.6
1994	24,602.3	32,542.9	31,289.3	39,355.8
1995	27,795.1	36,538.2	35,454.0	44,305.4
1996	31,370.7	40,847.3	40,016.1	49,583.4
1997	35,112.6	45,177.8	44,702.9	54,871.5
1998	39,051.3	49,360.2	49,812.9	60,253.8
1999	43,121.4	53,485.1	55,172.9	65,674.5
2000	47,632.8	57,697.7	61,017.8	71,242.5
2001	52,700.7	62,796.4	67,530.3	77,811.8
2002	58,756.4	68,876.8	75,227.4	85,562.4
2003	66,515.8	76,827.7	84,839.9	95,397.7
2004	75,379.2	86,285.6	95,947.7	107,141.6

TABLE 1.12   Time series of physical capital stocks: China, 1952–2014 (*cont.*)

Years	Productive capital K_{Pe}	Productive capital K_{Pl}	Fixed capital K_F	Total capital K_T
2005	85,142.8	96,529.8	108,219.8	119,948.5
2006	96,391.5	108,568.6	122,698.5	135,277.6
2007	109,205.4	122,666.6	139,853.3	153,803.6
2008	125,118.9	140,674.4	161,092.7	177,262.4
2009	144,911.7	161,807.0	187,010.4	204,637.2
2010	166,912.1	185,688.4	216,491.5	236,170.5
2011	190,906.3	212,474.7	250,047.2	272,874.3
2012	217,968.1	242,201.8	287,619.4	313,586.0
2013	246,723.8	273,716.7	328,421.7	357,710.2
2014	274,936.9	304,774.2	368,674.3	401,423.7

Notes: K_{Pe} = narrowly-defined productive capital stock (without built-up lands, without inventories);
K_{Pl} = broadly-defined productive capital stock (without built-up lands, with inventories);
K_F = fixed capital stock (with built-up lands, without inventories);
K_T = total capital stock (with built-up lands, with inventories).

Several arguments support that our capital series for China are of good statistical quality and that their construction constitutes a useful work for researchers wishing to undertake the macroeconomic study of the growth dynamics of this country, in addition to the time series currently available in the literature (Graph 1.5):

(i)   The initialization of our physical capital stocks is based on a less approximate (and lower) capital-output coefficient than those generally advanced.

(ii)   Our investment flows are consistent with the statistical perimeters of the initial stocks.

(iii)   Above all – and this is probably one of the original features of our current research – our investment price indices (Graph 1.2) are strictly adapted to the respective contents of these stocks, and the unit root tests show that these price indices are all non-stationary and integrated of order 2 – which means that they cannot be used in place of each other. Now, price indices represent the components most decisively determining the level

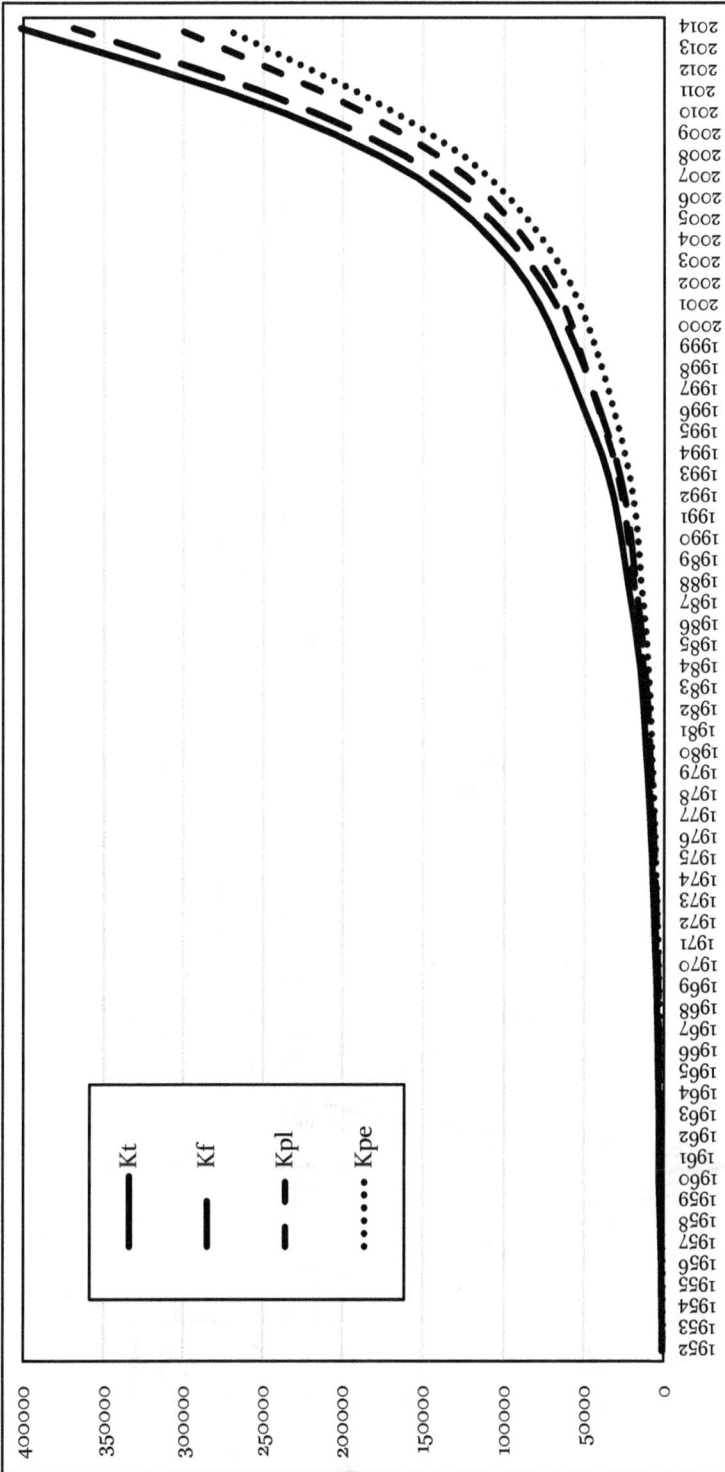

GRAPH 1.3 Levels of physical capital stocks (according to four selected definitions): China, 1952–2014

Notes: The monetary unit is hundreds of millions of yuan (RMB). All values are in 1952-base constant yuans.

K_{Pe} = narrowly-defined productive capital stock (without built-up lands, without inventories);

K_{Pl} = broadly-defined productive capital stock (without built-up lands, with inventories);

K_{F} = fixed capital stock (with built-up lands, without inventories);

K_{T} = total capital stock (with built-up lands, with inventories).

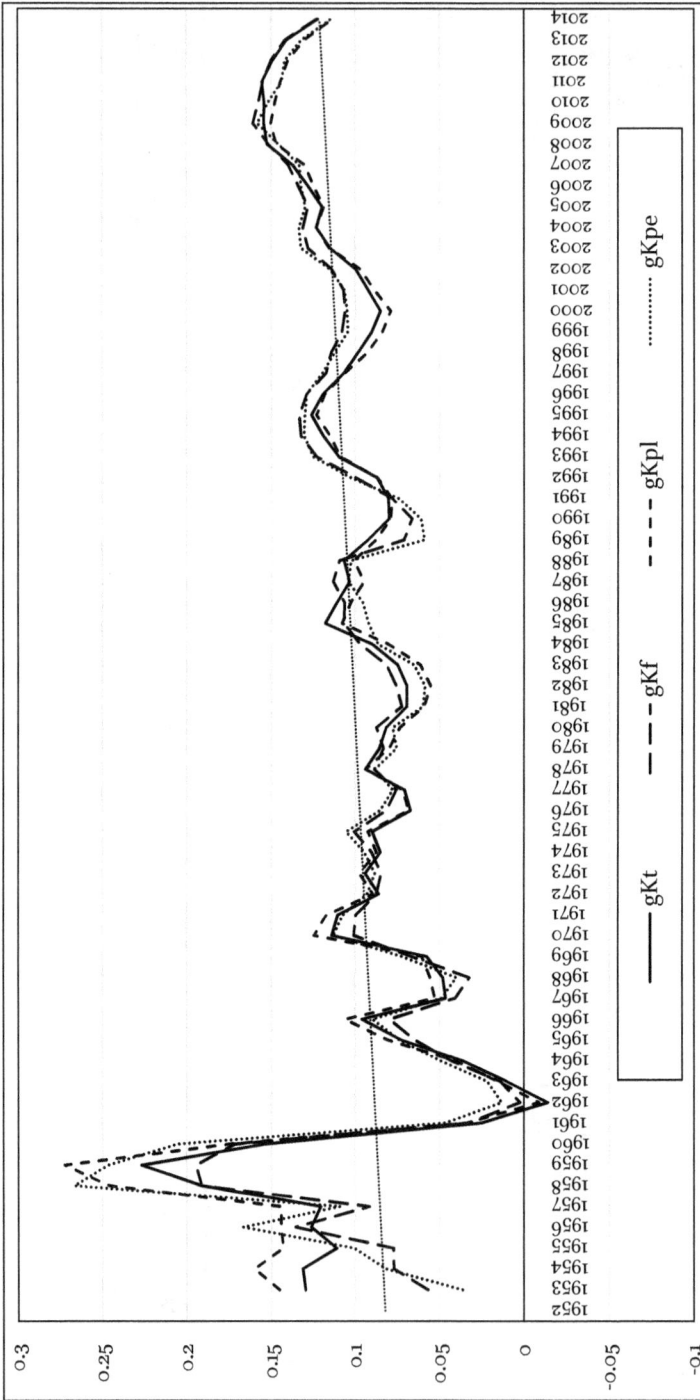

GRAPH 1.4   Growth rates of the four physical capital stocks: China, 1953–2014

Note: −0.05 = 5 percent decrease, +0.1 = 10 percent increase, for example.

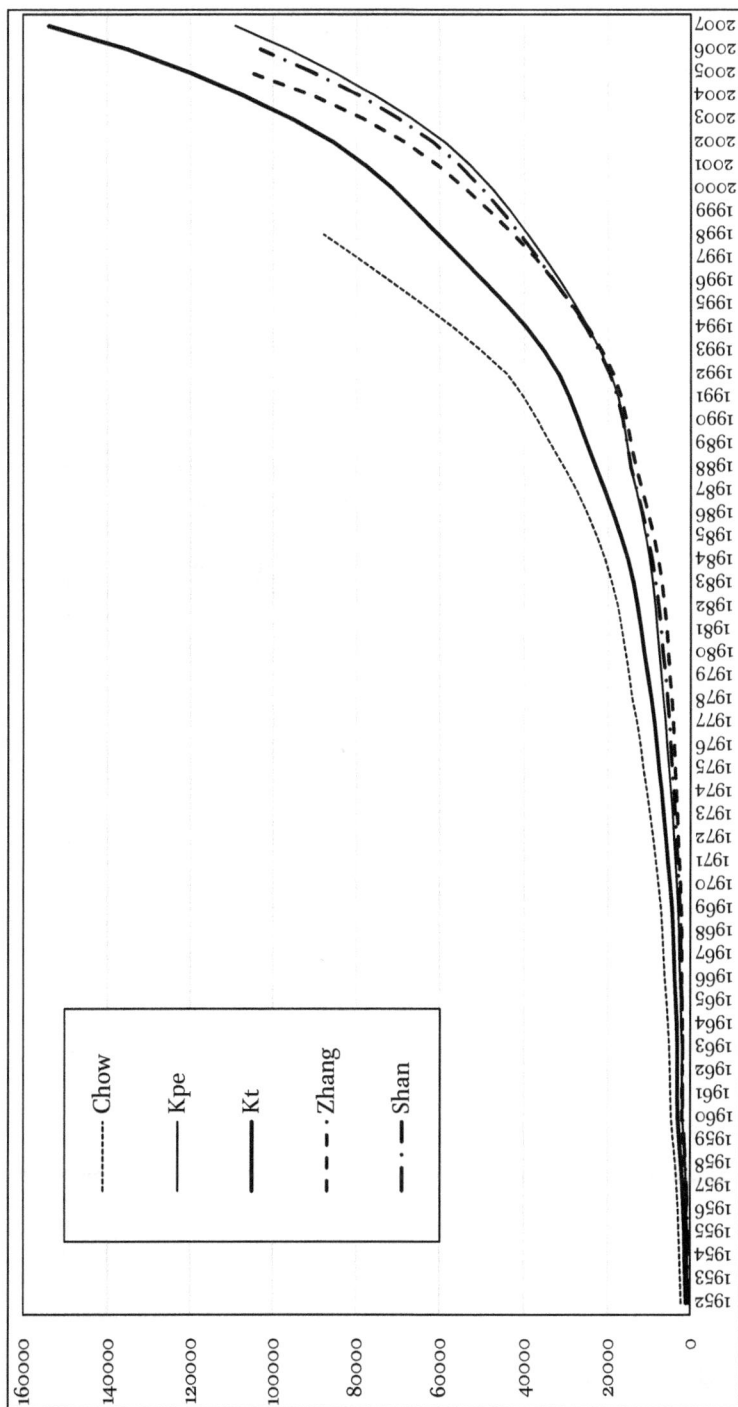

GRAPH 1.5   Comparison of the physical capital stock series for China since 1952

Notes: All trajectories of capital stock levels are expressed in hundreds of millions of yuan.
Zhang and Zhang (2003), Shan (2008), as well as our own estimates are at 1952 constant prices.
Chow (1993)'s series is at 1978 prices.

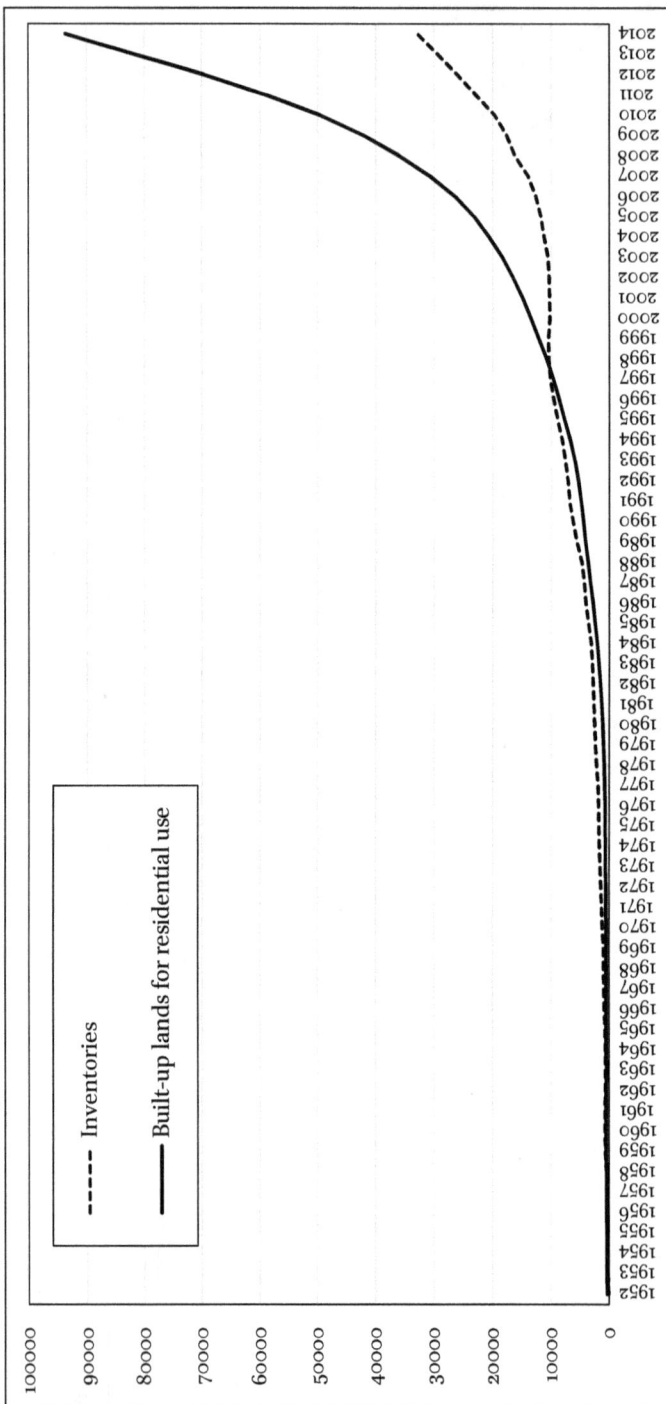

GRAPH 1.6   Values of built-up lands for residential use and inventories: China, 1952–2014

Notes: The monetary unit is hundreds of millions of yuans (RMB). All values are in 1952-base constant yuans.

Built-up lands for residential use correspond to the value of residential dwellings constructed and to that of their lands.

as well as the structure of the various categories of capital stocks. As a consequence, the care taken in their construction is therefore absolutely crucial.

(iv) Furthermore, our depreciation rates are estimated by type of capital goods, under compatible assumptions of age-efficiency and retirement, then the capital investment proportions are used to approximate the overall capital structure and calculate a total depreciation rate.

A parameterization error analysis confirms that these series of physical capital stocks are solidly built. So they could benefit the community of researchers wishing to make empirical works on China, and especially econometric estimates over a long period.

Finally, let us point out, among the intermediate variables considered for the elaboration of our capital stocks, the particularly dynamic evolution of built-up lands for residential use over the last two decades (Graph 1.6). We would be tempted to relate this phenomenon to the recently observed housing bubble in China and the significant role that housing has played in the country's economic growth. This dynamism is explained not only by the effects of land reform (1988) and tax reform (1993), which strongly pushed up the prices of real estate, but also by those, extremely powerful in the context of China's opening up to trade worldwide, of the so-called "compulsory foreign exchange settlement system" imposed from 1994 to 2012 on Chinese exporting companies, forced to deposit their cash in foreign currencies at an administered exchange rate with a specific network of State banks, facilitating thus the draining of these monetary liquidities by the Central Bank (*People's Bank of China*). As a counterpart, a considerable mass of liquidities was emitted into the national economy, fueling inflation, but also – for what concerns us here – the real estate bubble. China's land and currency regimes, however, are very complex issues that would require careful treatment, which we reserve for further research.

Building Time Series of "Human Capital" Stocks: 1949–2014

The very rapid growth rate of China's gross domestic product (GDP) over the past several decades has raised many questions about the contributions of various factors of production to this phenomenon, foremost among which is the stock of physical capital. This sustained economic growth contrasts sharply, however, with the moderation in China's demographic change, particularly in the labour force, due in large part to the official long-term policy of birth control implemented. In standard macrodynamic models applied to empirical estimation, which most commonly mobilize a Solowian theoretical framework, or a formalization very close to it, the use of the number of people employed to approximate simple labour frequently leads to a(n excessively) high coefficient of elasticity associated with labour as an input. This reflects a total factor productivity underestimation – and often, at the same time, an invalidation of the assumption of constant returns to scale in the production function.[1] There is little doubt that a statistical differentiation between simple and complex labour (or unskilled and skilled labor) is necessary in order to verify that a workforce with a higher level of education is actually much more productive.[2] We should instead use econometrically an indicator of China's so-called "human capital" as the labour factor – but being well aware of the conceptual and theoretical reservations to be made about this notion.[3] Nevertheless, for this, we will have to construct it, because, as we shall see, the data series available for this country are far from satisfactory. This is particularly true of those developed on the basis of the Kendrick *et al.* (1976) method (Appendix A.2.7) or on that of Jorgenson and Fraumeli (1989), or even data based on an average educational attainment, such as the Penn World Tables (PWT).[4]

---

1 Examples: Jefferson (1990), Zhang (1991), Su and Xu (2002), Guo and Jia (2005), Perkins and Rawski (2008).
2 Li, Loyalka, Rozelle and Wu (2017).
3 The critique of this concept of "human capital," which is not the specific object of this current work, focusing above all on the empirical dimension, has been carried out by us elsewhere. See in this regard: Herrera (2000a, 2010a).
4 *Cf.* https://ptw-sas.upenn.edu and, for the latest 8.1 version: www.rug.nl/research/ggdc /data/ptw.

In this chapter, we will first examine the different approaches used in the literature to estimate China's "human capital" and the main limitations of each, in order to identify precisely the points on which our efforts should focus. Then, using two distinct definitions of the stock of "human capital," respectively productive or total capital, we will present our own methodology, based on the permanent inventory method (PIM), and extended over the period from the founding of the People's Republic in 1949 until very recent data collected by the National Bureau of Statistics (NBS) of China, i.e., the year 2014. Therefore, after a brief presentation of the general conceptual and methodological framework, we shall successively explain the ways in which the depreciation rates of this stock are determined, for which mortality rates, retirement rates and unemployment rates are to be used; then the new increases in "human capital," requiring the calculation of the number of new graduates and the duration of studies for each type of education in order to obtain the new investments that raise these stocks; and lastly the values of "human capital" stocks corresponding to several base years chosen over the 66-year period covered by the present work, which implies identifying the average duration of studies by type of education for individuals and the number of the latter in the population concerned. Under these conditions, we will be able to provide the reader with two original series of "human capital" stocks for China's economy from 1949 to 2014, as well as those of the average educational level attainment of the population.

1 Estimates of Chinese Human Capital in the Literature: Advances and Limitations

1.1 *Evolutions of the Literature*
The most widely used measure of human capital stock today requires determining an average level of education attained or a number of years of learning per capita. The Penn World Tables (2013) estimated this indicator based on the number of years of study given by Barro and Lee (2018) and on Psacharopoulos (1994)'s educational returns. This latest author has indeed used the level of education to assess returns to human capital, while Barro and Lee (2018) have argued that the educational levels of workers reflect their levels of human capital. As regards the researches that have sought to apply the Barro-Lee method, it is first child school enrollment rates and adult literacy rates that have been employed as measures of human capital – which contributed to their real success in China, due to the availability of this kind of data and to the correlative lack of information on the number of years of study observed during a long time in this country.

It is with this in mind that Cai and Du (2003) estimated Chinese human capital, but using a succession of questionable hypotheses inspired by Cai (1999) who assumed, in particular, illiteracy equivalent to zero year of learning, primary education as corresponding to six years, lower secondary education to nine years, upper secondary education to 12, technical secondary to 13, high school to 14, and university to 16 years. However, the definition relating to the level of primary education of the total population given by the NBS is very precise: it refers to all the people whose highest level of education is primary school, whether they are still in school, already graduated, or even have dropped out of school. Consequently, for example, according to Table B0301a of the 2010 population census indicating the state of completion of studies, we can calculate that the primary educational level represents 4.942 years of study, and not six. Cai (1999) therefore probably overestimated the level of China's human capital.

1.2   Limitations of the Literature, Comparison of Databases and State of NBS Statistics

The empirical studies carried out with a methodology à la Barro-Lee by Chinese economists (Appendix A.2.4) present a number of serious limitations. The main ones in our opinion are the following: i) Most of them do ignore or disregard the definition that the NBS gives of the level of education attained by the total population. As a matter of fact, this definition refers to the highest educational level (called "cultural level" in the Chinese documents), which concerns not only graduates, but also pupils or students still at school, and even those who have dropped out of studies. However, virtually no work mentions this problem and, in general, it is the standard durations of studies which are used as numbers of years of education. ii) With few exceptions – including that of Cai and Du (2003), who take into account the impact of the Cultural Revolution through the interruption (or decline) of many training programs –, the effects on human capital of changes in the length of studies and successive educational reforms are almost never considered, even though it is a crucial question. iii) The importance of people educated in the first cycle of primary education prior to 1949 and its consequences on the evolution of human capital are not taken into account either. iv) Neither does the literature deal with the influence of adult education on human capital accumulation, nor with that relating to literacy campaigns. v) A very large majority of authors do not distinguish between the stock of human capital of the total population and that of the employed population (aged 16 years and over), although our tests show that these two indicators have markedly different trajectories. vi) As no distinction is made between productive human capital and total human capital, the issue of retirements is also neglected.

Added to this, we argue – and later demonstrate – that the (version 8.0) PWT (2013) data on China's human capital exaggeratedly and unduly understates these stock levels and *de facto* present considerably biased estimates of total factor productivity for this country. The Barro-Lee database is of better quality, but it does not start until 1970 and only has a five-year frequency, which is far from being sufficient for the requirements of the econometric analysis. And the one drawn up by UIS-UNESCO[5] experts, as to it, only offers three points, which is even more problematic (Graph 2.1). However, the fact is that China does not to date provide an official indicator of average level of education attained. We will therefore have to estimate it ourselves in order to be able to build series of human capital stocks in China.

To do this, numerous official data are available, but disparate and incomplete. In its *China Population Statistics Yearbook*, the NBS published in 1987, and subsequently from the year 1993 onwards, a table entitled "Population aged six and over by age, by sex and by level of education," which is based on the results of sample surveys. This yearbook changed its name in 2007 to now be called *China Population and Employment Statistics Yearbook*, which also includes, since 2006, a table on the "educational level of employed persons" (Table 3-1), established through labour force sample surveys. The information for year *t* is given in the yearbook *t+1*. Furthermore, for the years in which a population census was carried out (namely: in 1964, 1983, 1990, 2000 and 2010), there is more detailed, complete data on populations according to different educational levels. By combining the durations of each type of education, we can obtain the average level of education for the years in question, from official and homogeneous sources.

In other words, for the years 1964, 1982, 1987, 1990, then for the period 1993–2014, it is possible to have the average level of education reached by the population aged six years and over, and, in the next step, to multiply this level by the number of people making up the population aged six and over, so as to calculate the total human capital stock, i.e., that corresponding to the population aged at least six. From 2006 to 2013, we can also obtain the average educational level of employees, as well as productive human capital, again from official Chinese statistics. Barro and Lee (2018)'s database is relatively close to the latter, but only offers points spaced five years apart. By contrast, that of the PWT (2013) is notably lower (Graph 2.1).

Our effort will therefore consist in estimating for the missing years, quite numerous as can be seen, the values taken by two distinct stocks: i) the total

---

5   See here: http://data.uis.unesco.org/. To evaluate the quality of these different databases and their empirical consequences: de la Fuente and Doménech (2006, 2015), Cohen and Soto (2007), or Cohen and Leker (2014).

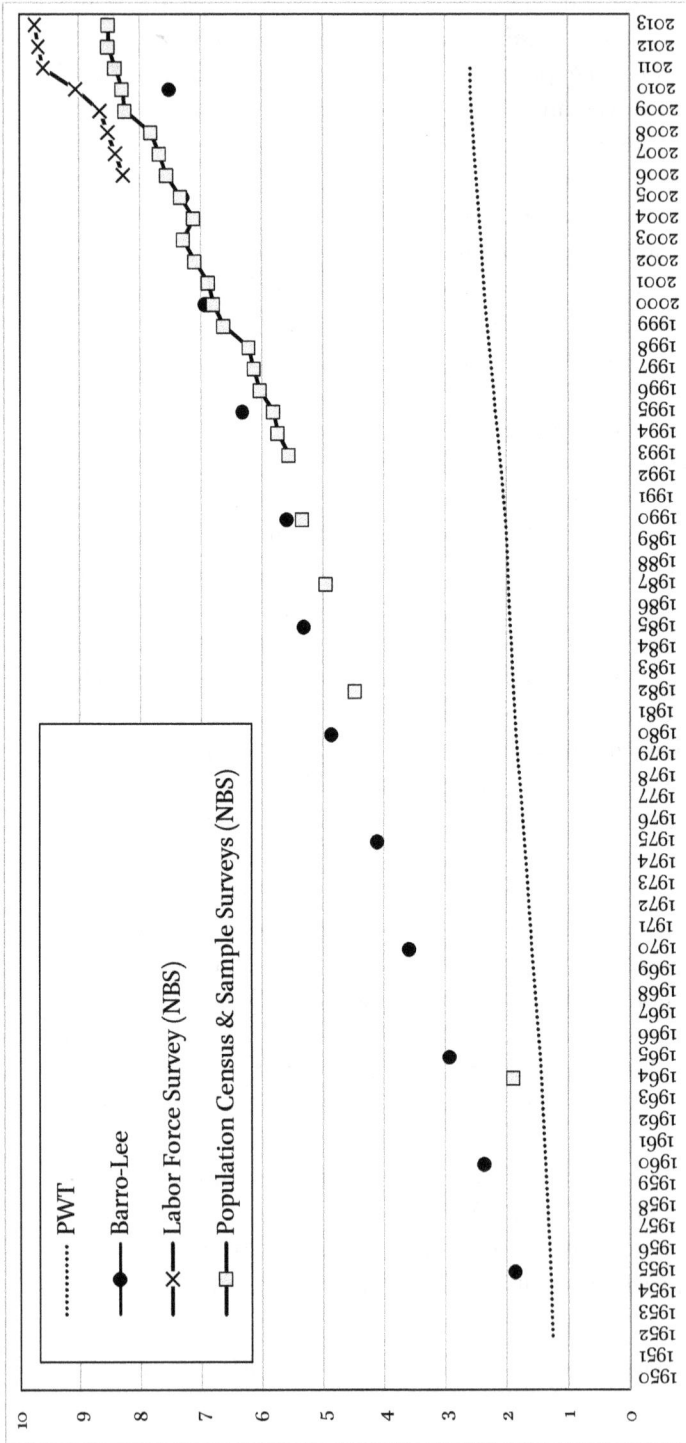

GRAPH 2.1   Average levels of education reached per person according to different sources: China,
1952–2014 (*in years*)
Notes: Data provided by the PWT (2013) are calculated on the basis of years of schooling (Barro
and Lee [2018]) and educational returns (Psacharopoulos [1994]). Barro and Lee (2018)'s data
relate to population aged 15 years and over. Data coming from the *Labor Force Surveys* by NBS
cover population of employed persons. Data from population census and NBS sample surveys
refer to total population.

human capital of the population aged six years or more, and ii) the productive human capital carried by the persons employed.

Before examining in detail the construction methods of our series, let us immediately indicate some significant differences concerning in particular the level of human capital and the growth rate of this capital which make the originality of our database compared to those currently available in the literature (Table 2.1). For example, between 1982 and 1990, the growth rate of our productive human capital was significantly lower than that of other statistical bases. This seems very logical to us, due to the fact that this period includes the events of Tiananmen which occurred in 1989 and are taken into account by our methodology, as we will see. In this very special historical context, and considering that before 1993, jobs were distributed by the State, many students, even well-educated, found themselves without diplomas nor jobs. We therefore believe that the growth rate proposed by the PWT (nearly 2.15 percent) is unrealistic and far too high. These differences are mainly due to the specificities of

TABLE 2.1   Comparison of the main databases available in the literature with our series of stocks of productive and total human capital

	Barro-Lee	PWT	UIS-UNESCO	Our own series of productive human capital	Our own series of total human capital
Most recent version	v. 2.2[a]	9.0	Publication in September 2018	–	–
Data Sample	1950–2010 (*13 points*)	1952–2014	Years of census (*4 points*)	1952–2014	1952–2014
Frequency	5 years	Yearly	10 years	Yearly	Yearly
Source of data	NBS Population Census Data	Barro and Lee	NBS Population Census Data	NBS Labor Force Surveys; NBS Yearbooks Population Census Data; Educational Yearbooks	NBS Population Census and Surveys
Age groups	More than 15 years	More than 25 years	More than 25 years	Employed persons[b]	More than 6 years

a   Precisely: *June 2018 and 2016, February 4 Update: Correction of estimates for China.*
b   Since the age groups of the persons employed vary over time, we have adjusted them according to the laws relating to labour or retirement.

TABLE 2.1   Comparison of the main databases available in the literature (*cont.*)

Comparison of data during census years

	Barro-Lee	PWT	UIS-UNESCO	Our own series of productive human capital	Our own series of total human capital
1982	Non-available	4.074772	3.97	5.143608	4.471453
1990	6.04	4.831018	4.31	5.263244	5.339319
2000	7.38	6.469095	6.61	6.680101	6.628803
2010	7.95	7.118676	7.33	9.050352	8.244960
Growth rate 1982–1990[c]	Non-available	2.15 percent	0.83 percent	0.29 percent	2.24 percent
Growth rate 1990–2000	2.02 percent	2.96 percent	5.5 percent	2.41 percent	2.19 percent
Growth rate 2000–2010	0.75 percent	0.96 percent	1.04 percent	3.08 percent	2.21 percent

c   Growth rates are calculated in geometric means.

our database; in fact, we have: 1) integrated different age groups; 2) estimated the effects of changes in the duration of studies and the consequences of the Cultural Revolution; 3) examined a large number of factors important to our topic, such as, for example, retirements, educational reforms, but also labour laws; 4) used abundant sources of information and fully exploited the original statistics; and 5) taken care to make completely transparent the methods of construction of our new database, much more than what is usually done in the literature.

2   Methodology for Building Human Capital Stocks in China from 1949 to 2014

2.1   *General Conceptual Framework*

In what follows, the term "human capital" refers to the product of, one the one hand, an average educational level attained, or the number of schooling years leading to a diploma expressed per capita, and, on the other hand, a population considered. This stock is assumed to accumulate in the following way: for a year t, the human capital H_t will be equal to that of the previous period H_{t-1} (after deducting a depreciation rate σ_{Et}), plus the investment in human capital I_{Et} made during year t:

$$H_t = (1 - \sigma_{Et}) H_{t-1} + I_{Et} \qquad (2.1)$$

In t, the increase in human capital I_{Et} is the sum of the products of the number of new graduates for each type of education i, denoted l_{it}, and the corresponding cumulative number of years of education, η_t:

$$I_{Et} = \sum_i l_{it} \eta_{it} \qquad (2.2)$$

Furthermore:

$$H_t = \sum_j E_{jt} L_{jt} \qquad (2.3)$$

where E_{jt} is the average number of years of education of individuals with the educational type j at date t, and L_{jt} their number of these persons in the population considered (E_{jt} and L_{jt} being different from η_{it} and l_{it}, respectively).

In this context, we will construct two distinct categories of human capital, using average levels of education corresponding to different populations: a total human capital stock, calculated for the population over six years of age; and a productive human capital stock, for all employed persons aged at least 16 years.

We therefore need to determine the values of the variables integrated in the composition of the two series of human capital stocks. The first of these variables corresponds to the depreciation rates used, which involve mobilizing different mortality rates, retirement rates, and also unemployment rates. Secondly, we will have to get information on the new increases in human capital, which requires knowing the durations of the educational cycles and, for each of them, the numbers of graduates. For total human capital stock, the mortality rate of persons aged six years or older is used as depreciation, and all new increases in human capital as investments. But for productive human capital stock, we retain as a depreciation rate the sum of the mortality rate of the population aged 16 or older, weighted between urban and rural areas, and of the rate of retirement; and as an incremental rise, the new increases in human capital of educational levels corresponding to the same age groups as those of employed persons. And finally, to determine the human capital stocks in the base years, we need to have the average levels of education and the numbers of people who have reached the various levels of education within the population. Thanks to the Chinese demographic yearbooks, it is possible to calculate the stocks of total human capital in 1964, 1982, 1987, 1990, and from 1993 to 2013, as well as those of productive human capital over the period 2006–2014. In this way, we can use these values as various crossing points in multiple bases in order to complete our series for their respective moments by retropolation from these years, from 1992 to 1952 for the first series, and from 2005 to 1952 for the second one. Since the necessary data are collected according to separate procedures, the equations used for their calculations are themselves different.

We can now turn to the details of the choices made.

2.2   *Two Concepts of Human Capital*

Let us begin with the stock of productive human capital.

First, it turned out that in China, diploma delivery is usually concentrated in the middle of the year, more precisely between the end of June and the beginning of July. The estimate of human capital by equation (*2.1*) actually shows its level in the middle of year t. However, if we perform econometric regressions mobilizing, as inputs, the stock of physical capital measured as usual at the end of year t, K_t, and that of human capital measured in mid-year t, H_t, then there will be a gap of 0.5 standard time between the two inputs, which will no longer be congruent and consistent with each other. To make these two inputs temporally coherent, the function of production should be:

$$Y_t = f(K_t, H_{t+0.5}) \qquad (2.4)$$

Nevertheless, in the usual modeling dealing with time series phenomena, non-integer lag orders are not accepted – with the exception of long-memory processes of the autoregressive type with fractional integration and moving average (ARFIMA) where real values are tolerated.[6] Faced with this difficulty,

---

6   See: Hosking (1981). Also: Lardic and Mignon (1999), or Mignon (1999). For example, let us consider a model:

$$\begin{cases} (1-L)^d y_t = \varepsilon_t \\ \quad d \in R \end{cases}$$

According to the binomial theorem, the rth term in the left side of this equation is:

$$C_d^r 1^r (-L)^{d-r}$$

If d is not an integer number, then the term L^{d-r} is associated with a non-integer lag operator. The application of ARFIMA models is however constrained by the requirement of series satisfying the fractional cointegration tests.

and in order to correct the temporal gap between the two inputs considered, we propose the following accretion formula for productive human capital stock:[7]

$$H_t = (1 - \sigma_{Et}) H_{t-1} + \left(1 - \frac{\sigma_{Et}}{2}\right) I_{Et} \qquad (2.5)$$

This amounts to retaining the following method of retropolation:

$$H_{t-1} = \frac{H_t - \left[1 - \dfrac{\sigma_{Et}}{2}\right] \cdot I_{Et}}{(1 - \sigma_{Et})} \qquad (2.6)$$

where the values of H_t are those of the calculated reference years.

Under these conditions, two implications are to be drawn from these equations:

1) Since human capital increases are scarce during the second half of the year, when the depreciation rate is not taken into account, the new increase in human capital in year t is equal to that of the same capital in the middle of the year

2) The new increase in human capital in the middle of the year should also be amortized when the time runs until the end of the year. It can be shown that if σ_t is small, the depreciation rate for half of the year is equal to half the depreciation rate for the whole year.[8]

---

7 Another method would be to use series in continuous time, but this requires more restrictive assumptions. Indeed, the discrete time series of the two inputs (physical capital stock at the end of the year and human capital stock at mid-year) could be transformed into continuous time in order to choose easily the points of time. However, we would have to assume stationarity over the year of the growth rates of the different variables used (that is, GDP and capital levels), which is quite difficult to accept given the impact of seasonal variations on these variables. The fact that diplomas are issued in June or July is sufficient to understand that the growth rate of human capital stock is higher during these two months and to discard the idea of the regular growth of H.

8 If σ_t^{mid} is the depreciation rate in mid-year noted t, and I_t^{end} is the increase in human capital at the end of t, then:

$$I_t^{end} = I_t \cdot (1 - \sigma_t)^{0.5} = I_t \cdot \left(1 - \sigma_t^{mid}\right)$$

In logarithmic form, we get:

$$0.5 \cdot log(1 - \sigma_t) = log\left(1 - \sigma_t^{mid}\right)$$

If x is small, one has the infinitesimal equivalence:

$$log\,(1 + x) \approx x$$

Let us now turn to the stock of total human capital.

The equation necessary for the calculation of total human capital stock in the first years must differ from those used previously because we will resort to the year 1964 as a basis for estimating this stock over the period 1949–1963, then the year 1982 in order to do the same for the period 1965–1981. However, the reference time for the 1964 and 1982 censuses is July 1, 00:00. If equation (2.4) is used to calculate the total human capital stock of the reference years, the values obtained will be those of the mid-year stock level, while equation (2.5) uses the increase of capital at the end of the year. More recent censuses have a reference time situated on November 1, 00:00. As a consequence, for the first years, we need to introduce a correction in the equation (2.5) used for total human capital stock, as follows:

$$H_t = (1 - \sigma_{Et})H_{t-1}(1 - \sigma_{E,t-1}/2) + (1 - \sigma_{E,t}/2)I_{Et} \qquad (2.7)$$

In other words, from the very beginning, the mid-year capital stock H_{t-1} is converted into its end-year level $H_{t-1}(1 - \sigma_{t-1}/2)$, then equation (2.4) is applied without adjustment for post-1990 censuses, since the reference time is close to the end of the year.

2.3   Structure of the Chinese Educational System and Schooling Categories

In our human capital calculations, we take into account all categories of education, with a few exceptions. The latter, not included in the stocks, correspond to types of education that do not lead to a diploma; even if, of course, most of them also play a positive role in the acquisition of basic knowledge, more in-depth skills, or even high-level qualifications, and undoubtedly exercising a beneficial influence on improving labour productivity. These are the cases, by instance, of pre-school level learning (nurseries, kindergartens, etc.), special education (i.e., establishments for the disabled, including medico-vocational structures enabling integration into the world of enterprises), "reform schools" (institutions for juvenile offenders with minor offenses), perfectioning centers for migrant workers (set up by local administrations), or training courses for workers directly in the workplace (more like apprenticeship by practice or learning-by-doing). On the contrary, the students who have returned home

---

Hence:

$$log(1+ (- x)) \approx - x$$

By substitution, it comes:

$$\sigma_t^{mid} = 0{,}5.\sigma_t$$

after having obtained their diploma(s) abroad are considered to be part of the country's human capital. In addition, and unlike Cai and Du (2003), we choose to include people who have participated in literacy programs or in adult training.

The structure of the Chinese education system can be presented according to two criteria (Table 2.2, and Appendix A.2.5): 1) the level of education (pre-primary, primary, secondary or higher) and 2) its nature (general, vocational, adult and other education).[9]

Table 2.2 groups together almost all the training courses leading to qualifications with diplomas since the founding of the People's Republic (1949). Some have disappeared or declined, others, more modern, have emerged. The durations of training were fairly stable, except in the early stages (especially in primary school, which experimented with several reforms), then at the time of the Cultural Revolution from 1966 to 1976, during which, in general, the durations of studies were shortened.

We will come back to this, but for now let us determine each of the variables that make up our human capital stocks.

3   Determination of the Calculation Variables (1): Depreciation of Human Capital Stocks

3.1   *Choosing the Depreciation Rates*
Our calculations will not take into consideration technical progress in depreciation, but only a phenomenon of attrition; or more exactly, the exit of productive units due to death or retirement – and not to a loss of working capacity. Here we put the hypothesis according to which the human capital defined by the number of years of studies requires the assumption that the years of education are homogeneous, which amounts to no longer taking into account the advance of knowledge and to prohibit distinguishing the quality between old and new capital.

With data coming all from the NBS, we use the mortality rate of persons aged six and over M_t^{6+}, m_t, as a depreciation of total human capital σ_t^{total}:

$$\sigma_t^{total} = m_t \qquad (2.8)$$

---

9   For English translations, see: "*Regulations of the People's Republic of China on Academic Degrees* (2004)."

TABLE 2.2   Synthetic presentation of the Chinese educational system

	General education	Vocational education	Adult education	Other education	Study abroad	Online courses
Pre-school	Nurseries and kindergartens					
Primary education	General elementary school		Literacy / Primary School	Special education / Other schools		
Secondary education	1st cycle / 2nd cycle	1st cycle / 2nd cycle / Workers schools / Specialized schools	1st cycle / 2nd cycle	Special education / Other schools		
Higher education	College / Under Graduate / Master & Ph.D.		College / Under Graduate	Other schools (*)	Returned graduates	Networks (**)

Notes: (*) = These part-time courses include the farm-schools, the "7th May University," and employed post-graduates, among others. (**) = Networks corresponding to network colleges, undergraduates ...

and the sum of the mortality rate of people aged 16 and over, weighted between urban and rural populations, and of retirement rates, r_t, as the depreciation rate of productive human capital σ_t^{prod}:

$$\sigma_t^{prod} = w_1 \cdot \sigma_t^{rural} + w_2 \cdot \sigma_t^{urban} \qquad (2.9)$$

under the constraint: $w_1 + w_2 = 1$, with w_1 and w_2 the respective proportions of the rural and urban employees in the total number of persons employed.

Since pensions generally do not apply to rural workers until now, we use the mortality rate of the rural population aged 16 years and over, m_t^{rural}, as a depreciation for persons employed in rural areas:

$$\sigma_t^{rural} = m_t^{rural} \qquad (2.10)$$

while for urban employees, we take into account the mortality rate of the urban population aged 16 and over, m_t^{urban}, and the retirement rates, as follows:

$$\sigma_t^{urban} = m_t^{urban} + r_t \qquad (2.11)$$

We must therefore estimate age-specific mortality rates and their distribution between rural and urban areas, m_t^{rural} and m_t^{urban}, as well as rates of retirement, r_t.

3.2   *Mortality Rates*

The respective values of m_t^{rural} and m_t^{urban} since 1994 can be calculated directly on the basis of the successive demographic yearbooks.[10] For the remaining years, data are lacking. However, we have observed that information on migration between rural and urban areas prior to the year 1983 provided by the NBS is biased, and that the resulting rural and urban calculations of m_t^{rural} and m_t^{urban} are unreasonable. Thus, while taking a maximum benefit of the available historical data, we had to select the optimal approximations when necessary (Table 2.3).

So, for the years 1992–1993, we replace the missing values by the mortality rates of the population aged 16 and over.[11] For the periods 1954–1965 and 1972–1985, we use the mortality rates of rural and urban populations,[12] m_t^{rural} and m_t^{urban}. On the contrary, information is rather rare for the years 1949–1953,

---

10   The 1995 data is based on the *Population Yearbook 1997*, while the 2000 and 2010 data are obtained thanks to demographic censuses (in Tables 6-4 A–C).

11   Data are from the *Population Yearbooks 1993* and *1994*.

12   Data provided by the *China Population Statistics Collection 1949–1985*.

TABLE 2.3   Mortality rates (by category of death) used in human capital stock calculations

Death	Selected mortality rate	Sources of data
Deaths of persons of 6 years or older	Mortality rate of the over six years, M_t^{6+}	
Deaths of persons with a 2nd level of primary education	Mortality rate of the over 10 years, M_t^{10+}	Data covering the period from 1992 to 2013 are calculated using the respective population
Deaths of persons with a 1st level of secondary education	Mortality rate of the over 12 years, M_t^{12+}	yearbooks (with 2000 and 2010 data directly coming from demo-
Deaths of persons with a 2nd level of secondary education	Mortality rate of the over 14 years, M_t^{14+}	graphic censuses).
Deaths of persons with a high school or higher educa-tion level	Mortality rate of the over 17 years, M_t^{17+}	Data covering the period from 1950 to 1991 are calculated using the *World Population Prospects*
Deaths of persons undergo-ing adult training	Mortality rate of the over 18 years, M_t^{18+}	yearbooks (in some years, the values of
Deaths during primary school enrollment	Average mortality rate of the 5–14 years old, M_t^{5-14}	M_t^{5-14}, M_t^{10-17} and M_t^{12-20} are negative, so that we need to
Deaths in the course of enrollment in lower second-ary education	Average mortality rate of the 10–17 years old, M_t^{10-17}	use moving averages over five years instead, while M_t^{6+} is the depreciation rate of total human
Deaths in the course of enrollment in upper second-ary education	Average mortality rate of the 12–20 years, M_t^{12-20}	capital in the same periods).
Deaths during schooling in high school or higher education	Average mortality rate of the 14–30 years old, M_t^{14-30}	

Note: It is assumed that children enter school at five to eight years of age; the duration of primary school is five to six years, that of lower secondary school is two to three years, as that of upper secondary education. In this way, we obtain the age groups for each educational level.

because of the wars preceding the creation of the People's Republic, and for 1966–1971, because of the Cultural Revolution.

As a result, in the case of m_t^{rural}, the value chosen for 1949 corresponds to the average of the data available in seven provinces of the country; the values for the years 1950–1953, to the averages of nine provinces; that of 1966, to the average of 21 provinces; and the values from 1967 to 1972, to the averages of 20 provinces.

For m_t^{urban}, the 1949 value is approximated by the mean of the data for eight provinces; those from 1950 to 1953, by the averages of 10 provinces; that of 1966, by the average of 22 provinces; and the values of the period 1967–1972, by the averages of 21 provinces.[13]

Since there is no information on m_t^{urban} and m_t^{rural} in 1987–1988, the mortality rate of the total population is used instead.

3.3   Retirement Rates

We calculate the retirement rate of urban employees, r_t, as:

$$r_t = P_t^{r,u} / P_t^{e,u} \qquad (2.12)$$

where $P_t^{r,u}$ corresponds to the number of people retiring in urban areas, $P_t^{e,u}$ and to that of urban employees.

According to the definition adopted:

$$P_t^{r,u} = P_t^{t,r,u} - P_t^{r,un,u} \qquad (2.13)$$

with $P_t^{t,r,u}$ the total urban population at retirement age, and $P_t^{r,un,u}$ the number of unemployed persons in urban areas who have reached that age.

Legal retirement ages differ between men and women, and, regulatorily, are linked to the socio-professional category of the persons concerned. They have been amended several times (Appendix A.2.6). As to it, the $P_t^{r,un,u}$ variable is calculated separately.

Four categories of socio-professional status (or "professional identity") make it possible to classify the population: workers, peasants, soldiers, and "cadres" or managers. Although this classification was almost completely abandoned following the 1978 reforms, it still continues to play a role in some areas. Strictly speaking, the term "cadres" refers to executives or leaders exercising senior positions and high responsibilities within the Communist Party of China or in governmental administrations, at provincial and national levels.

---

13   Data are from the *China Population Statistics Collection 1949–1985* (pp. 402–463).

In practice, we must add to this the top managers and senior leaders of public institutions[14] and State-owned enterprises,[15] who often also hold high-level political positions[16] – but not local administrative staff[17] (at the village level or neighborhoods committee level).

With the exception of jobs with very high responsibilities nationally, the retirement ages of men, workers or managers, have remained the same over time: 60 years. By contrast, there are differences and changes to be noted in the case of women depending on whether they are workers or "cadres" or managers – except during the Cultural Revolution, when women's pensions were received at the same age. In most years, the retirement age for female managers was 55, compared to 50 for female workers. As managers represent only a small fraction of female jobs,[18] the gap between women workers and managers can be considered to have had a negligible impact on the average retirement age. In terms of senior executive positions, their extreme scarcity makes this impact even more insignificant.

The retirement ages selected, distinguished by gender, are as follows (Table 2.4):

TABLE 2.4   Changes in the retirement age by gender: China, from 1952 to present (*in years*)

	Men	Women
From 1952 to 1957	60	50
From 1958 to 1977	60	55
From 1978 to the present day	60	50

14   Schools, research centers, hospitals, collective enterprises, institutes linked to central or local governments, etc.

15   In general, the socio-professional identity of an entrepreneur depends on his or her family register, or *Hukou* (see: Li *et al.* [2017]). If the latter is urban, this identity will be that of worker; if it is rural, it will be that of peasant.

16   As a general rule, workers tend to retire early, while executives often delay their departure.

17   In China, the various administrative levels are, in ascending order: village, town (sectional level), canton (divisional one), prefecture (departmental), province (ministerial), and the country itself (national).

18   In 2005, women executives accounted for only 5.3 percent of urban employees and only 1.0 percent of total employed persons (calculated from information provided by the *Xinhua News Agency* [2005]).

It is also necessary to calculate the urban populations of men aged 60 and women aged 50 (and/or 55), and those employed but of retirement age. The NBS yearbooks have only provided data on urban population by age and by gender since 1983. For structures prior to that date, only census years are available. As to them, the *World Population Prospects*'s age structures appear as five-year age groups with no specific indication of people of retirement age. We must therefore evaluate the urban population with the retirement age, $P_t^{t,r,u}$, before 1983.

To do this, we use information on adjacent censuses (in this case, those of 1953, 1964, and 1982) to estimate the series $P_t^{t,r,u}$ before 1983. We first define a three-dimensional function[19] of the depreciation rate:

$$\rho_t^{ij} = \rho\left(age, year, sex\right) \qquad (2.14)$$

ρ_t^{ij} representing the mortality rate of the population of age i, sex j, in year t; so as to obtain:

$$P_{t+\tau}^{i+\tau,j} = P_t^{i,j} \cdot \left(1 - \rho_t^{ij}\right)^{\tau} \qquad (2.15)$$

where $P_{t+\tau}^{i+\tau,j}$ and $P_t^{i,j}$ are the respective numbers of people in the same population group in two distinct censuses separated by τ years, so that we can calculate the depreciation rate between these adjacent censuses using a geometric mean.

Graph 2.2 shows the average depreciation rates of the population by age and by sex over the periods 1953–1964 and 1964–1982. The curves are in line with the traditional main findings of the demographic literature dedicated to China: 1) the depreciation rate of the population reaches its maximum near average life expectancy; 2) in the childhood period, the average mortality rate of girls is higher than that of boys; 3) at older ages, the mortality rate of women is generally lower than that of men. Moreover, ρ_t^{ij} is calculated for persons living at birth and does not take into account deaths of stillborn children. This underestimation of mortality at young ages does not affect our series, which concern the depreciation rates of populations aged 50, 55 and 60 years.[20]

---

19   It would be more appropriate to define a four-dimensional function, adding the urban and rural distribution. Nevertheless, since the urban–rural migration data of the NBS are biased, this urban–rural dimension is neglected. Thus, we first estimate the total number of people of retirement age, and then use a dynamic proportion of the urban population in the total population to calculate (indirectly) $P_t^{t,r,u}$.

20   Furthermore, it should be noted that the 1953 and 1964 censuses do not contain military personnel.

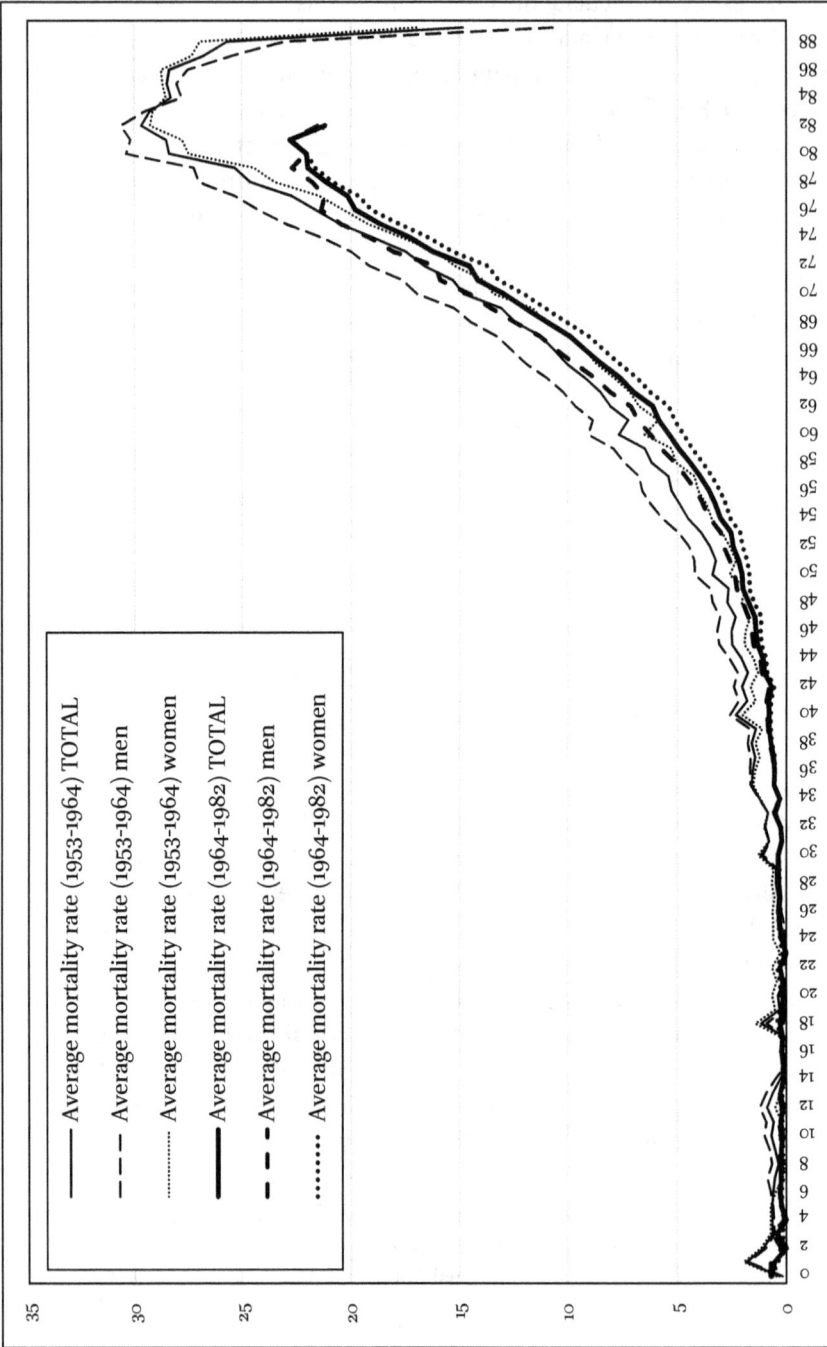

GRAPH 2.2   Average mortality rates of the population by age: China, 1953–1982
Note: The x-axis indicates the age (which ranges from 0 to 90 years) – the projection eliminating
time dimension.

Therefore, we can calculate the total population with retirement age $P_t^{t,r}$ before 1983, then obtain the urban population with the retirement age $P_t^{t,r,u}$:

$$P_t^{t,r,u} = \alpha_t \cdot P_t^{t,r} \qquad (2.16)$$

thanks to the proportion of the urban population in the total population for year t, α_t.

We also need to identify the unemployed urban population of retirement age. The NBS provides only the officially registered urban unemployment rate, and the number of urban unemployed only since 1978, without presenting the age structure of the unemployed. In fact, the Chinese data on unemployment are not of good quality. They consider as unemployment only the individuals who have taken steps to register with "civil affairs" agencies. This is quite logical, but since the amount of allowances paid is small, it does not encourage the registration of unemployed persons. It is therefore likely that the official urban unemployment rate is underestimated.

The dynamism of Chinese economic growth since 1978 has kept the urban unemployment rate at particularly low levels (around 3.5 percent in average over 36 years), and stabilized it around 4 percent since the beginning of the 2000s. There is every reason to believe that this variable was also contained during the period of the centrally-planned economy preceding the reforms of 1978.

Here, we assume that the unemployment rate of the urban population at the age corresponding to retirement was 4 percent before 1978. Values after that date are those of the officially recorded urban unemployment rate (see Graph 2.3).

Consequently, we have:

$$P_t^{r,u} = P_t^{t,r,u} \cdot \left(1 - r_t^{un,u}\right) \qquad (2.17)$$

where $P_t^{r,u}$ is the urban population which retires, $P_t^{t,r,u}$ that which is old enough to retire, $r_t^{un,u}$ and the unemployment rate of the urban population which is at retirement age.

Recalling equation (2.12), we obtain the legal retirement rate of persons employed in urban areas and, finally, using equation (2.9), the depreciation rate of the stock of productive human capital (Graph 2.4).

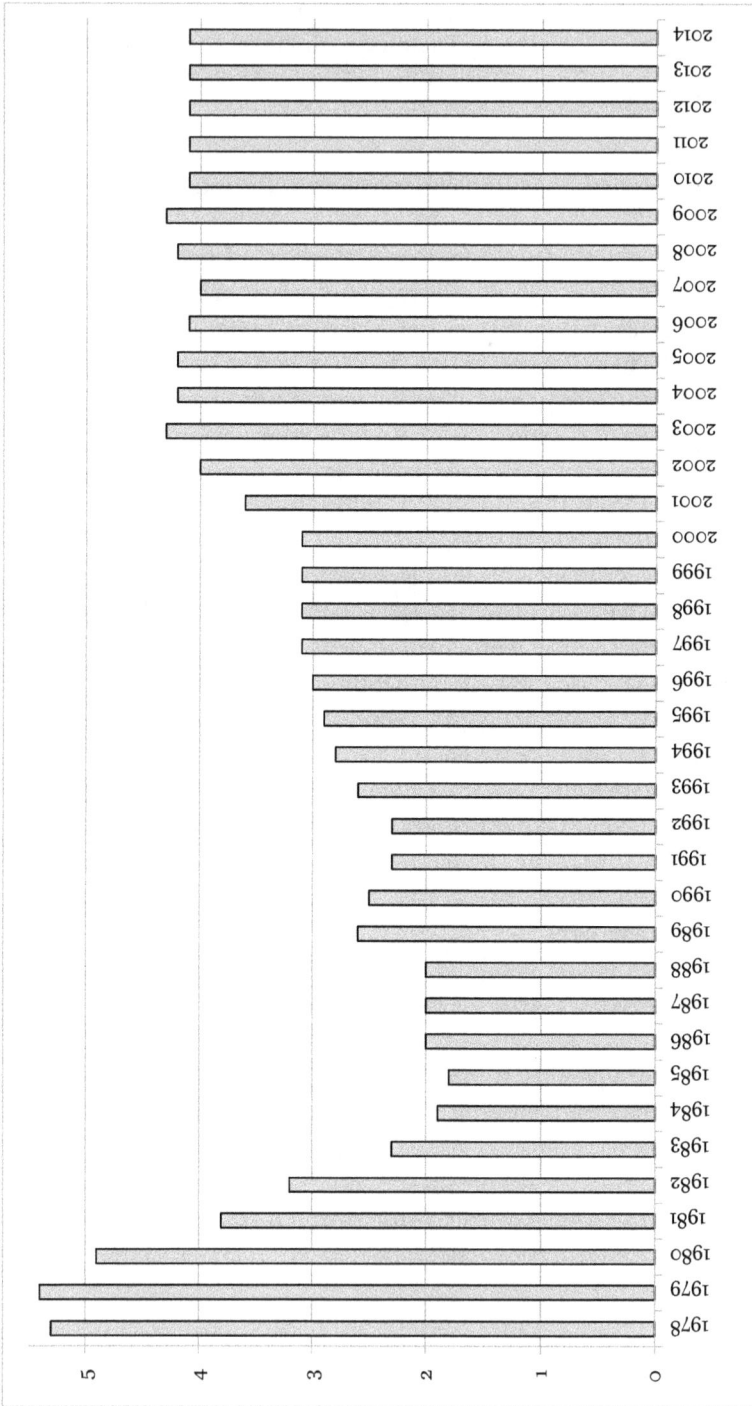

GRAPH 2.3   Changes in the officially registered urban unemployment rate: China, 1978–2013 (*as a percentage of the labour force*)
SOURCE: NBS (VARIOUS YEARS)

4 Determination of Calculation Variables (11): Increases in the Stock of Human Capital

We now have to construct the human capital increases I_{Et}, with equation (2.2). Consequently, we need to know the numbers of new graduates l_{it}, as well as the durations of education η_{it} of the different types of schooling presented in Table 2.2.

4.1 Numbers of Graduates
The NBS information on the numbers of graduates λ_{it} contains a lot of missing data. The latter sometimes have to take the value zero: as a matter of fact, some specific types of teachings did no longer exist, or did not yet exist, at the time of the statistical survey; or also certain establishments were closed, and courses interrupted during particular periods in the history of the country. Nevertheless, other values, undoubtedly non-zero, remain unavailable simply because the statistical data are non-existent.

The missing NBS data were completed, rebuilt or improved, for the following variables:

(1) Graduates of tertiary education during the period 1971 to 1977. Here, since all enrollments at this level were interrupted from 1967, and resumed in 1977 only,[21] the corresponding values are set to zero.

(2) Graduates of vocational schools from 1949 to 1958 and from 1966 to 1979. Their number is set at zero for the years in question, as these schools, which were opened in 1958, ceased to function during the Cultural Revolution.[22]

(3) Graduates of adult education over the period 1949–2003. Data from 1949 to 1981 come from the *China Education Statistical Yearbook 1949–1981*, and those between 1982 and 2003 from the *China Education Statistical Yearbooks* (various years).

(4) Graduates who studied abroad and returned to China after having completed their training between 1949 and 1952, and then from 1966 to 1973. These values are fixed at zero, due to particular historical contexts (the early years of the People's Republic, then the Cultural Revolution

(5) Graduates of online learning over the period 1949–2003. Before the year 2003 and the rise of the Internet, the values of online courses were obviously zero.

---

21 See: *China Education Statistical Yearbook 1949–1981*, p. 637.
22 See here the fourth *Administrative Work Meeting of the Ministry of Education* released in March 1958.

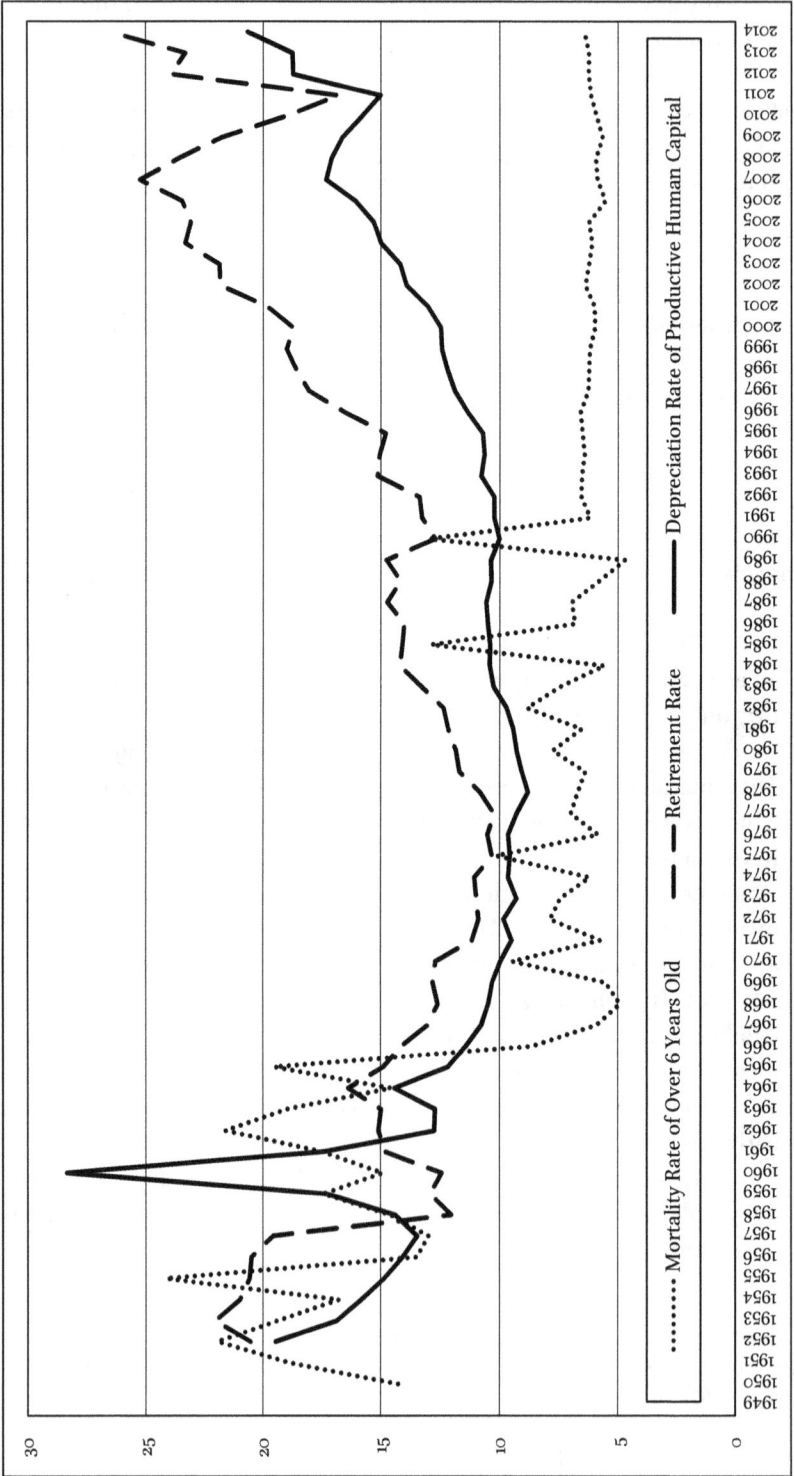

GRAPH 2.4   Rate of depreciation of productive human capital: China, 1949–2014 (*in percent*)

4.2 *Education Durations*

The standard durations of the different educational categories have remained fairly stable for each level (Table 2.5). In general, they were as follows:

TABLE 2.5   Standard course durations by level of education in China (*in number of cumulated years*)

Level of education	Level attained	Level of education	Level attained	Level of education	Level attained
General primary education	6	Primary education for adults	1	Literacy classes	1
1st cycle of general secondary	6 + 3 = 9	1st cycle of secondary for adults	1.5	1st cycle of vocational secondary	6 + 3 = 9
2nd cycle of general secondary	9 + 3 = 12	2nd cycle of secondary for adults	1.5	2nd cycle of vocational secondary	9 + 3 = 12
Specialized post-secondary college	12 + 3 = 15	Specialized college for adults	1.5	Training of skilled workers	1
1st cycle of higher education	12 + 4 = 16	1st cycle of adult higher education	2	Specialized secondary education	9 + 3 = 12
Master's degree	16 + 3 = 19	Online college	1.5	Education abroad	Dynamically calculated
Ph.D.	19 + 3 = 22	Online upper under-graduate	2	Uneducated	0

Let us note here that:
(1)   The educational level of the uneducated, persons not at school and/or illiterate, is set equal to zero. However, this does not mean that they will not appear among the inputs, because the uneducated will figure as a simple labour force.
(2)   We adopt a dynamic calculation method for the level of education achieved by students returning from abroad. Before the opening of the

country, almost all were Ph.D. students with scholarships provided by the Ministry of Education. Nowadays, these governmental allowances are no longer the only source of funding, and a majority of graduated students returning to China is currently composed of holders of Master's degrees, or even lower diplomas.[23] Between 1949 and 1999, graduates who returned after completing their studies abroad were considered to be mainly Ph.D. graduates with 22 years of education, then, from 2000 to 2004, graduates with 19 years of education. But from 2005 onwards, the *Open Doors Reports*[24] of the Institute of International Education (IIE) and available data from the *Chinese Service Center for Scholarly Exchange* of the Ministry of Education have been able to estimate the average level of education of this category of students.

(3) For adult education, what is to be calculated is the new increase in human capital, whereas the target of these courses is a group of adults already entered the labour market. Therefore, their previous education levels are not taken into consideration; we only have to account for the increase in the level of education corresponding to the training destined to improve or develop the knowledge of these workers. Moreover, since the courses are part-time, these years cannot be counted in full; we thus retain only half the duration of adult education as an increase in the educational level.

(4) For skilled workers' training, the assumptions are identical to those for adult education. However, admission to these schools does not necessarily lead to an increase in the number of new graduates, and time is split between work and study. The duration of the cycles is generally three years if the registered person is enrolled in junior secondary school, and two years if he or she is in the senior cycle of the same level – the last year being devoted to a training period. As a consequence, we suppose an increase of the educational level by one year.

(5) The increase in the level of education achieved for literacy courses is also assumed to be equal to one year, on the basis of the NBS definitions of

---

23 The *Chinese Returned Overseas Students Employment Blue Book 2014* indicates that 30 percent of the persons who have studied abroad have a Bachelor's degree, 63 percent a Master's degree, and only 6 percent a Ph.D.

24 As there were not enough time-series data about the structure of the diplomas by graduates returning to China from abroad, we had to use the diploma structure of the Chinese students in the United States as an approximation. As the U.S. is the main destination for Chinese overseas students, such an approximation is acceptable. Students returning from abroad being only a small proportion in the total number of graduates, the error remains quite negligible.

illiteracy or elimination of illiteracy. The first definition (illiteracy), which dates from 1953, considers as illiterate a person who can use less than 500 common Chinese characters; the second one (elimination of illiteracy), dating back to 1950, considers as literate an individual who increased his or her knowledge of the common Chinese characters to 1,000 in three years – a criterion that was raised in 1953 to 2,000 in urban areas and in 1956 to 1,500 in rural areas, which is equivalent, respectively, to a fourth or a second year (minimum) of primary education approximatively.[25] Thus, after three or four years of part-time literacy, the levels are equivalent to a minimum of the second year of primary school. To avoid overestimating the level reached at the end of these courses, it is reasonable to fix the increase at one year.

Let us now turn to ordinary education. Overall, the length of general and vocational education has remained fairly stable over time. However, during the first years of the People's Republic, a succession of reforms took place, involving frequent modifications of these durations, more especially in the primary.

Prior to 1949, the durations of education were determined by the *Renxu* system, established in 1922. Full primary education was then divided into two blocks, spanning six years: four years in the first cycle and two in the second cycle. In 1951, the State Council issued a decision on the reform of the education system, whereby the learning durations of primary education were uniformly reduced to five years, and those of high school and university reduced from four to three years, and from six to five, respectively. However, as soon as 1953, this reform was repealed, and the length of the primary school returned to six years. By 1958, a variety of regimes were tried throughout the whole country, with attempts of reforms entailing large-scale and irregular durations. In 1959, these experiments, with sometimes disorganized implications, were for the most part abandoned, but it was proposed to reduce the length of the primary and secondary cycles from 12 to 10 years in one or two decades from 1960. The attempts therefore resumed. Between January 1961 and May 1966 (on the eve of the Cultural Revolution), some schools also took part in the experiments carried out during the Great Leap Forward, the majority resorting to standard durations. Nevertheless, teaching was generally reduced during the Cultural Revolution. Up to 1973, in 14 provinces, the duration was nine years (five years in primary and four in secondary); and in seven others, it was 10 years (5 + 5 or 6 + 4); in nine others still, the schooling durations were different between cities and countryside (10 years for the former, and nine for the latter); and in Tibet,

25   See: *2011 Compulsory Education Curriculum Standards.*

primary schools of five or six years coexisted, with the first cycle of secondary schools of three years.

The durations of education have also been relatively stable in higher education – except during the period of the Cultural Revolution. We use for each year the proportions of graduates of curricula with different training durations in the total number of graduates in the same category as weightings, and then we calculate year after year the average durations of the first and second cycles of the primary and secondary education. Therefore, for the example of primary school, we have:

$$\eta_{prim,\, t} = 5\, \alpha_5 + 6\, \alpha_6 \qquad (2.18)$$

where α_5 and α_6 are the respective shares of primary school graduates of five or six years of age in the total number of primary school graduates, their sum being normalized, that is to say: $\alpha_5 + \alpha_6 = 1$.

We use a similar method to calculate the average durations of the first and second cycles of secondary education. The results are shown in Graph 2.5.

4.3   New Increases in Human Capital Stocks

It seems *a priori* possible, and even simple, to obtain the series of new increases in stocks of human capital, respectively total and productive, on the basis of the proposed equations. However, a difficulty arises in constructing the productive human capital stock when it comes to determining the ages of people employed. Series I_{Et} relating to total human capital does not pose any real problem, since it includes all the new increases. But the series associated with the productive human capital must exclude a part of the new investments due to the age entry into the labour market.

As a matter of fact, in view of the usual age of entry into primary school (at six), of the minimum compulsory duration of studies (nine years), and of the legal minimum age for work (16 years), graduates of the first cycle of secondary education, aged 15 or older, have generally reached the age of being employed. As a result, the series of new increase in productive human capital will have to include the graduates of first cycle of secondary education, but not those of the level of primary school. In China, however, the compulsory nature of education took on a legal form only with the 1982 Constitution, before being clarified by a Law on compulsory education, fixing its duration at nine years. This legislation was effectively implemented only from 1986 on. Therefore, before 1982, or more precisely before 1986, when using the series excluding the primary school graduates from our calculation of the new increases in productive

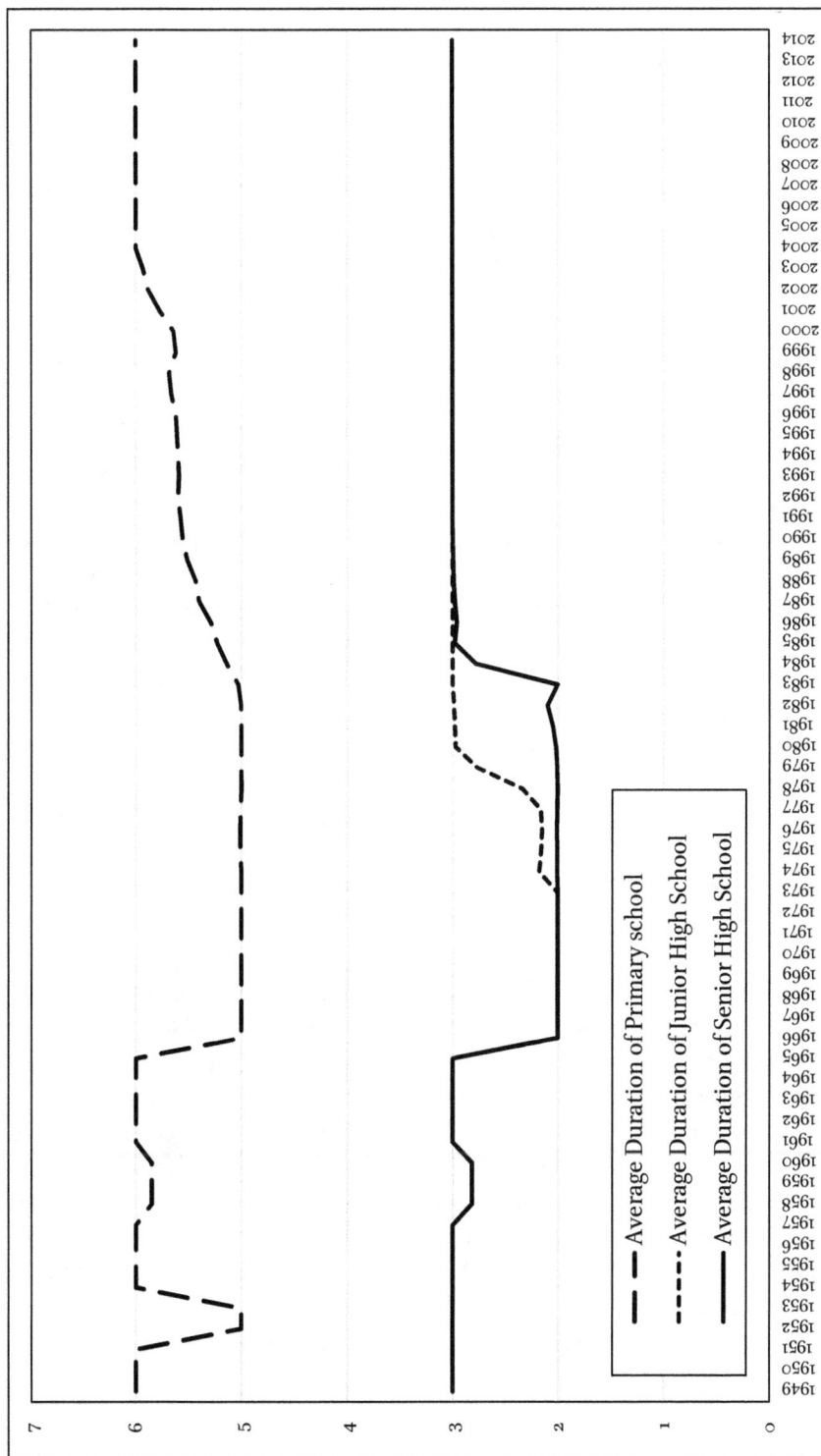

GRAPH 2.5 Weighted average durations of education levels: China, 1949–2014 (*in years*)

human capital, we risk underestimating the latter. Consequently, the level of education achieved in the initial years, obtained by retropolation, will be over-estimated. And because of the reduction in the duration of studies during the Cultural Revolution, graduates of lower secondary education may not have reached 16 years of age, while the usual age of graduates of upper secondary education is just attained around 16 years. We must thus improve this series; for which we will proceed by segmentation.

The application of the Compulsory Education Act (especially in its article 2) was only gradual. And in parallel, at the same time, the regulations relating to the legal working age resulted in two subsequent fundamental legal texts, namely: i) the law on the protection of minors (article 38 of the Juvenile Protection Act adopted in 1991) and ii) that of labour (article 15 of the Labor Act in 1994), which both formally prohibited the hiring of young people aged under 16. As a consequence, between the moment of the decision to impose compulsory education (in 1982, or rather in 1986), supplemented by the ban on child labour, and the full implementation of this compulsory education and the obligation to enroll, we use a (linear) smoothing function over the transition period. The degree of law enforcement is represented by the promotion rate T_p for primary school graduates: an increasing rate means that the law becomes effective; and the year for which it reaches 100 percent is the year in which its effects are generalized (that is to say, in 2006, precisely).

We thus obtain the adjusted series of new increases in productive human capital stock (Graph 2.6).

5   Determination of Calculation Variables (III): Values of Stocks
       for Base Years

The lack of historical data prevents determining human capital levels in the initial year of our series. Nevertheless, through the available demographic yearbooks mentioned above, we can gather information for recent years about the structure of the population aged six years and older, according to age, sex and educational level, as well as about the average level of education achieved by employees. Thus, we deduce the stocks of productive and total human capital for these years. Their values are used as bases to retropolize the two series to their respective origins, by resorting to equation (2.7) (total human capital) and to equation (2.6) (productive human capital), respectively. Our approach consists in using as much official data as possible to reduce the cumulative effects of possible errors – even minimal – caused by the approximations

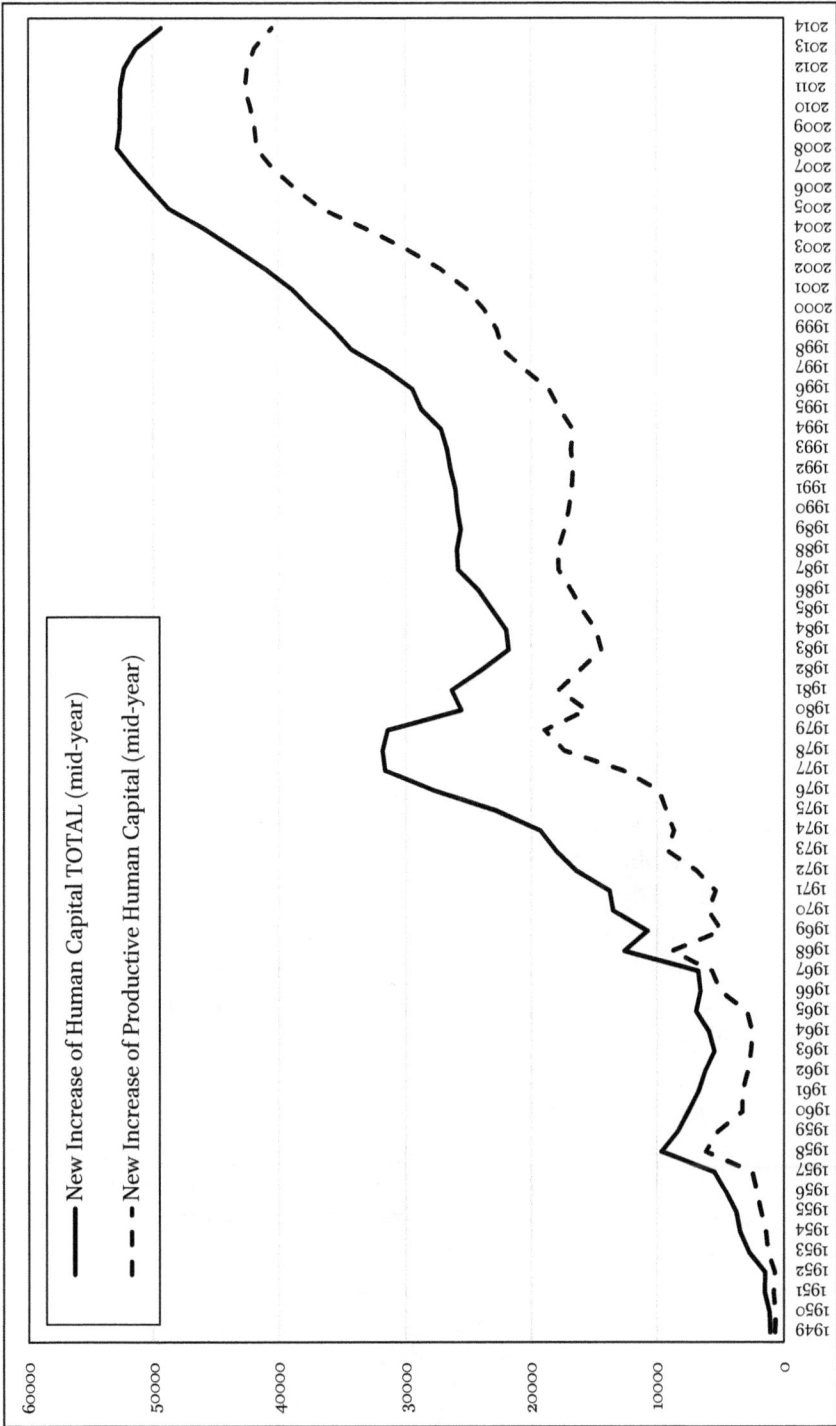

GRAPH 2.6 New increases in human capital stocks: China, 1949–2014 (*10,000 people × years*)

TABLE 2.6   Human capital for the base years and respective sources of data

	Period	Base years	Data sources for base years
Total human capital	1949–1963	1964	*Second Population Census*
	1965–1981	1982	*Third Population Census*
	1983–1986	1987	*China Population Statistics Yearbook 1988*
	1988–1989	1990	*Fourth Population Census*
	1991–1992	1993	*China Population Statistics Yearbook 1994*
	1993–2014		*China Population Statistics Yearbooks* for the corresponding years
Productive human capital	1949–2005	2006	*China Population and Employment Statistics Yearbook 2007*
	2006–2014		*China Population and Employment Statistics Yearbooks*

of depreciation rates and of investment flows. Here, we do not use the most recent year, which is available as a reference, but multiple crossing bases for a calculation by segmentation (Table 2.6).

As can be seen, the series of total human capital stock since 1993 and of productive human capital stock since 2006 can be directly calculated using the different demographic yearbooks available. In addition, the new increases of human capital and the depreciation rates previously defined are used in order to estimate stock levels for these years by applying equation (2.5). The observation of the two series obtained according to these separate methods shows that they are quite comparable, the differences between them being very limited, which indicates that the methodology employed is correct.

5.1   *Average Educational Levels*

To calculate the human capital stocks in the base years, we need the average educational level, E_{jt}. The demographic yearbooks give us the level of education reached by the population aged six-years or more, distinguishing five strata for total stock (Table 2.7). And as for productive stock, these same yearbooks provide the educational level attained by persons employed with seven strata (Table 2.8). We therefore assign the following values to E_{jt}:

TABLE 2.7 Standard educational level of population aged six and over: calculation of total human capital (*in years*)

Cultural level	No schooling	Primary	1st cycle of secondary	2nd cycle of secondary	High school and university
Educational level attained	0	6	9	12	15

TABLE 2.8 Standard educational level of employed persons: calculation of productive human capital (*in years*)

Cultural level	No schooling	Primary	1st cycle of secondary	2nd cycle of secondary	High school	1st cycle of university	1st cycle of university and more
Level attained	0	6	9	12	15	16	19

With regard to the educational level attained by employees, for which we have only post-2006 data, and standard schooling durations (Graph 2.6), the values of E_{jt} appear reasonable – except for those of graduates of the second cycle or more at the university who seem to be underestimated, as the number of studying years to complete a Ph.D. runs to 22 years, that is to say, more than the 19 years of a Master's degree. We therefore use the proportions of the cumulative numbers of Ph.D. or Master's graduates to improve our estimate of the education level reached by higher education graduates (Table 2.9):

TABLE 2.9 Average educational level of higher education graduates (*in years*)

Years	2006	2007	2008	2009	2010	2011	2012	2013	2014
Educational level attained	19.42	19.41	19.41	19.41	19.40	19.40	19.38	19.38	19.37

The cumulative numbers of Ph.D. and Master's graduates in the employed population are calculated using the corresponding depreciation rates and the numbers of Ph.D. or Master's graduates for each year. Here we resort to the following equations:

$$E_t^{diplo} = 22 \ w_t^{Ph.D} + 19 \ w_t^{master} \qquad (2.19)$$

with

$$w_t^{Ph.D} = L_t^{Ph.D} / (L_t^{Ph.D} + L_t^{master}) \qquad (2.20)$$

and

$$w_t^{Ph.D} + w_t^{master} = 1 \qquad (2.21)$$

Then, it comes:

$$L_t^{Ph.D} = L_{t-1}^{Ph.D} \cdot (1 - \sigma_t) + l_t^{Ph.D} \qquad (2.22)$$

where $l_t^{Ph.D}$ represents the number of Ph.D. holders in year t, and σ_t the corresponding rate of depreciation. Since the variable to be calculated is part of the employed population, we must deduct the Ph.D. holders who have died or who are retired. Estimation of cumulative numbers of Master's graduates is done using the same calculation method.

Nevertheless, with regard to the level of education of the population aged six years and over, the situation is considerably more complicated, for at least three reasons:

1) The educational level attained by the employed persons includes curricula that have been followed to completion and for which years of schooling and training are certain and complete. However, the calculation of educational level reached by the total population does not only concern the individuals who have actually completed these courses, but also those who are still in school, and even those who have dropped out of school. *De facto*, using standard schooling durations – as Cai and Du (2003), for example, do it – amounts to introducing a bias into the estimates. As a matter of fact, the definition of the level of primary education of the total population given by the NBS explicitly refers to the persons whose highest level of education does not exceed that of primary school, whether they are still in school, they have completed their studies, or even if they gave up. Standardizing the schooling duration to

six years leads to an overestimation of total human capital. Using *Population Census 2010*'s Table B0301a entitled "Population aged six years and over by sex, completion status and level of education," and by parameterizing the schooling durations of persons undergoing training as well as those who dropped out of school at the half-way stage of the full cycle, we can observe that the average number of years reached by the population with primary education was not six, but 4.94 years.

2) Besides, changes in the duration of schooling in the educational system should be taken into account. For productive human capital stock, the reference years begin in 2006, a date when the whole country had already re-adopted the standard durations of the educational system. But for total human capital stock, the base years are older (1964, 1982, 1987, 1990, 1993) and refer to periods when the durations of the studies were not the same. Accordingly, our estimates will have to take these differences into consideration.

3) Prior to the year 1949, primary education was divided into a first cycle of four years, and a second cycle of two – according to the *Renxu* system of school education, in particular. However, with the exception of the 1964 census, data of population with a cultural level equivalent to the primary school level coming from the other demographic surveys do not make it possible to distinguish between the first and second cycles of primary education. But the 1982 census shows that, for the "primary cultural level," there were about 83.6 million persons who were still studying in the first cycle of primary education during that year. This means that, if we do not pay attention to this problem, our results will be biased; or, more precisely, they will be overestimated.

Among the different E_{jt} needed, it is the level of education attained for primary education, E_t^P, which appears to be the most difficult to calculate. The question is how many years of education exactly correspond to an educational level of primary school. Indeed, E_t^P dynamically differs from year to year depending on the change in the training durations, in the promotion rates of primary school graduates, and in mortality rates. It is found that the values taken by E_t^P for the years 1964 and 1982 are decisive: on the one hand, the periods of the series estimated on the basis of these two dates are long; on the other hand, these are periods in a distant past, for which the historical problems mentioned above – that of the distinction between the primary cycles, among others – produce their greatest effects.

The values of E_t^P for these years must therefore be estimated with care. The 1964 census reveals that 195.82 million persons had a level equivalent to primary education at that date, of which 126.36 million were integrated into the first cycle, and 69.46 million into the second one. For the other years, however, these two cycles are no longer distinguished. For the recent period, particularly in the calculation of the values of E_t^P after 1993, this problem may be neglected to some extent. As a matter of fact, those educated in primary education prior to 1949 were aged 54 or over in 1993 (they were at least 10 years of age at the completion of this cycle before the year 1949).

However, at that age, with the exception of male executives or "cadres," the vast majority of workers had withdrawn from the labour market, without any more impact on productive human capital, and many people of that generation had even died during the half century that followed their schooling. Moreover, the extension of schooling and training, including for adults, had also raised the educational level that workers had been able to achieve for more than four decades. And after the year 1993, those with only an undergraduate level of primary education represented only a tiny fraction of the Chinese total population.

Nevertheless, for the first few years, the problem is unavoidable. To overcome this difficulty, we propose to use the following equation:

$$E_t^P = \beta_{p,P} \cdot E_t^{p,P} + \beta_{s,P} \cdot E_t^{s,P} + \beta_{A,P} \cdot E_t^{A,P} + \beta_{scol} \cdot E_t^{scol-p,S} + \beta_{drop} \cdot E_t^{drop-p,S} \qquad (2.23)$$

under the constraint: $\beta_p + \beta_S + \beta_A + \beta_{scol} + \beta_{drop} = 1$.

In these conditions, the population with the level of primary education thus comprises five components:

1) People in the first cycle of primary education: the proportion of persons in the population of primary level is $\beta_{p,P}$, and the educational level reached $E_t^{p,P} = 4$.

2) Those of the second cycle of primary education: by reasoning with completed studies and a corresponding fraction β_S, the level $E_t^{s,P}$ is the weighted average of educational duration $\eta_{prim,\, t}$ taking into account the variations of this schooling duration.

3) Adults with primary level: their share is $\beta_{A,P}$, and the level reached $E_t^{A,P} = 4 + 1$.

4) People currently in primary schooling: the proportion is β_{scol}.

And,

5) dropping out of primary school: of proportion β_{drop}.

We consider that the educational level reached by those enrolled and those who have dropped out of school corresponds to half the duration of full primary education.

Besides, at each stage of the educational system, we get an assumption of uniformity in the distribution between the population enrolled in school and that leaving school. In other words, we consider that:

$$E_t^{scol-p,S} = E_t^{drop-p,S} = 0,5 \cdot E_t^{s,P} \qquad (2.24)$$

We can therefore rewrite in the simplified form:

$$E_t^P = \beta_{s,P} \cdot \eta_{prim,t} + 4\beta_{p,P} + 0,5\, \eta_{prim,t} \cdot (\beta_{scol} + \beta_{drop}) + 5\beta_A \qquad (2.25)$$

5.2   Levels and Proportions of Educated Populations

The five proportions mobilized need still to be calculated, that is: the number of graduates of the first cycle of primary education $L_t^{p,P}$; that of graduates of the second cycle of primary $L_t^{s,P}$; the number of primary education pupils still in school $L_t^{scol,P}$; that of persons who dropped out at this level $L_t^{drop,P}$; and the number of adults who have graduated from primary school $L_t^{A,P}$. Thus, in its dynamics and logic, the population with a certain level of diploma corresponds to the number of persons registered at this level, less those who are still enrolled in education, or who have dropped out, or who have died.

Let us start with $L_t^{A,P}$, and move up the analysis of the variables up to $L_t^{p,P}$.

1) The number of adults with the level of primary education in the population, L_t^A, is calculated annually by the number of adults who graduate from primary school l_t^A, by that of adults enrolled in lower secondary education, $N_t^{A,insc2}$, and by the adult mortality rate M_t^{18+}:

$$L_t^A = L_{t-1}^A \left(1 - M_t^{18+}\right) + l_t^A - N_t^{A,insc2} \qquad (2.26)$$

This is however a problem: data of $N_t^{A,insc2}$ are missing, and those relating to adults enrolled in primary education after 1981 are only available since 2004. Added to this, the series by *China Education Statistical Yearbook 1949–1981* on enrolled adults do not make it possible to distinguish between the first and second cycles of secondary schools for adult education. Instead, we need to use the numbers of adults graduated from lower secondary education after two years, $N_t^{A,insc2}$. This means that adult students in primary and lower secondary education are all assumed to graduate and that the number of graduates is equal to that of enrollees two years earlier. This hypothesis is realistic insofar as the part-time adult education courses have relatively low-demanding examinations and a quasi automatic degree of qualification and delivery of diplomas:

$$N_t^{A,insc2} = l_{t+2}^{A,P} \qquad (2.27)$$

2) For $L_t^{drop,P}$, we use the cumulative numbers of enrollments in primary school, $\sum_{i=0}^{\infty} l_{t-i}^{P,insc}$ (less those of primary school graduates $\sum_{i=0}^{\infty} l_{t-i}^{P,diplo}$, and the pupils enrolled in primary education but deceased $\sum_{i=0}^{\infty} l_{t-i}^{P,dead}$), as well as the numbers of pupils in primary school L_t^{scol}, and the population of pupils promoted in lower secondary education $l_t^{p,S,insc}$. This allows the number of people who dropped out primary school to be calculated:

$$\sum_{i=0}^{\infty} l_{t-i}^{drop,P} = \sum_{i=0}^{\infty} l_{t-i}^{P,insc} - \sum_{i=0}^{\infty} l_{t-i}^{P,diplo} - \sum_{i=0}^{\infty} l_{t-i}^{P,dead} - L_t^{scol} - l_t^{p,S,insc} \qquad (2.28)$$

with

$$l_t^{P,dead} = l_t^{P,scol} \cdot M_t^{5-14} \qquad (2.29)$$

where M_t^{5-14} is the mortality rate of primary school pupils aged between 5 and 14 years.

If statistical data on dropouts are available for a census year, such as 2010, the calculation of the number of dropouts from primary education in the total population is as follows:

$$L_{t-1}^{drop,P} = L_t^{drop,P} - \left(\sum_{i=0}^{\infty} l_{t-i}^{drop,P} - \sum_{i=0}^{\infty} l_{t-i-1}^{drop,P} \right) \qquad (2.30)$$

where $\sum_{i=0}^{\infty} l_{t-i}^{drop}$ represents the cumulative numbers of the persons alive who have dropped out of school.

This equation posits that the number of people who dropped out of school in year t, $L_t^{drop,P}$, is equal to the population of the previous year,[26] noted, $L_{t-1}^{drop,P}$,

---

26   Since we have already considered this, there is no need to resort here to a "depreciation" of the variable L_{t-1}^{drop}.

plus the new increase in dropouts, i.e., $\left(\sum_{i=0}^{\infty} l_{t-i}^{drop,P} - \sum_{i=0}^{\infty} l_{t-i-1}^{drop,P} \right)$.[27] In order to use the most recent information, we retain 2010 as the base year in the calculation of $L_t^{drop,P}$.

3) The series of $L_t^{scol,P}$ is obtained very simply, because the NBS databases provide it directly since the year 1949.[28]

4) $L_t^{s,P}$ is calculated as the population of this group in the previous year (minus deaths), plus the new primary graduates, less the pupils promoted to the next level:

$$L_t^{s,P} = \left(1 - M_t^{s,P} \right) L_{t-1}^{s,P} + l_t^{s,P} \left(1 - P_t^{prim} \right) \qquad (2.31)$$

where $M_t^{s,P}$ is the mortality rate of the population of graduates of the second cycle of primary education for year t, $l_t^{s,P}$ the number of primary education graduates in t, and P_t^{prim} the promotion rate of pupils at the end of primary school.

The mortality rate $M_t^{s,P}$ is not the same as that of pupils enrolled in primary education M_t^{5-14}. The population distribution of the first rate is much broader than that of the second one, because it also includes adults who have attained an educational level equivalent to primary school, whereas the second rate corresponds to the mortality of pupils enrolled in primary school, which is, taking into account the age of admission, roughly equivalent to the mortality rate of the population aged five to 14 years.

Nevertheless, what we need to calculate is the number of people with a cultural level equivalent to the second cycle of primary education in the total population, which implies using $M_t^{s,P}$. Even in the cases where primary education lasts five years and the age of admissions is advanced, pupils are at least 10 years old when they finish the second cycle of primary education, completely. We then retain the mortality rate over 10 years,[29] i.e., $M_t^{s,P} = M_t^{10+}$.

---

27 If the difference $\sum_{i=0}^{\infty} l_{t-i}^{drop} - \sum_{i=0}^{\infty} l_{t-i-1}^{drop}$ is found negative, then this means that the number of dropouts is decreasing.

28 It should be observed that there is a discrepancy between the annual values of L_t^{scol} published by the NBS and the same series calculated from the census tables. In the case of NBS, this is the population enrolled at the end of the year, while the reference time is July 1 or November 1 for censuses. In addition, the latter have sampling biases. So we decide to use the NBS annual data.

29 In the absence of sufficiently solid empirical evidence, we decide not to consider that having a diploma – which may improve the income and living conditions of the graduate and of his or her family –, reduces the mortality rate.

A gross promotion rate must be used here, P_t^{prim}; a rate that may be greater than 100 percent.[30] Consideration is given to situations in which pupils who have completed a training cycle end their studies, and then resume them a few years later. Since the promotion rate data prior to 1978 provided by the NBS are only available in certain years, periodically, we have had to recalculate the gross promotion rates P_{jt} for each level of education from various sources, by identifying all possible promotion pathways:

$$P_{jt} = N_{j+1,t} / l_{j,t} \qquad (2.32)$$

$N_{j+1,t}$ representing the number of enrollments at education level $j+1$, and $l_{j,t}$ that of graduates from the previous level j.

5) As far as $L_t^{p,P}$ is concerned, the only usable data – which are quite rare – are those of 1964. In order to be able to apply the permanent inventory method without problems (the condition of constraint being: 1.086 > 1), we must write in this calculation:

$$L_t^{p,P} = L_t^P - L_t^{scol,P} - L_t^{s,P} - L_t^{drop,P} - L_t^{A,P} \qquad (2.33)$$

From this axiomatic, we deduced that the average level of primary education in the population was of 3.590 years in 1964. By comparison, for the same year, the levels of junior and senior secondary levels were 8.308 and 10.376, respectively.

For the reference years after 1993, the problem affecting the first cycle of primary education can be neglected, so that in the recent period, only three categories of populations having the primary educational level are considered, more precisely: pupils enrolled in school, graduates, and the persons who have given up.

Therefore, we can rewrite:

$$E_t^P = \beta_S \cdot \eta_t^{prim} + 0{,}5 \, \eta_t^{prim} \cdot (\beta_{drop,P} + \beta_{scol,P}) \qquad (2.34)$$

Due to the existence of a serious bias risk for the 1982 and 1987 reference years, which are situated far from the beginning and the end of the sample, as a consequence, we prefer not to retain them.

For the educational levels of the lower and upper secondary levels, as well as at those of college and university, calculations are simplified by the relative

---

30   For example, the rate of gross promotion from lower secondary education was 168.2 percent in 1952: the number of enrollments in upper secondary education was thus higher than that of graduates in the first cycle of this level.

abundance of data and by the low frequency of reforms in the education system. However, there are a number of problems to be underlined. About the first cycle of secondary schools, the series of dropouts calculated by the preceding equations present a bias. The value taken by these dropouts appears to be negative for the initial year 1949 – because the mortality rate M_t^{10-17} calculated on the basis of the census is itself biased for the younger generations of the more distant years in the past. Military personnel are absent from the statistics – in spite of several conflicts which have marked the early days of the People's Republic.[31]

In order to solve this difficulty, we use the following equation, assuming no dropouts in lower secondary education in 1948:

$$L_t^{D-J-S} = L_{t-1}^{D-J-S} + \left(\sum_{i=0}^{\infty} l_{t-i}^{D-J-S} - \sum_{i=0}^{\infty} l_{t-i-1}^{D-J-S} \right) \qquad (2.35)$$

In the end, out of 32.347 million people corresponding to lower secondary education for the year 1964, 7.294 million were enrolled in school, 17.415 graduates, and 7.638 had dropped out of school. The average cultural level reached by the population at this level $E_t^{p,S}$ was therefore 8.308 years in 1964. Since numbers of pupils enrolled in upper secondary education are unavailable before 2003, we used instead the sums of pupils involved in general, vocational and specialized schools, as well as skilled workers in training at this stage. Finally, at the highest levels of education, the number of people who have chosen to study abroad – a number indeed relatively large – must be removed from that of dropouts. Thus, we resort to the numbers of graduates at each degree as weights of dynamic calculations of the average levels of education attained.

6 Presentation of the Series of Productive and Total Human Capital Stocks

As a result, we obtain our two series of total and productive human capital stocks, constructed from alternative definitions of population, on the basis of crossing points supported by censuses at distinct reference times (that is, mid-year [July 1] or year-end [November 1]), and by using different statistical sources allowing to calculate all the components of these two indicators (see Graph 2.7 and Graph 2.8, and Table 2.10).

---

31 Especially, the Korean War in 1950–1953 (which led to more than 150,000 deaths on the Chinese side), or the war against Vietnam in 1979 (which made more than 25 000 deaths), etc.

TABLE 2.10   Levels of human capital stocks: China, 1949–2014

Years	Stock of productive human capital (10,000 people × years)	Stock of total human capital (10,000 people × years)
1949	52,975.3	75,499.1
1950	52,680.9	74,739.3
1951	52,574.0	73,932.2
1952	52,498.2	73,111.4
1953	52,968.2	72,358.4
1954	53,552.3	73,142.2
1955	54,531.1	74,169.1
1956	55,858.7	75,962.7
1957	57,534.8	78,974.9
1958	62,749.9	82,710.9
1959	66,829.9	90,232.8
1960	68,128.9	96,400.6
1961	70,138.6	101,468.7
1962	72,019.2	105,057.9
1963	73,667.3	108,027.6
1964	75,059.4	110,823.9
1965	77,006.3	113,882.9
1966	81,113.1	117,206.8
1967	85,882.7	122,216.7
1968	93,793.3	133,431.2
1969	97,765.2	142,736.1
1970	102,790.8	154,011.3
1971	107,130.9	165,383.3
1972	112,904.4	179,497.7
1973	120,995.8	194,711.2
1974	128,468.1	211,269.5
1975	136,471.4	230,573.6
1976	144,955.0	254,561.1
1977	156,230.6	282,816.9
1978	172,153.6	310,686.7
1979	189,451.0	337,959.2
1980	203,225.9	358,678.9
1981	219,066.8	379,827.1

TABLE 2.10   Levels of human capital stocks: China, 1949–2014 (*cont.*)

Years	Stock of productive human capital (*10,000 people × years*)	Stock of total human capital (*10,000 people × years*)
1982	232,979.7	397,864.7
1983	244,833.7	413,115.3
1984	257,097.0	429,656.2
1985	270,371.4	444,719.3
1986	284,389.9	460,150.9
1987	299,110.8	479,555.5
1988	313,759.2	499,277.4
1989	327,399.3	519,571.7
1990	340,789.8	519,004.0
1991	353,938.2	546,943.7
1992	366,300.0	567,634.0
1993	378,475.5	588,406.2
1994	390,471.4	585,191.7
1995	403,344.4	618,961.5
1996	416,612.5	650,678.7
1997	431,494.3	686,066.8
1998	447,778.4	707,340.1
1999	464,237.7	725,378.8
2000	481,535.1	781,887.2
2001	499,696.8	808,887.9
2002	518,978.2	827,069.2
2003	540,708.1	859,990.8
2004	564,910.1	889,849.1
2005	591,890.1	869,729.7
2006	620,794.6	903,994.8
2007	633,219.9	937,152.6
2008	644,286.7	956,839.5
2009	655,809.4	977,470.1
2010	688,777.0	1,024,474.0
2011	732,206.7	1,040,989.0
2012	741,271.0	1,060,084.0
2013	748,740.9	1,079,031.0
2014	758,714.8	1,083,728.0

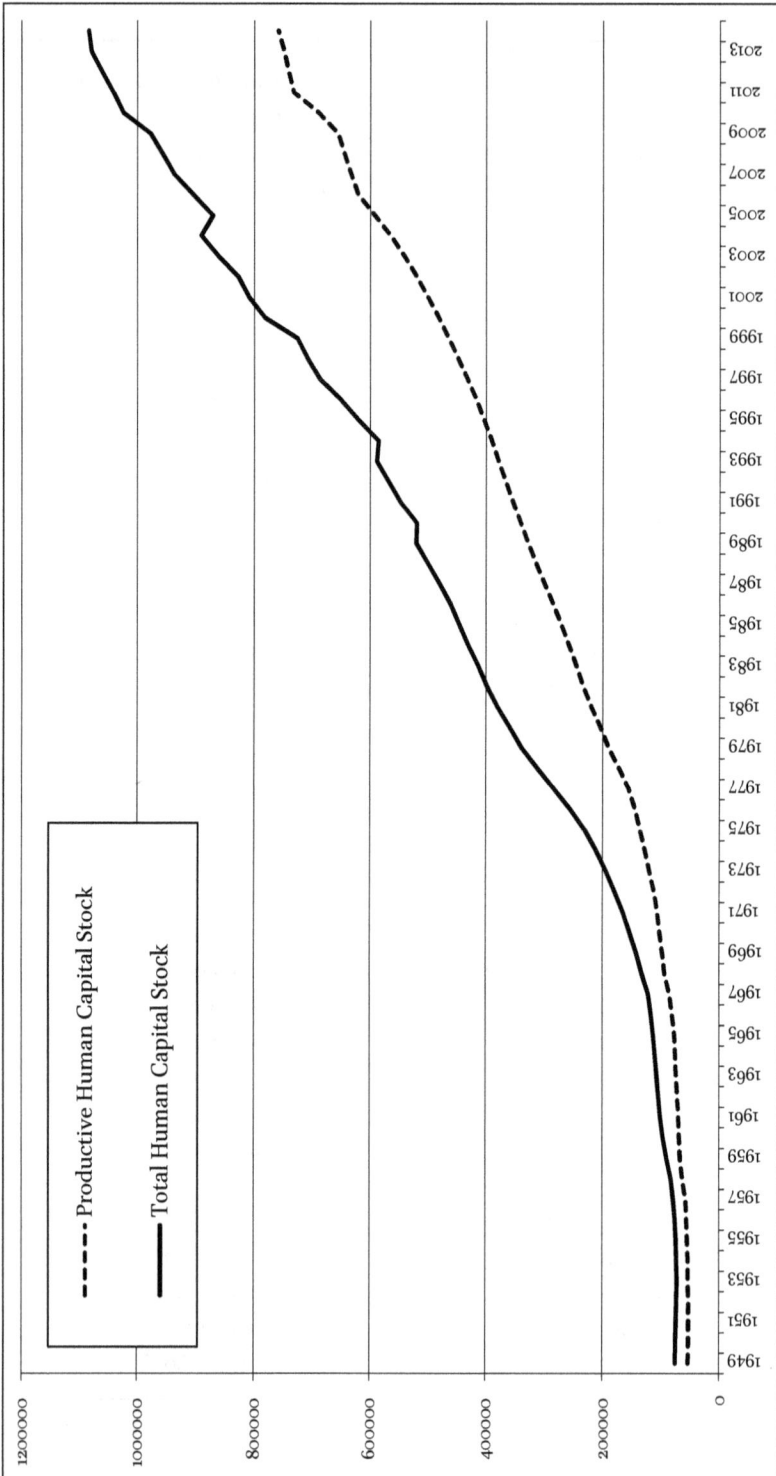

GRAPH 2.7   Stocks of productive and total human capital: China, 1949–2014 (*in 10,000 people × years*)

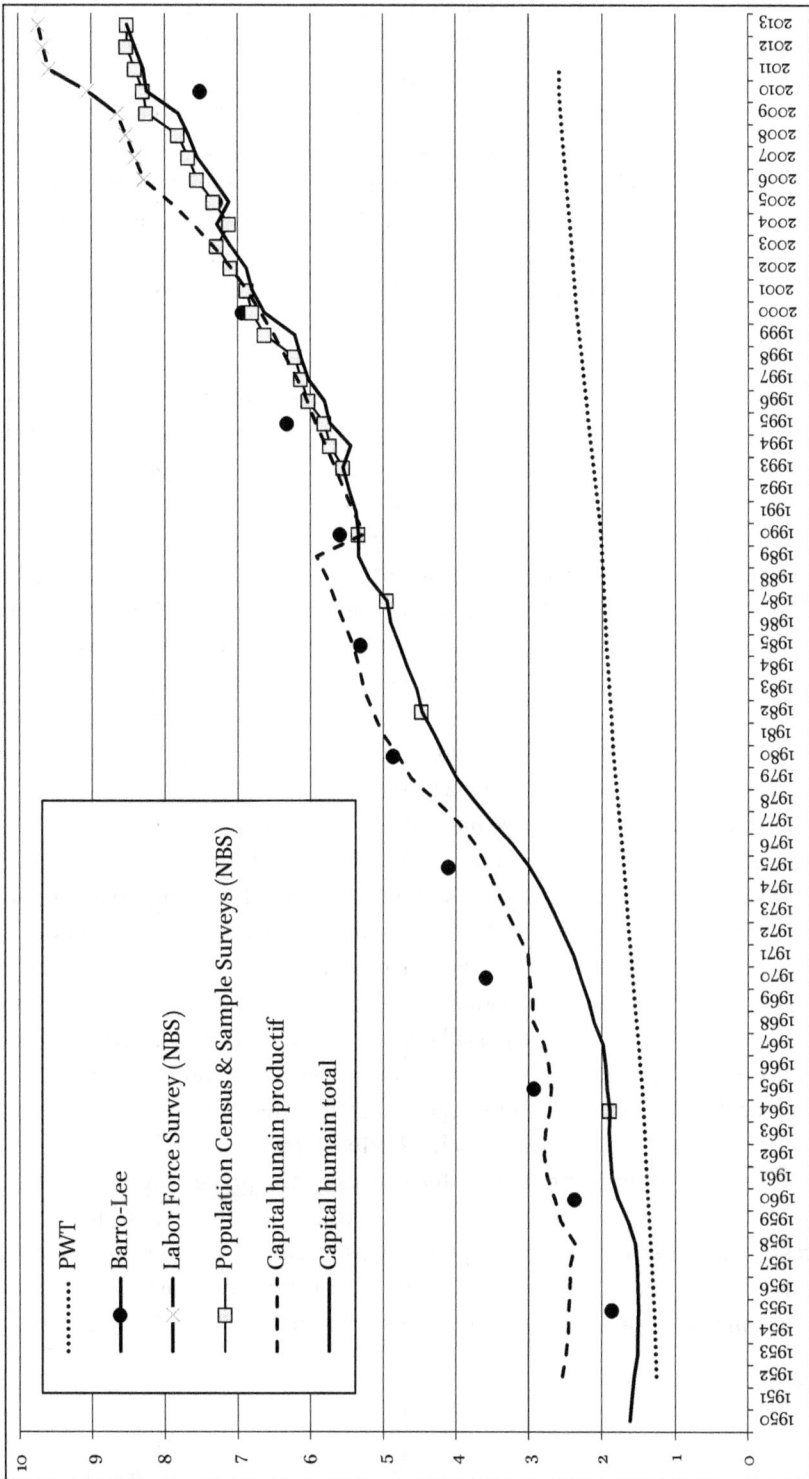

GRAPH 2.8   Average educational levels attained: a comparison between different databases China, 1949–2014 (*in years*)

By way of a conclusion, let us underline that the construction principle that we have adopted here has consisted in mobilizing as much as possible the official historical data released by the NBS, and in trying to limit the risks of errors, associated in particular with the determination of the flows of new human capital stock increases and of the depreciation rates of these stocks, thanks to a backward method by using retropolation, based on several crossing points in our series. The latter were calculated using the available population censuses. As a consequence, we have been able to provide two original series of stocks of human capital (productive and total) for China over the period 1949–2014, i.e., 66 years.

Compared to the current statistical literature (Graph 2.8), our estimates constitute a significant advance. They are more reliable than the series developed by the PWT (2013) which, in our opinion, very seriously underestimate the level of Chinese human capital stocks. This is mainly due to the assumption of the educational returns used by the PWT, following Psacharopoulos (1994). This hypothesis is inappropriate to China's reality, and *de facto* leads to biased values of human capital. But our new series also improve, in quality, in frequency and/or in length, those elaborated by Cai and Du (2003), and even those by Barro and Lee (2018), while remaining relatively close to the latter. To take just one example, according to our methodology using the NBS and census data, we have calculated that in 2010, the average educational level attained by China's total population was 8.24 years, whereas Barro and Lee (2018)'s database gives 7.51 years, and that of the PWT only 2.58 years.

To achieve such results, as we have seen, we have had to take into account the peculiarities of the Chinese educational system, as well as the political and historical changes of this country since the founding of the People's Republic in 1949. Our efforts have focused in particular on very strict compliance with the definitions provided by the NBS which make a clear distinction between pupils enrolled in education, graduates, and the individuals who dropped out of school. They concentrate especially upon the effects of educational system reforms related to learning durations; adult education and literacy; the examination of the issue of retirement departures; the integration of persons educated in the first cycle of primary school prior to the year 1949; and even the distinct reference time of demographic censuses. The processing of this huge mass of information was a thankless task – to put it mildly –, but it proved necessary in order to estimate as precisely as possible the stocks of Chinese human capital over the long period, and so to offer economists (or demographers and other researchers) renewed raw materials for their further work.

CHAPTER 3

Building Time Series of Research-and-Development (R&D): 1953–2014

In the econometric literature devoted to the growth of China's economy, a number of works carried out – in time series – have shown that the contribution of the total factor productivity to this economic growth is often quantitatively important and statistically significant. Therefore, this indicates clearly that we need to look carefully at this question of total factor productivity (for differentiated production factors), and even suggests the need for new indicators of technical progress, and more specifically those relating to research-and-development (R&D). This is the task we will tackle now.

In general, in China, activities described as "science and technology" (S&T) are now usually distinguished according to the following four main categories:

1) those of experimental research-and-development;
2) those relating to the application of R&D;
3) those of the various services associated to S&T; and
4) those of education and training in S&T.

In itself, R&D corresponds to systematic work aimed at improving knowledge and/or elaborating new forms of using it. Here, this is usually the most creative part of science and technology. Consequently, and in this circumscribed context, we will propose in this chapter two long series of R&D indicators as this constitutes a representation of quite essential components of technical progress.

It was the Organisation of Economic Cooperation and Development (OECD)'s *Frascati Manual* (1963) that first conceived the regulatory documents which have codified statistical series on these topics. This manual has been revised several times, then gradually adopted to become the standard internationally. Nevertheless, the Chinese authorities did not introduce the regulations in question until quite late: only in the mid-1980s – in the year 1986 to be exact. The very first national R&D sampling took place in 1988, while the first R&D census, as to it, dates from 2003; the second being organized in 2009. This means that the precise data that we need to build our R&D series are impossible to collect before 1987. It appears, however, that some of the indicators of the statistical system of the time turn out to be relatively close to what we would need, such as the number of people employed in science and technology activities, or S&T expenditures, as examples.

It is under these conditions that we could consider elaborating three types of technical progress indicators – those which are most frequently used in the literature –:

1) the number of people employed in R&D, or the conversion of this number into full-time working time equivalent (the unit used then being "person-years");

2) the number of patents registered or accepted; and

3) R&D expenses.

We summarize, in the specific case of China, the data sources and the length of the series currently available for these three indicators in Table 3.1.

TABLE 3.1   Sources and length of the series of technical progress indicators available

Indicator	Length	Data sources	Comments
Number of people working in the R&D sectors (or conversion into full-time working time equivalent)	From 1991 to 2014 + Several isolated years	Data from 1991: *China Statistical Yearbook on Science and Technology* (various years) + Data from 1995: NBS online database	In the early years, the number of people employed in S&T activities included the subentry "number of scientists and engineers" – which has disappeared since 2009. Data for 1952, for 1960, for population census years and after 1978 are all available in the directory *Statistics on Science and Technology of China 1949–1989*.
Number of patents registered (or accepted)	From 1986 to 2014	NBS online database + Data of the *State Intellectual Property Office*	The "Law on Patents" has been in force since April 1, 1985. Before that date, there was no legal system relating to patents which could be compared to this law.
R&D expenditure	From 1987 to 2014	NBS online database + Data of the Ministry of Science and Technology	The NBS has provided data since the year 1995, and the *China Science and Technology Statistics Network* of the Ministry of Science and Technology from 1987 on.

Let us take a look at these indicators in turn.

First, the data relating to the number of people employed in R&D activities, or those corresponding to the conversion of this number into working time equivalent, are those for which we have the longest time series, if at all we consider other very similar variables as acceptable surrogates, such as the number of people working in S&T activities, or the number of scientists and engineers. However, in these statistical series which are relatively longer than those of the other indicators, a lot of data has been missing, and this for quite a long time. Furthermore, the variable of the number of people working in R&D activities appears redundant compared to that of human capital, so that their joint use is not recommended in econometric tests.

Regarding the number of patents registered or accepted, some detailed data exist, and are even subdivided by sub-categories: "inventions," "utility models" and "designs." Nevertheless, it was not until the year 1985 that China passed a "law on patents." Prior to that date, there was no patent system in place, due to the grip of socialist public property. Basically, knowledge productions of a scientific and technological nature were all shared collectively and nationally, and no individual or institution could hold private title to knowledge or derive any monetary benefit from discoveries or inventions. The time series that we could elaborate is much too short, so this indicator is not likely to meet our expectations.

As for R&D expenditure, official Chinese data start from the year 1987. Gu and Lundvall (2006) have however proposed a series for this indicator since 1953. We therefore sought to go back to their primary sources and find the original version of the yearbook that these authors mention in their bibliographical references. The data they provide for the period 1953–1986 come precisely from page 202 of the collection entitled *Statistics on Science and Technology of China 1949–1989*. However, if we look closely at this document, we can see that it is not really a question of "R&D expenditure" in the strict sense insofar as, in reality, the amounts taken into consideration by Gu and Lundvall (2006) form only a part of the total sums corresponding to public spending allocated to science and technology at the national level. So it would be much better to call this series "S&T expenditure."

Indeed, as we have seen above, S&T activities include four categories, of which the one corresponding to R&D is only a part. Under these conditions, in our opinion, Gu and Lundvall (2006) would therefore overestimate the R&D expenditure during the first years of the period covered by their study. Moreover, since the application of the R&D accounting system by China starting in the mid-1980s, the statistical framework has not been the same as that for S&T activities. It is thus difficult to accurately assess an R&D indicator for the most distant years by having recourse to the instructions issued by the *Frascati Manual*. In such a context, we must therefore try to build ourselves a temporal series of R&D as rigorously as possible, by relying on the historical data that are available and starting from the exact definition of R&D.

Before the year 1986, R&D activities were primarily carried out by State-owned institutions and entities, with all R&D spending being public and allocated by the government. In 1985, the reform known as "the substitution of State appropriation by bank credits" was implemented, at the end of which the main mode of financing of companies owned by the State was profoundly modified, passing from the allocation of public subsidies at the national level to the granting of loans by certain specialized banking establishments for more targeted activities. Prior to 1986, the R&D expenses of both corporate and research institute were part of S&T expenditure. As a consequence, we construct the R&D expenditure series on the basis of that of S&T before the year 1986 – whereas Gu and Lundvall (2006) directly use S&T expenditure as if it were R&D expenditure.

What we observe in the S&T expenditure accounting system of that time is a breakdown of the type:

$$E_{S\&T}^{total} = F_{S\&T}^{3\ items} + E_{ops} + E_{cap} + E_{oth} \qquad (3.1)$$

where the term $E_{S\&T}^{total}$ corresponds to the total S&T expenditure, $F_{S\&T}^{3\ items}$ to a set of three items concerned by the allocation of S&T funds, E_{ops} to operational functionary expenses for science, E_{cap} to those for infrastructural constructions of research institutes, and E_{oth} to other administrative costs.

Important note: it should be observed that an additional difficulty arises from the fact that the titles of each of these items, which are relatively vague and unclear, do not always give a very precise idea of the respective contents of these various expenses.

So let us take a moment to examine this classification in more details.

The three items receiving scientific and technological funds, officially called "Expense on S&T Promotion," are listed as follows:

1) costs incurred by testing new products;
2) costs associated with intermediate experiments; and
3) governmental grants for major scientific research projects to promote the development of science and technology.

According to the definition of R&D, these three components fall within the scope of R&D activities. Let us see why.

First, most testing of new products can be thought of as R&D. Nevertheless, among all these activities, the manufacturing processes of new products through the importation of already existing technologies (with the use of patents, adaptations or technical tricks, design operations or prototypes of machines, among many other examples) do not constitute strictly R&D, since it is rather the duplication or application of prior R&D tasks. In our calculations, we must therefore deduct the amount of purchases of all scientific and technological goods that have been imported. But due to the authorities' guidelines for a self-sustaining development strategy, imports of technology remained very limited before the opening-up reforms. However, we are led to observe, by converting into national currency the budgets representative of the sums committed in U.S. dollars for the technology import contracts concluded during the first years of the People's Republic, that the available data on S&T expenditure did not include any import of foreign technologies. The difficulty that we have just raised is *de facto* resolved: the costs of testing new products which are mentioned are all within the scope of R&D.

Then, whether or not to include the costs of intermediate experiments should depend on the purpose of the latter. If such experiments are intended to improve the technology associated with the product or to gain more knowledge and information about it, then they should be incorporated into R&D activities. If, on the contrary, the objective is not this, but rather to collect certain production parameters aimed at only distinguishing the final appearance of the product, in this case, we are no longer really dealing with R&D, because they will not be any more in fact than simple applications of research carried out previously. The border between the two areas is nevertheless sometimes very ambiguous and extremely difficult to draw. So when the experiments were only carried out to obtain production parameters, what is actually observed most frequently is that there was a component to be modified – it often happens that products must be changed during the production process. In practice, there is no significant divergence between the two types of activities. It is not possible to distinguish their different purposes. Without much risk of making a mistake, it will be admitted that these intermediate experiments all come under R&D.

Finally, with regard to scientific research projects considered to be major, and corresponding to basic or fundamental research, there is no doubt that they fall within the scope of R&D activities.

Clearly, it will be understood that we consider that the three items concerned by S&T funds are to be selected and added to our time series of R&D expenditures.

In addition, funds for exploring potentialities and technical innovation of enterprises, officially called "Innovation Funds," must also be part of R&D expenditure. Their amounts can be found under various headings of fiscal documents in the succession of yearbooks and directories that we have been able to consult. These are governmental transfers granted to companies in order to promote technological innovations, including to renew certain fixed assets. Since a reform in 1983, these funds were gradually replaced by a range of subsidized and/or semi-subsidized loans – until these government allocations were withdrawn. Partial and disparate, this data is difficult to collect, having often been based in other budgets. They appear in the *Sixty Years Statistics Compilation of New China* under the name "Expense on S&T Promotion," are merged with the costs of testing new products in the *China Statistical Yearbook* for the year 1988; and then they disappeared in 2007. By comparing the different yearbooks and directories, we have pointed out some discrepancies in the registration of the Expense on S&T promotion and Innovation Funds of the *Sixty Years Statistics Compilation of New China*. Thus, data in this compendium prior to 1970 just report the costs of testing new products. In such circumstances, we use the data from the *China Statistical Yearbook 1988*, from which we have to deduct the "New Product Trial Fees" in order to obtain the expenses corresponding to these "Innovation Funds."

The amounts listed as "Operating Expenses for Sciences" are linked to the operational functionary costs of the research institutes, which has little to do with the creation of knowledge and should logically lead to not including them in R&D spending. Those known as "Expenses for Capital Construction of S&T Institutes" correspond to the expenses that accompany the infrastructural investments of these establishments, such as office buildings, and are no more than the previous ones at the origin of scientific creations; this which should also exclude them from R&D budgets. The same applies to the item "Other S&T Operating Expenses," which gathers together all administrative costs, and not directly R&D. We therefore understand that we are moving away from the core definition of R&D – centered on the notion of "creation."

We thus arrive at the following formula for R&D expenditure over the period 1953–1986:

$$E_{R\&D}^{prox} = F_{new\ prod}^{try} + F_{interm}^{expe} + S_{proj} + F_{innov}^{firm} \qquad (3.2)$$

where $E_{R\&D}^{prox}$ is an improved approximation of total R&D expenditure, while $F_{new\,prod}^{try}$ represents the costs of testing new products, F_{interm}^{expe} those of various intermediate experiments, S_{proj} subsidies intended for major scientific research projects, and F_{innov}^{firm} innovation funds for companies.

However, the approximation proposed here is not without some shortcomings. On the one hand, it does not take into account the R&D expenditure that has been made by the private sector. Nevertheless, let us remember that what we are evaluating is R&D expenses before the year 1986, that is to say for a period when almost all R&D activities were carried out by the State. But, on the contrary, from 1986 on, very important institutional changes were put in place, especially the reforms of "substitution of State appropriations by bank loans" and the "law on patents," which have one like the other powerfully encouraged private R&D activities to develop. Such a limitation can therefore be overcome before 1986. On the other hand, if the incorporation of intermediate experiments into R&D depends on their purpose and if the latter is not specified in the statistical system of S&T, we understand that this bias will prove impossible to correct. It appears that treating all intermediate experiments as uniformly "creative" will lead to overestimating R&D expenditure, while neglecting private sector costs in this area during the period prior to 1986 will lead to an underestimation of these same R&D expenses. These two opposing biases could eventually offset each other, at least to some extent, so that the error would ultimately turn out to be very small.

Information on R&D expenditure after the year 1995 could be obtained directly from the series provided by the NBS. As it happened that the online database of the Ministry of Science and Technology was unavailable (currently being updated), we sometimes had to use alternative sources in the form of yearbooks and directories – sources summarized in Table 3.2. Finally, our database itself is presented to the reader (Table 3.3), to which is attached its graphic representation (Graph 3.1).

TABLE 3.2   Data sources and components of R&D expenditure

Period	Components	Data sources	Comments
1953	Expenses for promoting science and technology	*55 Years Statistics Compilation of New China*	Data on innovation funds not available
1954–1970	Expenses for promoting science and technology	*55 Years Statistics Compilation of New China* + *China Statistical Yearbook 1988*	These expenses for promoting science and technology are calculated using the China Statistical Yearbook *China Statistical Yearbook 1988.* Innovation funds are incorporated into the costs of testing new products
1971–1985	Expenses of promoting science and technology + Innovation funds of enterprises	*55 Years Statistics Compilation of New China* + *China Statistical Yearbook 1988*	Expenses of innovation funds are calculated according to the *China Statistical Yearbook 1988*
1986–1988	R&D expenditure made on government budgets + R&D expenditure carried out by the higher education system	*40 Years Statistics of China's Science and Technology 1949–1989*	Transition period
1989–1994	Aggregate R&D expenditure	*China Statistical Yearbooks on Science and Technology* (various years)	After introduction of the accounting system for R&D activities
1995–2013	Aggregate R&D expenditure	NBS *China Statistical Yearbooks* (various years)	Corresponding period

TABLE 3.3   Time series database for research-and-development (R&D) expenses:
China, 1953–2014 (*in hundreds of millions of 1952 constant yuans*)

Year	R&D expenditure	Year	R&D expenditure
1952	n.-a.	1984	74.292
1953	0.257	1985	62.893
1954	1.032	1986	63.604
1955	1.796	1987	63.121
1956	3.306	1988	63.782
1957	2.720	1989	56.596
1958	6.691	1990	62.371
1959	11.345	1991	73.708
1960	20.360	1992	85.064
1961	12.016	1993	94.980
1962	7.911	1994	86.785
1963	10.964	1995	70.012
1964	14.484	1996	74.990
1965	16.865	1997	91.826
1966	16.219	1998	100.195
1967	11.488	1999	125.180
1968	9.555	2000	164.488
1969	9.000	2001	190.122
1970	12.385	2002	236.725
1971	22.144	2003	279.695
1972	21.313	2004	343.803
1973	21.317	2005	420.790
1974	22.589	2006	508.170
1975	26.031	2007	599.073
1976	28.320	2008	703.800
1977	31.679	2009	890.878
1978	50.429	2010	1,049.773
1979	56.180	2011	1,225.071
1980	58.565	2012	1,415.514
1981	46.377	2013	1,587.049
1982	48.057	2014	1,709.471
1983	53.730		

Note: "n.-a." = non-available.

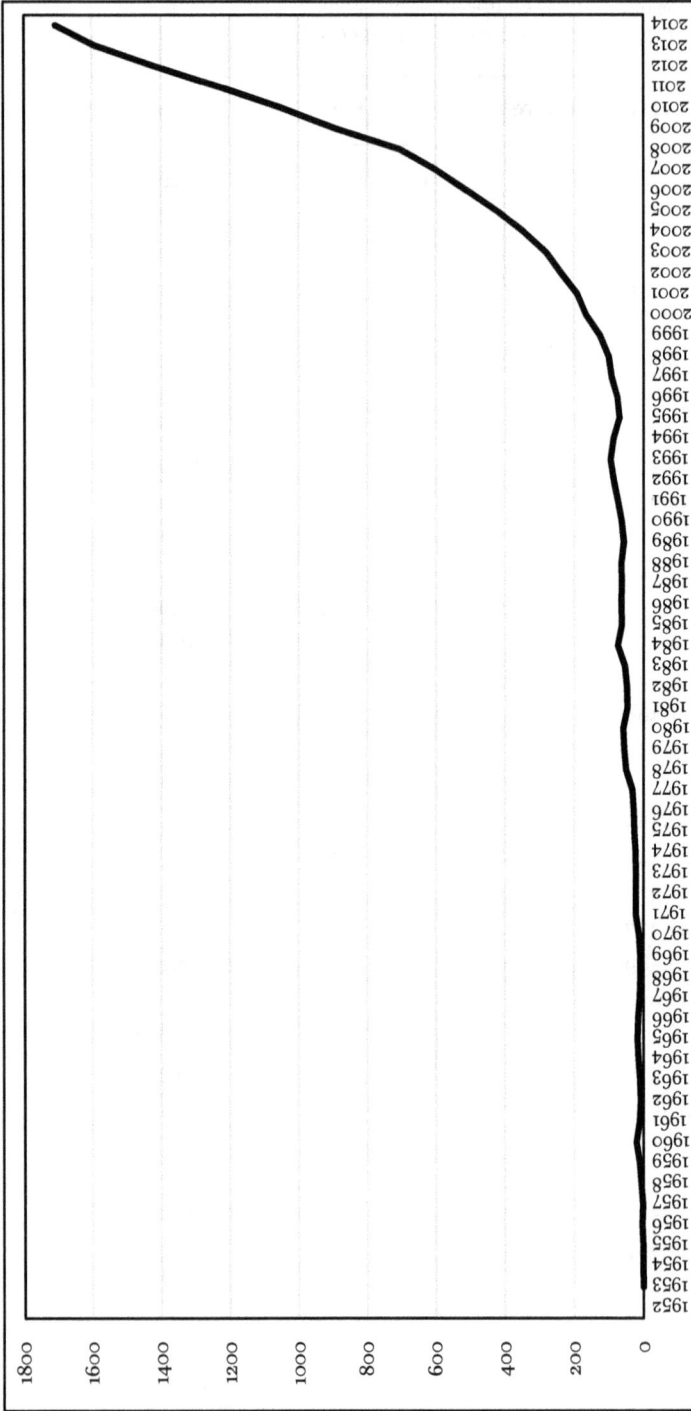

GRAPH 3.1   R&D expenditure series: China, 1952–2014 (in hundreds of million yuan, at constant prices, base year 1952)

Building Time Series of Gini Income Inequality Indicator: 1978–2014

The first surveys that the National Bureau of Statistics (NBS) of China carried out among Chinese households began in the year 1954, two years after the establishment of this institute. This logically means that it would have been possible, given the sufficient information available, to elaborate some indicators of income inequality from this date and, in particular, to calculate Gini coefficients – if only such had really been the will of the political leaders of the time.

However, the NBS did not begin to make public Gini coefficients until 2001. It did so, on the one hand, by distinguishing between urban and rural areas from 1978 onwards, and, on the other hand, for the entire population of the country over the period going from 1995 to 2000[1] (Table A.4.1). These indicators having risen sharply and reached relatively high levels in China, exceeding 0.4 since the 2000s in terms of the total Gini coefficient, it has not been published again – for political reasons, of course. It was in fact only recently (January 18, 2013, to be precise) that the NBS released a series of total Gini coefficient covering the period 2003–2012.[2] The *China Yearbook of Household Survey* again published a series of Gini inequality indicators spanning from 2000 to 2012, but only for rural areas (see page 4 of the 2013 yearbook).

It should be noted that, as the statisticians of the NBS (2001) themselves have quite rightly pointed out concerning the missing data for the total Gini coefficient from 1978 to 1999, the surveys which had been carried out among urban and rural households show some differences; so important in terms of statistical methods (regarding sampling and scope, more especially) that the information and result that come from them are no longer comparable at all. Strictly speaking, therefore, the corresponding data cannot be used directly to calculate indicators of Gini income inequalities.

Several authors, such as Chen (2007), Wu (2012) or Chotikapanich, Rao and Tang (2007), have nevertheless succeeded in constructing total Gini coefficients, relying on the databases released by the NBS. In general, they retain a

---

1 Here refer to: http://www.stats.gov.cn/tjzs/tjsj/tjcb/zggqgl/200210/P020130912449774536261.htm.
2 See: http://www.stats.gov.cn/tjzs/tjsj/tjcb/zggqgl/200210/P020130912449774383370.htm.

prior hypothesis according to which the distribution of income obeys a particular type of statistical law, then they proceed to filtering the parameters using
suitable techniques (in particular ordinary least squares method, maximum
likelihood estimation, or the method of generalized moments), on the data
provided by the NBS.

Chen (2007) assumes that the income distribution corresponds to a generalized logistic distribution, and therefore uses ordinary least squares to estimate
the parameters. For their part, Chotikapanich, Rao and Tang (2007) hypoth-
esize that incomes in rural areas follow a Weibull distribution law, while those
in urban areas follow a law of beta distribution of the second type, which leads
them to rather using maximum likelihood for parameter estimation. As for
him, Wu (2012) compares the sensitivity of the distribution laws by Weibull,
in log-normal and in beta II, and concludes that the use of the latter is more
suited to the case of China, which ultimately leads him to recommend the
method of maximum likelihood (and that of the multiples of the median) for
estimating the parameters.

These works, each in their own way, are quite excellent, and our criticisms of
them are only minor. For example, Chen (2007), who estimates the Gini coefficient in urban areas at 0.292 for the year 1964, only performs his calculations
on a very limited number of data, due to the scarcity of information available
at that time. However, it appears that the income data by group that are used,
all coming from the NBS, have been classified into only six categories (roughly
referred to as "quintiles"); namely household income: the lowest income (that
is, 10 percent of the total Chinese population), modest income (10 percent),
relatively low income (20 percent), middle income (20 percent), relatively
high income (20 percent), well-off income (10 percent) and the highest income
(10 percent). Nevertheless, such a classification of income seems to us much too
imprecise to be able to effectively filter the parameters of the distribution laws.

We argue that, taking into account the fact that we do not have more
detailed data and that the information for urban and rural households is not
comparable to each other before the year 2011, it may well be better to follow
the suggestion formulated by Li (2007) to limit oneself to calculating only a
total Gini coefficient. Therefore, we will apply a segmentation method, with
weighting of the Gini coefficients between rural and urban areas in order to
determine this indicator of total Gini income inequality, using statistical data
from the NBS.

So we will set:

$$Gini_t^{total} = w_1 . Gini_t^{rural} + w_2 . Gini_t^{urban} \qquad (4.1)$$

However, as Bourguignon (1979) and Shorrocks (1980) demonstrated it, the Gini coefficients do not satisfy the additive decomposability, so that the sum of the parameters w_1 and w_2 is not necessarily equal to unity. Under these conditions, we could not simply use the proportions of rural and urban populations as the respective weights of these two areas in the total indicator, unlike what we were able to do in Chapter 2 – when we built the stocks of "human capital." We therefore propose to use the average weights over the period 1995–1999 as substitutes for those of the period from 1978 to 1994. As a matter of fact, within the legal framework of the *Hukou* system, very strict, the mobility of Chinese citizens between rural and urban regions is hampered. Rural residents are unlikely to be allowed to come to work in the city. As a result, the respective changes in the rural and urban Gini coefficients are, so to speak, almost independent.

Added to this, from the household survey documents presented in the *China Labor and Wage Statistics 1949–1985* (page 244 and page 247, exactly), we were able to calculate approximate Gini coefficients for the urban and rural areas corresponding to the two years 1957 and 1964. However, the deep structures of society and the nature of social inequalities in China at the time are completely different from those of the present period, so our hypothesis related to weightings cannot be retained continuously for that long. As a consequence, we cautiously decide not to discuss the Gini coefficients before 1978 here. By selecting average weights calculated respectively at $\overline{w_1} = 0.54186$ for rural areas and at $\overline{w_2} = 0.72840$ for urban areas, we can finally draw the Kuznets curve at the national level (Graph 4.1).

Wang and Fan (2005) questioned whether the Kuznets curve could be validated in the case of China. In a study using panel data of both rural and urban Gini coefficients at provincial levels over the period 1996–2002, they showed that the trend of the Gini coefficients as they considered them exhibited certain mathematical characteristics of the Kuznets curve, while the gap between urban and rural incomes tends to increase over this period, without discontinuity. Their conclusion is therefore quite cautious, but sketches the idea that income inequalities will not necessarily reduce in China as this economy continues to develop.

According to our estimate, the Chinese Gini coefficient tends to decrease very noticeably (but extremely slightly) from the year 2008. This improvement cannot be taken for the argument of a forecast for the future. The most likely situation, however, is that China is still a "developing country"; consequently, it would still be in the first phase of the Kuznets curve, that is to say, the phase during which inequalities continue to increase. In other words – and

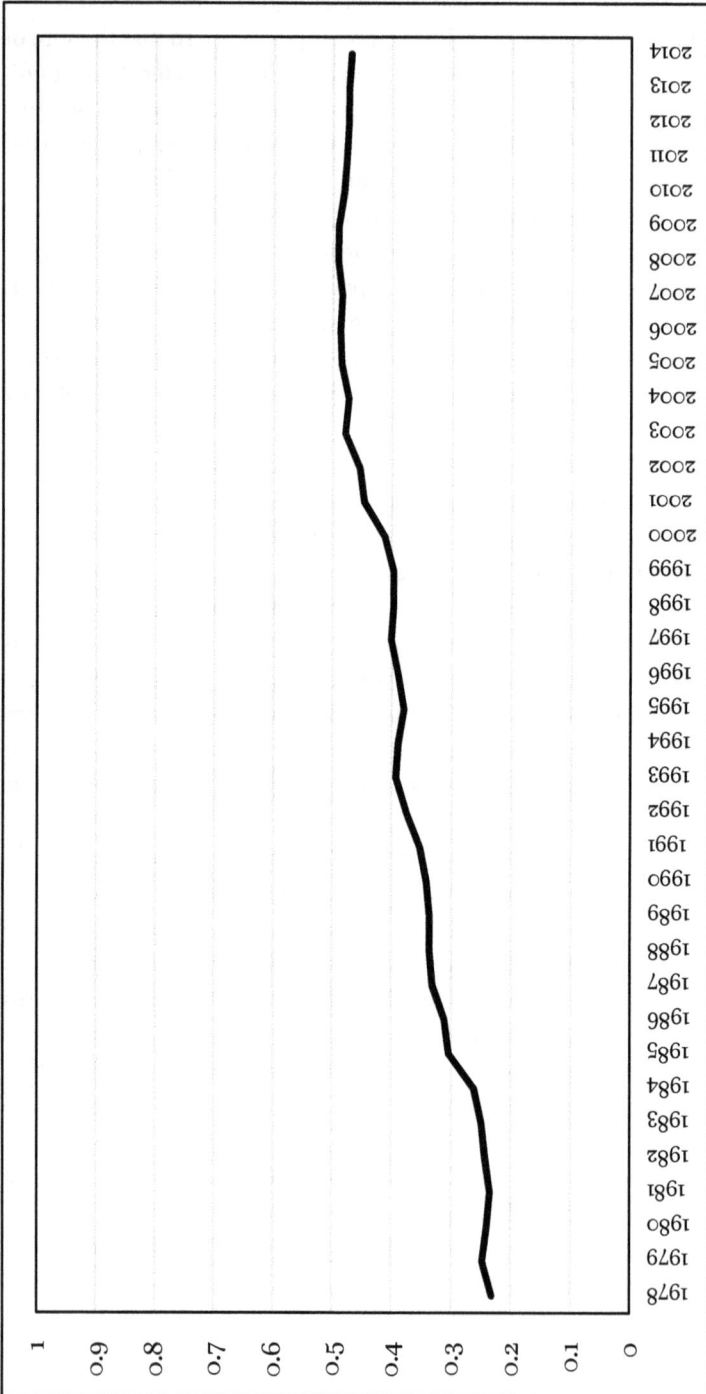

GRAPH 4.1 Gini inequality indicator: China, 1978–2014

remaining optimistic –, we would be approaching the turning point of the said curve, i.e., the point at which inequalities in the distribution of income would begin to decline.

After all, we have some reason to believe that the campaign currently being firmly and effectively conducted by the highest authorities of the State and the Party to fight corruption will help to propel such a reduction in social inequalities, and that, likewise, in this way, the ongoing process of "building the good institutions" will consolidate this trend evolution, so that the Kuznets curve may well be verified in the Chinese case.

TABLE 4.1   Time series of Gini inequality indicator: China, 1978–2014

Year	Gini coefficient	Year	Gini coefficient
1978	0.232	1997	0.401
1979	0.247	1998	0.397
1980	0.240	1999	0.397
1981	0.235	2000	0.412
1982	0.243	2001	0.447
1983	0.249	2002	0.454
1984	0.261	2003	0.479
1985	0.303	2004	0.473
1986	0.311	2005	0.485
1987	0.332	2006	0.487
1988	0.335	2007	0.484
1989	0.335	2008	0.491
1990	0.341	2009	0.490
1991	0.352	2010	0.481
1992	0.375	2011	0.477
1993	0.392	2012	0.474
1994	0.389	2013	0.473
1995	0.379	2014	0.469
1996	0.389		

Note: The NBS has not published a total Gini indicator for the years 2001 and 2002. The GNI series for 2001 comes from the World Bank (2004) and that for 2002 from the *Income Distribution Team of Chinese Academy of Social Sciences* (2003).

PART 2

Empirical Analyses of the Dynamics of China's Economy: From the Criticism of Neoclassical Mainstream (or Assimilated Currents) to the Marxist Perspective

∴

Identifying the Limits of the Neoclassical Explanations of China's Economic Growth: Econometric Tests of a Spectrum of Mainstream Macrodynamic Theoretical Models

We have to admit that, today, the possibilities of carrying out econometric estimates of long-term growth models over time series applied to the case of China, with all the rigor required, are still hampered by the incompleteness and/or the unsatisfactory nature of statistical databases relating to two key variables for understanding the dynamics of accumulation, namely data on the stock of physical capital and that of human capital. This is the case with official directories or yearbooks, in particular those of the National Bureau of Statistic (NBS)[1] of China, which to date do not provide series of physical capital stocks, but also databases made public and disseminated by researchers or networks of researchers, such as those of the Penn World Tables (PWT)[2] for physical capital, or that of Barro and Lee (1993, 2018) for human capital, both of which exhibit some inadequacies and worrying shortcomings.

As far as physical capital is concerned, the problems stem in particular from the scarcity of old data or, over the recent period, from the existence of statistical breaks, like the one that marked the transition from accounting frameworks according to the balances of the Material Product System (MPS) to the System of National Accounts (SNA) in the year 1993. Such a change makes difficult comparisons of time-series in Chinese data, and even more across countries. Some economists, including Gregory C. Chow (the inventor of the famous econometric test), have themselves reconstructed series of phsical capital stocks at national, regional or sectoral level. In our opinion, the most solidly elaborated chronological series are due to Chow (1993) and his co-authors (Chow and Li [2002], among others), but they have not been available since 1993, that is, the interruption of publication of the documents necessary for

---

their construction. The PWT include China, but the explanations given by their statisticians on several sensitive issues are vague, and do not distinguish the specificities of this country. As to the other available series, their calculation methods are frequently tainted with some estimation biases linked to an approximate interpretation of the perpetual inventory method (PIM) – which is the method we use here. Our criticism of this statistical and econometric literature, explained in Chapter 1 and several of our articles,[3] focus on the questionable parameterizations of the levels of initial physical capital stock or of the depreciation rates, but also on the indeterminate contents of the investment series and, above all, on the inappropriate choices of price indices used by most of the authors concerned.

The far fewer attempts at building databases on human capital stocks appear to be even more problematic. First, there are no official statistics in China measuring the average education attainment level. In addition, the PWT data, which were compiled from the series of average numbers of years of schooling by Barro and Lee (1993, 2018) and those of returns to education à la Psacharopoulos (1994), suffer from serious deficiencies and under-estimate, significantly in our opinion, China's level of human capital. And if the database provided by Barro and Lee (2018) is of better quality, the fact that it does not begin until 1970 and has a frequency of five years only still raises problems for the econometricians. As a consequence, we will have to build our own stocks, not only for physical capital, but also for human capital.

Accordingly, drawing on new statistical series relating to these two fundamental stock variables, this chapter will attempt to address some of the shortcomings mentioned above, and so contribute to improving the explanations of the Chinese economic growth over the long period. After having recalled the original databases over a period extending from 1952 to 2012 which will be used subsequently, it will offer econometric estimates taking into account the institutional changes that have occurred during China's growth trajectory, and carried out within the framework of a range of theoretical models spanning from standard or augmented Solowian specifications to more sophisticated log-linearized formalizations of endogenous growth, in order to shed light on the issue of how production factors have contributed to the Chinese GDP growth in the long run.

---

3   Long and Herrera (2016a) or Herrera and Long (2016b).

1   **Physical Capital, Human Capital and R&D Databases, and Determination of the Qualitative (Institutional) Variable**

Thanks to the original databases constructed in Chapters 1 and 2, there are in total four concepts of capital and labour (or human capital) respectively that we will retain, in an alternative or combined way, as inputs to the different production functions that we will now determine theoretically and test empirically; in this case:

Capital
$$\begin{cases} \textit{stricto sensu} \text{ productive physical capital stock (withhout lands, without inventories)} & K_{pe} \\ \textit{lato sensu} \text{ productive physical capital stock (without lands, with inventories)} & K_{pl} \\ \text{fixed physical capital stock (with lands, without inventories)} & K_F \\ \text{total physical capital stock (with lands, with inventories)} & K_T \end{cases}$$

and

Capital
$$\begin{cases} \text{employed population (or number of employed persons)} & L \\ \text{productive human capitals tock} & L_p \\ \text{total human capital stock} & L_T \\ \text{intermediary human capital stock} & L_I \end{cases}$$

Besides, it should also be noted that the series of Chinese GDP for the period 1952–2012, as to it, is taken from the *China Statistical Yearbooks* of the NBS (various years). Our series of R&D expenses, calculated in flows and expressed in hundreds of millions of constant yuan (based on 1952), is that which we constructed according to the methodology presented in Chapter 3.

The determination of the values of our qualitative (or institutional) variable or dummy variable, D, is not arbitrary. The choice of these values results from the application of a precise methodology, the steps of which are as follows:

Step 1: We regress the simplest form of a Solowian model, with a constant, but without dummy variable, and we get the residuals series.

Step 2: We test the residuals in order to know whether they are white noises. If so, then we do not add any dummy variable. However, if there is an autocorrelation problem in the residuals series, then we pass to the next step and build dummy variables. The autocorrelation problem is tested with the Lagrange Multiplier (LM) and Ljung-Box (LB) tests.

Step 3: We plot the residuals series and confidence intervals approximated at 95 percent for the null hypothesis of white noises. So we observe whether the residuals exceed the confidence intervals, and, when it happens, we denote a dummy variable for the corresponding point of time: +1 for values superior to the confidence intervals and –1 for values inferior to the confidence intervals. Numerous dummy variables can be generated, D_{1t}, D_{2t}, ... D_{nt}, but, if they are too many, a problem of multicollinearity may appear, or even a problem of singularity of the matrix of regressors. Thus, we have to test for the singularity and the collinearity.

Step 4: Let us begin by testing the singularity. With multiple dummy variables, if the pivot value of the sweep operation is less than the critical value, the matrix is deemed to be singular. In general, this diagnostic is automatically done by most econometric packages when performing regressions. If the matrix of regressors is singular, the econometric package refuses to execute the command. Thus, we do not need to write any specific program.[4] If there is a problem of singularity, then we continue with step 5; otherwise, we directly go to step 6.

Step 5: If too many dummy variables have caused a problem of singularity, then we do compress all these dummies into a single dummy, D, as follows: $D_t = D_{1t} + D_{2t} + ... + D_{tt}$. As this compressed dummy variable is probably close to the constant term, we also test the collinearity. This is what step 6 does.

Step 6: To deal with the multicollinearity problem with a compressed dummy variable, various tests are available, such as the Variance Inflation Factor proposed by Belsley, Kuh and Welsch (1980). If a multicollinearity problem appears, then we delete the constant term (which is always non-significant in our econometric estimations). Here, we do not recommend to use a "ridge regression" since the multicollinearity problem is caused by the similarity between the intercept and the compressed dummy variable. So, we just need to delete the constant to avoid such a problem.

Step 7: We test the new residuals series obtained from the regression with the compressed dummy variable (or with multiple dummies taken from step 4, if there is no singularity problem). If this series is already whited by the dummy variable, then we stop here. But if it cannot successfully pass the LM and LB tests, because of a symmetry between the positive and negative influences (in addition to the possibility of omitting explanatory variables of course), then, to cope with this problem, we propose an estimate through a scan method to deepen the determination of the values of some points in time of the compressed dummy variable. Example: for a negative shock, we take the

---

4   For example: SAS package suggests critical values at 10^{-7}. See here: http://support.sas.com
    /documentation/cdl/en/etsug/63939/HTML/default/viewer.htm#etsug_arima_sect022.htm).

values ranging from -1 to $-k$ (with $k > 1$) by successive small increments, until the residuals pass the LM and LB tests at a certain level of risk.

Moreover, if $D_t \neq 0$, the values of $\widehat{a_D}/D_t$ can be considered as those of an impulse response function after a political-institutional shock occurring at t, where $\widehat{a_D}$ is the coefficient of the estimate of the compressed dummy variable in the growth model taken into account.

It is true that in step 3, it seems somewhat arbitrary to select the dummies *a priori*, after simply viewing the residual plots. As a consequence, we propose here a Chi² test (or, alternatively, a Fisher test) in order to examine whether dummies should be included or not.

The idea makes sense: if the new dummy variable introduced is useful to explain the dependent variable, then: i) it should be significant in the model estimates, or ii) the R^2 should be improved. In other words, it comes down to considering:

either

i) $H_0 : \beta = 0$ vs $H_1 : \beta \neq 0$

or

ii) $H_o : R_o^2 = R_1^2$ vs $H_o : R_o^2 < R_1^2$

where β is the coefficient associated to the dummy variable; R_o^2 and R_1^2 are the coefficients of determination of, respectively, the null model [a] and the alternative model [b].

With D_t the dummy variable, $X_{1t} \dots X_{kt}$ the k explicative variables, with $\alpha_0, \alpha_1, \dots, \alpha_k$ their coefficients, and ε_t the Gaussian innovations series with mean zero and variance σ^2, these null and alternative models can be written:

[a] $Y_t = \alpha_0 + \alpha_1 X_{1t} + \dots + \alpha_k X_{kt} + \varepsilon_t$

and

[b] $Y_t = \alpha_0 + \beta D_t + \alpha_1 X_{1t} + \dots + \alpha_k X_{kt} + \varepsilon_t$

We can define the dummy variable in three different ways: as 1) instantaneous, the dummy takes the values $+1$ or -1 when a positive or negative shock occurs, and 0 for any other point of time; 2) permanent, the dummy takes the values $+1$ or -1 after a positive or negative shock, and 0 before; or 3) temporary, it takes the values +1 or –1 when a positive or negative shock occurs during a period, and o otherwise.

Now let us note:

$$N_t = \beta D_t + \varepsilon_t \qquad (5.1)$$

where $N_t = Y_t - (\alpha_1 X_{1t} + \dots + \alpha_k X_{kt})$.

With $D = (D_1, D_2, \dots, D_T)^T$ and $N = (N_1, N_2, \dots, N_T)^T$, under null hypothesis, N is a zero mean Gaussian vector with a variance covariance matrix $\sigma^2 \Omega$.

The generalized least squares (GLS) give:

$$\hat{\beta} = \frac{\delta}{\varkappa} \qquad (5.2)$$

and

$$\widehat{Var(\hat{\beta})} = \frac{\sigma^2}{\varkappa} \qquad (5.3)$$

where $\delta = D^T \Omega^{-1} N$ and $\varkappa = D^T \Omega^{-1} D$ are efficient estimators according to de Jong and Penzer (1998)'s method – or to that of Ansley and Kohn (1985). Here, σ^2 is obtained from the residuals series.

The empirical estimator of σ^2 is:

$$\hat{\sigma}^2 = \frac{1}{T} \sum_{t=1}^{T} \hat{\varepsilon}_t^2 \qquad (5.4)$$

When the sample size is small as compared to the number of parameters $k + 2$, we recommend to use the unbiased estimator:

$$\hat{\sigma}^2 = \frac{1}{T-k-2} \sum_{t=1}^{T} \hat{\varepsilon}_t^2 \qquad (V.5)$$

In case of problem of heteroscedasticity problem in the series of residuals ε_t, then we can recommend to use the robust correction by Findley, Monsell, Bell, Otto and Chen (1998):

$$\hat{\sigma}^2 = (1{,}49 \cdot Median(|\varepsilon_t|))^2 \qquad (V.6)$$

The Student statistics of $\hat{\beta}$,

$$\tau = \frac{\hat{\beta}}{\sqrt{\widehat{Var(\hat{\beta})}}} = \frac{\delta / \varkappa}{\delta / \sqrt{\varkappa}} \qquad (V.7)$$

approximately obeys to $t(T - k - 2)$, where T is the number of observations and k the number of explicative variables. The null model '2' includes the dummy variables and a constant term. We know that if $T - k - 2 \geq 25$, the distribution function of Student is close to a Gaussian form, that is: $\tau \sim N(0,1)$ approximately, when $T - k - 2 \geq 25$.

Consequently, $\tau^2 \sim \chi(1)$, and it is used to identify the significance of the dummy variable. If the latter is significant, then this is this dummy that is selected in step 3.

We can alternatively use another form of test, particularly:

$$H_0 : R_0^2 = R_1^2 \text{ vs } H_1 : R_0^2 < R_1^2 \qquad (5.8)$$

We know that:

$$R^2 = 1 - RSS/TSS \qquad (5.9)$$

Thus, we can define a Fisher statistics, such as:

$$F = \frac{(RSS_0 - RSS_1)/1}{RSS_1/(T-k)} \sim F(1, T-k) \qquad (5.10)$$

where k represents the number of parameters, RSS_1 the sum of squares of the residuals in the alternative model (with dummy), and RSS_0 the sum of squares of the residuals in the null model (without dummy).

However, this test is obviously less powerful than the previous one, because, in general, a single dummy increases the R^2 only very slightly; and if k is small, the effect of the explanatory variables on the overall significance of the model is much greater than those introduced by the dummy variable. As a result, we may well end up with a misleading conclusion about the effectiveness of dummies. Under these conditions, we recommend here to use the Chi^2 test as presented above.

Our compressed dummy variable has already whited the residuals series and therefore does not need a scan procedure. After having obtained the compressed dummy, we can finally draw from it the interpretations of the economic values. And, for our part, we argue that the exogenous shocks studied are likely caused by political-institutional changes. As can be seen in Graph 5.1, the different durations of these political-institutional changes show that their respective effects have not been identical over time.

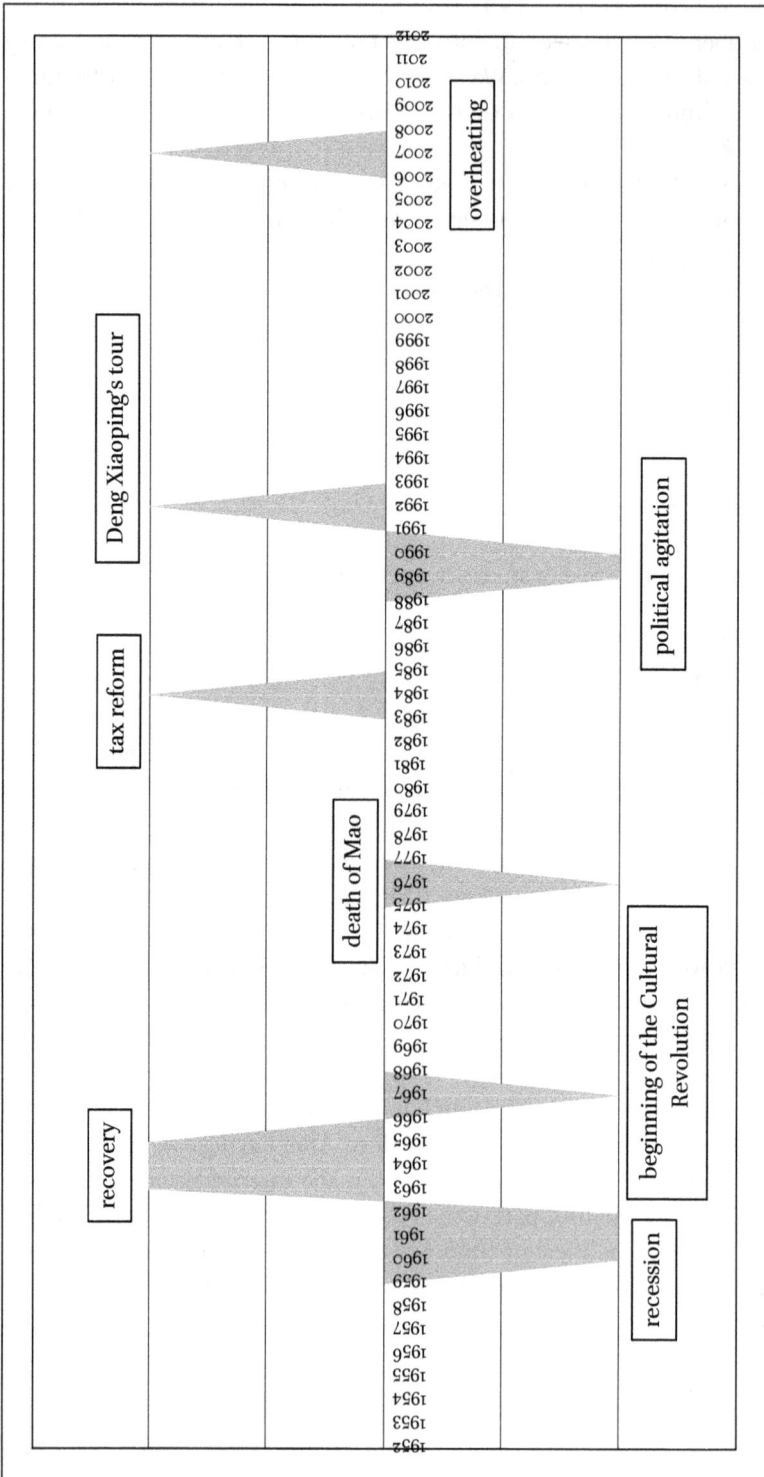

GRAPH 5.1   Representation of the qualitative (institutional) variable: China, 1952–2012

2 Econometric Estimates under Various Mainstream Growth Models

To perform our econometric estimates, we will choose here specifications derived from several mainstream growth models, including representations with endogenized technical progress *à la* Romer (1986, 1990), Lucas (1988), or Rebelo (1990) (see: Appendix A.5.1). The first of them, similar to a simplified version $Y = AK$, mobilizes a linear production function in a single input, which we limit to the sole stock of physical capital. The second theoretical framework is the standard Solowian model provided as a functional form of Cobb-Douglas type with two production factors, estimated in a standard way (physical capital and simple labour) or in an augmented specification (physical capital associated with human capital). The third approach adopted here integrates the R&D indicator, based on traditional writings of endogenous growth. The respective formalized frameworks of each of these three categories of specifications are presented mathematically in an appendix particularly dedicated to the theoretical foundations of these empirical studies (Appendix A.5.1.1).

In addition, an original Solowian model of endogenous growth is also proposed to emphasize the compatibility of these three theoretical frameworks (Appendix A.5.1.2). Indeed, mainstream growth theory is one of the fields that experienced the most significant advances over the last 35 years, especially under the influence of the so-called "new growth theory." Standard theory in macrodynamics, due to Solow and others in the late 1950s, has been newed thanks to various explanations of total factor productivity (TFP) and the analysis of the contributions of human capital and R&D, among other productive factors.[5] These works have remobilized some issues already studied by microeconomics for a long time, such as non-convexities. Nevertheless, as Solow (1988) himself indicated it, and some others with him, it would not really be fair to consider that the "new" growth models are very different from the "old" ones. Such is the case of the AK model (which revisits pioneer Keynesian dynamics). But this remark also applies to much more sophisticated non-linear models, resorting to increasing returns associated with the externalities of R&D or education. In fact, when they are empirically tested, the log-linearized specifications of these models are very close to extended Solowian formalizations. Besides, in another work, we had the opportunity to give a mathematical proof

---

5 Concerning the role of infrastructures in economic growth, see, by instance: Dessus and Herrera (1999, 2000).

that an endogenous growth can appear even within an augmented Solowian framework by remaining a convexity in technology.[6]

Consequently, to apply econometrically our original statistical series of capital stocks, we will use these three categories of models – Solow, AK-type endogenous growth, and endogenous growth with R&D and human capital –, taking into consideration their formal compatibility.[7]

The sources of growth will be explained more deeply when the model itself improves, that is, when the originally exogenous variables become endogenized:

$$y_t = f(x_{1t}, x_{2t}, \ldots x_{kt}) \tag{5.11}$$

If those variables have been endogenized, then the lagged values should also be included:

$$y_t = f(x_{1t}, \ldots, x_{1,t-p}, x_{2t}, \ldots, x_{2,t-p}, \ldots, x_{kt}, \ldots, x_{k,t-p}) \tag{5.12}$$

---

6 Let us say briefly that endogenous growth appears within an extended Solowian framework by keeping a concave production function, with constant returns to scale on all factors, be reproducible or not. For example, it would be the case with the following production function, combining two bifactorial symmetrical C.E.S. production functions, one for capital (K) and the other one for labour (L):

$$Y = K^{\alpha} (\Lambda L)^{1-\alpha} = \left(\mu_P K_P^{\sigma_K - 1 / \sigma_K} + \mu_G K_G^{\sigma_K - 1 / \sigma_K} \right)^{\alpha \left(\phi_K \frac{\sigma_K}{\sigma_K - 1} \right)} \cdot$$

$$\left[\Lambda^{\sigma_L - 1 / \sigma_L} \left(\mu_N N_Y^{\sigma_L - 1 / \sigma_L} + \mu_S S_Y^{\sigma_L - 1 / \sigma_L} \right) \right]^{(1-\alpha) \left(\phi_L \frac{\sigma_L}{\sigma_L - 1} \right)}$$

where Y is the output, K_P and K_G are the stocks of private and public capital, S_Y and N_Y skilled labour (human capital) and unskilled labour, and Λ is technical progress, with $0 < \alpha < 1$, unitary scale parameters ($\phi_K = \phi_L = 1$), the sums of intensity parameters normalized at 1 ($\mu_N + \mu_S = 1$ and $\mu_P + \mu_G = 1$), and elasticities of substitution between production factors characterized by $\sigma_K < 1$ and $\sigma_L > 1$ (with this last inequality being a *sine qua non* condition for the emergence of endogenous growth). For the complete mathematical presentation of this original growth model, see: Herrera (1998a, 2010a).

7 The purpose of this chapter is not to examine in detail the many theoretical problems related to the use of these endogenous growth models, discussed in depth by authors from diverse currents (DeLong y Summers [1991], Fine [2000], Salvadori [2003]). For a radical criticism of endogenous growth theory: Herrera (2000a, 200b, 2006a, 2010a, 2011).

However, this brings several econometric problems. First, the explicative variable x_{it} may also be correlated with other variables, so that we should have the simultaneous equation system:

$$yt = f(x_{1t}, ..., x_{1,t-p}, x_{2t}, ..., x_{2,t-p}, ..., x_{kt}, ..., x_{k,t-p}) \qquad (5.13)$$

and then k other equations, taking the form:

$$x_{it} = f(y_t, ..., y_{t-p}, x_{1t}, ..., x_{1,t-p}, x_{i-1,t}, ..., x_{i-1,t-p}, ..., x_{i+1,t}, ..., x_{i+1,t-p}) \qquad (5.14)$$

But with an increasing number of explicative variables k and a sufficient higher lag p to get white noise residuals, the possible combinations will sharply increase up to $(k + 1).(p + 1)^k$. For a model with a relatively small number of explicative variables and of lags (for example, $k = 10$ and $p = 3$), we will have around a dozen millions possible combinations. Although today it would not be an impossible task to run millions of regressions compared to 25 years ago, mainly because computer science is progressing fast, we would still need some time to interpret them all ...[8]

A second problem concerns the identification of such simultaneous equation systems, or VAR models. As indicated by Romer (2016), this identification is an extremely complicated issue in empirical macroeconomics, and almost no progress has been made over the past three decades. In other words, among the many million candidate models, all are not necessarily identifiable. In our opinion, the main reason is that in economics, the various variables are widely correlated, so simultaneous equation biases can be found everywhere. If the progress in economics just consists in continuing to endogenize previous exogenous variables, then an infinite number of variables to be added is available, and the identification problem will persist.[9]

In relation to those two problems, it should be recognized that Lucas (1976)' criticism according to which macroeconometric modeling should be based on economic theory rather than on statistical models is pertinent, because the statistical relationships are extremely sensitive. Thus, we decide first to derive

---

8 Contrary to the assertion of Sala-i-Martin (1997), who thinks that the variables do not need to be significant in each combination, we believe that they should be significant in a sufficient number of regressions tested. However, by excluding the many combinations which make no (economic) sense, we would be able to notably reduce their number.

9 In Chapter 8, we will see how to provide an analytical solution for this identification problem in the case of a system which does not contain too many variables. Our approach will imply the calculation of structural matrix determinants. However, for high dimensions, with determinants calculated in an iterative way, such resolution is much more tedious.

the specifications to be tested from explicit theoretical growth models; and secondly to perform our econometric regressions. As to the identification, we will impose stronger conditions than those of just-identifiable models.

Let us consider a dynamic structural model:

$$B_0 y_t = c + B_1 y_{t-1} + B_2 y_{t-2} + \ldots B_p y_{t-p} + u_t \qquad (5.15)$$

with B_p a $(n \times n)$ matrix, its row i–column j element being noted: $\beta_{ij}^{(s)} s = 1, 2, \ldots p$.

If we can order the variables in y_t to make B_0 be a lower triangular matrix, then the system is just-identified. But such an ordering generally has no theoretical economic foundations and is difficult to defend. Nevertheless, if we assume stronger restrictions on the coefficients matrix of the dynamic model, it can be much easier to justify these theoretical foundations. For example, if $n = 2$ and the matrix of coefficients B_p is lower triangular, then one of the system's variables is totally exogenous, so that the model will be over-identified. This strong restriction could be realized by a Granger causality test or an exogeneity Wald test.

Our regressions are performed in least squares on the first differences of the logarithmic forms in levels. As a matter of fact, we remember that Chow and Li (2002)'s regressions were made in least squares on the log forms in levels, and added a linear trend as a detrending method, like in many other studies in the macroeconomic literature. Nevertheless, Nelson and Kang (1981), following Chan, Hayya and Ord (1977), have showed that, in OLS estimates, the assimilation of a difference-stationary process (DS)[10] to a trend-stationary process (TS), as Chow and Li (2002) did it, can lead to a situation where the covariance of the residuals depends on the sample size, which artificially induces an autocorrelation of the residuals for the lags, as well as a cyclic movement into the series. By using such an inappropriate detrending method, the OLS estimator of trend will converge to zero in probability and the other OLS estimators will be divergent when the size of the sample tends to infinite.[11] Therefore, we recommend here to perform the regressions of the macrodynamic models in the first differences of the log-levels,[12] if the unit root tests indicate that the variables considered contain unit roots.[13] This choice is supported by econometric

---

10   DS is the most probable process for GDP, along with that of unit root, according to Nelson and Plosser (1982).

11   For the mathematical proof and Monte-Carlo simulations on a 1 million sample, see our article published in *Mathematics*: Long and Herrera (2020c).

12   This specification is also suggested by Hamilton (1994) for ARMA modelling.

13   We will see in the *Appendices* that our unit root tests show that the log of China's GDP has a unit root.

foundations: the logarithm might be useful in case of heteroscedasticity problems, and the difference operator[14] could avoid spurious regressions if there exists unit roots.

Unit root tests indicate that the growth rates of the variables are all stationary (Table A.5.2.1 to Table A.5.2.11 in Appendix A.5.2). The period studied is 60 years, from 1953 to 2012. Unlike Chow and Li (2002) who excluded years of strong fluctuations from their analysis – which we believe to be an unsatisfactory choice, because it is arbitrary, and with loss of information –, we decide for our part to include such years with fluctuations by introducing the qualitative variable, D, aimed at taking into account the political-institutional changes and their impact on growth in China. The years carrying the dummy variable, unique to preserve the maximum degrees of freedom, are those for which the residuals – of the estimate of a basic Solowian specification – exceed the confidence interval. In order to distinguish the positive or negative effects of such changes, D takes the value +1 in 1963–1965 (recovery), 1984 (tax reform), 1992 (Deng Xiaoping's tour) and 2007 (overheating), but the value –1 during the negative shocks of 1960–1962 (recession), 1967 (start of the Cultural Revolution), 1976 (death of Mao Zedong) and 1989–1990 (strong political unrest).

Under these conditions, the first set in the econometric estimates *à la* AK is conducted using the following equation:

$$g_{Yt} = c + \Theta D + \alpha g_{Kit} + \varepsilon_t \qquad (5.16)$$

where g_{Yt} and g_{Kit} are the growth rates of GDP and of one of the physical capital stocks (identified by i), as defined according to our four different conceptions, with or without the constant noted c (Table 5.1).

This set of model is derived from the Rebelo (1990) model, with an AK production function:

$$Y_t = A_t K_t^\alpha \qquad (5.17)$$

where Y_t is the output, K_t a composite capital input, and A_t its apparent productivity, that is, a technical factor assumed to follow the dynamics:

$$A_t = A_0 e^{ct} \qquad (5.18)$$

---

14   To avoid the over-differencing problem, we recommend to use the Inverse Autocorrelation Functions (IACF) to identify the order of integration together with unit root tests (Cleveland [1972], Chatfield [1980], Priestley [1981]).

TABLE 5.1   Classification of *AK* model regressions according to the physical capital input

Constant / Capital	Regressions with a constant	Regressions without a constant
Productive capital K_{Pe}	[1]	[2]
Productive capital K_{Pl}	[3]	[4]
Fixed capital K_F	[5]	[6]
Total capital K_T	[7]	[8]

Notes: See Chapter 1 for the details of the construction methods of the stocks of physical capital, with the following notations: K_{Pe} = narrowly-defined or *stricto sensu* physical capital stock (without lands, without inventories); K_{Pl} = largely-defined or *lato sensu* physical capital stock (without lands, with inventories); K_F = fixed physical capital stock (with lands, without inventories); K_T = total physical capital stock (with lands, with inventories).

where c is a constant.

By applying the difference-logarithm operator to this *AK*-type production function, we get the equation to be empirically tested.

From the eight tests of AK-type models carried out in least squares (Table 5.2), we can draw several comments. The elasticities of the physical capital stock are statistically significant and range between 0.60 (for productive capital stock, understood *stricto sensu*, with a constant) and 0.82 (total capital stock, without constant). Corresponding to the coefficients of the constants of the regressions which include them, the growth rates of technical progress – constant, with reference to a neutrality in the sense of Hicks – are between +0.61 and +2.06 percent, without however ever coming out significantly. In general, there is no autocorrelation in these estimates, but they present a slight problem with heteroskedasticity, even after adjustments.[15]

A second set of regressions is conducted on the basis of the following specifications:

$$g_{Yt} = \Theta D + \alpha g_{Kit} + \beta g_{Hjt} + \varepsilon_t \quad (5.19)$$

with g_{Hjt} the growth rate of the stock of human capital j, as one of its possible three forms (Table 5.3) – when it is not the simple labour which is used instead.

Such a set of formalizations is derived from an augmented Solow-Swan framework, but taking into account Lucas (1988)'s model. As a matter of fact,

---

15   Newey and West (1994).

TABLE 5.2   Results of eight regressions tested within the framework of AK models

	Constant	D	Capital	R^2	Autocorrelation	Heteroscedasticity	Correction
[1]	0.020621 (1.096374)	0.116241 (4.495805)	0.603389 (4.238478)	0.586267	0.8350 / 0.8219	0.0201 / 0.0214	Yes
[2]		0.115275 (4.282375)	0.782852 (13.67934)	0.576073	0.5897 / 0.6349	0.0135 / 0.0149	Yes
[3]	0.019631 (1.113699)	0.116347 (5.023654)	0.614105 (4.219976)	0.589707	0.5026 / 0.4766	0.0404 / 0.0410	Yes
[4]		0.115469 (4.935988)	0.785087 (12.14487)	0.580459	0.3161 / 0.3284	0.0369 / 0.0376	Yes
[5]	0.006394 (0.295208)	0.113428 (4.656443)	0.766911 (4.198741)	0.608815	0.9517 / 0.9474	0.0135 / 0.0149	Yes
[6]		0.112965 (4.435570)	0.825662 (17.98657)	0.608008	0.9559 / 0.9602	0.0121 / 0.0135	Yes
[7]	0.006124 (0.321922)	0.113964 (5.132911)	0.768219 (4.739061)	0.612600	0.5778 / 0.5529	0.0229 / 0.0241	Yes
[8]		0.113560 (4.963646)	0.824211 (16.70064)	0.611844	0.5715 / 0.5564	0.0218 / 0.0231	Yes

Notes: The first column gives the number of the regression using a physical capital stock with or without a constant (Table 5.1). In the next three columns, the numbers between parentheses are t-statistics. In the Autocorrelation column, the p-values are given (first for the Fisher test, then for the Chi² test) for the null hypothesis "no autocorrelation in the residuals series" with the Breusch-Godfrey Serial Correlation LM test. In the Heteroscedasticity column, the p-values are given (for the Fisher test and for the Chi² test) for the null hypothesis "no heteroscedasticity in the residuals series" with the Breusch-Pagan-Godfrey Heteroskedasticity test. The last column indicates whether a correction of heteroscedasticity à la Newey-West is introduced or not.

many endogenous growth models essentially look like augmented Solow models, and can be used for enriching the specifications to be tested. They also use a Cobb-Douglas production function, as Solow did it in the past:

$$Y_t = F(K_t, L_t) \qquad (5.20)$$

However, endogenous growth can appear here within the framework of a production function with constant returns to scale on all factors, whether reproducible or not, as in the original Solow model, by an asymptotic convergence towards a macroeconomic functional form characterized by an unitary elasticity of output to a composite capital stock.[16] We know that Jones and Manuelli (1990) have Reformulated a Solowian model, respecting the Kuhn-Tucker theorem, but without meeting the third Inada condition (according to which the *per capita* marginal productivity of capital tends to zero when *per capita* capital tends to infinity), and confirmed that – even if a convexity is maintained in the technology – the sole condition for the emergence of an endogenous growth is that this technology leads to an interest rate asymptotically bounded (inferiorly) by a non-zero, positive, and sufficiently high value. The production function can remain concave, and leads to a steady state similar to that of a model *à la AK*. Barelli and de Abreu Pessôa (2003) have demonstrated that any production function satisfying the Inada' conditions is an asymptotic Cobb-Douglas function, and can simply be deducted from the following well-known simple equation:

$$Y_t = A_t \, K_t^{\alpha} \, L_t^{\beta} \qquad (5.21)$$

Lucas (1988) proposed a model where human capital constitutes the driving force in the process of endogenous growth. All inputs of the production function are accumulable. By posing on them a constance of returns to scale, we re-find a self-sustained growth process of the AK-type where a broader, aggregated K includes physical capital and human capital. Thus, the issue of the emergence of an endogenous growth stays in the writing of an incentive to invest in human training which does not decrease with its accumulation. Then, an externality on human capital is added, which modifies the production function, by increasing its degree of homogeneity, but without leading to a situation where increasing returns are themselves necessary to obtain a permanent growth in the long period. As a consequence, the core of Lucas' model is that human capital is accumulated in a production function that associates

16   See: Herrera (1998a, 2010a).

non-decreasing returns to this same factor such that its marginal productivity remains constant. Thus, it is the linearity in the accumulation with respect to the level of individual human capital that precisely allows endogenous growth. Lucas used the following production function:

$$Y_t = A_t \, K_t^{\alpha} \, (lhL)^{1-\alpha} \qquad (5.22)$$

where l is the fraction of time allocated to training by the representative agent, and h the efficiency of labour. We define the product of the three terms as human capital stock, with the educational attainment as indicator:

$$lhL = H \qquad (5.23)$$

Therefore, we get the tested equations by applying to a difference-logarithm operator to the Cobb-Douglas function used.

Still in least squares and over the period 1953–2012, 16 other regressions are carried out in this framework, numbered from [9] to [24] according to the inputs selected (Table 5.3). We use a robust correction method (the one giving the best econometric results)[17] if the regression does not reveal white noises in the series of residuals. The R^2 are improved, now exceeding 0.60. Tests [9], [13], [17] and [21] using simple labour show very high (in fact, too high) coefficients for this factor, varying from 0.87 in the estimate [9] to 0.80 in the estimate [21], while those carried by the stocks of physical capital lie in an interval going from 0.63 to 0 67 respectively. As, in reality, the growth of the Chinese economy is much faster than that of demography, the strong contribution of labour input to product growth turns out to be overestimated – due to a likely underestimation of the dynamics of total factor productivity. The assumption of constancy of returns to scale can no longer be defended, however. It therefore becomes relevant to use the stock of human capital, whose productivity is higher, as a labour factor.

The estimates [10] and [14], selecting the productive versions of human capital and physical capital, in the alternately narrow or broad conceptions of the latter, offer interesting results, after Newey-West corrections: the elasticities of the two physical stocks hover around 0.64, those of human capital are from 0.35 to 0.38, their sums thus yielding – without constraint – almost exactly constant

---

17   The Breusch-Pagan-Godfrey (BPG) and Glejser tests reveal that there is a problem with heteroskedasticity in all the regressions performed, but those of Harvey and ARCH say the opposite, while the White test is rather ambiguous. As a precaution, we only present here the results that are the most unfavorable to us (namely, those of the BPG test).

TABLE 5.3   Classification of Solowian model regressions according to the inputs of physical capital and
human capital (or labour)

Capital		Labour	Employed population L	Productive human capital H_P	Total human capital H_T	Intermediate human capital H_I
Productive capital	K_{Pe}		[9]	[10]	[11]	[12]
Productive capital	K_{Pl}		[13]	[14]	[15]	[16]
Fixed capital	K_F		[17]	[18]	[19]	[20]
Total capital	K_T		[21]	[22]	[23]	[24]

Notes: See Table 5.1 for the definition of the physical capital variables and Chapter 2 for details of the methods of constructing human capital stocks, the notations of which are as follows: L = employed population (or number of employees); H_P = productive human capital stock; H_T= total human capital stock; and H_I = stock of intermediary human capital.

returns to scale. Overall returns also appear constant in the estimates [18] and [22],[18] but with noticeably lower elasticities of productive human capital and, above all, statistically not significant. The stocks of fixed and total physical capital include too many non-productive elements (such as land) to fit a strictly productive definition of human capital. None of the coefficients of the total human capital stock appear with the significance required in [11], [15], [19] and [23], exhibiting the worst results by far – human capital even carrying a negative sign, of course not significant, when the concepts of physical and human capital stocks that are the most distant from their respective productive "core" are considered. On the contrary, the indicator of intermediate human capital, integrated as an input of a Solowian production function tested according to formulas [12], [16], [20] and [24], leads to elasticities of physical capital stocks from 0.64 to 0.69 and to elasticities of human capital stocks from 0.31 to 0.28, both passing the thresholds of statistical significance – albeit extremely narrowly, for the H_I in [24]. In the last regression [24], the positive contribution of human capital could be explained by the productive effect, direct or not, of some of its components considered "non-productive" (retirees, for example).

Finally, we test a third set of equations derived from linearized forms of endogenous growth models incorporating research-and-development (R&D) expenditure, alongside physical capital and human capital stocks, as follows:

---

18   For these estimates as well as for the previous ones, the constant overall returns are confirmed by the Wald tests.

$$g_{Yt} = \Theta D + \alpha g_{Kit} + \beta g_{Hjt} + \gamma g_R \&_{Dt} + \varepsilon_t \qquad (5.24)$$

with $g_R\&_{Dt}$ the growth rate of this R&D spending, which has been preferred to the number of scientists, already incorporated in human capital stocks, or to the number of patents, intellectual property being regulated in China only since 1986.

This set of equations is also derived from the Lucas (1988) model, with a dynamic technical progress allowed here, as follows:

$$A_t = A_{t-1} e^{a_t} \qquad (5.25)$$

where a_t is a dynamic random variable of technical progress replacing the constant.

The R&D expenditure series was previously found to be stationary by unit root tests (see Table A.5.2.10 and Table A.5.2.11 in Appendices), converted into 1952-based constant prices and expressed in first differences of the logarithmic forms in levels, as for the input variables above. It is also the same principle of correction which is adopted: apart from the cases where the residuals are white noises, a correction is made when at least one of the tests carried out reveals a risk of heteroskedasticity (at 5 percent), using White's method or that of Newey-West, in order to obtain robust regressions.

It should be remembered that China did not begin to fit into the international standardized system of accounting for R&D activities until the year 1986 – without it being possible to have a homogeneous series before that date, as established by the *Frascati Manual*.[19] Faced with this constraint, we distinguish two indicators of R&D expenditure (Table 5.5): on the one hand, $R\&D_1$ (see Table 3.3 in Chapter 3), constructed according to the budgets of Science and Technology[20] (1952–1985), of R&D of the public entities and of higher education (1986–1988), and of aggregate R&D from the *Statistical Yearbooks of Science and Technology* (1989–1994), then from the NBS (1995–2012); and on the other hand, $R\&D_2$ (see Table A.3.1.1 in Appendix A.3.1), corresponding to the financing of the various fundamental or applied components of science and technology (1952–1970), to which are also added those of the technical

---

19   See: OECD (2015).
20   *Cf.* Gu and Lundvall (2006). These authors used the database of the Chinese Academy of Science and Technology for Development (*Chinese Science and Technology Statistics Network*), a mission institution of the Ministry of Science and Technology whose site (http://www.sts.org.cn) has not been accessible since mid-2015.

TABLE 5.4   Results of 16 regressions tested within the framework of Solowian models

D	Capital	Labour	R²	Autocorrelation	Heteroscedasticity	Correction
[9] 0.118987	0.628570	0.878810	0.670247	0.4807	0.0396	No
(9.191989)	(9.184534)	(4.034677)		0.4604	0.0415	
[10] 0.117659	0.647430	0.353519	0.590207	0.7844	0.0207	Yes
(4.572008)	(7.927187)	(2.253730)		0.7732	0.0231	
[11] 0.115308	0.781568	0.003115	0.576075	0.5970	0.0329	Yes
(4.289987)	(10.58792)	(0.022544)		0.6360	0.0350	
[12] 0.120679	0.641063	0.312691	0.603007	0.6562	0.0480	Yes
(4.996345)	(6.400047)	(2.113660)		0.6361	0.0496	
[13] 0.118850	0.635180	0.814565	0.657805	0.2100	0.0598	No
(9.012558)	(8.900340)	(3.589385)		0.1911	0.0607	
[14] 0.118036	0.639539	0.384885	0.598272	0.4210	0.0538	Yes
(5.204937)	(6.764899)	(2.169106)		0.3951	0.0551	
[15] 0.115739	0.774578	0.025680	0.580565	0.3336	0.0853	No
(7.854788)	(7.146692)	(0.120211)		0.3361	0.0847	
[16] 0.120640	0.647743	0.301266	0.605157	0.3561	0.0933	Yes
(5.600580)	(5.821833)	(2.042065)		0.3323	0.0922	
[17] 0.117048	0.669931	0.860514	0.698997	0.5233	0.0128	Yes
(6.428302)	(12.87299)	(6.341289)		0.5767	0.0152	
[18] 0.114836	0.729801	0.237664	0.614015	0.8945	0.0165	Yes
(4.629540)	(9.431224)	(1.546768)		0.8889	0.0189	
[19] 0.112852	0.829714	−0.009556	0.608023	0.9560	0.0292	Yes
(4.458757)	(11.59976)	(−0.067975)		0.9607	0.0314	
[20] 0.118473	0.687704	0.295727	0.632773	0.8513	0.0318	Yes
(5.124221)	(8.582082)	(2.230495)		0.8658	0.0340	
[21] 0.117250	0.673494	0.801219	0.687650	0.3303	0.0215	Yes
(6.934376)	(10.77296)	(5.563952)		0.3297	0.0239	
[22] 0.115546	0.719935	0.261628	0.619435	0.4851	0.0309	Yes
(5.150099)	(8.444532)	(1.547888)		0.4624	0.0331	
[23] 0.113437	0.828719	−0.010682	0.611863	0.5762	0.0536	Yes
(4.987187)	(10.06643)	(−0.070797)		0.5561	0.0549	
[24] 0.118628	0.694134	0.277166	0.633069	0.5277	0.0511	No
(8.533138)	(7.324835)	(1.815775)		0.5132	0.0525	

Notes: The first column gives the number of the regression carried out by combining capital and labour inputs (Table 5.3). For the rest, see Table 5.2's notes.

TABLE 5.5   Classification of the regressions of endogenous growth models according to the indicator of R&D associated with productive human capital and physical capital

Capital	Constant	Productive human capital H_P associated with variable $R\&D_1$	Productive human capital H_P associated with variable $R\&D_2$
Productive capital K_{Pe}		[25]	[26]
Productive capital K_{Pl}		[27]	[28]
Fixed capital K_F		[29]	[30]
Total capital K_T		[31]	[32]

Note: See Chapters 1 and 2 for the building of physical and human capital stocks, respectively. We note: K_{Pe} = narrowly-defined or *stricto sensu* physical capital stock (without lands, without inventories); K_{Pl} = largely-defined or *lato sensu* physical capital stock (without lands, with inventories); K_F = fixed physical capital stock (with lands, without inventories); K_T = total physical capital stock (with lands, with inventories). And: L = employed population (or number of employees); H_P = productive human capital stock; H_T = total human capital stock; and H_I = stock of intermediary human capital. For the series $R\&D_1$, see: Chapter 3. And for $R\&D_2$: Appendix A.3.1.

innovation by companies (1971–1985), before the profiles of the two series were joined in the year 1986.

The calculation of the average growth rates of R&D expenditure (of the order of 14.5 percent over the period 1952–2012) gives values that are much higher than those we obtain elsewhere for the expressions of total factor productivity, however we define it as a Solowian residual, with neutral technical progress in the Hicks acception. Nevertheless, in general, the contribution of this total factor productivity does not come out statistically significant. This supports a result already highlighted by Su and Xu (1999), among others.[21] It is also much more than the growth rate of the term of total factor productivity (+ 2.5 percent) advanced by Chow and Li (2002), in a framework that remained a Solowian model, explaining in logarithms a GDP expressed per capita and integrating a linear trend. Their sample is however more limited[22] than ours and, what is more, divided into sub-periods. But it is above all because we doubt not only the magnitude of this trend, which we believe is underestimated, but also the relevance of its introduction into OLS estimates – due, in

---

21   See also here: Jefferson, Rawski and Zheng (1996).

22   This is also the case with the study by Ding and Knight (2009), which only covers the years from 1980 to 2004.

particular, to the observation of the presence of statistical breaks in the series of Chow and Li (2002), even "cleaned" from the years considered to be "problematic" (precisely those from 1958 to 1969) –, that we ultimately opted for first difference regressions of logarithmic forms in levels on various specifications going beyond the strict Solowian framework in order to mobilize endogenous technical progress models.

The results of regressions [25] to [32] (Table 5.6) show that R&D, as represented by our two alternative indicators, contributes positively to Chinese GDP growth, with coefficients between 0.088 and 0.093 for $R\&D_1$, and between 0.041 and 0.048 for $R\&D_2$, most frequently being statistically significant. Nevertheless, the coefficients of the stocks of physical capital are now clearly lower than those recorded in the previous tests, but still situated within completely satisfactory ranges. This conclusion is all the more interesting as the sum of the elasticities borne by the inputs of directly productive capital and labour turns out to be, almost always, close to unity. Furthermore, taking into account the institutional qualitative variable contributes a lot to the overall consistency of the estimates that we propose to the reader.

One might be concerned that there may exist some feedback effects between the dependent and explicative variables: the output may also have an influence on the input factors. In such a case, the explicative variables associated with the residuals would be endogenous. Consequently, the estimations of the coefficients would be biased due to a simultaneous equation bias. We examined the causality between dependent and explicative variables through pairwise Granger causality tests (bivariate and VAR) – expecting that the explicative variables do cause g_Y, but that g_Y does not cause the explicative variables. These tests show that all explicative variables are non-endogenous – except technical progress, which appears weakly endogenous. In addition, it should be observed that the institutional variable significantly improved the residuals and the exogeneity Wald test results in VAR models.

We have therefore econometrically estimated, on the basis of time series entirely reconstructed for the occasion of physical capital stocks and human capital stocks for China from 1952 to the present day, several specifications derived from a fairly wide range of macrodynamic models, ranging from simplified AK-type versions to more complexified representations of endogenous growth with R&D indicators, and passing through standard or augmented Solow formalizations. The best empirical results are obtained when we retain the concepts of stocks of physical capital and human capital closest to their respective productive "cores." As a matter of fact, in our final econometric regressions, the most complete ones, we indeed clearly observe positive and statistically significant contributions of *stricto sensu* productive physical

TABLE 5.6   Results of eight regressions tested within the framework of endogenous growth models

	D	Capital	Labour	R&D	R^2	Autocorrelation	Heteroscedasticity	Correction
[25]	0.102881	0.404455	0.586624	0.088078	0.678216	0.0763	0.0147	Yes
	(5.613430)	(2.100353)	(2.438769)	(1.791943)		0.0654	0.0181	
[26]	0.111416	0.517774	0.473772	0.043268	0.641996	0.4090	0.0369	No
	(7.850935)	(4.008071)	(1.921720)	(1.719731)		0.3761	0.0403	
[27]	0.102657	0.348890	0.687569	0.093257	0.660638	0.0400	0.0372	Yes
	(6.557960)	(1.716261)	(2.527576)	(1.963446)		0.0348	0.0406	
[28]	0.112510	0.480750	0.563337	0.040806	0.617048	0.3195	0.0899	No
	(7.646198)	(3.381593)	(2.181051)	(1.479169)		0.2899	0.0903	
[29]	0.100381	0.486869	0.456239	0.089661	0.702461	0.2638	0.0057	Yes
	(5.400343)	(3.399253)	(2.556562)	(2.184299)		0.2385	0.0083	
[30]	0.108274	0.583992	0.368676	0.048289	0.663837	0.7553	0.0197	No
	(7.889510)	(4.547741)	(1.515083)	(2.077384)		0.7500	0.0233	
[31]	0.101239	0.446507	0.532977	0.090019	0.684656	0.1356	0.0249	Yes
	(6.122867)	(2.733372)	(2.417058)	(2.152730)		0.1174	0.0285	
[32]	0.109988	0.559597	0.432362	0.043125	0.642348	0.5361	0.0503	No
	(7.764226)	(4.016805)	(1.697882)	(1.714445)		0.5052	0.0531	

Notes: The first column gives the number of the regression combining stocks of productive physical capital and human capital with R&D (Table 5.5). For the rest, see Table 5.2's notes.

capital (K_{Pe}), of productive human capital (H_p), but also of R&D, to the Chinese product growth over the long period (60 years); and this in theoretical frameworks where constant returns to scale are often accepted.

While capturing economic information relating to the institutional changes that characterized the contemporary history of China, the introduction of the qualitative variable D clearly reduces the autocorrelation of the residuals, which probably derives from the breaks caused by the presence of strong fluctuations in the variables studied in certain periods of this history (especially during the 1960s and 1990s), and greatly improves the explanatory power of our econometric estimates. The persistence of a slight heteroskedasticity problem at the end of this work, in some tests, suggests the need to analyze in more depth the question of the existence of possible cycles in the growth trajectory of the Chinese economy, which opens up new research perspectives.

However, as we have had to justify this choice over and over again times and, in several publications,[23] these are mainly the conceptual, methodological and theoretical limits of the neoclassical axioms and formalizations – in our view definitively insurmountable – that make us turn away from the mainstream. Expanding here the detail of these shortcomings would make us deviate from our course.

---

23   Read, for example: Herrera (2000a, 2010a, 2011, 2015a).

Capital in the Twenty-First Century to the Test of China: About Thomas Piketty's "Fundamental Laws"

The success of the book *Capital in the Twenty-First Century* by the French economist Thomas Piketty has been staggering, including in China, where it was published in 2015, shortly after its French (2013) and English (2014) editions. In this book, the author defines "capital" in a very broad sense and makes a presentation of what constitutes, in his eyes, "fundamental laws" of the dynamic functioning of the capitalist system – or rather some regularities of the latter over the long term. The purpose of this chapter is to reconstruct, for the case of the economy of the People's Republic of China, a statistical series of capital stock as close as possible to the concept given by T. Piketty, in order to test the validity of these "laws."

A preliminary question is whether the Chinese economic system can be assimilated or likened to capitalism or not. A vast majority of authors, both abroad and in China, argue that since it has opened to the world system in 1978, China's economy has moved considerably closer to capitalism;[1] enough anyway to allow, from a methodological point of view, to try to apply to this country the framework proposed by Piketty. Therefore, we will provisionally assume the generally accepted hypothesis according to which such a system constitues one of the forms of today's capitalism. In this case, the expression "State capitalism" might be the most appropriate.[2] Moreover, the concept of capital used by Piketty could be able to be applied, according to him, to any patrimonial system, as the suggested mode of regulation would correspond to any ownership system, even public.[3] As a consequence, it seems relevant to us to wonder about the scope and the limits of the analysis Piketty has applied to the developed capitalist countries concerning the very singular case of China.

This chapter offers the reader a statistical method for constructing data on capital for China in the manner of Piketty, over a relatively long period, from

---

1 For French authors, by instance, see: Aglietta and Bai (2012), Dufour (2012). Let us mention, on the Chinese side: Cheung (1998), Zhang (2000), Lin, Cai and Li (2001).
2 Our fundamental position, however, is that China is not a capitalist country. Read: Herrera and Long (2019c).
3 Piketty (2013), p. 83.

1952 to 2012. The methodology gradually expands the contents of a capital stock from narrowly-defined productive physical capital – elaborated in Chapter 1 – to include the inventories necessary for production, agricultural lands and buildings for commercial use, but also the values of various not-directly productive components, such as developed real property and built-up lands for residential use (housing buildings and the value of their lands), as well as monetary elements representative of the country's net asset position vis-à-vis the rest of the world. We will call this capital à la Piketty the "stock of general capital" (K_G), reasoning as he does on an open economy.

Thereafter, the elasticity of this general capital is estimated econometrically with specifications which integrate, alongside this aggregate stock, human capital, research-and-development (R&D), and a variable of institutional change. These empirical tests are performed within the framework of modern neoclassical macrodynamic models;[4] an analytical framework that this author explicitly claims to be his, although not exclusively so. On this basis, we will calculate an implicit rate of return on such capital in order to verify, or to refute, what Piketty presents as a "fundamental inequality," supporting that the rate of return of capital would have to be higher than the income growth rate over the long period. Then, the "second economic law" that Piketty states, arguing that the coefficient of capital, or capital-income ratio, would be tendentiously equal to the ratio of savings rate to income growth rate in the long run, is examined, by comparing several indicators of savings.

The results obtained by this method are confronted with a new set of econometric estimates performed this time for a sub-period: 1978–2012. This sub-period is shorter but corresponds much more clearly to what many observers consider to be that of "capitalism with Chinese characteristics." In conclusion, we touch on the issue of the inequalities in China today, which is a crucial but extremely complex question that cannot be really examined in more detail in this chapter.

1   Construction of a Time Series of General Capital à la Piketty for China

1.1   The Concept of "Capital" According to Piketty
First of all, we need to conceptually grasp what Piketty means by "capital." The latter, as it is understood by this author in his bestseller, as well as in other

---

4   About such models applied to China, see: Perkins (1988), Gu and Lundwall (2006), Ding and Knight (2009).

publications signed or co-signed by him in the past,[5] is a particularly broad notion, expanded well beyond that of the usual physical capital stock. The conception selected by Piketty is closer to that of "assets," or rather that of "patrimony" – which could be used, *"to simplify the presentation,"*[6] as a synonym of "capital" –, or even that of "wealth."[7] In fact, this notion actually means everything (or almost everything) that can bring money to its owner – with the main exception being human capital. In other words, "capital" would be any asset which allows its owner(s) to earn any monetary return. It thus corresponds to all the assets to which it is possible to give a price, whether material or not (intangible assets), be it of a real nature or not (financial). In this definition, capital may or may not have a productive function (it may not be directly productive or may even be unproductive). In addition, such capital may exist as private property, but it may also be public or collective ...

Capital therefore concerns all *"non-human assets* (...), *owned and traded in markets"*[8] by *"individuals or groups of individuals"* – including the State. *"In practice, capital may be owned either by private individuals (private capital), or by the State and the public administrations (public capital)."*[9] In other words, it includes *"all furniture capital* (...) *used for housing, as well as financial and professional capital (buildings, equipment, machines, patents, etc.) used by the enterprises and the administrations."*[10] Similarly, and in more detail, Piketty's capital represents *"the sum of the non-financial assets (housing, land, commercial property, buildings, machinery, equipment, patents and other business assets held directly) and the financial assets (bank accounts, savings accounts, bonds, companies' shares, and other financial investments of any kind), less the financial liabilities (i.e., all debts)."*[11] Nevertheless, despite its extremely heterogeneous character, this capital is clearly seen as a factor of production, and therefore is supposed by Piketty to be remunerated at its marginal productivity. The latter depends on the substitutability between capital and labour, which would be, according to him, superior to one. In this way, this economist can register distinctly, at the conceptual, methodological and analytical levels, in the neoclassical framework – among other references (especially Keynesian and institutionalist), also mobilized.

---

5   See, for example: Piketty (2003), Piketty and Saez (2003), Atkinson, Piketty and Saez (2011).

6   Piketty (2013), p. 54.

7   Piketty and Zucman (2014).

8   Piketty (2013), p. 82.

9   *Idem*, p. 83.

10   *Idem*, p. 86.

11   *Ibidem*, p. 86.

Thus, in our own perspective, the challenge to take up will be for us to reconstruct a series of Chinese capital stock defined *à la* Piketty. China is indeed incorporated in the databases made publicly available on Piketty's website[12] – without, however, that the curious visitor can find any capital stock for China. Creating capital stock series is certainly a difficult task, in particular because of the specificities of this economy, which still retains some features of the socialist system even today. This is the case, for example, of the status of the agricultural lands within an original tenure system that is still considering them to be "public"; or of intellectual property, that has only been recognized and regulated in China since the second half of the 1980s. More generally, the values of the various capital goods to be calculated are influenced by changes in prices set by markets in which the interventions of the State are very energetic, multifaceted, and therefore, to say omnipresent.

1.2   *Method of Construction of a Chinese General Capital Stock* à la *Piketty*

To succeed in constructing statistically-rigorous data on an overall general capital in the sense of Piketty (K_G) for China, the method we have followed, step by step, consists in:

1) relying on a stock of physical capital defined as productive *stricto sensu* (K_{Pe}), comprising equipment, machines, tools, commercial property and buildings for business purposes, as well as agricultural lands, but excluding built-up lands for residential use (T) and inventories (V);

2) to extend it to a *lato sensu* or largely-defined productive physical capital (K_{Pl}), corresponding to the previous stock to which inventories (V) are added, but without built-up lands for residential use (T);

3) then to a fixed physical capital (K_F), which corresponds for its part to the narrowly-defined productive capital plus built-up lands for residential use (T), but without inventories (V);

4) and then to expand capital even further to a total physical capital stock (K_T) including both inventories (V) and built-up lands for residential use (T);

5) in order to finally obtain the desired general capital stock, within the meaning of Piketty (K_G). This global capital is an extremely large aggregate that brings together the various components of the previous fixed capital stock, stretching from equipment, machinery and tools to

---

12   See: piketty.pse.ens.fr.

buildings, industrial facilities and plants, and including the values of residential housing, of agricultural lands and livestocks, of raw materials and energy commodities, but also intangible elements (e.g., software, in addition to computer hardware), with regard to domestic assets.[13] And it is to these already very heterogeneous assets that are added the foreign exchange currency and gold reserves (*M*) owned by China's authorities and estimating in monetary terms, as a first approximation, the cumulative balances of trade with the rest of the world. The unit used is hundreds of millions of yuan.

We have seen that it is the permanent inventory method (PIM) that is used to build our capital series:[14]

$$K_{i,t} = (1 - \sigma)\, K_{i,t-1} + I_{i,t} \,/\, P_{i,t} \qquad (6.1)$$

where $K_{i,t}$ is the capital stock of category i at the end of year t, $I_{i,t}$ the corresponding investment flow, $P_{i,t}$ the appropriate price index and σ the rate of stock depreciation, with the following alternative capital stocks:

$$\left\{ \begin{array}{l} K_{Pl} = K_{Pe} + V \\ K_F = K_{Pe} + T \\ K_T = K_{Pe} + V + T \\ K_G = K_{Pe} + V + T + M \end{array} \right. \qquad (6.2)$$

The initial levels of these five capital stocks are estimated for the base year 1952, that is, the furthest possible date in time; that also which corresponds to the completion of the reunification of mainland China's continental territory and the founding of the National Bureau of Statistics (NBS) of China. Lacking historical data on physical capital stocks or even sufficiently reliable investment series from statistical yearbooks prior to 1952, we were forced to derive our initial levels of physical capital from an estimate of a capital-output ratio. Here, we remember from Chapter 1 that our calculation procedure by iterations of the initial stock of physical capital converged towards a K_0 close to

---

13   On the composition of the fixed assets, read: Xu (1999), who uses as sources the statistics of fixed assets by the NBS and other various ministries. And on their repartition between productive and non-productive capital, see: Intersecretariat Working Group on National Accounts (http://unstats.un.org/unsd/nationalaccount/aeg.asp).

14   See, again, Chapter 1.

1025 in 1952, i.e., equivalent to the capital-output ratio of 1.5, and avoided having to resort to the hypothesis – delicate, because improbable, but usual[15] – of steady state reached as soon as the base year.[16]

Through this iterative method and using the productive investment series, we find an initial productive capital K_{Pe} of 623.25 hundred million yuan; and, again by this iteration process, from the gross capital formation series, that the total initial capital is worth 1018.50×10^8 yuan. By comparison, our stock of productive capital is quite close to the capital estimate established for that same year by Chow (1993). And by considering the inventories (73.00) as they appear in the series of GDP calculated according to the extended approach,[17] we can obtain a large productive stock of China (K_{Pl}) at 696.25. Total capital (K_T), including built-up lands for residential use, is estimated by assuming that the stylized Kaldorian fact of a constant capital-output ratio (of 1.5) for the entire country is verified: 1018.50×100 million yuan. After deduction of built-up lands for residential use (322.25), we thus arrive at a fixed capital K_F of 945.50. And by adding to K_T the reserves accumulated in gold and foreign currencies converted into 1952-based national currency (3.92 and 2.45×100 million yuan, respectively), we finally get the value of the general capital stock understood as from Piketty, K_G: 1024.87 hundreds of millions of yuan. We recapitulate the calculation of the Chinese 1952 initial capital stock *à la* Piketty in Box 6.1.

---

15   See: Harberger (1978) or Nehru and Dhareshwar (1993).

16   To apply the PIM, we need the initial capital stock. With the method of Nehru and Dhareshwar (1993), one would have to assume that the economy was in a steady state from the base year 1952. However, this assumption is clearly not in accordance with reality. Instead, we use the coefficient of capital α to estimate this initial level. If we knew the coefficient of capital α_0 in 1952, we could use the equation:

$$K_0 = I_0/\alpha_0$$

If the unknown variable α_0 is ergodic on average, we could use its temporal average as a replacement for its mathematical expectation:

$$E(\alpha_0) = \frac{1}{T}\sum_{t=1}^{T}\alpha_t$$

So we will get the initial stock by the formula:

$$E(K_0) = I_0/E(\alpha_0)$$

This ergodicity on average is verified by the stationarity of α_t and the speed of convergence of its autocorrelation function. So behind this iterative procedure, the mathematical hypothesis is that of ergodicity, and the implicit economic hypothesis that the economy tends towards a steady state in the long term.

17   Source: *China Statistical Yearbooks* du NBS (various years).

Box 6.1 Steps in calculating the initial stock of capital *à la* Piketty: China, 1952

For the whole of China, we obtain by iterations, based on the series of productive investment:

Narrowly-defined productive physical capital: $K_{Pe1952} = 623.25 \times 10^8$ yuans

+ Inventories: $V_{1952} = 73.10 \times 10^8$ yuans

= Broadly-defined productive physical capital: $K_{Pl1952} = 696.25 \times 10^8$ yuans

Iterative procedure: convergence towards a capital
coefficient for China of 1.5

By iterations, using gross capital formation series, it comes:

Total physical capital: $K_{T1952} = 679 \times 1{,}5 = 1{,}018.50 \times 10^8$ yuans

→ Built-up lands for residential use: $T_{1952} = K_{T1952} - K_{Pe1952} - V = 322.25 \times 10^8$ yuans

Fixed physical capital: $K_{F1952} = 1{,}018.50 - 73{,}00 = 945.50 \times 10^8$ yuans

Total capital = $1{,}018.50 \times 10^8$ yuans

→ + Gold and currency reserves: M = $2.45 + 3.92 = 6.37 \times 10^8$ yuans

= General capital defined *à la* Piketty: $K_{G1952} = 1{,}018.50 + 6.37 = 1{,}024.87 \times 10^8$ yuans

Once these initial stocks have been calculated, the perimeters of capital series must be strictly compatible, concerning in particular the integration or not of built-up lands for residential use and of inventories, with the flows allowing them to be increased. Several investment series are available, but only those of gross capital formation and gross fixed capital formation of China have been complete since 1952. The first of these two notions (gross capital formation), which comes from the breakdown of GDP according to the extended approach, adapted to the MIP's definitions, includes the second one (gross fixed capital formation), plus changes in inventories. Nevertheless, a part of gross fixed capital formation concerns flows linked to non-productive investments. So we use here the series of gross capital formation F_{BC}, which contains built-up lands for residential use as well as inventories, in order to construct that of total capital, K_T; and that of gross fixed capital formation F_{BCF}, with built-up lands but without inventories, for fixed capital, K_F.

However, to reconstitute the productive stocks, K_{Pe} and K_{Pl}, it is necessary to deduce from F_{BCF} the flows of non-productive components. To this end, we use a series of investments in residential housing construction, including built-up lands and other unproductive items; a series taken from the *Finance*

Yearbooks of China (since the year 1982). And for the previous period, we take the series of investments in non-productive buildings, which includes housing. But this last series only covers investments by State-owned enterprises, and not those of collective or private entities. We must therefore assess the investments in non-productive buildings made throughout the economy. In order not to underestimate non-productive investments (from 1952 to 1981), we take into account the relative weight of State-owned enterprises in successive national plans. The shares of the fixed capital investment of State entities in domestic investment are assumed to be equal to those given by the series of non-productive investments, on a five-year average.

In the end, the general capital stock K_G, defined in the sense of Piketty, within an open economy, is therefore calculated by adding to the total capital (K_T) the net wealth that the country holds vis-à-vis the outside world and such that it is represented by the stocks of gold[18] and foreign currency reserves[19] accumulated by the Chinese monetary authorities; stocks which have been converted into national currency at the average annual official exchange rate and expressed at constant prices in 1952. Captured by China's Central Bank as part of its "Compulsory Foreign Exchange Settlement System" – device remained in force until 2012 –, these gold and foreign currency reserves allow us to approximate the cumulative balances of exports and imports of China with other countries.[20] The series of general capital *à la* Piketty from 1952 to 2012 is shown in Graphs 6.1 and 6.2.

As China is far from being a "pure" market economy, a PIM-capital stock, based on production prices, is better than a capital estimated by market values – used by Piketty, Yang and Zucman (2017). Indeed, the reasons to use the PIM are solid. 1) Before 1993, there is no market price for assets, so estimating capital stocks is possible only with the PIM. 2) Using book values before 1993 and market values after this date would cause a statistical break. 3) Even after 1993, market prices are never at the equilibrium, and assuming that the Tobin's Q is equal to 1, as supposed by Piketty *et al.* (2017), is not a convincing hypothesis. 4) As we work on low frequency (annual) time series and as the market values of assets fluctuate sharply within a year, the PIM provides a

---

18   We retain here the average annual gold price in U.S. dollars on the London market since 1978 and use, prior to that date, the historical gold price tables of the World Gold Council (Green [1999]).

19   See: NBS (various years). And, prior to the year 1985: People's Bank of China (1992), p. 79.

20   The incompleteness of Chinese data on foreign direct investments (available since 1983 only) and the uncertainty surrounding the wealth held by China abroad have forced us to use the reserves of the monetary authorities to approximate the net asset or patrimonial position of the country.

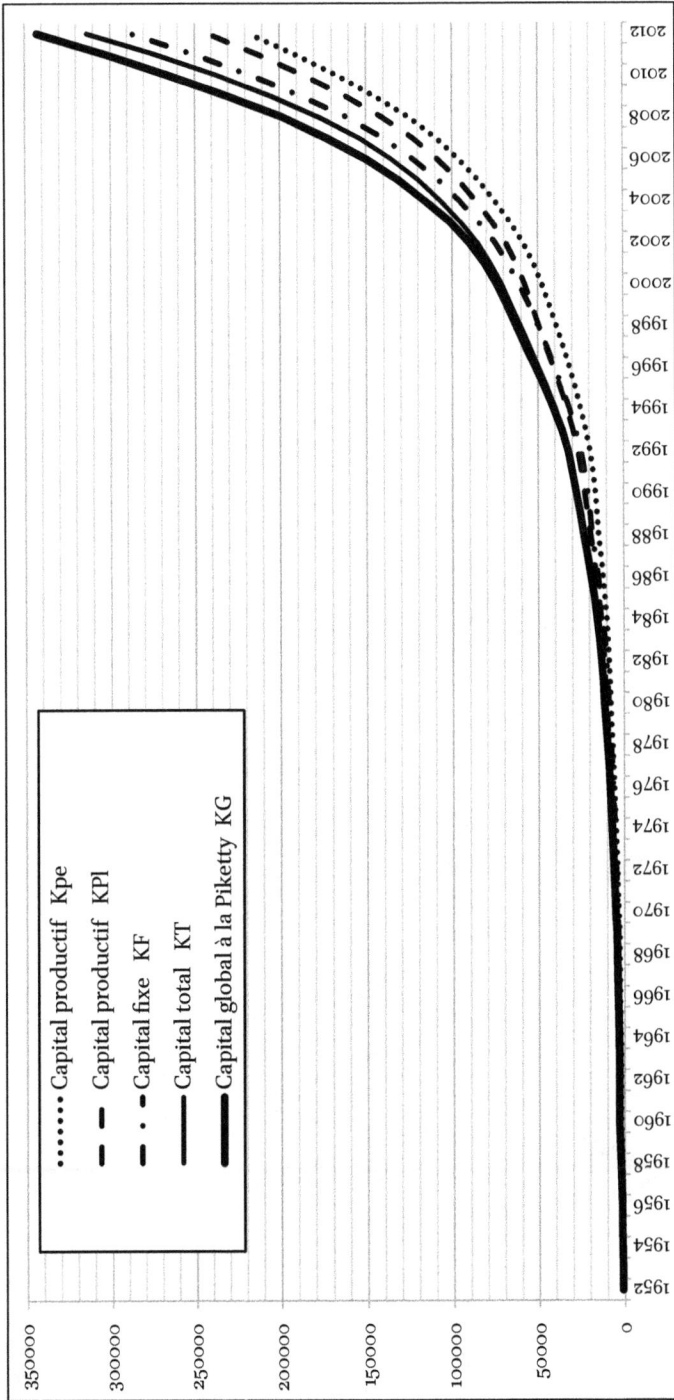

GRAPH 6.1   Level and composition of the stock of general capital *à la* Piketty: China, 1952–2012
(*in hundreds of millions of yuans*)

Legend:

...... Capital productif Kpe

– – – Capital productif KPl

–··– Capital fixe KF

—— Capital total KT

——— Capital global à la Piketty KG

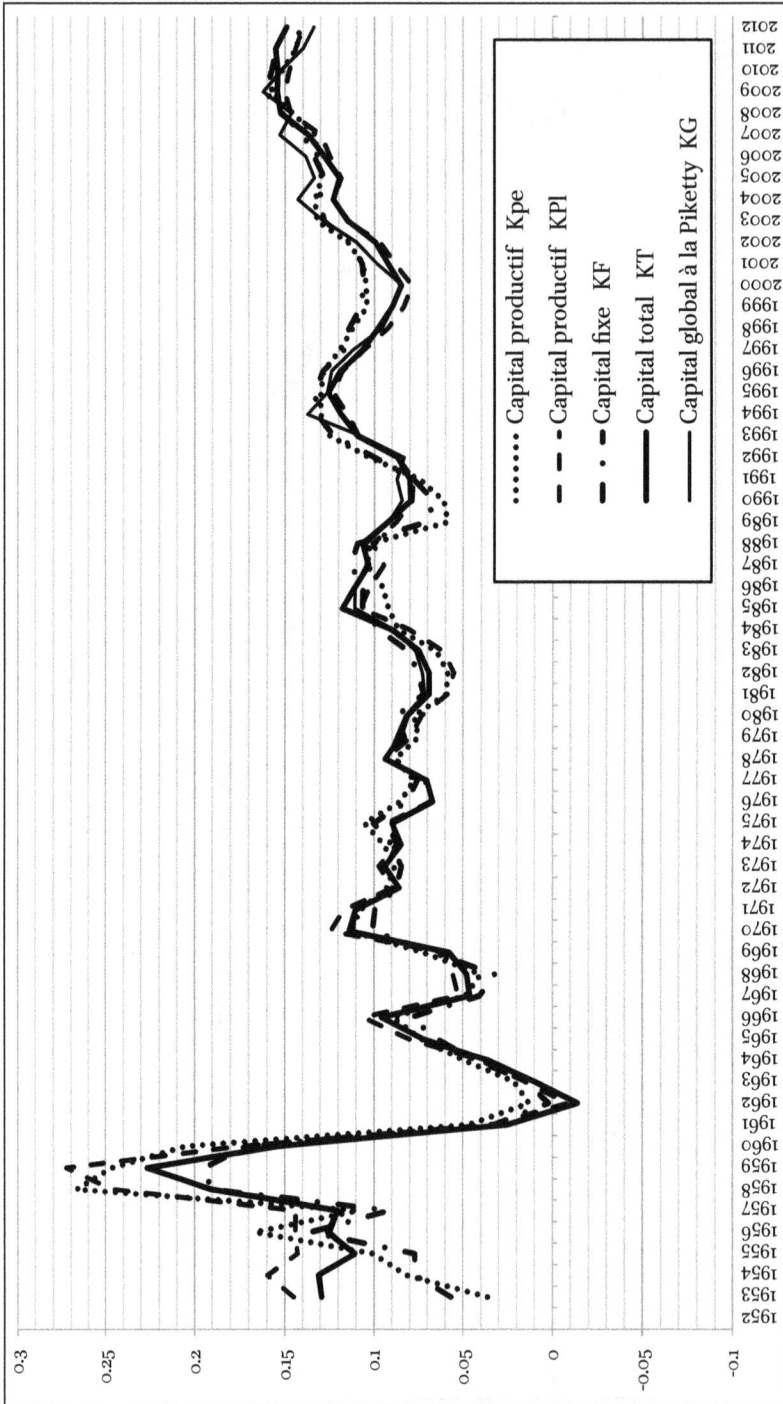

GRAPH 6.2   Growth rate of the general capital stock *à la* Piketty: China, 1952–2012 (*in percentages*)

more stable value of capital. 5) The PIM makes it feasible to estimate capital series as long as possible, allowing to take into account the importance of capital accumulation during the early years. But Piketty's classification of capital and ours are consistent (Table 6.1),[21] both methods being based on the System of National Accounts (SNA).

2   Do Piketty's Dynamic "Laws" of Capital Function in China?

2.1   The "Fundamental Inequality" between the Return on Capital and Income Growth

In *Capital in the Twenty-First Century* – a work combining economic research and committed positions –, Piketty (2013) sets out a number of economic "laws," or long-term regularities. He thus argues that the return on capital, noted r_{KG}, as we have just defined it, must be superior to the income growth rate, g_R, that is, $r_{KG} > g_R$, in order to impulse the dynamic mechanisms of (capitalist) economy. Otherwise, this would "*kill the engine of accumulation*,"[22] because the capitalists would see their profits shrink – to the point that they no longer invest enough. The first "law" that he formulates – as an accounting relationship, in reality – maintains that the share of profits in national income is equal to the product of the profit rate and the capital-income ratio. Thus we will calculate this ratio (Graph 6.3) on the basis of our series of general capital stock, K_G and from data of gross national income R (Graph 6.4) supplied by the *China Statistical Yearbooks* of the NBS (various years).

To define the rate of return on general capital *à la* Piketty, r_{KG}, we use the formula:

$$r_{KG} = \alpha_{KG} \cdot \frac{R}{K_G} \qquad (6.3)$$

where $\alpha_{KG} = \partial R / \partial K_G \cdot K_G / R$ is the elasticity of income with respect to capital stock.[23]

---

21   A difference between Piketty's studies and ours concerns land. As there is no real market price for agricultural land in China, we use accumulated and depreciated "land improvement" as implicit value of agricultural land.

22   Piketty (2013), p. 943.

23   For a theoretical justification of this writing, see: Gramlich (1994), Dessus and Herrera (2000).

TABLE 6.1   Consistency of the classification of capital: Piketty's studies and ours

Piketty (and co-authors) (*)	Our classification	Corresponding System of National Accounts (SNA) data used as investment series for different types of capital		
Housing	Land (built-up lands)	Housing investment	Gross capital formation	Gross capital formation
Farmlands	K_{Pl} — K_{Pe} — Agriculture land	Land improvement	Gross capital formation − Housing investment	
Other domestic capital	Others / Inventories	Gross capital formation − Housing investment − Land improvement		
Net foreign assets	Total reserves or net international investment position	Reserves and gold or net foreign direct investment		

Note: (*) = See here Piketty and Zucman (2014) and, more recently, Piketty, Yang and Zucman (2017).

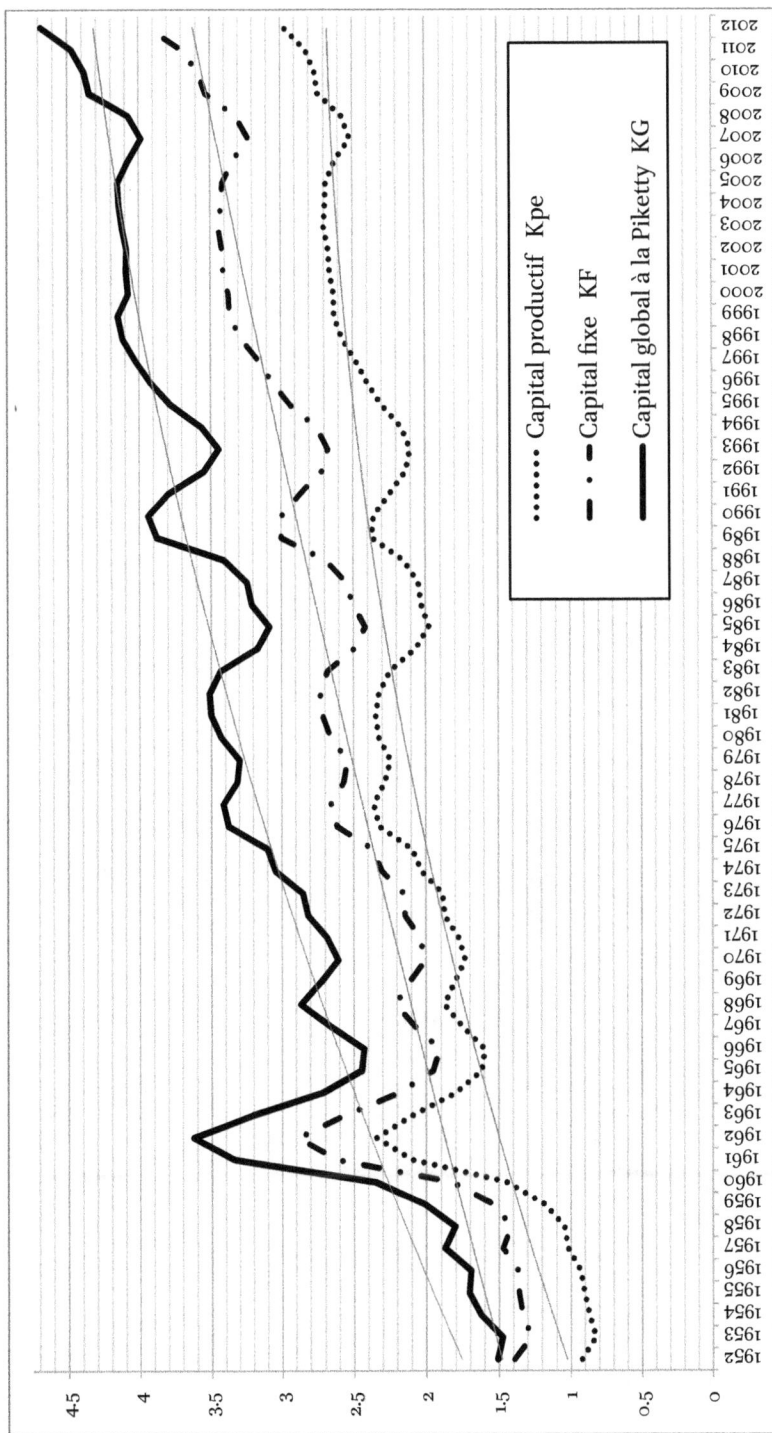

GRAPH 6.3   Ratio capital / national income, according to different capital stocks: China, 1952–2012 (*capital measured in years of income*)

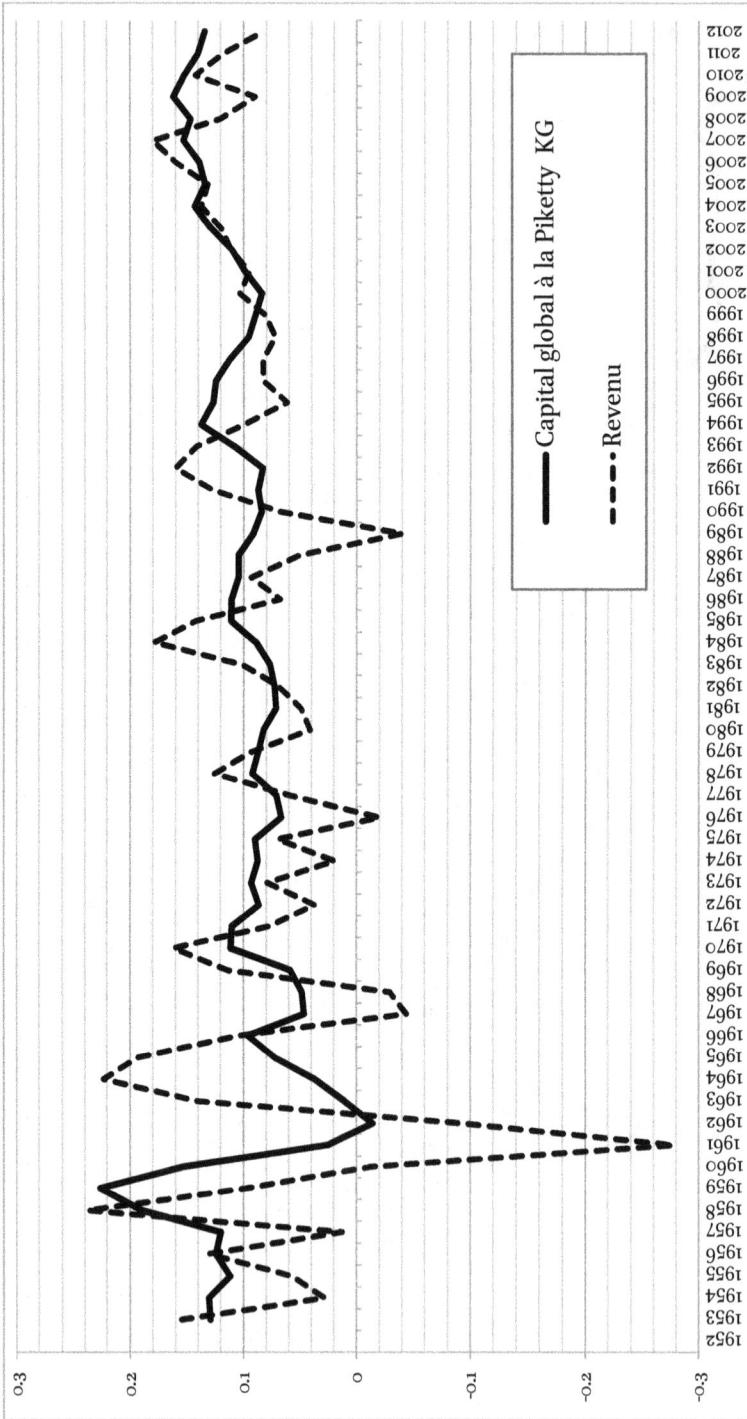

GRAPH 6.4   Growth rate of gross national income: China, 1952–2012 (*in percentages*)

To estimate this elasticity, we need to test econometrically a production function in which this general capital stock is considered to be one of the production factors in the sense of Piketty. To do this, we choose to use various specifications derived from several theoretical neoclassical frameworks, and precisely from log-linearized functional forms of: (1) simplified models, *à la* AK, where the single input is general capital in Piketty's sense; (2) standard models, *à la* Solow, where the two production factors considered are general capital and simple labour; and (3) more complex models, augmented to integrate, alongside general capital, an input of human capital, but also R&D expenditure, in the manner of a formalization with endogenous growth (see Chapter 5).[24]

We therefore consider successively the following three equations, corresponding to these (linked, but distinct) categories of models:

$$g_{Rt} = \Theta D + \alpha_{KG}\, g_{KGt} + \gamma\, g_{R\&Dt} + \varepsilon_t \qquad (6.4)$$

$$g_{Rt} = \Theta D + \alpha_{KG}\, g_{KGt} + \beta\, g_{Lt} + \gamma\, g_{R\&Dt} + \varepsilon_t \qquad (6.5)$$

$$g_{Rt} = \Theta D + \alpha_{KG}\, g_{KGt} + \beta\, g_{Ht} + \gamma\, g_{R\&Dt} + \varepsilon_t \qquad (6.6)$$

where g_R, g_{KG}, g_L, g_H and $g_{R\&D}$ are respectively the growth rates of gross national income (GNI), general capital stock *à la* Piketty (including total reserves of the monetary authorities), simple labour (L), a human capital stock (H), and spending on *R&D*. The national income series for the period 1952–2012 is taken from the NBS *China Statistical Yearbooks* (various years).

In addition, a qualitative variable, D, destined to take account of the institutional changes and their impact on economic growth, is introduced. Distinguishing between positive and negative shocks, this dummy variable will take the same values as in Chapter 5, that is: +1 in 1963–1965 (recovery), 1984 (tax reform), 1992 (Deng Xiaoping's tour) and 2007 (overheating), but -1 in 1960–1962 (recession), 1967 (beginning of the Cultural Revolution), 1976 (Mao's death) and 1989–1990 (political unrest).[25]

The variable of simple labour corresponds to the workforce, namely all employed persons aged over 16 years, according to the NBS *China Statistical Yearbooks* (various years). The absence of official series of human capital stocks in China, and, in our view, the relatively unsatisfactory character of the

---

24   See also: Aghion and Howitt (1998).

25   The choice of the values of the dummies is obtained by a scan method in seven steps inspired of the ridge regression and the outlier test of X-12-ARIMA (Findley *et al.* [1998]). For the detail, see: Long and Herrera (2015b).

available international databases – including those of the Penn World Tables (PWT [various years]) –, led us to reconstruct such an indicator ourselves, using a methodology we have explained previously in detail, and in all its complexity (Chapter 2).[26] Let us limit ourselves to indicating here that "human capital" is supposed to accumulate in the manner of physical capital, and that it corresponds to the product of an average level of education (or the number of years of studies leading to diplomas per head) by a specific population (employed or total). For the year t, the stock of human capital is equal to that of the previous period (net of a rate of depreciation, which is variable and triggering mortality rates, retirement rates and unemployment rates), plus the investment in human capital of t. The increase in the latter in year t is the sum of the products of the number of new graduates for each type of education and the number of cumulated years in each category. The stock of human capital used in our estimates is termed "productive," since it is calculated for the workforce of employed persons – and not for total population.

We have also built cautiously the series of expenditure in R&D (Chapter 3), according to the budget data of Science and Technology (1952–1985), R&D by public entities and higher education (1986–1988), and aggregated R&D from the *Statistical Yearbooks of Science and Technology* (1989–1994), then from the NBS (1995–2012).

Our regressions (Table 6.2) are performed in ordinary least squares (OLS) on first differences of the logarithmic forms in levels. The time series we estimate here cover the period 1953–2012, or 60 years of China's economic history. The preliminary unit root tests indicate that the growth rates of the variables used are all stationary. When at least one of the tests carried out reveals a risk of heteroskedasticity (at 5 percent), a correction is made using the White method or that of Newey-West to get robust regressions. The coefficients associated with the different variables taken into consideration are presented in Table 6.2.

The elasticities of national income to general capital designed in the sense of Piketty, α_{KG}, statistically very significant, are found at 0.69, 0.57 and 0.46, respectively, according to the equation tested in AK growth, Solow growth, or endogenous growth with capital human, and integrating R&D as an indicator of technical progress. As can be seen in Table 6.3, they are within the orders of magnitude of the values proposed in the empirical literature. Thanks to these three elasticities, which we multiply by the values of the national income / general capital ratio (R/K_G) calculated over the period 1953–2012, we are able

---

26   Compared with the current literature, the original series of human capital that we provided are much more reliable than those of PWT. They also improve those by Cai and Du (2003), and even those by Barro and Lee (2018).

TABLE 6.2 Results of the estimates of three theoretical models: China, 1953–2012

Equation	D	General capital	Simple labour	Human capital	R&D	R^2	Auto-correlation	Hetero-scedaticity	Correction
(1)	0.099596	0.686832	—	—	0.075111	0.6654	0.1181	0.0337	Yes
	(5.456165)	(7.683111)			(1.802472)		0.1135	0.0358	
(2)	0.104944	0.571319	0.725271	—	0.064459	0.7271	0.0729	0.0555	No
	(8.195789)	(7.587738)	(3.525905)		(2.604417)		0.0629	0.0581	
(3)	0.100767	0.459334	—	0.504085	0.090485	0.6908	0.1479	0.0256	Yes
	(5.998232)	(3.002002)		(2.414623)	(2.209519)		0.1286	0.0292	

Notes: In the first column is indicated the number of the equation tested, integrating the general capital stock *à la* Piketty and, possibly, other variables (simple labour or human capital, and R&D). The *t*-statistics are given between parentheses in the following five columns. The *p*-values (of the Fisher test and Chi² tests) are presented in the columns *Autocorrelation* (for the null hypothesis "there is no autocorrelation of the residuals" for the Breusch-Godfrey LM Test) and *Heteroscedasticity* (for the null hypothesis "there is no problem of heteroscedasticity of the residuals" for the Breusch-Pagan-Godfrey Test). The last column mentions whether a correction *à la* Newey-West for the heteroscedasticity was necessary or not.

TABLE 6.3   Some estimates of the elasticity of the output with respect to capital in China

Authors	Elasticity values	Comments
Zhang (1991)	0.70	Data taken from various sources
Guo and Jia (2005)	0.69	Data from 1979 to 2004, with cointegration methods
Jefferson (1990)	0.65	Data on the steel industry from 1980 to 1985
Su and Xu (2002)	$0.65 > \alpha_K > 0.40$	Estimates of AK models on data from 1952 to 1998
Chow and Li (2002)	0.61	Tests of a Solow model in the form of a Cobb-Douglas production function, with introduction of a linear trend
Zheng, Bigsten and Hu (2009)	$0.60 > \alpha_K > 0.50$	Method inspired by Chow and Li (2002), with TFP
Chen et al. (1988)	0.54	Data relative to State-owned enterprises from 1953 to 1985
Jefferson, Rawski and Zhang (2008)	0.38	Data on industrial sectors from 1998 to 2005
Zhang, Shi and Chen (2003)	0.37	Estimates made with introduction of constraints
Perkins and Rawski (2008)	$0.13 < \alpha_K < 0.93$	Wide range (lowest point: 1952–1957; highest point: 1957–1965)

to provide a range of several estimates of the rate of return on capital *à la* Piketty r_{KG} – a capital shown in (Graph 6.5) –, then to compare the changes to that of the growth rate of national income, g_R (Graph 6.6).

The "fundamental inequality" between the rates of return on capital and the growth of income ($r_{KG} > g_R$), as Piketty puts it, seems apparently to be verified on our database for China over the 60 years considered. This statement should however be qualified, for at least three reasons. First, the more complete the model making it possible to theoretically base the specification that is tested empirically – in this case, equation (*6.6*), which integrates not only general capital stock, but also human capital, R&D, as well as the dummy variable capturing institutional changes –, the more the coefficient of capital *à la* Piketty tends to become low (0.46), and the less clearly the said "inequality" is validated. Then, for even lower values of the same coefficient (inferior to 0.40, of the order of those proposed by some authors),[27] Piketty's "law" is no longer verified. In the econometric work that we conducted previously (Chapter 5), we ourselves have sometimes highlighted elasticities associated with various stocks of capital ranging between 0.35 and 0.40, by focusing on "productive cores" of physical capital, which are more compatible with the use of production functions – this amounts *de facto* to contesting the relevance of Piketty's definition of capital as "patrimony." Finally, we observe that this "inequality" has started to be called into question, tendentially, during the last decade (Graph 6.7); and so even for high elasticity values (0.57).

2.2   Piketty's "Fundamental Law" in China: Savings, Growth and Coefficient of Capital

According to Piketty, besides the two relationships concerning the "accounting law" of the share of profits and the "inequality" between the rate of return on capital and the income growth rate ($r_{KG} > g_R$) studied before, there is a "second law" on the dynamics of capitalist economies that is said to be "fundamental." This "second law" occupies an important place in Piketty's explanation of the evolution of cumulative social inequalities, and it affirms that the ratio of general capital stock, or patrimony, to national income (a ratio noted $\beta = K_G/R$) would tend asymptotically to the value of the quotient of the savings rate (s) and the income growth rate (g_R, the latter being very close to that of

---

27   Econometricians such as Zhang *et al.* (2003), Jefferson *et al.* (2008), or Perkins and Rawski (2008).

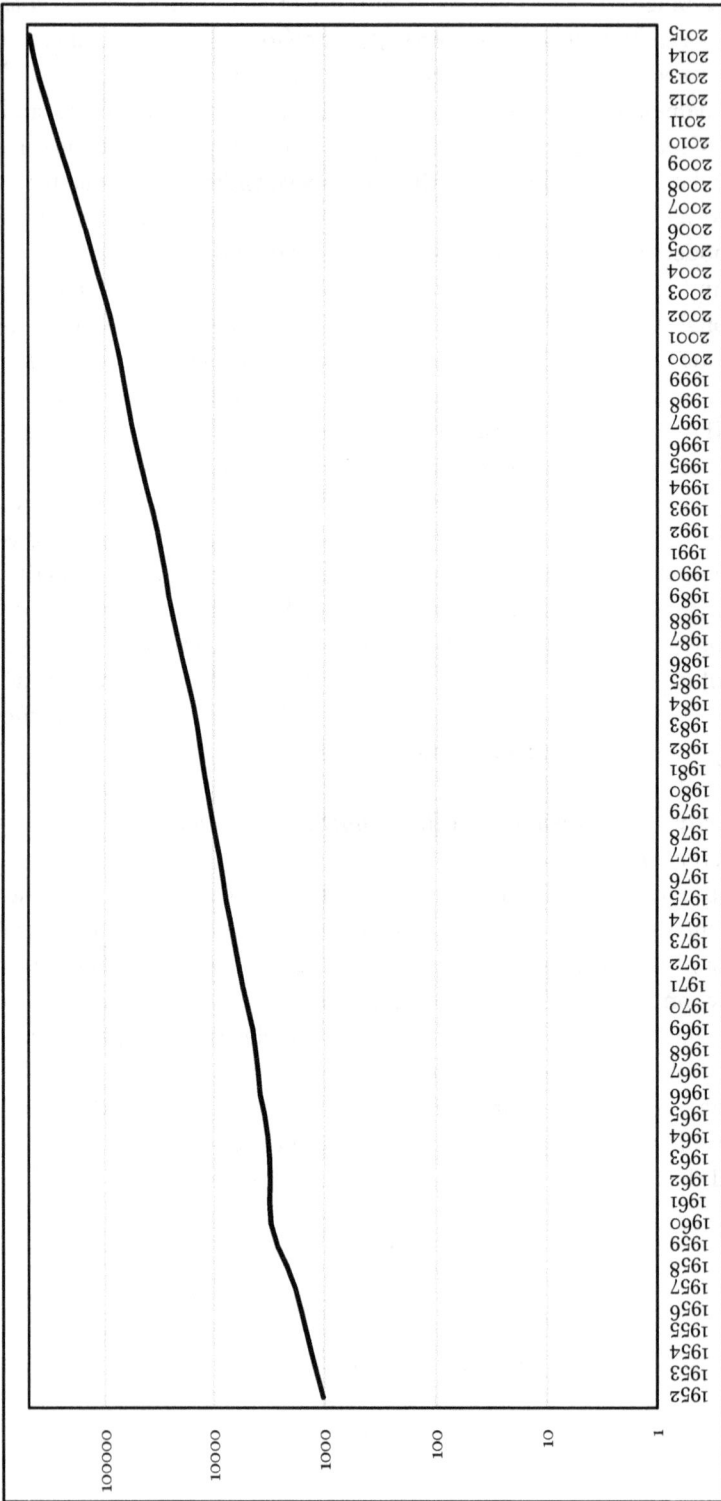

GRAPH 6.5   General capital *à la* Piketty (including gold and foreign exchange reserves) in logarithmic
scale: China, 1952–2015 (*hundreds of millions of yuans, constant prices, base 1952*)

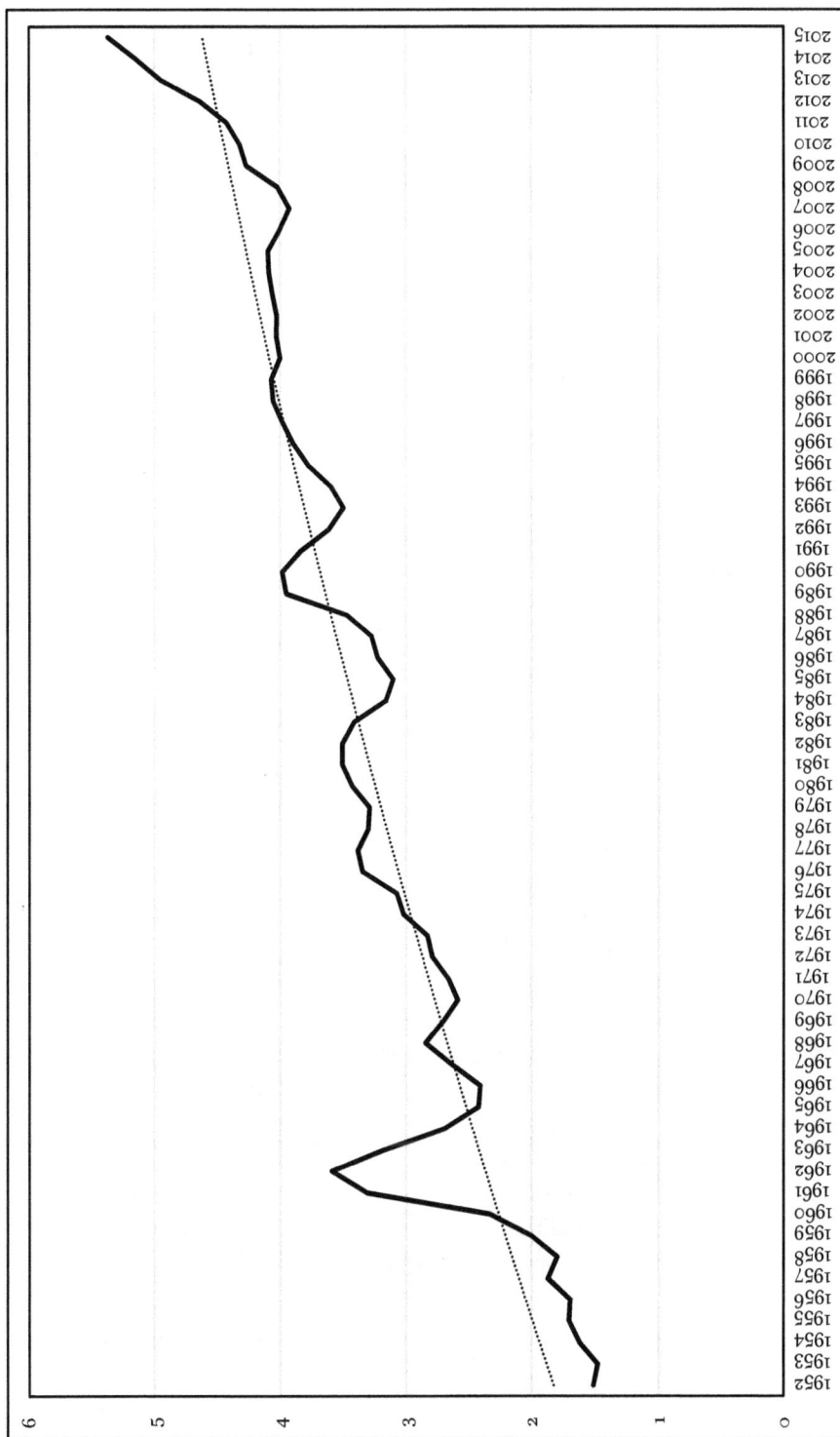

GRAPH 6.6   Ratio general capital *à la* Piketty / gross national income: China, 1952–2015

production). This can be written as: $\beta = K_G / R = s / g_R$. In this section, we will thus attempt to empirically confirm or disprove this "law."[28]

To do this, for China from 1952 to 2012, we must have a largely-defined conception of the savings rate, encompassing all the different "economic agents." Nevertheless, no series that corresponds to such a variable exists for this country over the period studied. Several options are then available to us to reconstruct it. The best of them consists in considering savings as the difference between national income and total final consumption; the latter being the sum of public and private consumptions in the calculation of the GDP according to an expenditure approach, as established by the SNA, that is to say: $s_{(1)} = (1 - C)_G / R$. This method has the advantage of consistency, since the construction of the general capital stock K_G also resorts to the series of flows provided by the SNA (that is, those of investment, or gross capital formation). We preferred to use this indicator $s_{(1)}$ because of the drawbacks that have accompanied the elaboration of the other savings rates we were able to conceive.

As a matter of fact, a second savings rate, $s_{(2)}$, considered the level of the households' per capita consumption, divided by the rate of available income per head, from NBS source. Nevertheless, as this series only starts in the year 1978, it is too short, especially since a recent change in the statistical methodology prevents extending it beyond the year 2012.

A third savings series, $s_{(3)}$, made the choice to replace the available income by the national income. The latter too is expressed in per capita terms, in order to expand the previous series by extending it both backwards before 1978, and forwards after 2012. In doing so, however, an overestimation bias has been introduced, because what is obtained is a savings rate of households, which is significantly higher in China than that of the economy taken as whole.

A fourth savings indicator, $s_{(4)}$, could be designed from data published by the Central Bank (or People's Bank of China), relative to bank deposits. The annual variations of the latter, concerning not only households and companies, but also the various entities of the State, can be interpreted as corresponding to the flows of net savings of the year. This time, however, this new savings rate series is underestimated, since all the savings do not take the form of money – there are also physical reserves, including strategic raw materials, energy resources or agricultural stocks –, and even money saved is not itself found only in bank deposits – part of monetary savings is also seen in the form of cash held at home by households. In addition, disaggregated data from financial accounts, expressed as flows, are also available, making it possible for us to distinguish

---

28   On the importance and theoretical implications of Piketty's second "law," see, among others: Krusell and Smith (2015).

different savings rates between sectors (households, non-financial enterprises, financial institutions, State, foreigners and the rest of the world), but this can only be done for figures since 2000.

All things considered, this is indeed the savings rate $s_{(1)}$ we choose to be used for calculating the ratio s / g_R, by taking the gross national income (GNI) growth rate as the denominator. If we compare this ratio to the coefficient of general capital over the complete period (1953–2012) (Graph 6.8), we observe a certain tendency of s / g_R to converge towards β. Piketty describes this "law" as a long-term relationship, which would require at least 30 years to be assessed. As a consequence, we follow him[29] by using a moving average over ten years (not centered, but backward or retroactive), in order to represent the rate of savings over the long period, smoothing out by this way its strong fluctuations observed in the short term. A cursory view, omitting the sharp volatility of $s_{(1)} / g_R$, suggests that a convergence does in fact take place. In addition, the more extensive the length of the moving average, the more this convergence appears to be "obvious."

Nevertheless, we must go beyond appearances or intuition. As we are dealing with a long-run relationship, "equality" may not be confirmed by a simple Wald test. Therefore, we need to examine whether a cointegration relationship exists between the series of $\beta = K_G / R$ and of s / g_R with a moving average (Table 6.4). We start by testing a univariate approach à la Engle and Granger (1987). This method consists in performing – to begin with – unit root tests on the variables considered. These tests reveal that the series of coefficient of capital and of ratio savings rates to income growth are non-stationary, regardless of the duration of the moving average selected. Moreover, the first differences of these series, stationary, are found to be integrated with an order of 1: $\beta \sim I(1)$ and $s_{(1)MM} / g_R \sim I(1)$. Six types of tests are carried out on these series for the whole of the period 1952–2012 studied (see, in Appendices, from Table A.6.2.1 to Table A.6.2.11): Augmented Dickey-Fuller (ADF), Elliott-Rothenberg-Stock (ERS), Phillips-Perron (PP), Kwaitkowski-Phillips-Schmidt-Shin (KPSS), Phillips-Ouliaris (PO), and Ng-Perron (NP).[30]

Then, in a second step, we test the following equation: $s_{(1)MM} / g_R = c\,(0) +$ $c\,(1)\,\beta$, with the restriction of a null constant: $c\,(0) = 0$ – for it, the Wald test checks if $c\,(1)$ is unitary (first block). After that, the stationarity of the series of

---

29   *Cf.* the spreadsheets on the site: piketty.pse.ens.fr. Here, our goal is, in first analysis, to mobilize a method of smoothing short-term fluctuations similar to that proposed by Piketty (non-centered moving averages) to allow a comparison; before suggesting an alternative approach (with filter).

30   See: Dickey and Fuller (1979), Elliott *et al.* (1996), Phillips and Perron (1988), Kwaitkowski *et al.* (1992), Phillips and Ouliaris (1990), Ng and Perron (2001).

the residuals then obtained is estimated by an ADF test (second block), using the critical values (with lags or not) proposed by Engle-Granger (1987) – those by Mackinnon (1991) are more precise, but require at least 50 observations, and cannot be mobilized without a bias due to the insufficient size of the sample tested, when the chosen moving average exceeds 15 years.

TABLE 6.4   Results of tests according to the univariate approach *à la* Engle-Granger with smoothing through a Hodrick-Prescott (H.-P.) filter for s / g_R and β

		Level
c (0)		0.16565
Wald Test		
p-value (Fisher)		0.8689
p-value (Chi²)		0.8683
t-statstics ([−1.68, 1.68] at 10% Gauss.)		0.16581
Scale coefficient	c (0) = 0	
c (1)		0.83056
Wald Test		
p-value (Fisher)		0.5674
p-value (Chi²)		0.5652
t-statstics ([−1.68, 1.68] at 10% Gauss.)		2.81960
Scale coefficient	c (1) = 1	
ADF Test		−4.60282
Lags		1
Model		None
Criterion		AIC
Critical values at 1% (*) to 5% (**)		−3.37*
Relationship of cointegration		Yes
		$s / g_R = 0.16565 + 0.83056 . \beta$
Sample size		60

Note: The first two horizontal blocks give the results of the Wald test and the scale coefficient; the third block, those of the ADF test for the cointegration relationship.

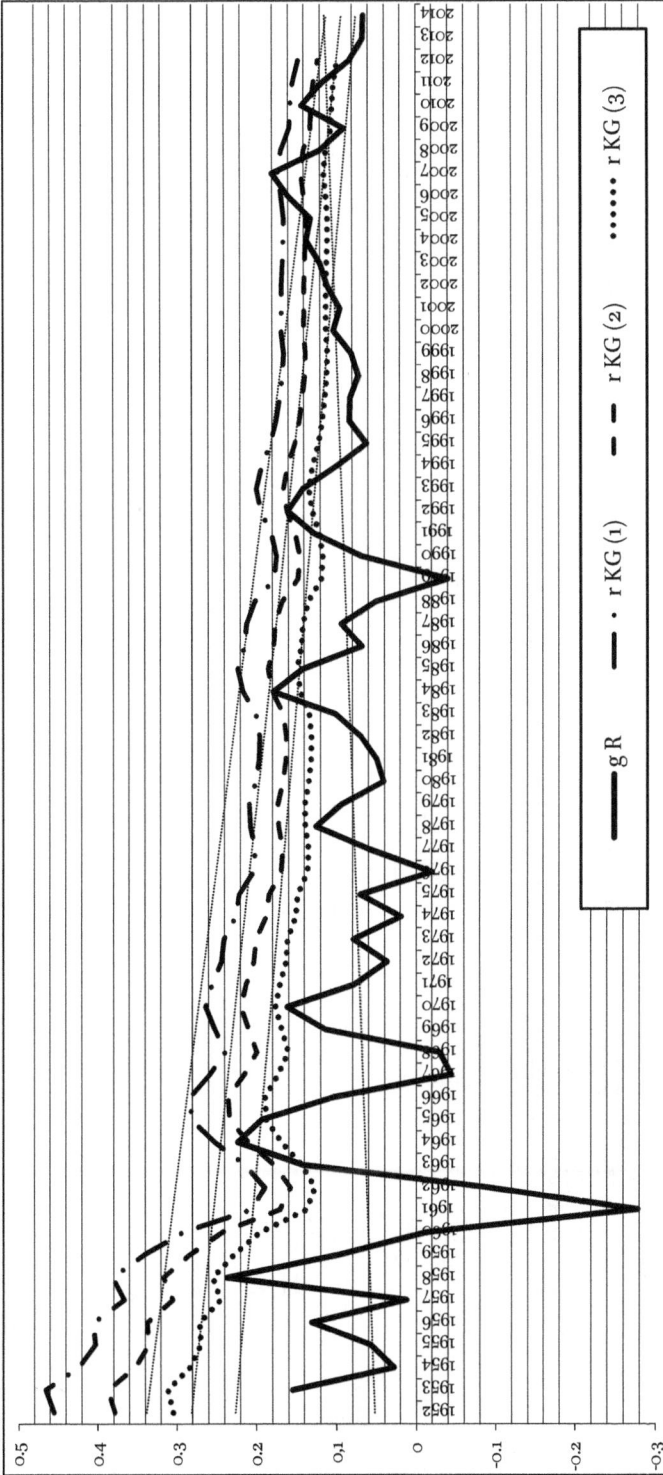

GRAPH 6.7   The "fundamental inequality" between income growth rate and rate of return on general capital: China, 1953–2012

Notes: Here income corresponds to GNI. All rates are to be read in percentages (e.g., 0.1 = 10 percent).

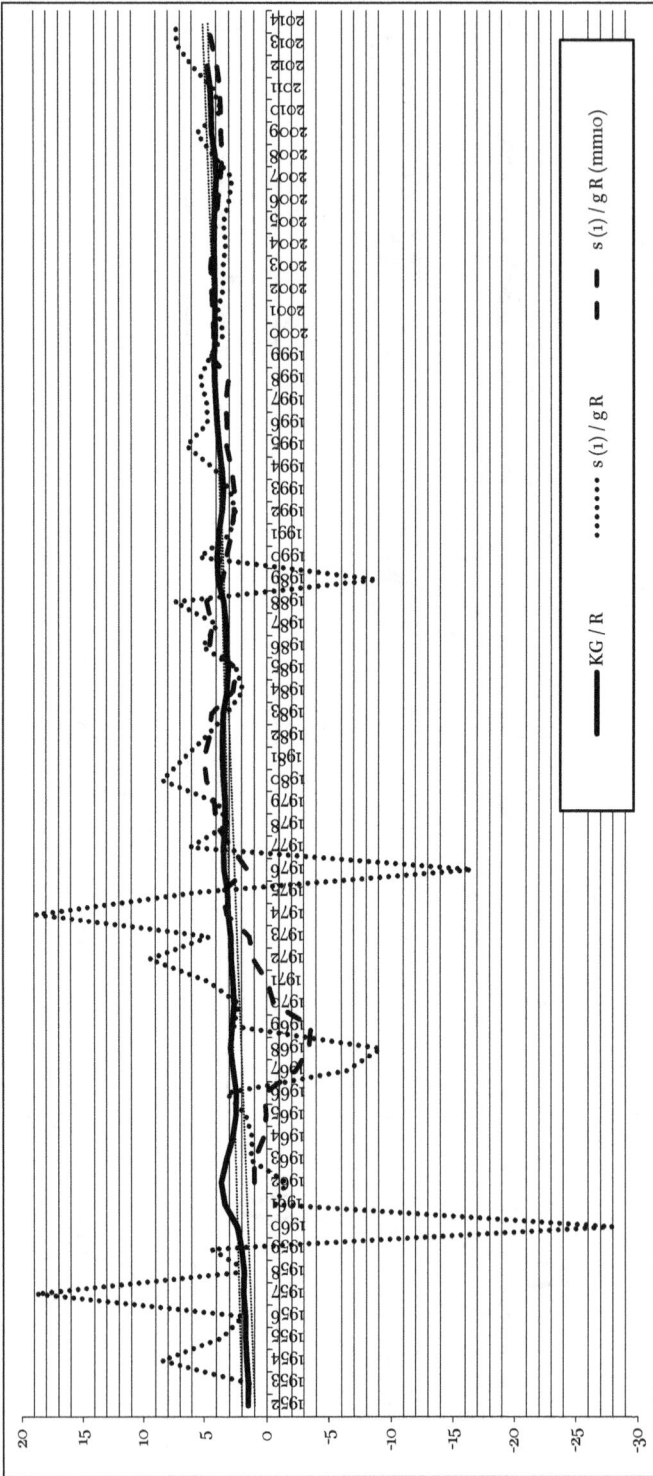

GRAPH 6.8   Coefficient of capital and ratio of savings rate and income growth rate: China, 1953–2012

Note: K_G/R measures capital in years of income; $s_{(1)}/g_R$ is to be read in percentages

While the graphical representations look like indicating that the longer the duration of the moving average, the more "visible" the tendency of $s_{(1)MM} / g_R$ to converge towards K_G / R, the econometric tests carried out show the opposite: the cointegration relationship does exist between the series of $s_{(1)MM} / g_R$ and β when the savings rate is calculated in moving averages of five, seven, and 10 years. However, beyond these durations, the residuals of our regressions are no longer stationary; which means that the cointegration relationship is rejected for terms of moving averages greater than 15 years. This – negative – result can be explained by the relatively small size of the samples studied, especially because the number of observations decreases when the length of moving average increases (46 points for 15 years, for example). This reduces the credibility of our tests, even by standards of Engle-Granger.

Another reason for such rejection beyond 15 years might be related to the presence of a zero constant constraint ($c(0) = 0$). Including a non-zero constant in our tests indeed brings results that allow us to accept the existence of a cointegration, with notably higher R^2, for all moving average durations of the ratio of savings rate to income growth, including up to 30 years.[31] Then, however, this is the coefficient associated with $c(1)$ that is no longer found to be equal to unity by the Wald test, since it exceeds one almost always (except for five years) and rather widely so (1.90 for seven years, 2.36 for 10 years, 2.03 for 15 years, 1.68 for 20 years, 1.53 for 25 years, 1.57 for 30 years), in contrast to the values achieved with a null constant – these remained close to 1, or just below. The empirical conclusions are therefore, as we can see, relatively ambiguous.

Such an ambiguity is confirmed by the results obtained by applying the multivariable approach *à la* Johansen (1988), the advantage of which is to allow us to introduce into a Vector Error Correction Model (VECM), particularly suitable for studying long-term relationships, deterministic components and qualitative variables of the type of the dummy that we have previously used to account for political and institutional changes in China (see Chapter 5). Once we have constructed a VAR(p) making white noises the residuals, and incorporated the dummy variable if necessary, we use the information criteria to choose the optimal number of lags p and we estimate the cointegration thanks to a VECM (p-1), with specific deterministic components. In agreement with the unit root tests which were carried out on β and $s_{(1)MM} / g_R$, we will choose to retain a linear trend in the cointegration equation (long term), but not in the VAR (short term).

---

31   For example, for a moving average calculated over 30 years, the ADF test statistic is
     −5.28045, while the critical value is of −3.37, without trend nor constant, and with a lag
     chosen at zero according to the AIC information criterion.

TABLE 6.5   Results of tests according to the multivariate approach *à la* Johansen with smoothing through a Hodrick-Prescott (H.-P.) filter for s/g_R and β

	Level (with trend in the equation of cointegration)	Level (without trend in the equation of cointegration)
Lags	4	
Criterions	Minimum lag causing white noise residuals	
Dummy	Without	
p-value (**Jarque-Bera test**)	0.7806	
Trace test (p-value)	1 (0.0376)	1 (0.1631)
Max-Eig test (p-value)	1 (0.0376)	1 (0.1631)
Cointegration	Yes (at 1 percent), no (at 5 percent)	Yes
(*t*-statistics between parentheses)	$\dfrac{s}{g_R} = \dfrac{1.461631\ \beta}{(1.7802)} + \dfrac{0.006457\ .t}{(0.1967)}$	$\dfrac{s}{g_R} = \dfrac{1.622610\ \beta}{(6.7053)}$

Faced with this indeterminacy, we decide to repeat our tests, but this time introducing a method of smoothing fluctuations by a filter. The Kalman filter (1960), which makes full use of the information from complete samples, generally gives good linear predictions, but requires first building a state-space model for s/g. However, since the structures and values of the matrix of coefficients of the equations of states are unknown, it is not possible to opt for a particular matrix structure without the risk of new biases. Under these conditions, it is better to apply the H.-P. filter method (Hodrick-Prescott [1981]).

Our results are significantly improved (see: Table 6.4 and Table 6.5): the cointegration relationship between the series β and $s_{(1)}/g_R$ appears clearly. Our conclusions must nevertheless remain cautious. The tests with moving averages are quite divided, even if they lean rather in favor of the existence of cointegration relationships of order 1 between β and $s_{(1)MM}/g_R$, verified at least up to 10 years – without the rejection of cointegration being able to be taken for assured on the moving average durations of more than 15 years. Introducing the H.-P. filter supports the existence of such relationships, but in all cases the scale coefficient evidenced by the Wald tests deviates from unity. Therefore, it is extremely difficult to validate Piketty's "fundamental law" – which can only be interpreted, at best, as a long-term asymptotic convergence process.

2.3   The $r_{KG} > g_R$ Inequality and the $\beta = s / g_R$ Law over the "Capitalist" Sub-period 1978–2012

Obviously, our estimates are problematic when considering the entire economic history of China since 1952. This is precisely because after 1949, its political leaders tried to experience for several decades a break with the "laws of capitalism," more or less successfully, by attempting to create a socialist economic system. As we know, a decisive orientation towards greater openness was decided and put into practice after the end of the year 1978, which a lot of authors in economics or other social sciences have analyzed as an inflection a shift in the direction of a "capitalism with Chinese characteristics" or "Chinese-style capitalism." If this hypothesis is accepted,[32] then it is necessary to examine what happens to the results of our econometric estimates previously performed when applied only to this recent time, i.e., the post-1978 period – until the year 2012.

The elasticities of national income to capital understood *à la* Piketty, presented in Table 6.5, are estimated in the same way as above, according to the three mainstream models used, that is: AK, Solowian, and in growth with an endogenized technical progress derived from R&D. As can be seen, the coefficients obtained over the 1978–2012 sub-period are all statistically significant, and those of the general capital stock even higher – as will also logically be the corresponding rates of return on overall capital – than over the entire period previously studied. Furthermore, the structure of the production function remains consistent, revealing roughly constant returns to scale, whether one considers simple labour or human capital as labour input. As the sub-period was marked by less political upheaval, it is not surprising to note a decrease in the impact of political-institutional changes on the post-1978 economic growth trajectory. Almost perfectly Gaussian, the residuals of the regressions no longer present a problem of heteroskedasticity – due to the clear attenuation of economic fluctuations[33] –, which reinforces the robustness of our results, despite the relative smallness of the size of the new samples: between 1978 and 2012, Piketty's "fundamental inequality" is thus tendentially verified (Graph 6.9).

The rates of return on general capital found over the sub-period 1978–2012 are high (from 15 percent to 18 percent), but not exaggerated for China. First, the economic growth recorded by this country has been quite extraordinary

---

32   This hypothesis can however be contested. See: Herrera and Long (2019c).

33   It was because of these sharp disturbances that Chow and Li (2002) decided to exclude from their study the years going from 1959 to 1969. For our part, we have chosen to integrate this "problematic" period into our quantitative analysis – despite the difficulties generated.

TABLE 6.6   Results of the estimates of various theoretical models: China, 1978–2012

Eq.	D	General capital	Simple labor	Human capital	R&D	R^2	Auto-correlation	Hetero-scedasticity	Correction
(1)	0.056470	0.734504	—	—	0.143396	0.643515	0.2187	0.4190	No
	(4.932871)	(13.39682)			(3.721595)		0.2023	0.3907	
(2)	0.069553	0.661446	0.449290	—	0.143870	0.727430	0.3564	0.7212	No
	(6.313409)	(12.21600)	(3.089311)		(4.202882)		0.3026	0.6859	
(3)	0.059175	0.596055	—	0.363500	0.139853	0.692934	0.3359	0.1901	No
	(5.447685)	(7.384775)		(2.233636)	(3.845574)		0.2826	0.1792	

Notes: The first column contains the number of the equation tested, integrating the stock of general capital *à la* Piketty and the other variables, simple labour or human capital, as well as R&D. The *t*-statistics are given between parentheses in the following five columns. The *p*-values (of the Fisher test and Chi² test) are indicated in the columns *Autocorrelation* (for the null hypothesis "no autocorrelation of the residuals" for the Breusch-Godfrey LM Test) and *Heteroscedasticity* (for the null hypothesis "no problem of heteroscedasticity of the residuals" for the Breusch-Pagan-Godfrey Test). Finally, the last column mentions whether a correction *à la* Newey-West for heteroscedasticity was needed or not.

for more than three decades (in the order of 10 percent per year on average); it is therefore not surprising to find that Chinese capital exhibits high profitability. Second, a number of other authors who have calculated such returns quite often found values higher than ours – although it is true that they did not use the same definition.[34] Finally, the relatively weak result (of approximately 8 percent) highlighted by Delozier and Hochraich (2007), for example, is for the period 1998–2003, which corresponds to the moment of greatest difficulties experienced by State-owned enterprises.[35]

As for the "fundamental law," making the quotient of the savings rate and the income growth rate asymptotically converge towards the ratio of the general capital stock to national income, its validation can only be assumed, that is to say, left to the "visual" interpretation (therefore at the discretion of each) of the long-term trends of these two variables in Graph 6.10. The ambiguity of the results of the cointegration tests between the series of $s \, / g_R$ and β already underlined is aggravated on the sub-period 1978–2012 by the substantial reduction (by 27 years) of the size of our samples, removing any statistical strength for the attempts to estimate the cointegrating relationships between the two series. Taking into account the reservations already mentioned, and the fact that the Wald tests do not make it possible to maintain unitary scale coefficients (their values estimated between 1978 and 2012 remaining close to those obtained previously over the complete period at 0.83 for the Engle-Granger univariate approach and at 1.46 for Johansen's multivariate approach, with trend), it seems unreasonable to us – despite the relative attenuation of the volatility of the ratio savings rate to income growth rate, which accompanies that of fluctuations in the country's economy (and institutions) – to suggest verifying Piketty's "fundamental law" from 1978 to 2012.

3   On Inequalities in China

In his book *Capital in the Twenty-First Century*, Thomas Piketty insists on the role of inheritance and the dynamics of the patrimonies in the reproduction of social inequalities, which would constitute a sort of "third law." Yet it is not

---

34   To cite just one study here, Bai, Hsieh and Qian (2006) found a rate of return on capital of around 20 percent between 1978 and 2005. For a discussion of their article, see: Blanchard (2006).

35   For example, the *China Labor Statistical Yearbook 2006* states in this regard that more than 32.43 million Chinese workers lost their jobs during the reforms that were adopted from 1998 to 2004.

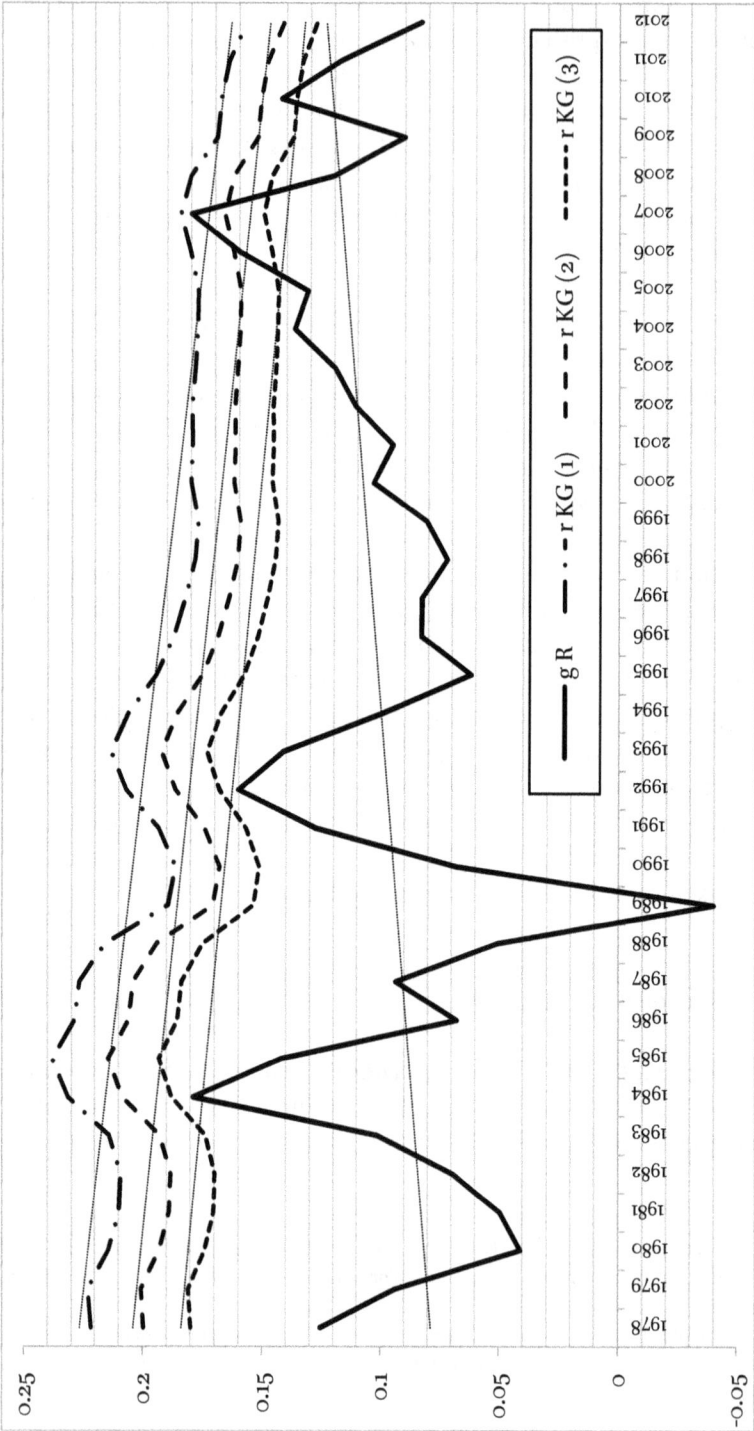

GRAPH 6.9   Rate of return of capital and income growth rate: China, 1978–2012
Note: The rates are to be read in percentages (example: 0.1 = 10 percent).

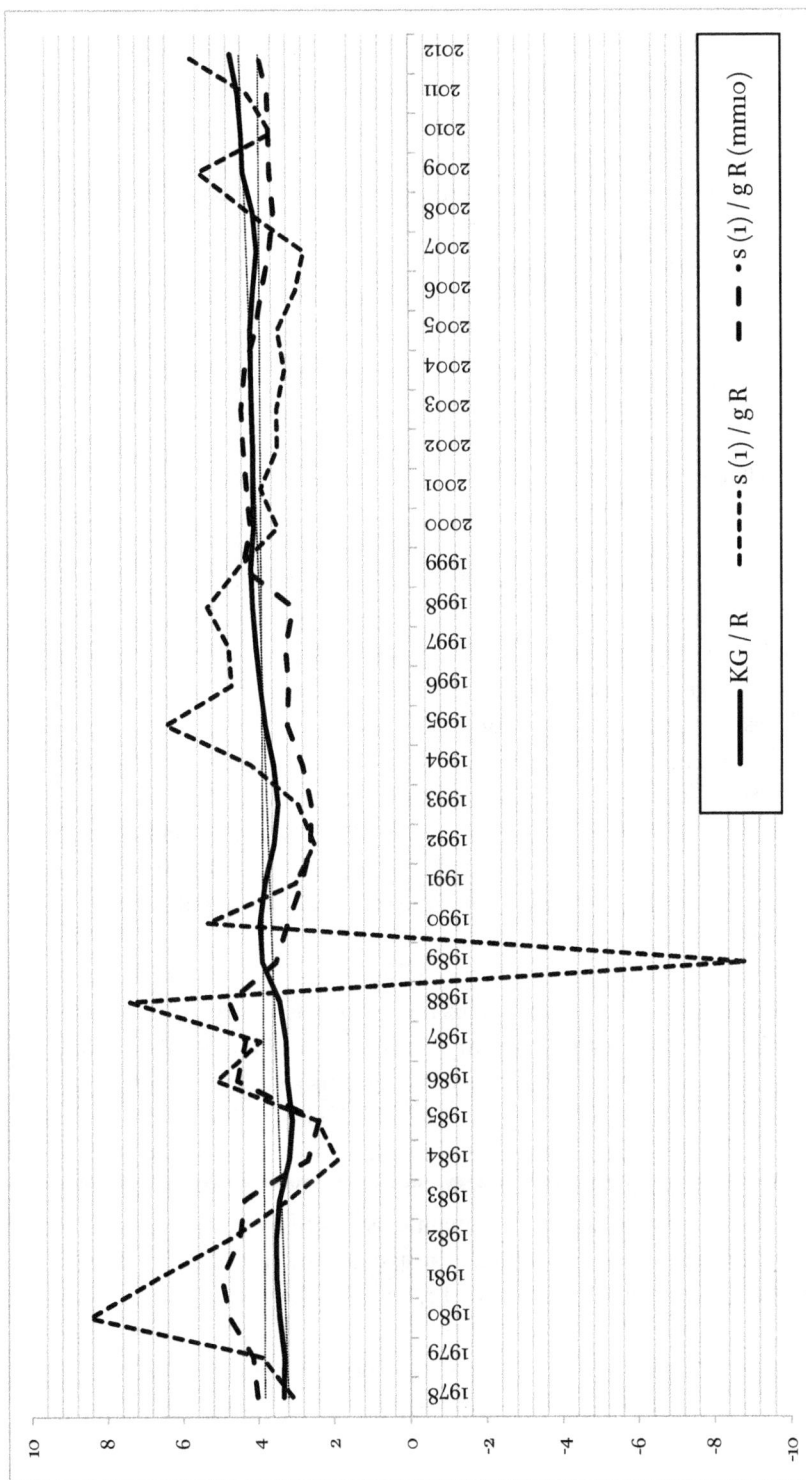

GRAPH 6.10   Coefficient of capital and ratio of savings rate and income growth rate: China, 1978–2012

Note: K_G/R measures capital in years of income; $s_{(1)}/g_R$ is to be read in percentages.

possible for us to assess the latter, as it stands, in the case of China. This, for several reasons.

First reason: in China, there is no statistical data available which allows the calculation of the amounts of estates concerning the succession files for inheritance. So far, there is no inheritance tax, and therefore no notarial documents as abundant as they can exist in Northern capitalist countries, for example. Chinese legislation does not impose property taxes – with the exception of the few measures implemented as part of the experiments carried out in Shanghai and in Chongqing since 2011. In this context, we have no access to any information relating to the average wealth of individuals at the time of their death in order to calculate the ratio between this average wealth at the time of death and the average wealth of living people.

Second reason: while there is little doubt that patrimony inheritance transmission will become a serious problem in the relatively near future of China, we argue that, until now, this is not the main cause of inequalities in this country.

At the current stage, social inequalities mainly find their origin in an unfair income distribution system – where the effect of inheritance from parents' fortunes has little influence –, as well as in phenomena of corruption, largely linked to the rise of capitalist mechanisms in the economy – hence the absolute necessity of the anti-corruption campaign launched in 2012, which is likely to reduce inequalities more quickly and directly than the introduction of a possible inheritance tax. Following the famous "get rich first" slogan once promoted by Deng Xiaoping, the 30-year-rich Chinese entrepreneurial generation has generally started from nothing. Most of them are still alive today, with their businesses still flourishing. Few of the inherited patrimonies intervened in these enrichment processes.

Furthermore, although in the future inheritance will most likely worsen inequalities in China, the relaxation of the "one-child policy" following decisions adopted in 2015 at the 5th plenary session of the 18th Central Committee of the Communist Party of China (October 29, 2015) acts as a counterweight. After the effective softening of birth control which was imposed until that date, and that the Chinese authorities have recognized as being too strict and not exempt from negative consequences, the rise in fertility rates will probably be able to somewhat reduce the inequalities induced by inheritance. Indeed, if a couple does have several children, the assets to be shared by both sides of their parents will have to be divided – in the case where the latter have some possessions.

In practice, the main wealth of Chinese families takes the form of real estate. Nevertheless, ownership is found to be limited by the "70-year-old right of use" legislation. As a matter of fact, in China, land ownership is public – i.e., property of the State or of a local collectivity – with individual owners of their homes having only a right to use the land on which buildings or individual houses are erected. The exact contents of future land ownership laws are quite unclear. Many uncertainties remain on this subject. In other words, and so far, especially since the 1988 land reform, the Chinese government has not provided a clear explanation of how it intends to renew the 70-year-old user rights when the latter will expire. In the event that this renewal of the right of use would involve relatively high costs, then the inheritance of real estate could become a burden, and no longer a wealth, for the next generation.

Constrained by a lack of data, Piketty and Qian (2009) only studied the richest 1 percent of incomes in China using the NBS survey series related to urban households (*Urban Household Survey: 1986–2003*). They assume that over the period 2004 to 2015, income levels and income tax schedules can be considered to have followed constant trends compared to the period 2003–2008, and they then estimate the data for other years. These authors, however, did not use the data related to rural households (namely, *Rural Household Survey*), and assert that excluding them is not problematic insofar as, they note, in 2000, 97 percent of rural incomes were exempt from income taxes.

Nevertheless, the situation seems to have changed notably over this past decade. The income growth rate, on average, has slowed down: at constant prices, it was 14.1 percent between 2003 and 2008 (i.e., the authors' reference period), but 11.7 percent between 2009 and 2014 (that is, their forecast period). The reason is mainly due to the fact that recent years have seen, from the systemic crisis of 2008, a slowdown in the GDP growth rate – slight and very relative, because the dynamism of the Chinese economy has remained quite marked. In addition, Piketty and Qian (2009) assume that income brackets have remained the same over time. But the changes made by the Act of 30 June 2011 on the individual income tax (*Individual Income Tax Law*) have led to significant modifications for these income brackets. Above all, it is the restrictions associated with the *Hukou* device that have been eased, to the benefit of rural households, with significantly increased possibilities of mobility from rural to urban regions for them. As a result, people from rural areas can now come to live and work in cities much more easily than before, without risking being excluded, so that their average incomes have been able to increase considerably. In this context, the documents on which these authors relied date from the year 2000, but the evolutions observed over the last decade have thwarted their expectations.

Since 2011, the NBS published a yearbook dedicated to a specific household survey, entitled *China Yearbook of Household Survey*. This collection contains precisely the statistical base used by Piketty and Qian (2006, 2009) and provides other information, even more complete. The values related to the period corresponding to that of their forecasts can therefore be compared with the actual data collected in this source. However, we are not inclined to follow these authors when they select only the top 1 percent of income, as a significant part of the latter probably comes from corruption and is not reflected in statistical databases nor revealed in the various household surveys available. Wang (2010) estimated that this "gray" income derived from corruption could represent around 17 percent of Chinese GNI in 2008. But it is likely to think that such an estimate underestimates the seriousness of this phenomenon. In any case, what we can see is that the income distribution tables substantially underestimate the income levels of the upper strata of society.

Even if we disregard corruption, the point is that neither tax data – under current tax laws – nor household surveys – given the Chinese cultural context – today allow to have information which is fully consistent with the reality of the income levels reached by the richest in the country. If the regulations came to tax the income of individuals on transfers of property, the profits earned on the stock exchange market from the resale of securities remain until now exempt from income taxation. As the wealthiest households derive on average a much higher proportion of their income from capital gains compared to other families in the total population, their real income is *de facto* considerably underestimated in tax documents.

Furthermore, although the sample size of the NBS household surveys seems large enough (500,000 families in 2001 and 2002, plus another 140,000 in 2012), in China as elsewhere, the rich are accustomed to hide a proportion quite large of their fortunes, to the point that the rigorous estimation of their wealth entails risks of errors significantly more serious than for those of other social categories. So many reasons that militate in favor of examining the evolution of inequalities over the past decades by means of Gini coefficients, such as those we proposed to construct in Chapter 4.

Let us conclude. Our econometric estimates of the verification of what the author of *Capital in the Twenty-First Century* states as "fundamental laws" in the long run leads to revealing rather mixed results, both over the period 1952–2015 and over the sub-sample corresponding to what numerous researchers, economists or social scientists, consider to be a "Chinese capitalism." The indeterminacy of the conclusions of the estimation of the "law" $\beta = s/g_R$, which requires some precautions, can probably be partly explained by the structural instability of the underlying model used by Piketty (close to a dynamics *à la* Harrod-Domar), but also by the small size of the samples studied, especially over the sub-period 1978–2012, yet the most able to verify this law. Here, the reservations that we believe it appropriate to formulate also extend to the definition of "capital" defended by Piketty, which is in itself questionable and moreover difficult to reconcile with its own theoretical framework – a framework which refers explicitly to a production function, but with a "capital" input that has not really been built to be a strictly "productive" factor. Our nuances also target the fragility of some results of econometric tests validating in the long term the existence of cointegration relationships between the series of capital coefficient and of the savings rate / income growth rate ratio.

That said, the reader might feel – rightly – some frustration of not seeing us address more in our arguments and econometric work the issue of inequalities in China, which is absolutely crucial to Piketty (this is in fact his so-called "third law"), and many others.[36] However, it does not seem relevant to us, in our view, to formulate the problem of the inequalities which characterize China's current development in the terms used by Piketty – due to the fact that he gives excessive importance to the transmission of patrimonies of wealth, through inheritance and donation. The origins of these inequalities, as well as the mechanisms and channels by which they operate, are quite different, and require explanations whose technical details cannot occupy the few lines that remain to us. The same will apply to the criticism, which we deem necessary, of the work that Piketty, in co-signing with Nancy Qian, has devoted to this subject and applied to the case of China[37] – along with to that which must also target the statistical data used, and more specifically the NBS *China Yearbooks of Household Survey*, which significantly underestimate the incomes of the upper deciles and percentiles in the distribution tables. This would be however a separate and new research.

---

36   Read, among many others: Bourguignon (1979), Lambert (1993), or Sen (1997).
37   Piketty and Qian (2011). See also: Piketty, Li and Zucman (2017).

Capital Accumulation, Profit Rates, Cycles and Crises in China's Economy: A Marxist Analysis through Industrial Profit Rates (1952–2014)

The growth path of China's economy has been remarkable for its strength and its relative stability in recent years. However, along with numerous academic studies,[1] this phenomenon has raised many questions. The latter concern not only the causes, the mechanisms and the engines of such dynamism, but also its sustainability and the likely consequences of the rise or "emergence" of China in the hierarchy of countries within the capitalist world system. Most of these issues relate to the *sui generis* – and complex – nature of this economy, which has known in practice how to adopt some features of capitalism since its opening in 1978, while it retained certain characteristics of socialism. This is particularly true, as we mentioned it in Chapter 6, of land tenure, intellectual property, or massive participations and proactive interventions by the State. And in addition, this State itself remained under the authority of a very powerful Communist Party. So, in the case of China, our interpretation encourages us to speak of a "market socialism," rather close to a "State capitalism," but under conditions which still remain those of a transition to socialism.[2]

This chapter does not attempt to define the nature of the current Chinese economic system; and still less to deal with all the facets that such a definition would require. It will aim more modestly to offer some elements of reflections on the role played by the rates of profit in the dynamics of capital accumulation in China's economy over the long period. As a matter of fact, our premise is that today, the functioning of this economic system shares sufficiently (and increasingly) common features with capitalism to allow us to methodologically use the concept of "profit rate" in order to study it. Such research will be conducted within a Marxist framework, quite original in this school of thought, because it is performed through two methods; more precisely, and alternatively, using both "microeconomic" and "macroeconomic" analyzes. Here, we conceive these two levels of analysis very simply: "microeconomic" means led by statistical data taken from the accounts of the enterprises, and

---

1   For example: Chow (1993), Maddison (1995), Chow and Li (2002), or Ding and Knight (2009).
2   See: Andréani and Herrera (2013a, 2013b, 2015a), Andréani, Herrera and Long (2018c), Herrera and Long (2019c).

"macroevonomic" by using data from series characterizing the national economy. These two methods intersect at the level of the industrial sector, but studied from two distinctive angles. We chose such a methodological approach after having written a series of research contributions on China's economic growth, presented in the two previous chapters, in which we emphasized the limits – insurmountable, we believe – of the tools provided by the neoclassical mainstream, or its dependencies.[3]

First, it should be stressed that the different indicators of profit rates that we will build, by comparing a surplus or "profit," and a stock of capital or of fixed assets, cannot be interpreted in the same terms as in the cases of developed capitalist countries. Nevertheless, the attention devoted to profit rate indicators is fundamental if we are to explain the reproduction dynamics of the Chinese economy in the long term, even over the period when it was largely and centrally planned. Consequently, once the core of our subject is clearly identified – namely, the industry –, our efforts will focus on the calculations of profit rates of industrial enterprises at the microeconomic level, and of profit rates of the industrial sector at the macroeconomic level. Then we will explain the changes in these indicators, as well as those in their technical and economic decompositions, shedding light on a succession of cycles which has punctuated the capital accumulation process of China's economy over the last six decades.

1   The Industrial Sector in Chinese Accounting Systems

The contours of the "industrial sector" should be carefully delimited, because this concept has been understood in different ways in the successive accounting systems in China (Table 7.1). Similar to the Soviet planning model, the scheme of balances of the Material Product System (MPS) remained in force from 1952 to 1992. It recognized the productive contributions of both agriculture and industry, but not services – whose added values were not integrated then in the calculation of the national income. Therefore, all non-agricultural activities identified in the classification of that period could be considered as "industrial." Following the reforms of the late 1970s, the MPS was gradually replaced by the System of National Accounts (SNA), which has introduced a distinction between three economic sectors: primary for agriculture, secondary for industries and construction, tertiary for everything else (that is, among

---

3 For a theoretical (and radical) critique of the "new" neoclassical growth: Herrera (2000a, 2000b, 2006a, 2011).

TABLE 7.1   Evolutions in the scope and classification criteria of industrial activities

Period	Scope	Criteria	Comments
1952–1992	All activities, except agriculture	Material Product System (MPS)	Non-recognition of the productive contribution of activities in the tertiary sector by the NBS
1993–2003	Sections B + C + D, excluding construction	System of National Accounts (SNA) "GB / T4754-1994"	Recognition of the productive contribution of activities in the tertiary sector by the NBS
2004–2011	Sections B + C + D, excluding construction	"GB / T4754-2002" and "2003 Three-Sector Classification Rules"	Redistribution of the divisions in the secondary sector and significant changes in the tertiary sector
2012–present	Sections B + C + D, excluding construction	"GB / T4754-2011" and "2012 Three-Sector Classification Rules"	Some divisions in the secondary sector moved to the tertiary sector, more identified with services

other activities, transport, post and telecommunications, commerce, social services, etc.).

The complete transition from the MPS to the SNA was achieved in 1993 and, as soon as the following year, the National Bureau of Statistics (NBS) of China released an "Industry Classification of National Economy." In this classification, codified as "GB / T4754–1994" (in Chinese: 国民经济行业分类), the secondary sector had been divided into four main sections under the titles called "B" for mining and extractive industries, "C" for manufacturing industries, "D" for the production and distribution of electricity, gas and water, and "E" for construction. Thus, aggregation of the sections B, C and D fits well with the traditional conception of "industry." In 2004, a new "GB / T4754–2002" classification was adopted, based on the typology of the "2003 Three-Sector Classification Rules" (三次产业划分规定).[4] The modifications then introduced (with renewed delimitations of subsections, or "divisions," within the secondary sector, or between the latter and the tertiary sector) did not call into question the previous definition of industry. And the same applied to the changes which accompanied the very last "GB / T4754–2011" classification,[5] in application since 2012,

---

4   http://www.stats.gov.cn/tjgz/tjdt/200305/t20030519_16460.html.

5   http://www.stats.gov.cn/tjsj/tjbz/201301/t20130114_8675.html.

and mostly concerned agricultural activities (section "A") and services (strictly identified with the tertiary sector, and including additional divisions trans-ferred from the secondary sector).

The statistical consistency of the "GB / T4754" classifications and the relative stability of the scope of industry in the different periods of their formulation led us to define the "industrial enterprises" as those belonging to all the sec-tions B + C + D, as the NBS conceives them. Clearly, we retain here the produc-tive entities whose activities are primarily performed within the sections of "mines" (B), "manufacturing industries" (C) and "production and distribution of electricity, gas and water" (D), that is, all the secondary components, except construction. This is an interpretation that is relatively close to that of the *2008 International Standard Industrial Classification* (ISIC). Finally, we see that the successive adjustments recorded in the Chinese accounting systems have had only limited impacts on the contours of the fundamental concept of industry.

2   Calculation of Industrial Profit Rates: Microeconomic Level

First of all, we will calculate microeconomic profit rates from data collected at the level of the enterprises in the industrial sector, as defined above. This calculation requires the availability of two types of variables: the profits of these companies, and the value of their capital stocks. Regarding these capital stocks, we follow the method proposed by Gregory C. Chow (1993), which used cumulated data in order to determine the stocks of fixed assets of industrial enterprises. The aim of this author was to evaluate stocks at the national scale. Nevertheless, the series that he used are no longer made available to the public by the NBS since the transition from the MPS to the SNA; so that it is no longer possible to extend them beyond that date after the year 1993. However, thanks to the existence of standardized business accounting balances (i.e., *Enterprise Accounting Standards*), continuous data on cumulated depreciations allow us to reconstruct the stocks of fixed assets of the industrial enterprises, as under-taken by Chow (1993). The *Enterprise Accounting Standards* that we use are those established for 2006 (in Chinese: 会计准则 2006). All productive entities are indeed supposed to comply with this accounting system, but a significant number of them are still registered with reference to the 1992 standards in the documents of the NBS, as well as in those of the Ministry of Finance.

The capital stocks which are considered here are those of material assets with a serving life of more than one fiscal year. These are, among others, build-ings, equipment, machinery, tools, means of transport, which are held by enter-prises for their production of goods and services, or for rental or administrative purposes. Concerning the value of fixed assets of the industrial companies, noted K_{AT} and recorded at year-end values in the *Tables of Assets and Liability of Enterprises*,[6] the *Enterprise Accounting Standards 2006* adopt the following definition:

$$K_{AT} = K_{AO} - A_C - L_A \qquad (7.1)$$

with K_{AO} the original value of fixed assets,[7] corresponding to their initial cost, that is to say, to the total expenditure spent by the enterprises through the purchase, construction, installation, transformation, expansion or technical upgrading of these tangible assets. From this value are deduced the cumulated depreciations during the years of functioning[8] and the impairment losses of assets recorded in the accounts over the period. When the NBS did not provide data on these impairment losses, these were recalculated for the missing years.[9]

The total profits realized during the accounting period,[10] noted P_T, are calculated by the following formula:

$$P_T = B_E + R_E - D_E \qquad (7.2)$$

where R_E and D_E represent the operating revenues and expenses respectively, while B_E corresponds to the operating benefits, to be interpreted themselves as corporate income (including those earned from investments), less the sum of the charges, various taxes, other expenses of the financial year, as well as impairment losses of the assets.

Therefore, we are able to calculate four profit rates for industrial enterprises to be distinguished at the microeconomic level. Two criteria are retained here (Table 7.2):

i)   whether the cumulated depreciations are included in the capital of fixed assets (nominal rate of profit) or not (real rate of profit), and

---

6   For the *Enterprise Accounting Standards*, the data come from the *Tables of Assets and Liability of Enterprises*.

7   This value is reported at the end of the year and according to the debit balance of fixed assets in the accounting records.

8   Value reported according to the year-end credit balance of cumulated depreciations in these same accounting records.

9   In most cases, the NBS provided the data of "total value of fixed assets" and "original value of fixed assets."

10   The amounts of total profits are found in the *"Profit Tables"* in the accounting records of the enterprises.

TABLE 7.2   Definitions of the four microeconomic profit rates of industrial enterprises

Criterion 2: Taxation *Criterion 1*: Depreciation	Taxes not deduced from profits	Taxes deduced from profits
Cumulated depreciations included in the capital of fixed assets	Nominal profit rate before taxation: r_1	Nominal profit rate after taxation: r_2
Cumulated depreciations excluded from the capital of fixed assets	Real profit rate before taxation: r_3	Real profit rate after taxation: r_4

ii)   whether taxes are deducted from the profits (profit rate after taxation) or not (before taxation rate).

These different profit rates of the industrial enterprises are written:

Microeconomic rate of profit

$$\text{in nominal terms, before taxes:} \quad r_1 = \frac{P_T}{K_{AO}}$$

$$\text{in nominal terms, after taxes:} \quad r_2 = \frac{P_T - T_E}{K_{AO}}$$

$$\text{in real terms, before taxes:} \quad r_3 = \frac{P_T}{K_{AT}} \qquad (7.3)$$

$$\text{in real terms, after taxes:} \quad r_4 = \frac{P_T - T_E}{K_{AT}}$$

where T_E represents income taxes on the industrial enterprises.

In China, tax regulation has undergone significant changes since the founding of the People's Republic in 1949. These changes have accompanied those of the ownership structure of the whole economy. The "Great Socialist Transformations" were launched in 1952; they consisted more notably of expanding the scope of the State and collective enterprises, which extended to almost all the productive entities of the country (more than 99 percent) as soon as at the end of the year 1956. A major tax reform was implemented in 1984; it was established in parallel to the Chinese government's decision to allow private property in the industrial sector – once again. We will use as an indicator of taxation the "industrial" component of the series of the industrial and commercial tax between 1952 and 1984. From 1985 onwards, that is, just after the introduction of the tax on corporate income, levied on the State-owned enterprises and collective units of production,[11] we have chosen this last tax. However, after 2001, all national companies were subject to this tax.[12]

In a large majority of cases, the statistical series provided by the NBS are incomplete and only allowed the calculation of rates of profit since 1978. Thus, we ourselves had to add all the missing data by rebuilding them. For those of the "total value of fixed assets" prior to 2000, we used instead the "net value of fixed assets," which is a very similar series. The latter is recorded at year-end value in the yearbooks of the NBS prior to 1993 – as is also recorded the "total value of fixed assets." Nevertheless, between 1994 and 1999, the "net value of fixed assets" is presented as an average annual indicator. To correct the bias that characterizes this period and to be able to recalculate "net values of fixed assets" at the end of the fiscal year, we assume here that the growth rate of one half-year is equal to half the growth rate of the year.

As indicated in Table 7.3, the accounting documents which were available to build our series of microeconomic capital stocks do not include the enterprises of a size smaller than a certain threshold of fixed assets. As the weight of these "small" production units is relatively limited in the Chinese economy – even if they are very numerous –, our calculations can be seen as acceptable approximations of the profit rates of the industrial enterprises, taken as a whole. However, this omission of the smaller companies is probably sufficiently significant to induce a bias in our results for the microeconomic profit rates – but this is rather limited to the period after 1998 and remains under control. We will come back to that.

Let us say for the moment that three arguments can be formulated in support of this choice:

i)   the data used for "large companies," relatively detailed, are complete and consistent, with clear conceptual criteria and stable statistical perimeters;

ii)   the thresholds for the definition of "large companies" (of "5 million yuans" [in 1988–2010]) or "20 million yuans" [in 2011–2014]) are relatively modest and can refer in reality to (included) medium-sized production units at the China level, particularly in the industrial sectors;

iii) the share of these large or medium-sized companies is around three-quarters of the total value of the fixed assets of industrial enterprises in China, sometimes even exceeding them since the 2000s (Table 7.4).

---

11   See the "Notes" in the *China Finance Yearbook 2012* (p. 452).

12   *Cf.* The *China Finance Yearbook 2000* (p. 401).

TABLE 7.3   Types of enterprises taken into account for the calculation of profit rates by period

	r_1	r_2	r_3	r_4
1952–1978	All industrial enterprises owned by the State			
1979–1984	All industrial enterprises	All industrial enterprises owned by the State		
1985–1997	All industrial enterprises, whatever their accounting system			
1998–2006	All state-owned enterprises with annual revenues from their main business exceeding 5 million yuans			
2007–2010	All enterprises with annual revenues from their main business exceeding 5 million yuans			
2011–2014	All enterprises with annual revenues from their main business exceeding 20 million yuans			

TABLE 7.4   Share of large and medium-sized enterprises in China from 2000 to 2014 (*in percentages of the total value of the fixed assets of industrial enterprises*)

2000	2001	2002	2003	2004	2005	2006	2007	2008	2009	2010	2011	2012	2013	2014
72.95	75.38	74.72	76.62	74.55	75.08	74.92	74.51	71.61	72.52	72.92	74.69	73.67	72.59	70.76

SOURCE: NBS (VARIOUS YEARS)

3   Calculation of Industrial Profit Rates: Macroeconomic Level

In a second step, we will calculate macroeconomic profit rates, again for the industrial sector, in order to compare them to the microeconomic results previously obtained. Such profit rates are ratios which compare a numerator representing the aggregate surplus of the industrial sector or "profit," and a denominator corresponding to the capital stock of the same sector. Regarding this stock, we rely on our original statistical series of physical capital, reconstructed in Chapter 1 for China over the long period 1952–2014. We remember that our database includes various time series of physical capital stocks that are called "productive" or "core" – that is to say, without residential buildings and the value of their lands –; stocks which are conceived according to more or

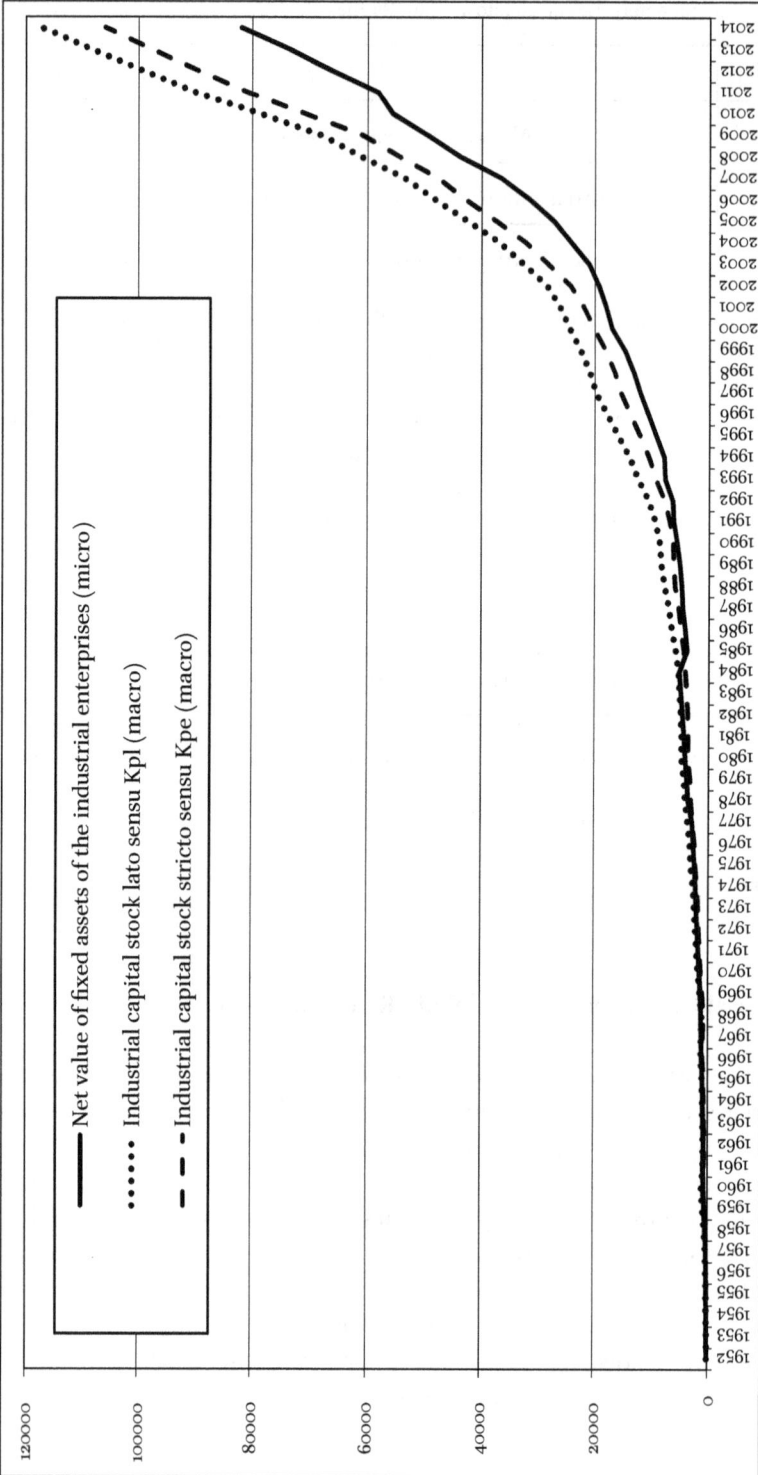

GRAPH 7.1   Levels of micro- and macroeconomic industrial capital stocks: China, 1952–2014 (*in hundreds of millions of yuans, at constant prices, base 1952*)

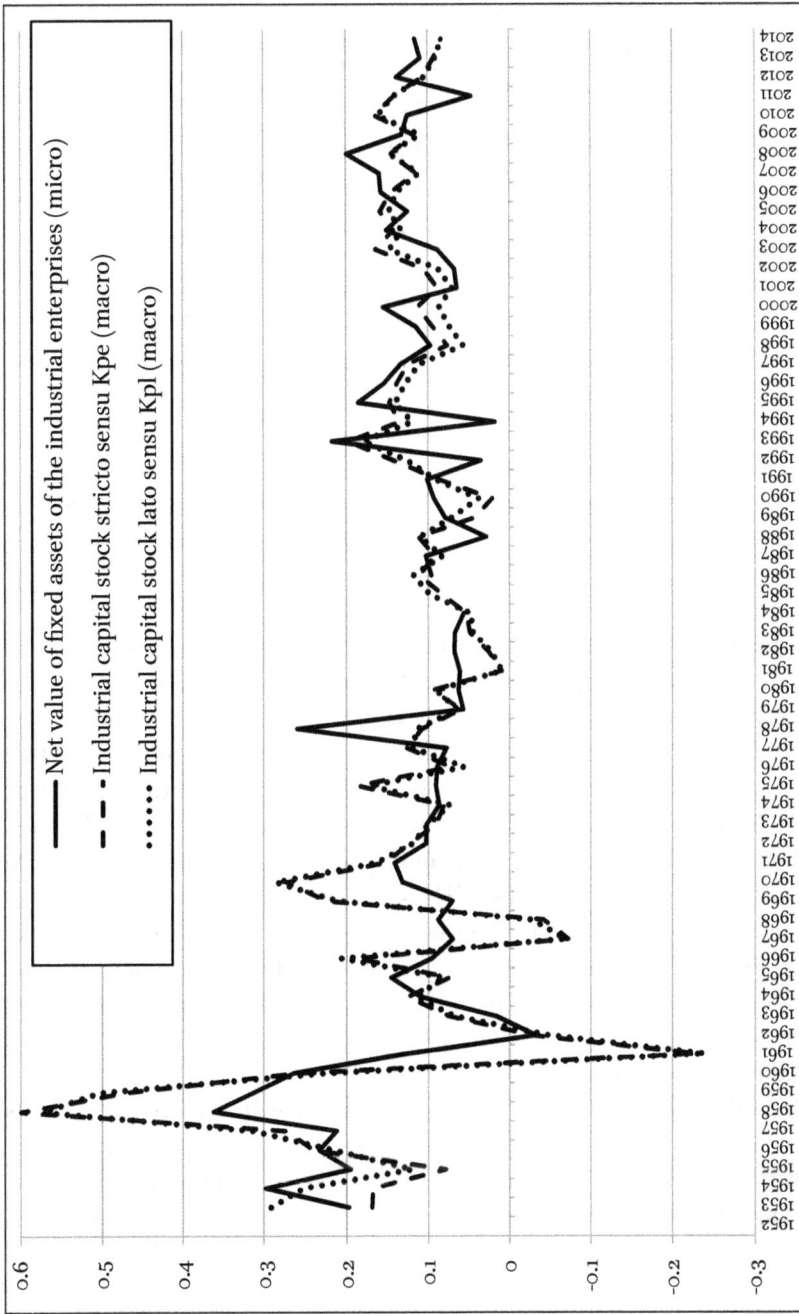

GRAPH 7.2 Growth rates of the micro- and macro-industrial capital stocks: China, 1952–2014 (in percentages [0.1 = 10 percent], at constant prices, base 1952)

TABLE 7.5   Calculated or actual proportions of the investment in State-owned enterprises'
fixed assets as compared to the national investment in fixed assets in a five-year
average: China, 1953–1980

Period	Years	Calculated average proportion	Actual proportion
First Plan	1953–1957	83.95 percent	–
Second Plan	1958–1962	99.00 percent	–
Period of recovery	1963–1965	81.82 percent	–
Third Plan	1966–1970	79.57 percent	–
Fourth Plan	1971–1975	89.62 percent	–
Fifth Plan	1976–1980	87.09 percent	–
Sixth Plan	1981–1985	66.98 percent	66.70 percent
Seventh Plan	1986–1990	64.48 percent	64.80 percent
Eighth Plan	1991–1995	65.58 percent	59.00 percent

less broad definitions. In particular, there are: a *lato sensu* or broadly-defined productive capital stock, K_{Pl}, including the inventories, and a *stricto sensu* or narrowly-defined productive capital stock, K_{Pe}, which does not include these.

We should mention again that several arguments allow us to maintain that our macroeconomic series are of good quality compared to those currently available in the literature. First, our initial stocks of capital are calculated through an iterative process which converges towards a capital-output ratio that is less approximate (and lower)[13] than those generally advanced. Besides, our investment flows are consistent with the statistical scopes of these initial stocks (Table 7.5). In addition, the depreciation rates are estimated by type of capital, under consistent assumptions on age-efficiency and retirement, in order to deduce the calculation of a total depreciation rate from the overall structure of the capital.

Our efforts have focused on constructing price indices of investments strictly tailored on the content of these capital stocks. The unit root tests that we performed have shown that, contrary to what many authors think,[14] with extremely rare exceptions,[15] the price index of capital investment – an index

---

13   See, for example: Zhang (1991), and He, Chen and He (2003).
14   Among others: Jefferson, Rawski and Zheng (1996), Wu (1999), Zhang and Zhang (2003), Shan (2008), etc.
15   We can quote here: He (1992) and Chow (1993).

that does not appear continuously and homogenously from 1952 to 2014 for the whole of China in the yearbooks of the NBS – cannot be replaced by another price index. This issue is indeed fundamental to the extent that price indices are the components that most decisively determine the level and the structure of the stocks of capital. Their careful construction is therefore crucial.

Under these conditions, four industrial profit rates are calculated at the macroeconomical level, as follows:

$$\text{Micro rate of profit} \begin{cases} \text{\textit{stricto sensu} productive capital, before taxes:} & r_5 = \dfrac{Y_{(I)} - R_{(I)}}{K_{Pe(I)}} \\[3ex] \text{\textit{stricto sensu} productive capital, after taxes:} & r_6 = \dfrac{Y_{(I)} - R_{(I)} - T_{(I)}}{K_{Pe(I)}} \\[3ex] \text{\textit{lato sensu} productive capital, before taxes:} & r_7 = \dfrac{Y_{(I)} - R_{(I)}}{K_{Pl(I)}} \quad\quad (7.4) \\[3ex] \text{\textit{lato sensu} productive capital, after taxes:} & r_8 = \dfrac{Y_{(I)} - R_{(I)} - T_{(I)}}{K_{Pl(I)}} \end{cases}$$

where $Y_{(I)}$ represents the product of the industrial sector, $R_{(I)}$ the income of workers in this same sector, $T_{(I)}$ the taxes on corresponding companies, $K_{Pe\,(I)}$ and $K_{Pl\,(I)}$ the industrial components of the respectively narrowly- or broadly-defined stocks of industrial productive physical capital (Graphs 7.1 and 7.2).

In the same way that, at the microeconomic level, we have defined the industrial sector taken as a whole as all enterprises in the sections "B + C + D," excluding construction (section "E"), logically, it is a productive capital stock without residential buildings nor the value of their lands that we use in addressing the macroeconomic level. We assume here that the proportion of the industrial capital stock $K_{(I)}$ in the total productive capital stock K is equal to that of industrial production $Y_{(I)}$ (i.e., the sum of the industrial added values) in the gross domestic product (GDP, minus the added value of the construction sector), noted Y^*, that is to say:

$$K_{(I)t} = \frac{Y_{(I)t}}{Y_t^*} \cdot K_t = \alpha_t \cdot K_t \qquad (7.5)$$

where K_t is the total stock of productive physical capital respectively conceived *stricto sensu* (or narrowly-defined) K_{Pe}, or *lato sensu* (or broadly-defined) K_{Pl}.

Therefore, we associate with the trajectory of α_t an assumption of constant returns to scale in production.[16] The calculation of this variable is allowed through the online series of the NBS (NBS online database) after 1978 and, before 1978, thanks to the "Comprehensive Statistical Data and Materials on 50 Years of New China" (or 新中国 50 年五十年统计资料汇编).

China's GDP comes from the calculations performed by the NBS according to the production approach, aggregating the added values of the three economic sectors (primary, secondary and tertiary). Total incomes (both direct and indirect, including premiums and specific allocations) received by the workers in all industrial sections, $R_{(I)}$, and expressed before taxation, are also extracted from the NBS's databases. However, only data after the year 2003 are provided. So, for those prior to that date, we recalculate them by multiplying the remunerations of the urban (i.e., non-rural) employees by the proportion β_t of the industrial added values $Y_{(I)t}$ in those of the secondary $Y_{(S)t}$ and tertiary $Y_{(T)t}$ sectors, as follows:

$$\beta_t = \frac{Y_{(I)t}}{(Y_{(S)t} + Y_{(T)t})} \qquad (7.6)$$

the sources being here identical to those of α_t.

The series related to these remunerations come from the "Comprehensive Statistical Data and Materials on 50 Years of New China" before 2000, and from the the NBS's online database after that date. The comparison of actual and estimated income of the industrial workers over the period after the year 2003 shows a gap of around +35% between the latter and the former; this leads to a downward correction in remunerations before 2003. Here, the consumer price index is used to convert current income into 1952-base constant income (Appendix A.7.2.1).

Data on taxes of the industrial enterprises, $T_{(I)}$, was much more difficult to obtain, especially because the NBS disseminates little statistical information about them. Published by the State Administration of Taxation, the *Tax Yearbook of China* (中国税务年鉴) provides data on such taxations by economic sections only since 2001. Before the tax reform in 1993, the first fiscal yearbook (called *Tax Yearbook of China 1993*) gives data on the "Industrial and

---

16   Although carried out under a very different methodology to that developed in this chapter, our previous studies (in Chapters 5 and 6) on China's economic growth has shown that such an assumption of constant returns to scale in production is defensible under certain conditions.

commercial tax" of industrial sections for the period 1952–1993, while the *Tax Yearbook of China 2001* indicates income taxes on enterprises by sections only since the year 2000.

Consequently, the series of $T_{(I)}$ are incomplete between 1993 and 1999. Over those years, it is assumed that there is a relationship of proportionality between the taxation of industrial sections and the total product, $\gamma_t = Y_{(I)t}/Y_t$. This assumption is acceptable for the taxes on sales (value added tax or VAT), but not for those on the enterprises' incomes, because of the existence of various tax incentives implemented by the Chinese authorities in favor of foreign firms.[17] It was therefore necessary to distinguish the years of application of this policy in order to take them into account, by using the table of "Taxes on corporate revenues by section and by nature of enterprises for the whole country" in the corresponding yearbooks (全国企业分项目分企业类型所得税情况) (Appendix A.7.2.1).

4   Changes in Micro- and Macroeconomic Profit Rates: A Comparison

The evolutions of industrial profit rates calculated at the micro- and macroeconomic levels are presented in Graphs 7.3 and 7.4. The results obtained at the macroeconomic level are higher than those found microeconomically. Indeed, on average, the microeconomic profit rates are respectively 17.9 percent for r_1 (pre-tax nominal profit rate of industrial enterprises), 13.0 percent for r_2 (nominal profit rate after taxes), 26.2 percent for r_3 (real profit rate before taxes) and 18.2 percent for r_4 (real profit rate after taxes) over the entire period from 1952 to 2014. The average macroeconomic profit rates are found at 42.2 percent for r_5 (profit rate of the narrowly-conceived productive industrial capital stock before taxes), 30.4 percent for r_6 (profit rate of the *stricto sensu* productive capital stock after taxes), 32.9 percent for r_7 (profit rate of the *lato sensu* capital before taxes) and 23.7 percent for r_8 (profit rate of the capital defined in a broad sense after taxes) during the same period 1952–2014.

As we see it, the averages of the two profit rates which can be considered to be the most representative of the effective activity of the Chinese industry, that is, r_4 at the microeconomic level (calculated by subtracting taxes and excluding the cumulated depreciations of fixed assets of industrial enterprises) and r_8 at the macroeconomic level (calculated from the productive capital stock

---

17   *Cf.* Article 8 of the 1991 Act on the taxation of companies' revenues with foreign investment and foreign enterprises (中华人民共和国外商投资企业和外国企业所得税法 1991).

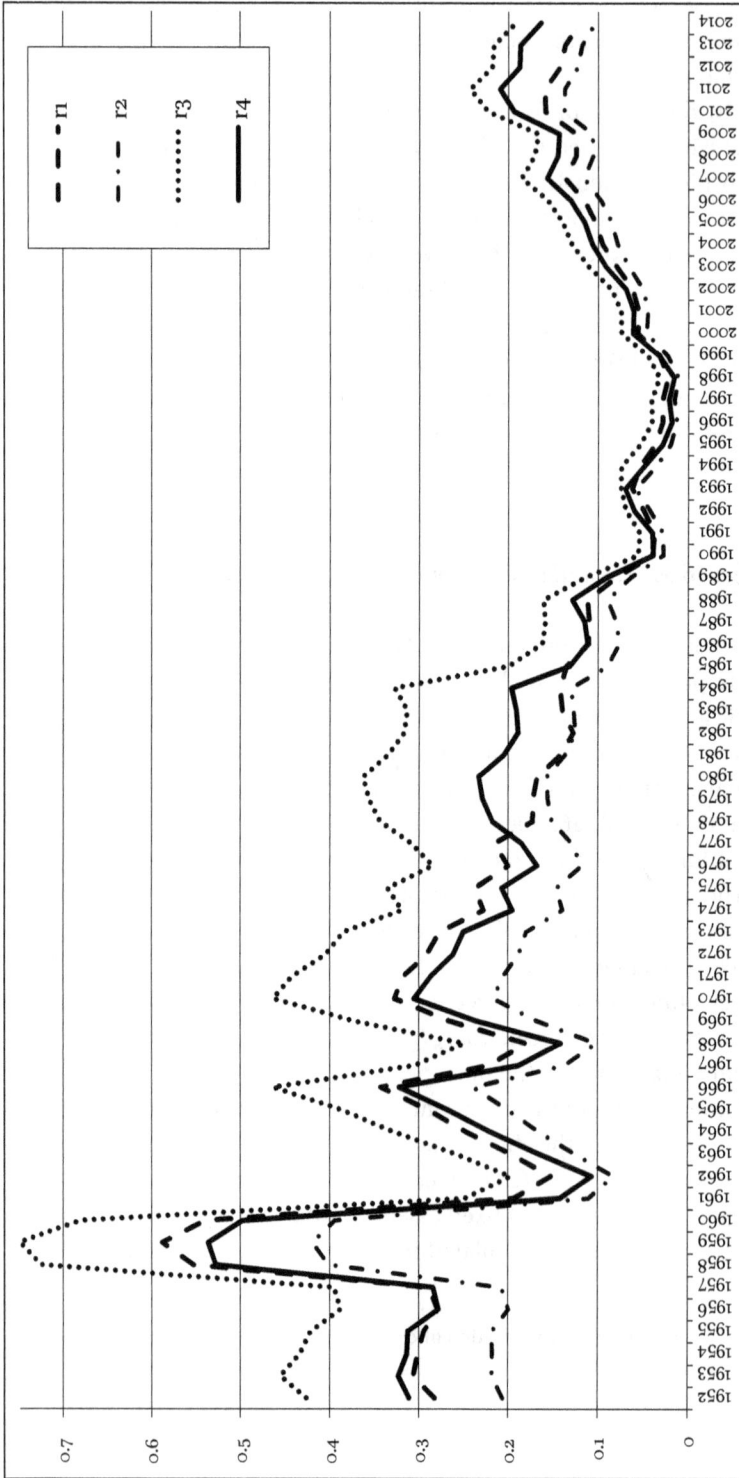

GRAPH 7.3 Changes in the profit rates of industrial enterprises at the microeconomic level: China, 1952–2014 (*in percentages* [*0.1 = 10 percent*])

Notes: r_1 = nominal profit rate before taxes of industrial enterprises at the microeconomic level;
r_2 = nominal profit rate after taxes of industrial enterprises at the microeconomic level;
r_3 = real profit rate before taxes of industrial enterprises at the microeconomic level;
r_4 = real profit rate after taxes of industrial enterprises at the microeconomic level.

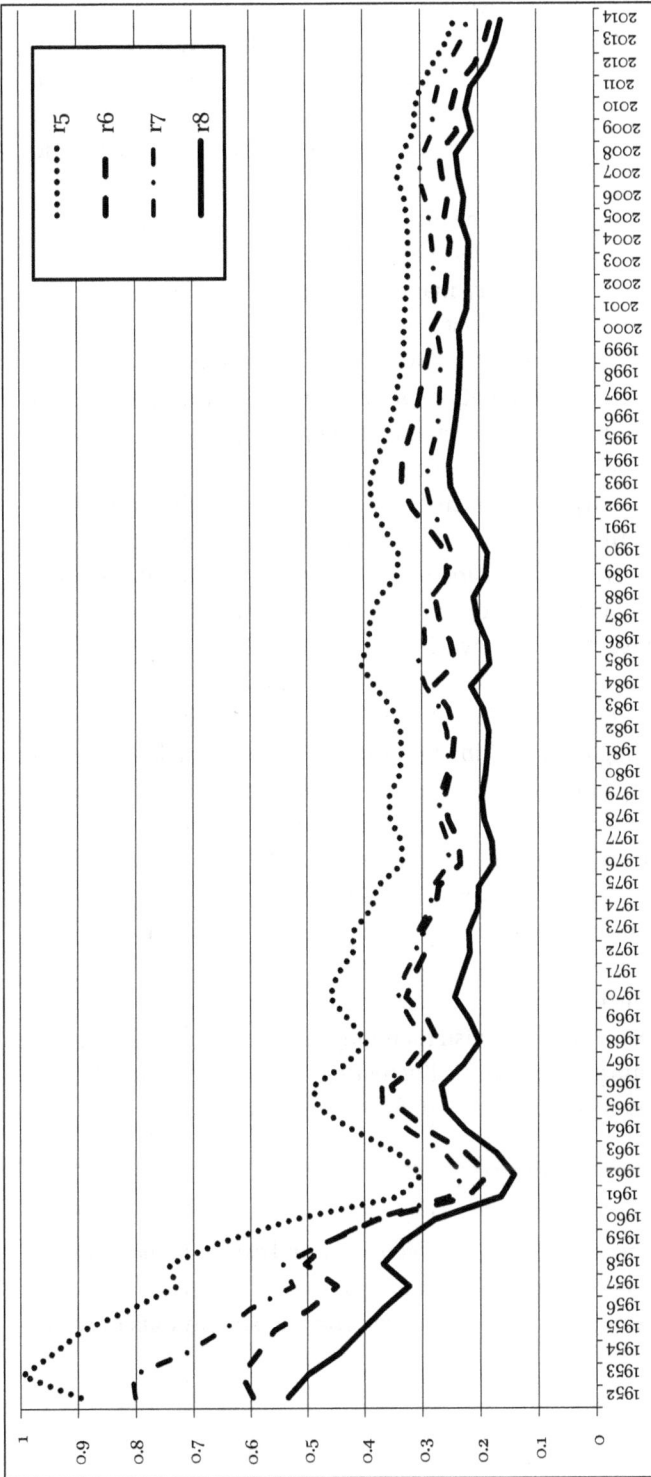

GRAPH 7.4   Changes in the profit rates of the industrial sector at the macroeconomic level: China, 1952–2014 (*in percentages* [*0.1 = 10 percent*])

Notes: r_5 = profit rate of narrowly-defined capital stock before taxes for the industrial sector at the macroeconomic level;

r_6 = profit rate of narrowly-defined capital stock after taxes for the industrial sector at the macroeconomic level;

r_7 = profit rate of broadly-defined capital stock before taxes for the industrial sector at the macroeconomic level;

r_8 = profit rate of broadly-defined capital after taxes for the industrial sector at the macroeconomic level.

of the industrial sector including inventories, but not residential buildings and the value of their lands), are of the same order of magnitude: 18.2 percent for the first profit rate, and 23.7 percent for the second one. Both profit rates still remain rather close to one another, or let us say not so far from each other, over the sub-period 1978–2014, that is to say, after the reforms: 12.0 percent and 21.2 percent respectively.

In general, the overall profiles of the micro- and macroeconomic profit rates are quite similar; i.e., they are basically characterized by a downward tendency over the long term (Graph 7.5). Very marked fluctuations are observable for the two levels of analysis during a first stage, going from the founding of the People's Republic to the break with the Soviet Union (1952–1961). Accompanying this downward trend, the oscillations in profit rates continue, albeit in a much less harsh way, until 1978, and even until the 1990s, but with these gradually diminishing. It was from there that things seem to have changed somewhat. Indeed, the trajectory of the macroeconomic profit rate appears to move upward, slightly, from the early 1990s, while that of the microeconomic profit rate continues its descent, before rising more strongly at the end of the same decade. The micro- and macroeconomic curves meet again in the first years of the 2010s, and move together downward more noticely. These sequences are clearly visible in the case of the indicators r_4 and r_8 (Graph 7.6).

Beyond the "reassuring" or "safe" result – at least, for a Marxist economist – brought about by highlighting a falling profit rate trend over the long term (a trend which is measured in logarithmic terms for r_4 and r_8 in Graph 7.6), however, the findings of a sharp rise in the trajectory of r_4 from 1999 until 2007 (or rather until 2011), on the one hand, and, on the other hand, of a relative stability for that of r_8, extended over fifty years (from 1963 to 2011 approximately), require the introduction of some complexity in these over-intuitive interpretations.

Consequently, for further analysis, we perform a technical decomposition of the rates of profit in order to distinguish their long-term trends and their cyclical components, capturing short-term fluctuations. Such a technical breakdown can be obtained by writing these profit rates, as follows:

$$r_t = \Psi_t + \Theta_t + \varepsilon_t \qquad (7.7)$$

where Ψ_t represents the trend – which is decreasing and can take a polynomial form –, Θ_t the cyclical component – that is to say, a stationary process (of a sinusoidal type, for example) –, and ε_t an error term – a random walk or white noise.

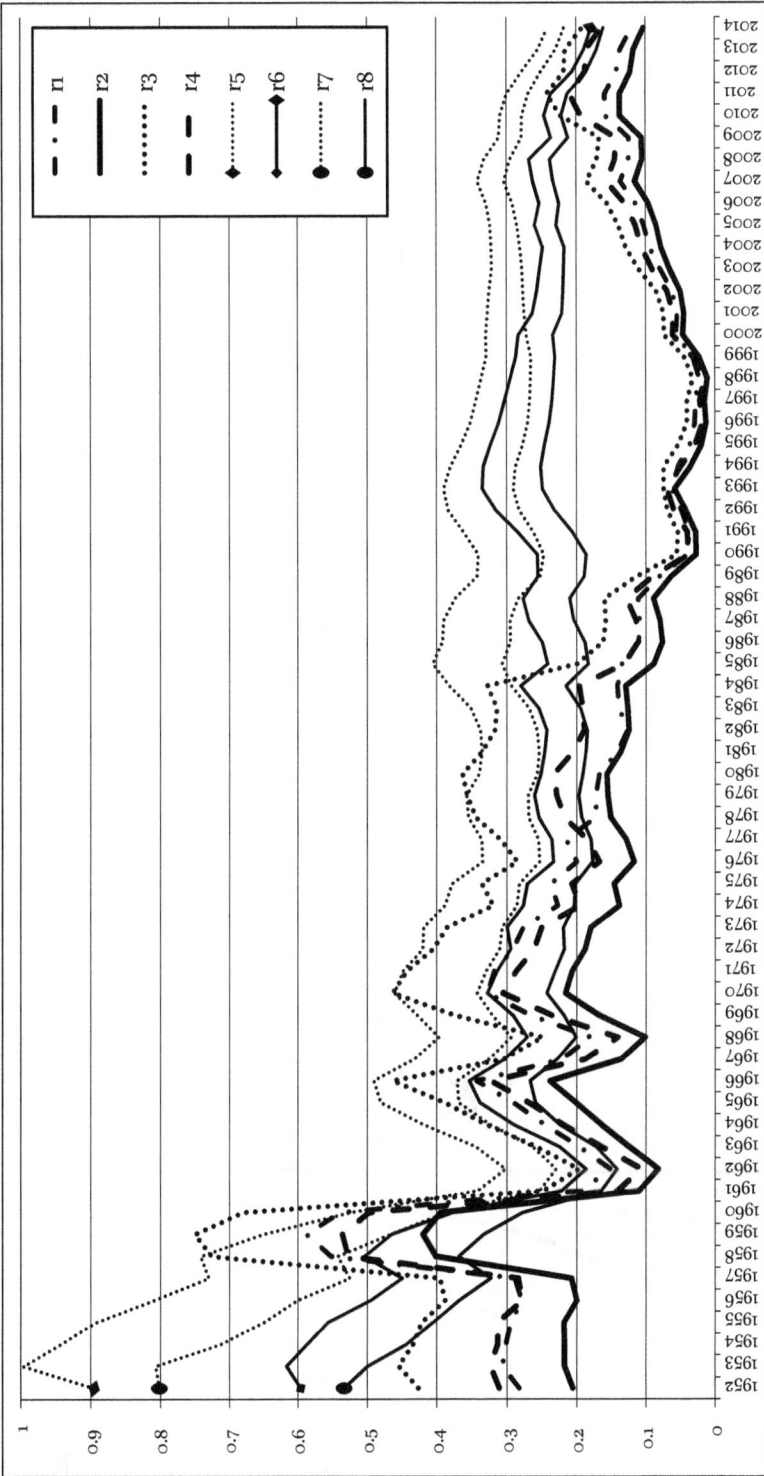

GRAPH 7.5   Comparison of the changes in profit rates at the micro- and macroeconomic levels: China, 1952–2014 (*in percentages* [*0.1 = 10 percent*])

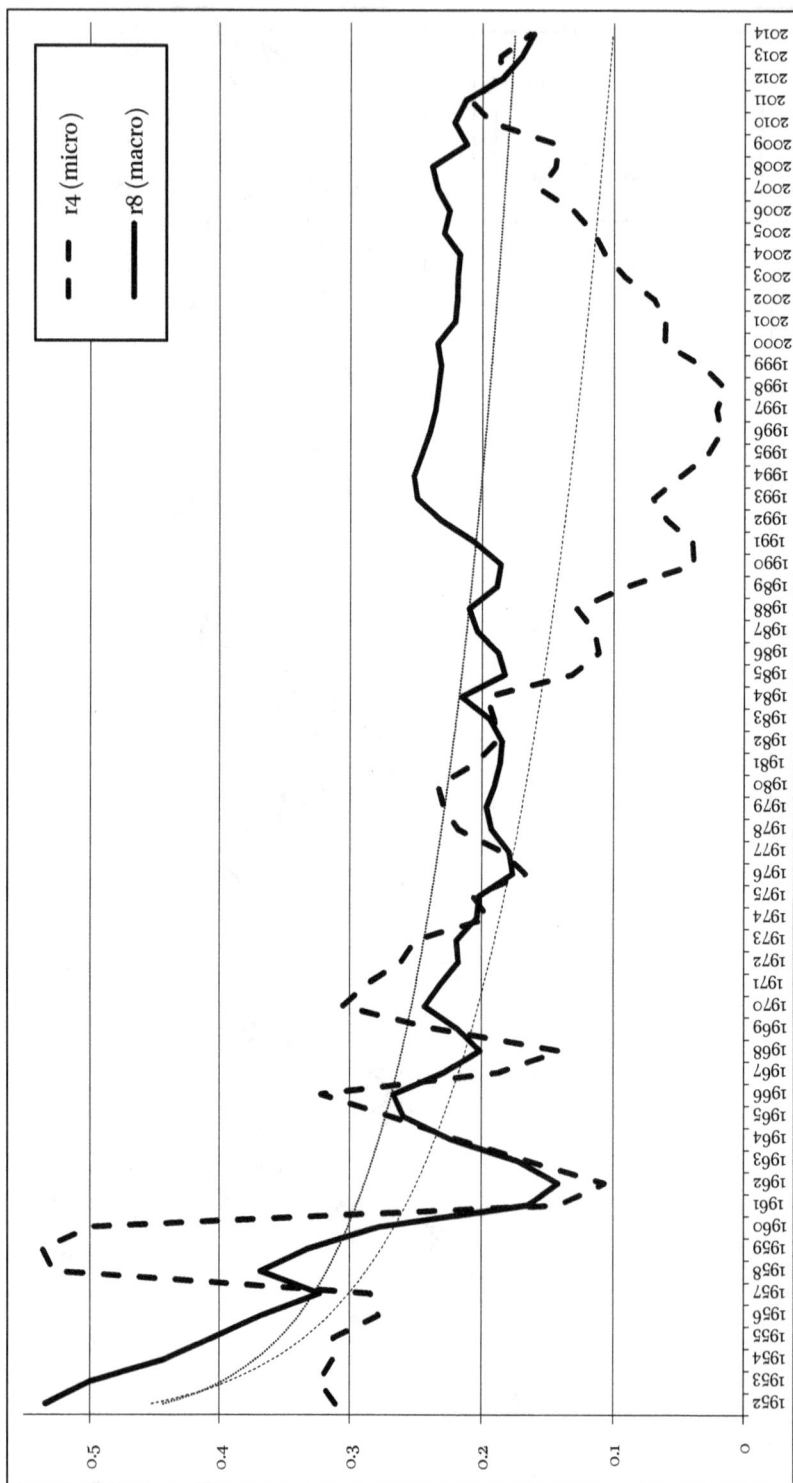

GRAPH 7.6   Comparison of the trends in profit rates at micro- and macroeconomic levels: China, 1952–2014 (*in percentages* [0.1 = 10 percent])

A simple formulation of this breakdown is, among many other possibilities:

$$r_t = [a_1 t + \dots + a_n t^n] + [a_0 + A\sin(\omega t + \varphi)] + [b_1 r_{t-1} + \dots + b_p r_{t-p} + u_t] \qquad (7.8)$$

with $a_1 < 0$, and where the three components (polynomial trend, sinusoidal functional form of the cycle, and error term) are shown in square brackets.

Here, we present the application of this technical decomposition to the cases of macroeconomic rates of profit r_6 and r_8 only. For this, the breakdown is performed by using the method of the Hodrick-Prescott filter (Graph 7.7); the setting of its own parameters being completed by those suggested by Ravn-Uhlig (Graph 7.8).[18] Other breakdowns into trend and cycles have also been tried in time series.[19] They give similar results and confirm the solidity of findings.

Graph 7.8 shows that the short-term cycles of the macroeconomic profit rates see the magnitude of their fluctuations diminish over time, from the early 1950s until the end of the 2000s – however, from the onwards they seem to widen again. Thus, these fluctuations fairly regularly alternate up and down periods. For the macroeconomic profit rates r_6 and r_8, with two parameter settings for the filters (Hodrick-Prescott and Ravn-Uhlig parameters), the years of common recession, marked by the first differences of the cyclical components recording a negative sign, are observed 24 times. Such a negative sign happens more specifically in 1957, 1961–1963, 1968, 1976–1977, 1981–1982, 1985–1986, 1989–1991, 1998–1999, 2001–2004, 2009, and 2012–2014. This corresponds to more than a third of the 63 years of the total period studied from 1952 to 2014 – even if the GDP growth rate can sometimes simultaneously achieve quite a speed rhythm.

Through these 11 sequences of recession, we readily recognize the successive slowdowns that have characterized China's economic history since the founding of the People's Republic.[20]

i)   After the huge difficulties experienced in the early period (1949–1952), mainly due to the wars and convulsions through which the country has gone during the decades before the revolution, we find traces of the recessionary period that began in 1954 and whose low point was in 1957.

---

18   See: Hodrick and Prescott (1981), then Ravn and Uhlig (2002).

19   Alternative techniques are those with – fixed length – symmetrical filters (Baxter and King [1995], Christiano and Fitzgerald [1999]) or with – time-varying – asymmetric filters. The other methods that we used are those provided by Beveridege and Nelson (1981), Harvey (1985), Watson (1986), Clark (1987), Quah (1992), and also Morley (2002).

20   Read: Herrera and Long (2019c), as well as Wen (2021).

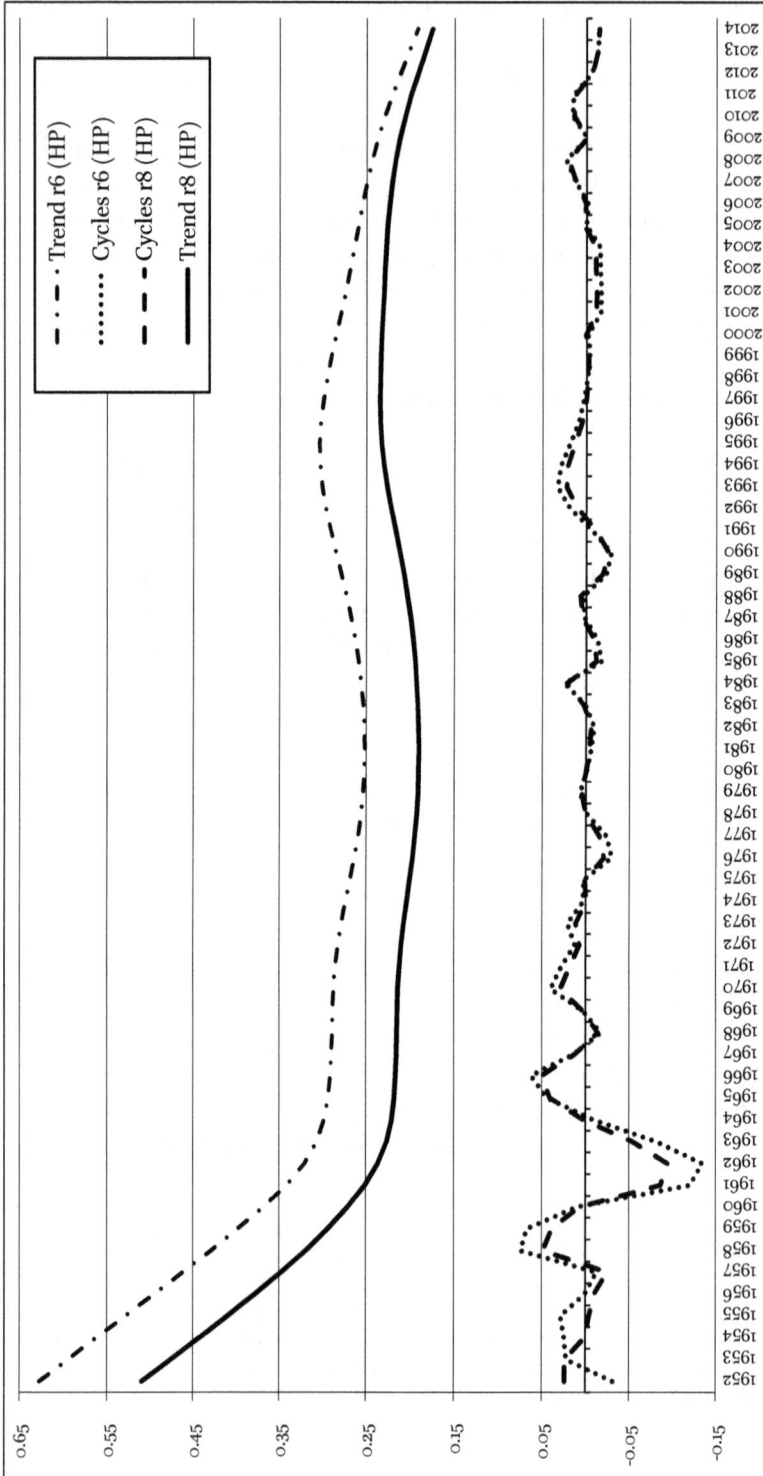

GRAPH 7.7   Technical decomposition of the macro profit rates r_6 and r_8 into trend and cycles: China, 1952–2014 (*in percentages* [*0.1 = 10 percent*])
Note: The technical breakdown is performed using the method of the Hodrick-Prescott filter (H.-P. filter).

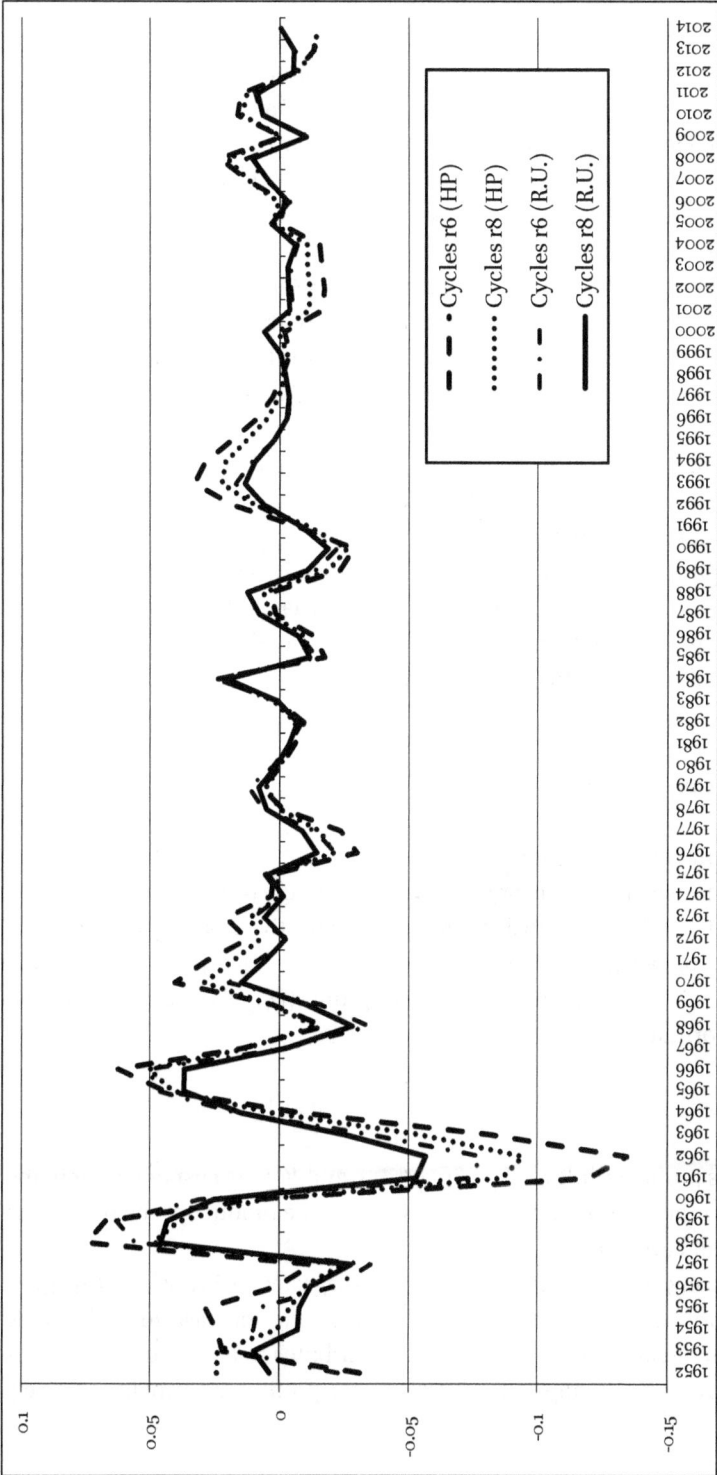

GRAPH 7.8 Changes in the cyclical components of the macro profit rates r_6 and r_8 according to several methods of technical decomposition: China, 1952–2014 (*in percentages*)

Note: The technical breakdown is performed by using the method of the Hodrick-Prescott filter with its own parameters (power = 2, lambda = 100) or those suggested by Ravn and Uhlig, R.U. (power = 4, lambda = 6.25).

ii)   The crisis of the early 1960s, the worst ever for the People's Republic of China, has resulted from the combined effects – clearly visible in 1961–1962 – of the interruption of the USSR's aid after the Sino-Soviet conflict, the relative failure of the "Great Leap Forward," and various disasters that occurred at that time (particularly on the Yellow River).

iii)   Another low point, the year 1968, coincides with the hardening of the Cultural Revolution, launched two years earlier.

iv)   The serious problems encountered in 1976–1977 reveal those of the transition following the death of Chairman Mao Zedong.

v)   1981–1982 were years of implementation of the structural reforms of "openness" adopted after the XIth Congress of the Communist Party,

vi)   and 1985–1986 those of application of the 1984 tax reform – one of the turning points towards China's market economy.

vii)   Amid the collapse of the USSR, a brief "neoliberal" experiment was attempted and resulted in a sharp slowdown in the economy (1989–1991) – accompanied by corruption cases.

viii) In a (quite paradoxical) context of the strong dynamism of China's GDP, the declines recorded from 1998 onwards are largely attributable to exogenous (or imported) shocks, linked to the generalized spread of regional or global crises: Asian crisis (1998–1999),

ix)   then the "new economy" and "post-September 11" crises (2001–2004), and the so-called "financial" crisis of 2007–2008, whose global effects have been felt in China on two occasions:

x)   in 2009,

xi)   and from 2012 to the present.

Finally, we proceed to an economic decomposition of the macroeconomic profit rate (here r_8) in order to distinguish the respective changes in the organic composition of capital (i.e., the inverse of $R_{(I)}^* / K_{Pl(I)}$), the productivity of the labour cost unit ($Y_{(I)} / R_{(I)}^*$), and the share of profits ($\Pi_{(I)}/Y_{(I)}$), using the following simple formula:

$$r = \Pi_{(I)} / Y_{(I)} \cdot Y_{(I)} / R_{(I)}^* \cdot R_{(I)}^* / K_{Pl(I)} \qquad (7.9)$$

where $\Pi_{(I)}$ is profit, with $\Pi_{(I)} = Y_{(I)} - R_{(I)} - T_{(I)}$; and $R_{(I)}^*$ the cost of labour in the industrial sector (without taxes), approached by the product of the number of employees and average earnings.

Theoretically, this formula is close to that suggested by Weisskopf (1979).

Graph 7.10 indicates that it is mostly the strong increase in the organic composition of capital ($K_{Pl(I)} / R_{(I)}^*$), that contributes to largely explaining the downward trend of the long-run profit rate. If the profit share remains relatively

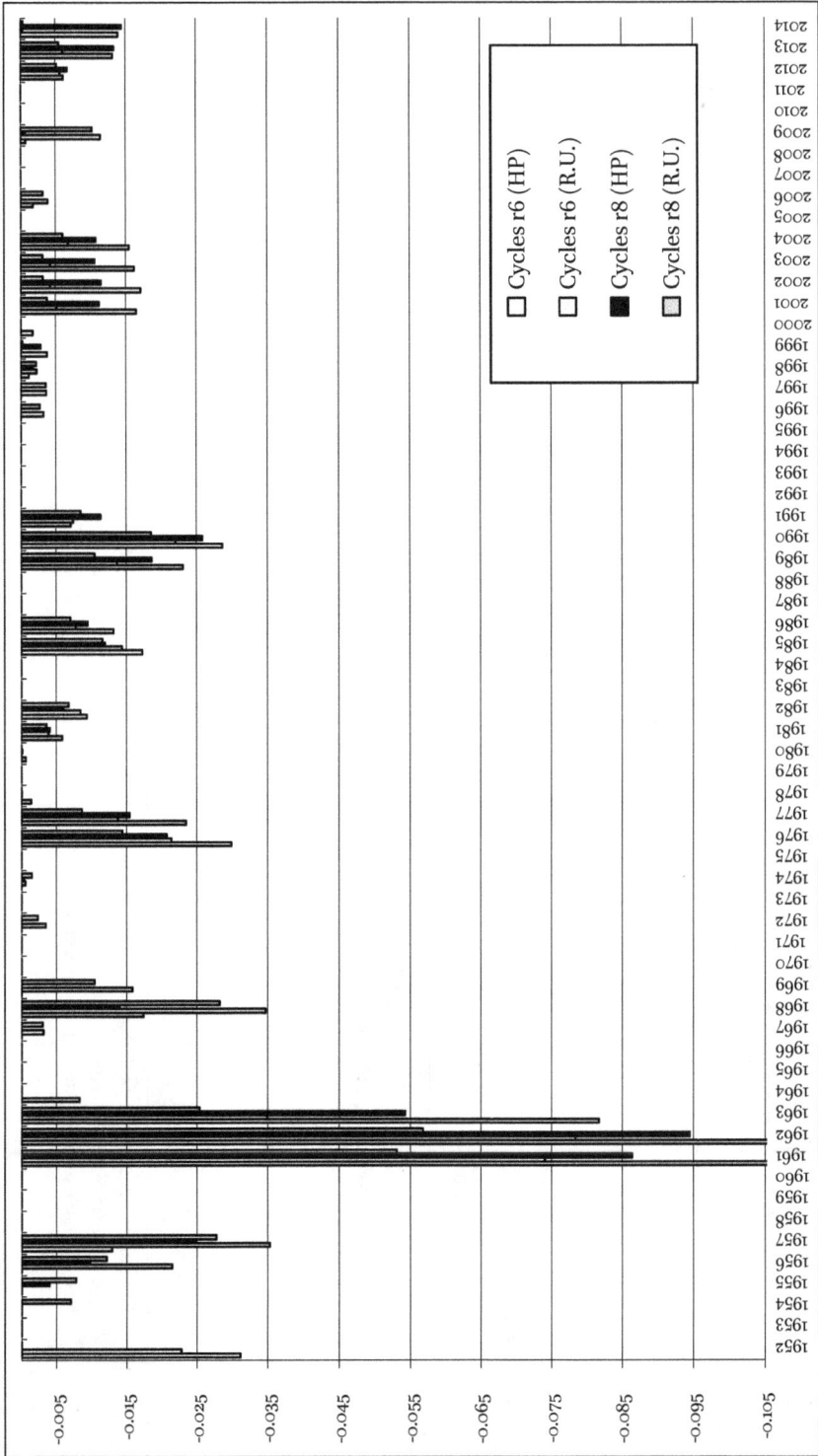

GRAPH 7.9 Negative values of the cyclical components of the macro profit rates r_6 and r_8; China, 1952–2014 (*in percentages* [$1 = 1952$])

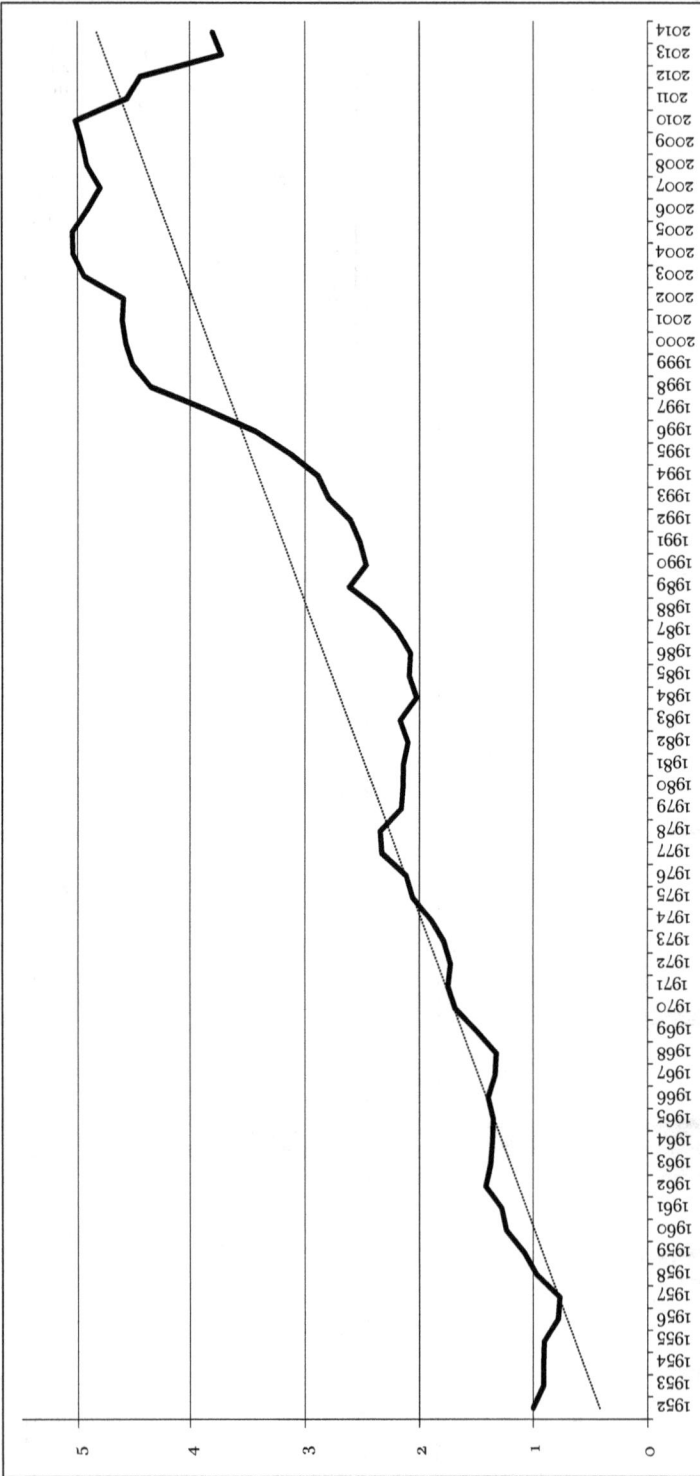

GRAPH 7.10   Organic composition of capital derived from an economic decomposition of r_8: China, 1952–2014 (*in indices* [1 = 1952])

Note: Variable presented with its linear trend.

stable, the upward trend of the productivity of the labour cost unit is slightly more pronounced – but the latter begins to decline over the last decade.

Based on a definition – as rigorous as possible – of the scope of the industrial sector, and the construction of original stocks of fixed assets of industrial enterprises (Appendix A.7.1.1), complementing the series of productive physical capital stocks presented in the first chapter of this book, we have calculated profit rate indicators for China at the micro- and macroeconomic levels from 1952 to 2014 (see respectively Appendix A.7.3.1 and Appendix A.7.3.2). The results obtained using the two alternative methods selected (micro/macro), are quite similar, and can be summarized as follows:

1)   a tendency of the rate of profit to fall is observed over the long period, for the two levels of analysis.

2)   The short-term fluctuations in profit rates exhibit, at the macroeconomic level, a succession of cycles – rarely completely achieved – whose range is decreasing with time.

3)   More than a third of the total period (1952–2014) is concerned with recessive years of the profit rate cyclical components.

4)   Regarding these cyclical components of the rate of profit, the largest declines are recorded, in descending order, after the rupture between China and the Soviet Union (1961–1963), during the Cultural Revolution (1968), in the course of the 1950s (especially in 1957), in the post-Mao transition (1976–1977), when a "neoliberal" experiment was attempted (1989–1991), and finally with the dissemination of the crises of capitalist globalization (which affected China in 1998, 2001 and 2009, then again after 2012). And

5)   it is essentially – much more than the evolutions of the profit share in value added and of the productivity of the labour cost unit – the increasing organic composition of capital that pushes the macroeconomic profit rate down tendentiously.

However, a number of difficulties of interpretation persist at the end of this exercise. First, it is the analysis of this decline in the profit rate itself that raises a problem, to the extent that this long-term trend does indeed find part of its explanation in the extreme scarcity of physical capital that characterized the People's Republic of China at the beginning of the revolution. In addition, over rather long periods of time, at the macroeconomic level, we can very distinctly observe intervals of relative stability in the industrial profit rates, or even phases of increases in these rates, as it was the case in the first half of the 1990s. The microeconomic analysis also highlights a clear recovery in profit rates, but from the end of the 1990s – until the moment when the country suffered the effects of the 2007–2008 global crisis. Such an increase in the profit rate at the microeconomic level since the end of the 1990s is not only due to State-owned enterprises' reforms. One of the explanations is also, very probably, the recent acceleration of China's integration into the global economy.[21] Indeed, its over-production problem has been eased by the opening of new outlets in external markets. Nevertheless, at the same time, this integration also involved the exposure of the Chinese economy to exogenous fluctuations, and its relative vulnerability to imported cycles, or even to crises, such as from 2007–2008 onwards. Thus, our conclusion of a long-term downward tendency in the profit rate must tolerate some nuances.

Moreover, and apart from the disturbances of the very first period of the Chinese revolution, the most notable gap between the trajectories of the micro- and macroeconomic profit rates can be observed after the adoption of the structural reforms (1978) – and of the tax reform (1984). The deep causes of such a discrepancy, which lasted until the late 2000s (i.e., until the outbreak of the most recent stage of the capitalist world systemic crisis in 2007–2008),[22] are to be found in differences in our angles of study – that is to say, also in the statistical sources used –, in the perimeters and contents of the industrial sector (for example, the scope of large industrial enterprises is changing at the microeconomic level and, in addition, it does not integrate small units of production which generally have higher rentability rates than those of registered large State-owned enterprises), but also in the indicators related to taxation. Furthermore, even if the gap previously noted between the micro- and macroeconomic levels seems to narrow when the effects of the world systemic crisis impact the Chinese economy at the end of the 2000s, once again directing downwards both the micro- and macroeconomic profit rates, the question remains of how to qualify recessive phenomena that negatively affect the rates of profit in overall economic contexts where very high GDP growth rates are recorded, as was still the case recently in China, even in 2015 – before the Covid-19 pandemic. The answers to these questions, as well as to those, among others, related to the functional forms that are able to translate as pertinently as possible the long-term trends and short-term fluctuations of China's economy, thus call for further research.

---

21   The export of Chinese capital has considerably increased from the very beginning of the 2000s. Added to this, China joined the World Trade Organization in 2001.

22   For a theoretical and political interpretation of the current systemic crisis (which is not only a "financial" one), from a Marxist perspective, see: Herrera (2014).

One of the main lessons to be drawn from this chapter concerning the future is that, beyond an impressive GDP growth rate of more than 10 percent over several decades, the Chinese economy is paradoxically not immunized against sudden short-term economic downturns or adverse cycles, and even, in relation to the transformations of its structures in the long term, against "crises" – as the severe disruptions in its stock markets during the Summer of 2015 have shown.

CHAPTER 8

Study on the Evolution of China's Economic Structure from 1952 to 2014: Analysis of the Role of Profit Rate by Impulse Response Functions

Debates about the nature of the Chinese economic system have sparked prolific – and controversial – literature. However, the great majority of these works take the form of essentially descriptive analyses, and few of them examine the issue from a modeling and/or statistical point of view. Even fewer studies grant the profit rate the place it deserves in the reflection. This chapter suggests emphasizing the crucial role of the profit rate in the economy and attempts to discuss its effects on some key macroeconomic variables. The basic postulate is that this concept can be used in the case of China as soon as its content and meaning are specified rigorously and adapted both to the complex specificities and to the transformations that have characterized this country since the 1950s. Though the current functioning of the Chinese system has many points in common with capitalism, the interpretation of its nature remains compatible with market socialism, or socialism with a market (Herrera and Long [2019c]).

Our purpose is to examine the changes in the structure of this economy from the very beginnings of the People's Republic of China to the present day. To do this, we first explain our method to calculate, from a database of physical capital stock that we have built previously, a profit rate for all economic sectors, taken as a whole. We then develop a system representative of the economy and, in stochastic process analysis, use structural vector autoregressive models (SVARs) to follow the evolution of its structures. Using impulse response functions, we estimate the influence of profit rate on different variables, namely the growth rates of investment, capital accumulation, and GDP. Then, we test whether various *a priori* restrictions hypotheses are verified or not over the entire period (1952–2014), taking into account the transformations that have occurred over these six decades. The impulse response functions are also calculated using a Bayesian approach. After that, we apply our econometric modeling to the forecast for the year 2015, i.e., one year beyond the limit of our sample. Finally, we draw conclusions about the evolution of the Chinese economic system in the long period.

1   Profit Rate Calculation

It is on the basis of our new series of productive physical capital that we calculate a profit rate (r) of this capital stock as the ratio of a surplus (Π) to the sum (K_T) of constant capital and variable capital:

$$r = \Pi/K_T \qquad (8.1)$$

where the surplus, or "profit," (Π), is written:

$$\Pi = Y - (R + B + T) \qquad (8.2)$$

that is to say, as the product (Y) minus the direct and indirect income of workers (R), all social welfare allowances from which they benefit (B), and taxes (T).
Total advanced capital K_T is then given by:

$$K_T = K + R + B \qquad (8.3)$$

The formula for calculating the total profit rate used (r) is, therefore:

$$r = \frac{Y - R + B + T}{K + (R + B)} \qquad (8.4)$$

We have chosen to mobilize here a total rate profit, calculated on the whole economy, rather than limiting ourselves only to industries. As we are interested in the influence of profit rate on macroscopic variables concerning all the sectors, this approach is justified – even if it is not necessarily the most common.
    To calculate r, we use data from different but homogeneous sources. We first use a series of GDP – defined according to the production approach – as published by the NBS (various years). Workers' direct and indirect income are provided by the same NBS yearbooks but according to a decomposition of GDP by the income approach. They include the total remuneration received by the workers, including in the form of bonuses and payments in kind. The series "total wage bills of employed persons in urban units" before 1978, "total earnings of employed persons in urban units" from 1995 to 2008, and "compensations of employees" after 2008 are selected. However, two corrections are introduced: one to minimize the bias due to the gap existing between the different GDP series (of approximately 5 percent on average between the national aggregate

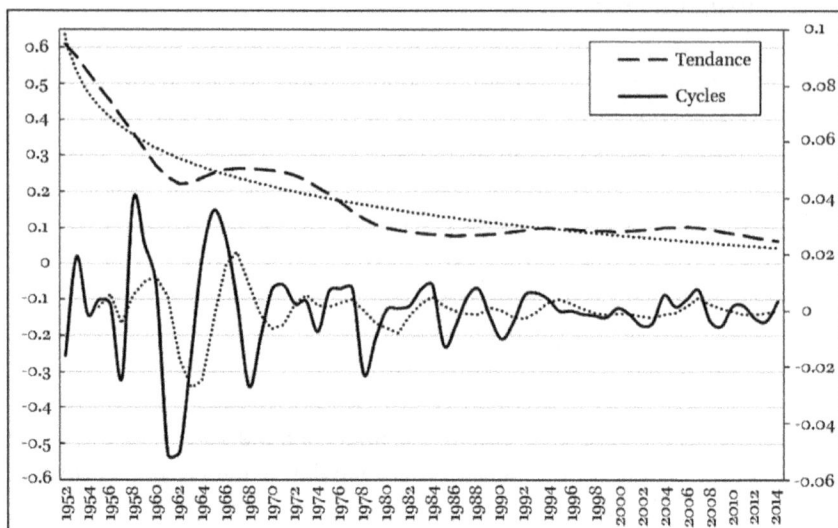

GRAPH 8.1   Profit rate decomposition into trend and cycles: China, 1952–2014
             Note: The scale on the left is that of the trend; and the scale on the right, that of
             cycles, with their five-year moving average.

and the sum of provincial GDP), and the other to take account of the modifications in the administrative map of the regions. Welfare allowances, considered as part of the production costs of enterprises, correspond not only to the
transfers of social security, pensions and unemployment benefits but also to
transport subsidies, housing aid, etc. This series has been reconstructed from
NBS data, supplemented by other sources (*China Labor and Wage Statistics* and
China Labor Yearbooks). Finally, *T* incorporates all taxations, including import
taxes. All data are expressed at 1952 constant prices, with the index being that
of consumer prices.

Graph 8.1 shows the trajectory of profit rate calculated thus for China from
1952 to 2014. As we can see, its trend is downward, with three fairly distinct
sub-periods: a fall is observed for three decades, up to the late 1970s, corresponding to the Maoist period; then comes a phase of slight recovery in the
profit rate, until the beginning of the 1990s, marked by an accentuation of the
reforms; finally, after a stabilization at a rather low level, there is a new phase
of decline from the 2007 crisis.

This downward trend in the profit rate over the long term is to be distinguished from short-term fluctuations. The profit rate statistical decomposition,
carried out by the H.-P. filter method (Hodrick and Prescott [1981]), reveals
oscillations with a certain regularity. The amplitude of these economic cycles

tends to decrease over time, but the frequency of their recurrence seems to be accelerating. The years for which the component of profit rate attributable to cycles, expressed in first differences, registers a negative value are equivalent to almost half of the number of observations over the whole sample (Herrera and Long [2017]).

2   Econometric Modeling Framework

Once these new statistical series have been presented, and the arguments for their reliability have been outlined, we propose to build a system representative of the economy to evaluate the impact of profit rate on three fundamental macroeconomic variables, in this case, the investment dynamics, capital accumulation, and GDP growth rate, with the aim of interpreting the changes in the economic structures during the period 1952–2014 studied. To achieve such a goal, vector autoregressive (VAR) modeling can provide an appropriate analytical framework. Here, methodologically, we select impulse response functions, which enable us to measure the effects produced by exogenous shocks in the profit rate on the various other variables of the system. Obviously, however, a simple VAR statistical model lacks theoretical foundations, and the coefficients of such an a-theoretical framework will lead to biased estimators due to the presence of bias in estimating the simultaneous equations' systems. As a consequence, the model will have to be constrained to make the system identifiable. Thus, we seek to build an SVAR model and to adequately determine the structure linking its macroscopic variables and satisfying the required identification conditions.

Thereafter, to explore these structural relationships, we proceed in three steps:

Step 1: First, we develop a multivariate VAR model, with which we test the coefficients that we have constrained, and then we calculate the impulse response functions of the various endogenous variables to profit rate shocks (r_t) in order to dynamically assess the impact of the profit rate on these variables $(I_t, K_t,$ and $Y_t,$ expressed in growth rate).

Step 2: Second, we establish bivariate VARs within the system, associating the profit rate and another variable. We test the variables two by two for Granger causality and then calculate the impulse response functions to analyze their links more precisely. The null hypothesis of this causality test is strong and quite delicate to verify on this structure, because it supposes the total exogeneity of the variable considered. If this were the case, we could impose several constraints on the VAR models. However, these results are sensitive to the order of lags, and the hypothesis used generally appears excessive, so it is difficult for us to reach the expected conclusions.

Step 3: Third, we can examine some of the structural interconnections between variables. On the basis of the preceding hypotheses and results, in accordance with economic theory (and logic), we can impose restrictions on the structure of the VARs to make the system identifiable. It is possible to estimate one (or more) SVAR model(s) and to find the economic structure to finally calculate the orthogonal impulse response functions of the variables to the innovation shocks of r_t, which will allow more reliable conclusions to be drawn about the role of the profit rate.

Problem: it appears from the correlograms and graphs corresponding to r_t that the profit rate time series is non-linear and non-stationary. Consequently, we need to choose an appropriate way to detrend it and thus work on a stationary series.

Several alternative methods are possible for such a transformation:

1) First, using an H.-P. filter, we can distinguish the long-term trend of r_t from its cyclical component, which appears to be stationary on average (Graph 8.1), while the heteroskedasticity could be treated by the Box-Cox transformation (Box and Cox [1964]).

2) The first difference of the series is stationary, which means that the variations in profit rate are stationary.

3) The first difference of the logarithm of r_t is also stationary; in other words, the growth rate of profit rate is itself stationary.

Let us see which detrended time series of profit rate constitutes the best solution here. The H.-P. filter method is not the most appropriate. By using the sole cycle component, only the effects of the periodic movements of r_t on the other variable will be highlighted. But the information provided by the downward trend in profit rate over the long term, which also turns out to be fundamental, would then escape analysis. In Graph 8.1, we observe that if the cycle component of r_t is effectively stationary on average, its fluctuations have the characteristics of a harmonic movement, which suggests that there may be a heteroskedasticity problem attached to this component. Therefore, we must have recourse to another method, of the Box-Cox transformation type, to overcome this difficulty. It is further understood that the expression of r_t in growth rate will provide more information than in variations. The same variation of +1 percent in the rate of profit will have very different effects on the economy and the behavior of agents depending on the configuration in which it operates (for example, from 10 to 11 percent or from –1 to 0 percent, asking the question of situations of loss or surplus, absolutely crucial for the production processes). Thus, we use the first difference of the log of r_t (logarithm that exists over the entire sample, as r_t always has a positive value), that is, the growth rate of the profit rate Gr_t.

Therefore, we seek to econometrically estimate the following dynamic structural model:

$$B_0 y_t = c + B_1 y_{t-1} + B_2 y_{t-2} + \ldots + B_p y_{t-p} + u_t \qquad (8.5)$$

where the system variable y_t, the structural shocks u_t, the matrix B_0 (with terms of the main diagonal normalized to 1) and the vector of constants c are written as, respectively:

$$y_t = (Gr_t, GI_t, GK_t, GY_t)' \qquad (8.6)$$

$$u_t = (u_t^r, u_t^I, u_t^K, u_t^Y)' \qquad (8.7)$$

$$B_0 = \begin{bmatrix} 1 & -\beta_{12}^{(0)} & -\beta_{13}^{(0)} & -\beta_{14}^{(0)} \\ -\beta_{21}^{(0)} & 1 & -\beta_{23}^{(0)} & -\beta_{24}^{(0)} \\ -\beta_{31}^{(0)} & -\beta_{32}^{(0)} & 1 & -\beta_{34}^{(0)} \\ -\beta_{41}^{(0)} & -\beta_{42}^{(0)} & -\beta_{43}^{(0)} & 1 \end{bmatrix} \qquad (8.8)$$

$$c = (c_1, c_2, c_3, c_4)' \qquad (8.9)$$

B_p being a (4×4) matrix, where the element of line i and column j is noted $\beta_{ij}^{(s)} = 1, 2, \ldots, p$.

We assume a lag p large enough for u_t to be a vectorial white noise:

$$E\left(u_t u_t'\right) = \begin{cases} D, & f \text{ or } t = t \\ 0, & \text{in all other cases} \end{cases} \qquad (8.10)$$

Therefore, in this framework, it will be a question of calculating the impulse response functions:

$$\frac{\partial y_{t+s}}{\partial u_t^r} \qquad (8.11)$$

which will allow to measure the effects of a deviation of an innovation unit impulsed by the growth rate of r_t at time t (u_t^r) on the values of the system variable in $t + s$ (y_{t+s}), keeping the other innovations constant at all times.

Let us reformulate the proposed system in a reduced form, like the following VAR model:

$$y_t = \Pi' x_t + \varepsilon_t \qquad (8.12)$$

with

$$\Pi' \equiv -B_0^{-1} \begin{bmatrix} c & B_1 & B_2 & \cdots & B_p \end{bmatrix} \qquad (8.13)$$

$$x_t \equiv \begin{pmatrix} 1 & y'_{t-1} & y'_{t-2} & \cdots & y'_{t-p} \end{pmatrix}' \qquad (8.14)$$

$$\varepsilon_t \equiv -B_0^{-1} u_t \qquad (8.15)$$

$$\Omega = E(\varepsilon_t \varepsilon_t') \qquad (8.16)$$

The SVAR identification conditions are relatively complicated to satisfy, because it is necessary here to collect the parameters to be estimated in B_0 as a $(n_B \times 1)$ vector θ_B and those in D as a $(n_D \times 1)$ vector θ_D.

The system is identifiable if both conditions are met:

1) Order condition:

$$n(n+1)/2 \geq n_B + n_D \qquad (8.17)$$

where n is the number of system variables. This assumes that there are at least as many constraints as parameters in the structural matrix.

2) Rank condition:

$$\text{rank}(J'J) = n_B + n_D \qquad (8.18)$$

where

$$J = \left(\frac{\partial \text{vech}(\Omega)}{\partial \theta_B'} \quad \frac{\partial \text{vech}(\Omega)}{\partial \theta_D'} \right) \qquad (8.19)$$

Thus, J must be linearly independent in column, which requires that the maximum likelihood estimator (MLE) is unique (local maximum). Giannini (1992) provided a numerical algorithm for verifying the rank condition for J.

Identification can be performed by means of short-term constraints – the most commonly used, and which, here, will result in the imposition of *a priori* restrictions on the structure of B_0 – or in the long term (we will come back to this later). As we know, such restrictions arouse criticism of SVAR models. Often, however, the assumptions required to meet the identification conditions are difficult to defend and lack a solid theoretical foundation. In addition to this, as we want to calculate impulse response functions, we also need to evaluate their standard errors.

Nevertheless, Runkle (1987) and Lütkepohl (1990) have shown that the precision of the standard errors of such functions based on VARs is frequently of bad quality. Therefore, formalization and the successive steps that we suggest aim to offer both reliable restrictions and as few parameters as possible in order to increase this precision.

A possible improvement would consist of ordering the variables within y_t to make the matrix B_0 lower triangular, so that the system can be identified. We would then simply need to estimate the MLE of the unconstrained VAR model, and then decompose the matrix of the covariances of the VAR residuals, Ω, according to:

$$\Omega = ADA' \qquad (8.20)$$

The uniqueness of this orthogonal decomposition – Giannini (1992) using Cholesky's (1910) factorization: $\Omega = PP'$ – would then lead to: $A \equiv B_0^{-1}$. This would make it possible to obtain the estimators of the dynamic structural model. Such an ordering seems possible.

By noting $Z_t = \{Gr_{t-1}, ..., Gr_{t-p}; GI_{t-1}, ..., GI_{t-p}; GK_{t-1}, ..., GK_{t-p}; GY_{t-1}, ..., GY_{t-p}\}$ all past information available at time t until lag p, let us consider four alternative hypotheses:

H_1: The producers will anticipate what the future profit rate will be based on the past, that is to say that Gr_t can be written as a linear projection of past useful information:

$$Gr_t \equiv \hat{E}(Gr_t | Z_t)$$
$$= c_1 + \beta_{11}^{(1)} Gr_{t-1} + \beta_{11}^{(2)} Gr_{t-2} + ... + \beta_{11}^{(p)} Gr_{t-p}$$
$$+ \beta_{12}^{(1)} GI_{t-1} + \beta_{12}^{(2)} GI_{t-2} + ... + \beta_{12}^{(p)} GI_{t-p}$$
$$+ \beta_{13}^{(1)} GK_{t-1} + \beta_{13}^{(2)} GK_{t-2} + ... + \beta_{13}^{(p)} GK_{t-p}$$
$$+ \beta_{14}^{(1)} GY_{t-1} + \beta_{14}^{(2)} GY_{t-2} + ... + \beta_{14}^{(p)} GY_{t-p} + u_t^r \qquad (8.21)$$

In other words, we set the restrictions:

$$-\beta_{12}^{(0)} = -\beta_{13}^{(0)} = -\beta_{14}^{(0)} = 0 \qquad (8.22)$$

H_2: In this case, the producers determine their investment behavior based on their expectations of the future profit rate, as well as on past information:

$$GI_t \equiv \hat{E}\left(GI_t | Gr_t, Z_t\right)$$
$$= c_2 + \beta_{21}^{(0)}Gr_t + \beta_{21}^{(1)}Gr_{t-1} + \beta_{21}^{(2)}Gr_{t-2} + \ldots + \beta_{21}^{(p)}Gr_{t-p}$$
$$+ \beta_{22}^{(1)}GI_{t-1} + \beta_{22}^{(2)}GI_{t-2} + \ldots + \beta_{22}^{(p)}GI_{t-p}$$
$$+ \beta_{23}^{(1)}GK_{t-1} + \beta_{23}^{(2)}GK_{t-2} + \ldots + \beta_{23}^{(p)}GK_{t-p}$$
$$+ \beta_{24}^{(1)}GY_{t-1} + \beta_{24}^{(2)}GY_{t-2} + \ldots + \beta_{24}^{(p)}GY_{t-p} + u_t^I \qquad (8.23)$$

Thus, the constraints this time are only:

$$-\beta_{23}^{(0)} = -\beta_{24}^{(0)} = 0 \qquad (8.24)$$

H_3: The producer's investment for year t will determine the level of capital stock for that same year t, as suggested by the key PIM equation:

$$GK_t \equiv \hat{E}\left(GK_t | GI_t, Gr_t, Z_t\right)$$
$$= c_3 + \beta_{31}^{(0)}Gr_t + \beta_{31}^{(1)}Gr_{t-1} + \beta_{31}^{(2)}Gr_{t-2} + \ldots + \beta_{31}^{(p)}Gr_{t-p}$$
$$+ \beta_{32}^{(0)}GI_t + \beta_{32}^{(1)}GI_{t-1} + \beta_{32}^{(2)}GI_{t-2} + \ldots + \beta_{32}^{(p)}GI_{t-p}$$
$$+ \beta_{33}^{(1)}GK_{t-1} + \beta_{33}^{(2)}GK_{t-2} + \ldots + \beta_{33}^{(p)}GK_{t-p}$$
$$+ \beta_{34}^{(1)}GY_{t-1} + \beta_{34}^{(2)}GY_{t-2} + \ldots + \beta_{34}^{(p)}GY_{t-p} + u_t^K \qquad (8.25)$$

the only restriction imposed being:

$$-\beta_{34}^{(0)} = 0 \qquad (8.26)$$

H_4: Classically, the level of capital stock determines the level of production. If there is enough labour supply available, more capital will mean that more labour can create more value.

$$GY_t \equiv \hat{E}\left(GY_t | GK_t, GI_t, Gr_t, Z_t\right)$$

$$= c_4 + \beta_{41}^{(o)} Gr_t + \beta_{41}^{(1)} Gr_{t-1} + \beta_{41}^{(2)} Gr_{t-2} + \ldots + \beta_{41}^{(p)} Gr_{t-p}$$

$$+ \beta_{42}^{(o)} GI_t + \beta_{42}^{(1)} GI_{t-1} + \beta_{42}^{(2)} GI_{t-2} + \ldots + \beta_{42}^{(p)} GI_{t-p}$$

$$+ \beta_{43}^{(o)} GK_t + \beta_{43}^{(1)} GK_{t-1} + \beta_{43}^{(2)} GK_{t-2} + \ldots + \beta_{43}^{(p)} GK_{t-p}$$

$$+ \beta_{44}^{(1)} GY_{t-1} + \beta_{44}^{(2)} GY_{t-2} + \ldots + \beta_{44}^{(p)} GY_{t-p} + u_t^Y \qquad (8.27)$$

So, we assume a set of identification restrictions recursively. Before applying them to SVAR models, let us test these constraints by estimating beforehand the unrestricted dynamic system (8.6), or its reduced form in unrestricted VAR model (8.13), and then let us check if the following equation is validated:

$$-\beta_{12}^{(o)} = -\beta_{13}^{(o)} = -\beta_{14}^{(o)} = -\beta_{23}^{(o)} = -\beta_{24}^{(o)} = -\beta_{34}^{(o)} = 0 \qquad (8.28)$$

3 Empirical Estimations

3.1 Wald Tests in Unrestricted Dynamic System

For this, we perform a Wald test, after determining the order of the lags in the reduced form, i.e., the p value of the unrestricted VAR(p) model. For a maximum lag fixed at 5 years (equivalent to an electoral cycle), the information criteria give the optimal lags:

TABLE 8.1   Optimal lags by information criteria on unrestricted VAR(p)

	LR	FPE	AIC	SC	HQ
Lag	3	3	5	1	1

Notes: LR = modified sequential likelihood-ratio test statistic (at the 5 percent level); FPE = final prediction error; AIC, SC and HQ = information criteria, respectively, of Akaike, Schwarz, and Hannan-Quinn.

TABLE 8.2   LM tests for residuals' series correlation on unrestricted VAR(p)

h	VAR(1)	VAR(2)	VAR(3)
1	0.0106	0.0751	0.8019
2	0.0380	0.0479	0.4998
3	0.0402	0.1098	0.3946
4	0.5528	0.6092	0.4983
5	0.0867	0.2855	0.3588
6	0.8125	0.2641	0.1022
7	0.4149	0.0861	0.0688
8	0.6191	0.7269	0.8652
9	0.2566	0.5209	0.4917
10	0.9123	0.4376	0.9075

Note: Probability of null hypothesis = absence of correlation of the series with the lag order h.

TABLE 8.3   Wald test for the restrictions in VAR(3)

Test statistic	Value	DF	Probability
Chi^2	470.4833	6	0.0000

The Lagrange multiplier (LM) tests show that until a lag $p = 3$, there is no correlation in the series of VAR model residuals. Therefore, it follows that p = 3. Nevertheless, in the estimation of the unrestricted dynamic system, the Wald test rejects the null hypothesis of short-term constraints:

$$H_0 : -\beta_{12}^{(0)} = -\beta_{13}^{(0)} = -\beta_{14}^{(0)} = -\beta_{23}^{(0)} = -\beta_{24}^{(0)} = -\beta_{34}^{(0)} = 0$$

This result is not surprising. As the unrestricted dynamic system is an a-theoretical statistical model, a problem of potential endogeneity could lead to biased coefficients and, thus, to unreliable Wald test results. Added to this, the structure chosen incorporates only four variables, whereas the real economy turns out to be infinitely more complex. The innovations contain the influences of other omitted variables. So, our quadrivariate structure is only a part of an unknown system. Therefore, it is preferable to test the corresponding restrictions in a bivariate setting.

Several methods are available to us. One is based on this unrestricted quadrivariate dynamic system, but the order of the variables of y_t is changed to make the new form of B_0 lower triangular. The other uses the same restrictions' hypotheses, but uses them to test bivariate VARs, the arguments for which are sought by retaining only bilateral relationships and by ruling out the effects of other variables.

To begin with, let us follow the first method. The t tests show that the form of B_0 looks like this:

$$B_0 = \begin{pmatrix} 1 & o & o & X \\ o & 1 & X & o \\ o & X & 1 & o \\ X & o & o & 1 \end{pmatrix} \qquad (8.29)$$

where X indicates a significant coefficient (at 5 percent) and o that we cannot reject the null hypothesis according to which the coefficient located in this place is zero.

We immediately understand that this matrix represents an analytically non-identifiable system, because if we suppose that the MLE $\hat{\Pi}$ is found, then the maximum value of the log-likelihood function should be:

$$\mathcal{L}\left(B_0, D, \hat{\Pi}\right) = -\left(T/2\right)\log\left(2\pi\right) + \left(T/2\right)\log\left|B_0\right|^2 - \left(T/2\right)\log\left|D\right|$$
$$- \left(T/2\right)trace\left\{\left(B_0'D^{-1}B_0\right)\hat{\Omega}\right\} \qquad (8.30)$$

Assuming that the matrix B_0 is such that:

$$B_0 = \begin{pmatrix} 1 & o & o & a \\ o & 1 & b & o \\ o & c & 1 & o \\ d & o & o & 1 \end{pmatrix} \qquad (8.31)$$

we will get:

$$|B_0| = abcd - ad \qquad (8.32)$$

We can note here that the elements a and d are strictly equivalent: if we modify their positions, the determinant of B_0 remains unchanged. Therefore, there are at least two different forms of B_0 that lead to the same maximum value $\mathcal{L}(B_0, D, \hat{\Pi})$, and it is not possible to distinguish them by the same probability of distribution of data. As a consequence, the model is not identifiable. Hence, the relevance of carrying out short-term restrictions tests in bivariate systems is confirmed.

3.2   *Granger Causality Tests and Wald Tests in Bivariate* VAR *Models*

It might be inappropriate to estimate these restrictions by Granger causality tests because short-term constraints only require that B_0 be a lower triangular matrix. However, the null hypothesis of these tests assumes that in given bivariate VARs, the matrices B_0, B_1, ..., B_p are all of lower triangular shapes. These are singularly radical ways of seeking restrictions and are, moreover, very sensitive to the lag order, which can lead to contradictory conclusions. As can be seen, however, Granger causality tests provide little useful information. Consequently, we try to test equation (*8.28*) on the respective bivariate VARs. Mobilizing our four variables, we establish the unrestricted bivariate dynamic systems with $C_4^2 = 6$, and then we test the corresponding restrictions in each system by Wald tests.

TABLE 8.4   Granger causality tests *p*-values for pairwise bivariate VARs

Null hypothesis	Lag = 1	Lag = 2	Lag = 3	Lag = 4	Lag = 5	Conclusio
GI does not Granger-cause Gr	0.2730	0.1650	0.0442	0.0102	0.0279	H_0 rejecte
Gr does not Granger-cause GI	0.0101	0.0826	0.6387	0.6632	0.7155	H_0 accept
GK does not Granger-cause Gr	0.0040	0.0139	0.0321	0.0171	0.0303	H_0 rejecte
Gr does not Granger-cause GK	0.0047	0.3755	0.1914	0.3536	0.3251	H_0 accept
GY does not Granger-cause Gr	0.2796	0.5077	0.0706	0.0917	0.1458	H_0 accept
Gr does not Granger-cause GY	0.1864	0.7499	0.9188	0.5913	0.7224	H_0 accept
GK does not Granger-cause GI	0.0013	0.0004	0.1587	0.2605	0.0138	H_0 accept
GI does not Granger-cause GK	0.0006	0.2018	0.0014	0.0015	0.0001	H_0 rejecte
GY does not Granger-cause GI	0.0018	0.0031	0.4328	0.1628	0.1848	H_0 accept
GI does not Granger-cause GY	0.2484	0.1335	0.1019	0.0055	0.0156	H_0 accept
GY does not Granger-cause GK	2.00^{E-05}	0.2145	0.0051	0.0050	0.0162	H_0 rejecte
GK does not Granger-cause GY	0.0007	0.0481	0.0441	0.0170	0.0703	H_0 rejecte

TABLE 8.5   Wald tests on the constraints of bivariate VAR models

Null hypothesis	Bivariate system variables	Lags								Wald test p-values
		Information criteria					Test of lag exclusion	Tests LM	Final p used	
		LR	FPE	AIC	SC	HQ				
$-\beta_{12}^{(0)}=0$	Gr, GI	2	3	3	1	2	1	2	2	0.0281
$-\beta_{13}^{(0)}=0$	Gr, GK	2	2	2	1	2	1	2	2	0.1283
$-\beta_{14}^{(0)}=0$	Gr, GY	1	2	2	1	2	1	2	2	0.0000
$-\beta_{23}^{(0)}=0$	GI, GK	5	5	5	3	3	3	3	3	0.0000
$-\beta_{24}^{(0)}=0$	GI, GY	2	3	3	2	2	3	3	3	0.0000
$-\beta_{34}^{(0)}=0$	GK, GY	3	3	4	1	1	1	3	3	0.0000

Notes: 1) The results of the lag exclusion tests keep the significant common minimum lag, while the maximum lag is fixed at 5. 2) The results of the LM tests keep the minimum lag for which there is no correlation in the series of residuals up to a lag of 12.

The forms taken by the bivariate dynamic systems appear far from our expectations. The variables Gr and GY on date t influence each other, as also do GI and GK, mutually. If the PIM equation offers an interpretation, this does not mean that K determines I. As a matter of fact, the PIM (equation [1.1] in Chapter 1) can be rewritten as:

$$I_t/P_t = K_t - (1 - \sigma)K_{t-1} \qquad (8.33)$$

so that K_t then "determines" I_t on the same date. Here is a formal representation, though it is illogical, because it is investment that determines the level of capital stock and not the reverse. The rate of capital accumulation should rather be taken as a forward-looking indicator of the investment dynamic: the expectation of a faster accumulation rate then leads to more savings intended to be invested and, consequently, to an accelerated investment growth rate. In other words, the rate of capital accumulation in t could be useful in forecasting (and not "determining") the current or contemporary growth rate of investment.

3.3   *Conditions of the Long-Term Constraints*

Faced with this difficulty in identifying the system by the use of short-term restrictions, we now turn to long-term constraints, in the manner of either Blanchard and Quah (1989) or Blanchard and Diamond (1990), whose method is based on the properties of impulse responses: the cumulated response (over the period considered) of the *i-th* variable to the *j-th* structural shock will be zero in the long term. This means that we test $c_{i,j} = 0$, where $c_{i,j}$ is the element of row i and column j in matrix C, the latter being defined as:

$$C = \Psi'_\infty B_0^{-1} D^{1/2} \qquad (8.34)$$

Using Cholesky decomposition ($C = \Psi\infty P$), this matrix C with long-term restrictions is lower triangular, as was the matrix B_0 with short-term restrictions – the two matrices thus having to give the same impulse response functions.

In this context, testing the previous *a priori* restrictions will now amount to checking whether:

$$c_{1,2} = c_{1,3} = c_{1,4} = c_{2,3} = c_{2,4} = c_{3,4} = 0 \qquad (8.35)$$

We define the long term as the largest possible number of observations on the sample of 63 years studied, and we calculate the impulse responses functions up to 30 years to examine the long-term restrictions' conditions. If zero is always within the 95 percent confidence interval in the impulse response functions over 10–30 years, we conclude that the long-term constraints are validated. For these calculations, we use the generalized impulses due to Pesaran and Shin (1998). Their main advantage is that they do not make innovations depend on VAR ordering. We obtain the following structure of C:

$$C = \begin{pmatrix} X & 0 & 0 & a \\ 0 & X & ? & ? \\ 0 & X & X & X \\ 0 & 0 & 0 & X \end{pmatrix} \qquad (8.36)$$

where *?* indicates that even if zero is within the 95 percent confidence interval over 10–30 years, the zero on the horizontal axis is very close to the limit tolerated by the confidence interval (see Graph 8.2 to Graph 8.17).

If relatively large standard errors of the impulses are taken into account, then it can be seen that the equality $c_{2,3} = c_{2,4} = 0$ will be exposed to wide

Accumulated Response to Generalized One S.D. Innovations ?2 S.E.

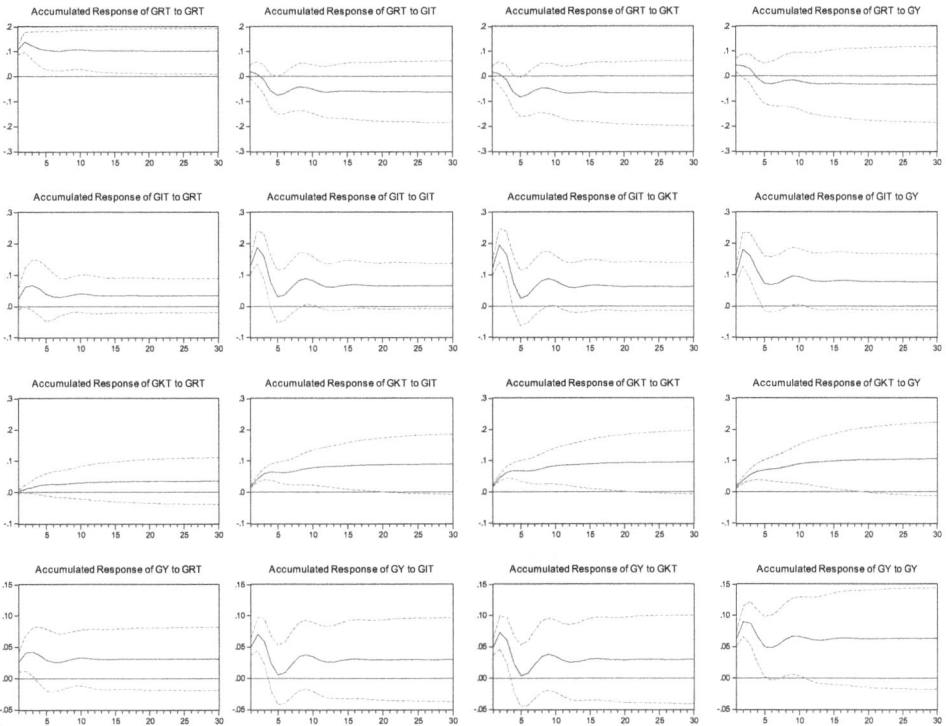

GRAPHS 8.2–17   Cumulated responses to generalized impulses produced by a standard deviation of the respective innovation

uncertainty. If we constrain these elements to be equal to zero, the model will be over-identified (because, to satisfy the order condition, we need to restrict only six coefficients to zero) and we will then get the same impulses as with a matrix C constrained to be lower triangular. Nevertheless, releasing the restriction $c_{2,3} = 0$ would make the model unidentifiable (its rank condition no longer being satisfied), but still would go against economic theory (investment determining capital, for sure). Consequently, this leads us to an over-identification of the model, which is likely to increase the precision of the estimates – a just identified system, with a single solution, having a low probability. Although this overidentified model provides useful information, the likelihood-ratio test (LR) reveals that an excess of constraints is not validated (Table 8.6).

TABLE 8.6   LR test for over-identification

Chi^2(3)	Probability
22.17044	0.0001

Note: The null hypothesis is that excessive constraints are validated.

We argue that the main cause of the difficulty encountered in validating both short-term and long-term restrictions lies in the variability over time of the structure of the economy under study – in formalized terms, in the instability characterizing the matrices B_0 and C. As a matter of fact, major institutional changes have upset China's economic system, so the restrictions imposed *a priori* could be accepted over one period, but not over another one. By instance: the assumption that Chinese enterprises' investment behavior obeys profit rate expectations seems a reasonable hypothesis in a market economy, that is, after the reforms opening up China to market mechanisms, but not in a planned economy, where producers decide not only on the basis of this rate – which will no longer be, at least temporarily, the decisive argument for investment – but also and above all according to the choices made by the political leaders. The latter, faced with a slowdown in activity, will have to promote new investments to stimulate GDP growth, which will thus become a forward-looking indicator of the investment growth rate ($\beta_{24}^{(0)} \neq 0$). Such changes in economic structure over time can be understood either by periodizing the trajectory of the Chinese economy since 1952 or through the introduction of dummy variables of institutional changes.

3.4   *Institutional Dummies and Periodization*

Graph 8.18 provides several important lessons, that we can synthetize in three points:

1)   Before 1978 (i.e., the year of the launch of the reforms, under the impetus of Deng Xiaoping), the extreme values of *Gr* and *GY* can be observed on the same dates, which indicates that these variables have simultaneous influences on each other.

2)   From 1978 to 1993 (the latest date on which, in addition to a change in the national accounts system, a very important tax reform, initiated by Prime Minister Zhu Rongji, occurred that redefined the modalities of the distribution of tax revenues between central and local governments, as well as the governments' respective fiscal responsibilities), the extremums of *Gr* follow those of *GY*.

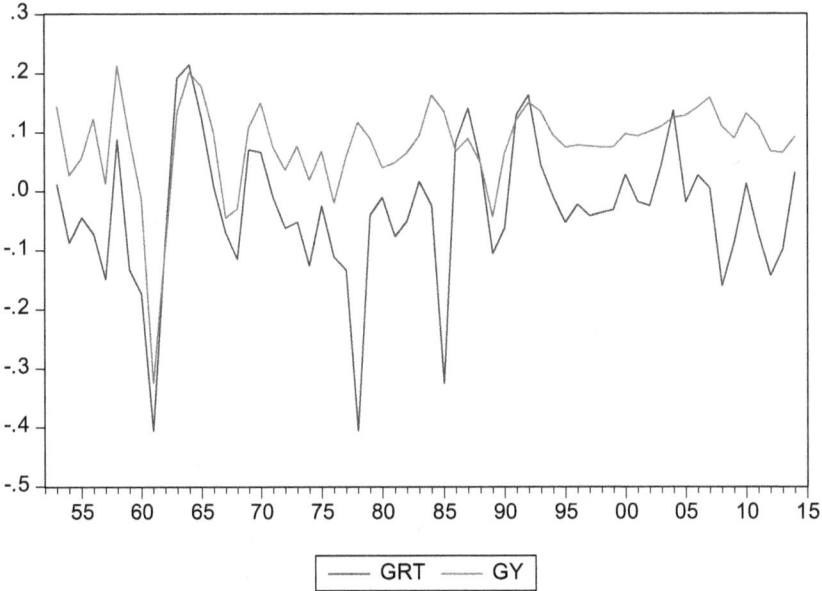

GRAPH 8.18   Changes in *Gr* and *GY* in China over the period 1952–2014

3)   After 1993, the extremums and movements of *Gr* precede those of *GY*,
      which corresponds to the features of a market economy – and, much
      more adequately, to the *a priori* constraints' hypotheses adopted. We are
      dealing with distinct economic structures, which need to be analyzed
      period by period. If the economic opening began in 1978, the period
      1978–1992 still seems to be comparable to that of the planned economy.
      Therefore, it would only be after the 1993 tax reform that China began to
      undergo its profound transformation, turning its economy more toward
      market mechanisms.

Let us first look at whether exogenous dummies would improve the examination of structures, so that the restrictions' hypotheses could be better met in a
market economy.

$$B_0 y_t = c + d_t + B_1 y_{t-1} + B_2 y_{t-2} + \dots + B_p y_{t-p} + u_t \qquad (8.37)$$

The results of the tests carried out allow us to answer in the affirmative. To
take into account the time evolution of B_0, a dummy is insufficient. We should
estimate the model:

$$[B_0^{(1)}(I - D) + B_0^{(2)} D] y_t = \Gamma y_t + u_t \qquad (8.38)$$

where

$$D = \begin{cases} 0 & \text{over period 1} \\ 1 & \text{over period 2} \end{cases} \qquad (8.39)$$

As long as the sub-samples have enough observation points, we can distinguish several periods, at least three. We think indeed that the structures of B_0 differ according to those of the economy:

$$B_0 = \begin{cases} B_0^{(1)} & \text{over period 1} \\ B_0^{(2)} & \text{over period 2} \end{cases} \qquad (8.40)$$

If the matrix B_0 can evolve over time, Γ should be assumed to be able to adopt a specific matrix form per period. This amounts to estimating SVAR models also for each period. Nevertheless, if there are many sub-periods, and if p is large, the number of parameters will increase sharply, and the size of our sample may not be sufficient to estimate as many. The resolution of this problem recommends that:

1)   the number of sub-periods should be as limited as possible;
2)   the lags should also be few, if the residuals are white noises; and
3)   we should use a Bayesian approach for each of the sub-samples to increase the precision of the estimators.

We first consider three dummies: d_1, equal to 1 from 1952 to 1977 and to 0 in the other years, representing the era of planned economy; d_2, which is equal to 1 from 1978 to 1992 and 0 otherwise, for the transition; and d_3, fixed at equaling 1 from 1993 to 2014 and 0 otherwise, corresponding to the period of market economy. Obviously, these variables are linearly dependent and cannot be used in the same regression. Then, compacting two of them and removing the constant term, we redefine two dummies that could be present together: du_1, posed as being equal to 0 from 1952 to 1977 and to 1 otherwise, indicating that the periods differ before and after 1978; and du_2, equal to 0 from 1952 to 1992 and to 1 between 1993 and 2014, marking the distinction between the before and after tax reforms of 1993. We use a stepwise method to find the equivalent combinations by fusion, allowing us to obtain the maximum R^2 in VAR(3) model, and check if the long-term constraints are validated (Table 8.7). It is expected that once the dummies are introduced, the R^2 and the log-likelihood will increase, the determinant of residuals' covariance will decrease, and the AIC and SIC information criteria will be weaker. If this is the case, then we can say that the exogenous dummies have improved the estimates.

TABLE 8.7   Results of VAR(3) model estimates with exogenous dummies

Exogenous terms	c	(c, d_1) / (c, du_1)	(c, d_2)	(c, d_3) / (c, du_2)	(c, d_2, d_3) / (c, du_1, du_2) / (d_1, d_2, d_3) / (c, d_1, d_3)
Average R^2	0.5635	0.5752	0.5648	0.5861	0.5904
Lowest R^2	0.3817	0.3939	0.3836	0.4182	0.4205
Determinant resid covariance (dof adj.)	7.07^{E-012}	6.15^{E-012}	7.45^{E-012}	6.37^{E-012}	6.02^{E-012}
Log-likelihood	451.9258	458.6055	452.9472	457.5917	461.9242
AIC	−13.5568	−13.6476	−13.4558	−13.6133	−13.6246
SIC	−11.7258	−11.6757	−11.4839	−11.6414	−11.5118
Test LM	Accepted	Accepted	Accepted	Accepted	Accepted
Structure of C	$X o o o$ $o X ? ?$ $o X X X$ $o o o X$	$X o o o$ $o X ? ?$ $o X X X$ $? o o X$	$X o o o$ $o X ? ?$ $o X X X$ $o o o X$	$X o o o$ $o X ? ?$ $o X X X$ $o o o X$	$X o o o$ $o X ? ?$ $o X X X$ $o o o X$
Identification	over-identified if $c_{2,4} = 0$; if not, unidentified	over-identified if $c_{2,4} = 0$; if not, unidentified	over-identified if $c_{2,4} = 0$; if not, unidentified	over-identified if $c_{2,4} = 0$; if not, unidentified	over-identified if $c_{2,4} = 0$; if not, unidentified

Notes: Average R^2 of the four equations. H_0 of the LM test: no autocorrelation of the residuals until a lag of 12.

Several remarks on the results of Table 8.7. First, the R^2 of systems with dummies, whatever the number and combinations of variables, are higher than are those of regressions without a dummy, which means that these institutional indicators have efficiently improved our models. Then, the more dummies there are, the sharper the rise in R^2, suggesting not only that each period is relatively independent and has its own characteristics, but also that our chronological division is rather successful. However, the integration of d_2 does not provide a clear improvement, which means that even if the intermediate period (1978–1992) stands out from the others, it is closer to that of the preceding planned economy. Therefore, to limit the number of estimated parameters, we will limit the number of periods by merging the first two into an extended one (from 1952 to 1992) under the name of a planned economy with Chinese characteristics or with "the market in supplement." Finally, according to the form of C, the economic structure is stable, but the condition for identification remains: $c_{2,4} = 0$. Our intuition was well founded. When the Chinese political leaders observed some slowdowns in economic activity, they may have been led to accelerate the pace of investment. The hypotheses of *a priori* restrictions relating to the period of market economy are not verified: we have: $c_{2,4} \neq 0$. The impact of GDP growth rate on investment dynamics is not found to be zero in the long term. Thus, the system is not identifiable. We can only apply the *a priori* assumptions to the 1993–2014 period, that of the transition to a market economy. We see that if we take only this period into account, the sample size decreases sharply (from 61 to 22 points). On this sample, if the model is just identified, we use 88 points to estimate $4 \times (4p + 1) + 10$ parameters. The lags should not then exceed 4. The optimal lag found at 3 satisfies this condition. However, the large number of parameters casts doubt on our empirical exercise. Would the estimates be more precise with a Bayesian approach?

3.5   *Bayesian Analysis and Sub-periodization (1993–2014)*

Bayesian analysis requires a distribution of probability of parameters beforehand. We have two choices: the first is to directly use the information from 1952 to 1992 as a pre-sampling, and then to estimate BVARs between 1993 and 2014; the second is to mobilize a certain type of *a priori* specifications, as in either Litterman (1986) or Sims and Zha (1998). Both of these methods have their drawbacks. If the periods before and after 1993 are of a different nature, it seems to be unreasonable to use information collected during the period of planned economy as a pre-sampling intended to estimate the structure characterizing a market economy. Besides, these specifications require to consider that the parameters have a singular probability distribution. The success of the Bayesian analysis depends on whether the chosen distribution is close to "reality." There is still room for some adhocity. According to Litterman (1986), the *a priori* specification makes it impossible to predict changes in variables (the first difference of a variable being white noise, constant included):

$$y_t - y_{t-1} = c + \varepsilon_t \qquad (8.41)$$

where ε_t is not correlated with the lagged values of any of the variables.

This amounts to assuming that the markets are in perfect competition and that the growth rates of r_t, I_t, K_t, and Y_t follow random walks. In this configuration, predicting changes in Gr seems impossible. Such an assumption is unrealistic for China. Even after 1993, state intervention has remained omnipresent, and it is obvious that the competitive situation is illusory. Furthermore, we must assume that the standard errors of the parameters carried by the lagged variables tend to zero – the reduction chosen being hyperbolic by Litterman (1986) with standard errors such as: $\gamma / 1$, $\gamma / 2$ ... γ / p; linear for Kadiyala and Karlsson (1997) with a reduction parameter of 1; or of 2 in Koop and Korobilis (2009).

We try different Bayesian specifications, summarized below (Table 8.8):

TABLE 8.8   Comparison of the BVAR estimates for the period 1993–2014

	With 1952–1992 data As a pre-sampling	Litterman – Minnesota's method	Sims – Zha's method	With 1993–2014 data in traditional VAR
A priori	Coef. matrix: thetao (*) Cov. matrix: varianceo	Mu: 0, L1: 0.1, L2: 0.99, L3: 1	Lo: 1, L1: 0.1, L3: 1	Not available
Average R²	0.667647	0.468692	0.446659	0.793736
LM Test	Rejected	Rejected	Rejected	Accepted

Note: (*) = VAR is estimated over 1952–1992, then information driven from the sub-sample is used as *a priori*.

However, what we see is that in practice, the Bayesian approach does not lead to significantly better results than those given by traditional statistical tools. In fact, in the Bayesian framework the impulse response functions are quite similar to those of SVARs. In sum, the assumptions made on the *a priori* are too strong. The information provided by the pre-sampling from 1952 to 2014 is of better quality than is that of the other *a priori*, but it is not as good as that given by the sub-sample itself. This means that, although the information provided by the enlarged period of planned economy (1952–1992) is useful, it is not suitable as *a priori* for that of the market economy (1993–2014); especially since the *a priori* distribution hypothesis is too strong and not valid in Bayesian analysis. Standard errors of the impulses could be significantly large. Thus, as we observe from Graph 8.19 to Graph 8.26, the impulse response functions calculated from BVARs are quite similar to those obtained from the 1993–2014 sub-sample, suggesting that, despite a quite limited sample size, the structures derived from traditional econometric methods are stable and relatively reliable.

We finally present the results of the traditional VARs with the sub-sample 1993–2014, even if its size is small (22 observations). The impulses are calculated up to 20 years. As seen in Graph 8.27 to Graph 8.32, all cumulated responses tend toward zero and verify the equation (8.33). In other words, the system that we have modeled is identifiable.

Response to Cholesky One S.D. Innovations ?2 S.E.

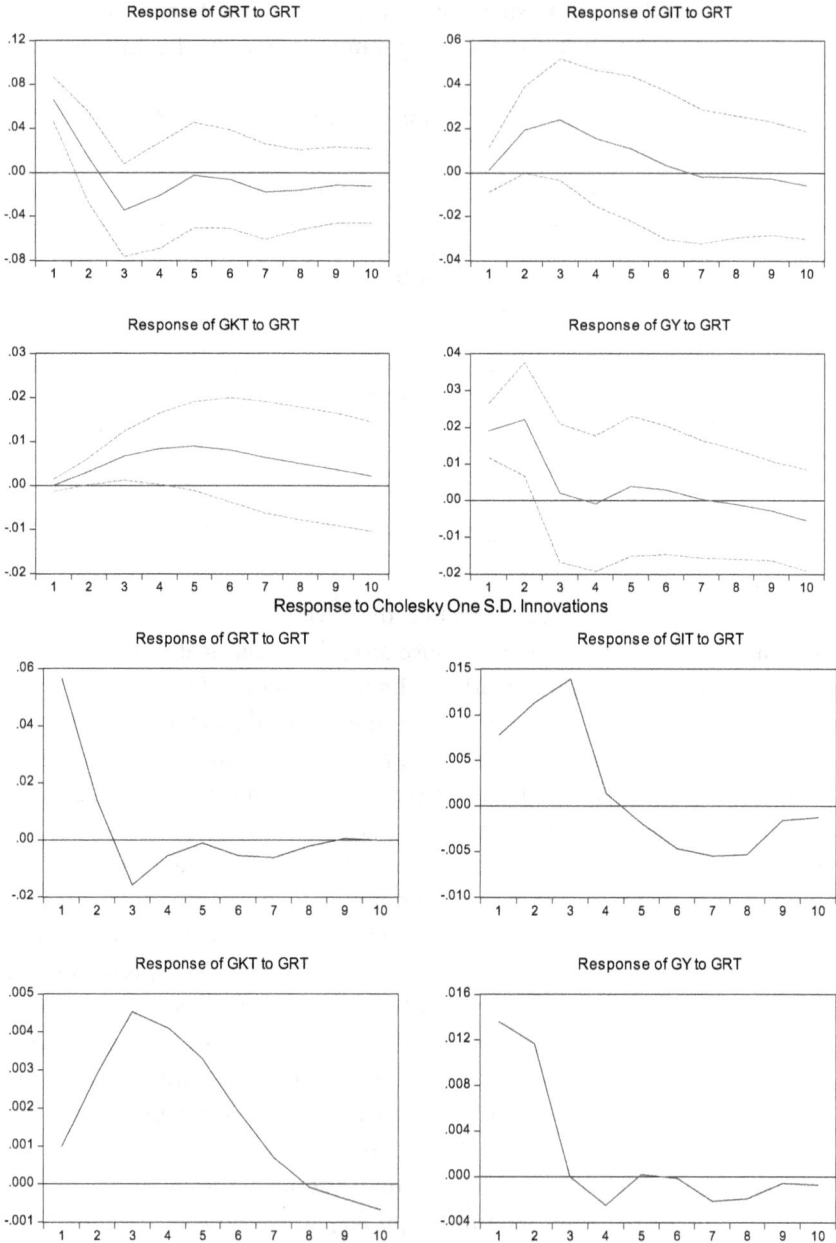

Response of GRT to GRT

Response of GIT to GRT

Response of GKT to GRT

Response of GY to GRT

Response to Cholesky One S.D. Innovations

Response of GRT to GRT

Response of GIT to GRT

Response of GKT to GRT

Response of GY to GRT

GRAPHS 8.19–26   Impulse response functions of VARs and BVARs for the period 1993–2014
Note: The above block corresponds to VARs; the block below
corresponds to BVARs with pre-sampling as *a priori.*

Accumulated Response to Cholesky One S.D. Innovations ?2 S.E.

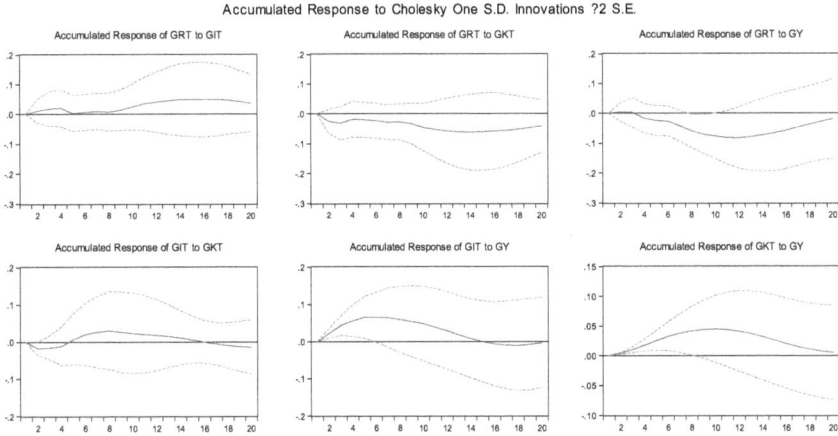

GRAPHS 8.27–32   Cumulated impulse responses of the models over the period 1993–2014

With the 1952–1992 sub-sample also revealing valuable information – about the evolution of the same economy studied –, we present the SVAR responses for 1952–2014 (from Graph 8.33 to Graph 8.40).

The key condition for identifying the system on the full sample is $c_{2,4} = 0$. However, the results of our tests indicate that the verification of this condition remains ambiguous. This suggests that when the Chinese leaders faced a slow-down, they were able to take the shutter of the economy, and had the initiative to accelerate investment as an anti-crisis policy, rather than to entrust to the rate of profit the task of convincing business leaders whether to invest more. We recognize here one of the fundamental features of "Chinese governance": the public authorities intervene very powerfully to fight against the crisis.

4   Application: Forecasts for the Year 2015

Finally, let us investigate forecasting and – according to Box and Jenkins' (1976) method – try to rely on the SVAR models in the full sample and in the sub-samples in order to predict our four macroscopic variables for the year 2015. Their relevance in our prevision application will be assessed by comparing them to NBS data as they appear in the *China Statistical Yearbook* (2016).

As seen in Table 8.9, the forecasts drawn from all three versions of our models give negative values for the growth rate of r_t in 2015, which would, therefore, continue to decline – despite the fact that it was already low in 2014 (at 5 percent). This worsening of the fall in the total profit rate of China's economy brought *per se* a risk of crisis to come; especially as *Gr* concerns all sectors,

Response to Cholesky One S.D. Innovations ?2 S.E.

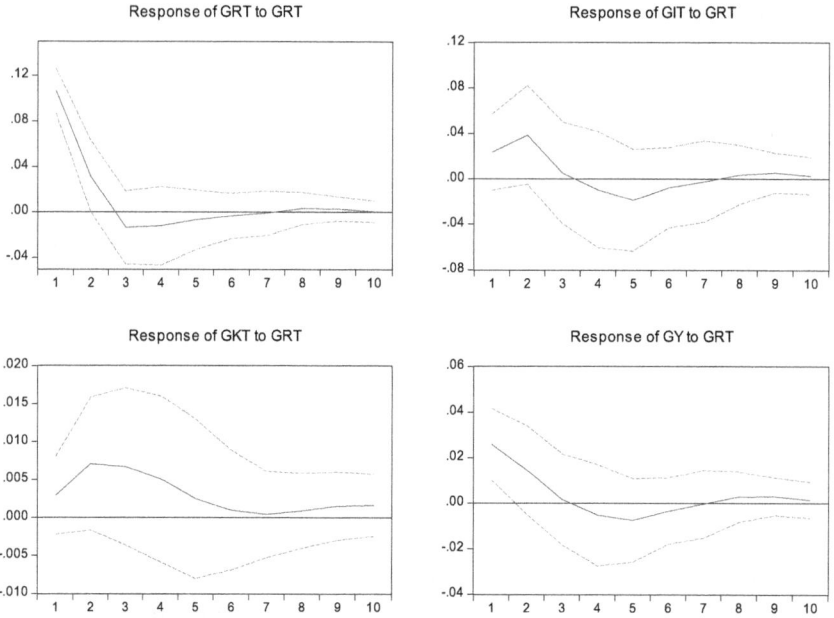

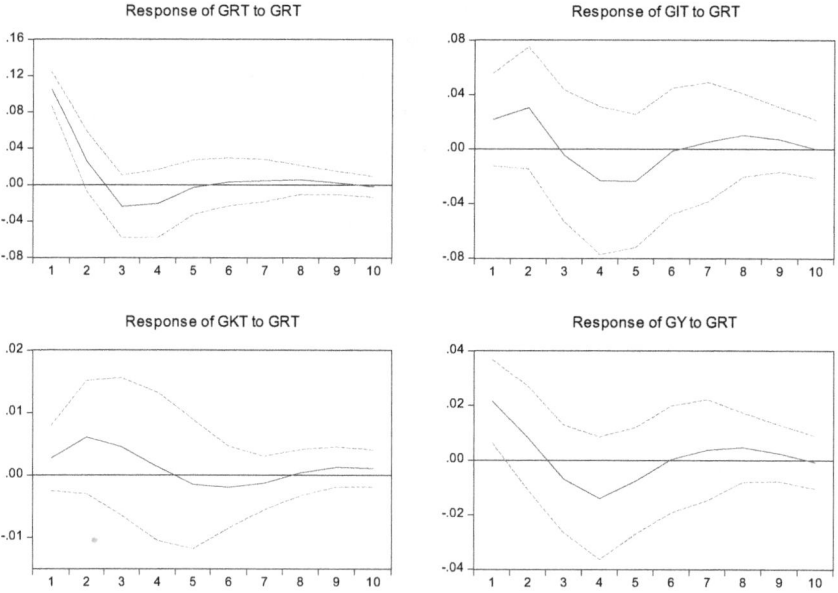

Response of GRT to GRT

Response of GIT to GRT

Response of GKT to GRT

Response of GY to GRT

Response to Cholesky One S.D. Innovations ?2 S.E.

Response of GRT to GRT

Response of GIT to GRT

Response of GKT to GRT

Response of GY to GRT

GRAPHS 8.33–40   Impulse responses from SVARs on the full sample (1952–2014)
Note: The above block corresponds to SVARs with three dummies; and the
block below corresponds to SVARs without a dummy.

TABLE 8.9   Forecasts of macroscopic variables for 2015 from 1952–2014 data

		Gr	*GI*	*GK*	*GY*
Data provided by NBS		Not available	3.4%	Not available	6.9%
Forecast	Value	–4.8%	4.4%	10.9%	6.6%
on full sample	RMSE	0.158432	0.049955	0.165162	0.031903
of the model	MAE	0.137710	0.042965	0.156112	0.024935
without dummy	MAPE	165.2387	39.37974	2500.854	0.945150
	Theil	0.031903	0.024935	34.42076	0.162895
Forecast	Value	–2.3%	5.6%	11.0%	8.6%
on full sample	RMSE	0.164466	0.050130	0.149755	0.029137
of the model	MAE	0.146229	0.043092	0.137604	0.023604
with three dummies	MAPE	146.7758	39.07008	1248.364	24.69899
	Theil	0.793943	0.200322	0.903595	0.139841
Forecast	Value	–2.7%	9.9%	11.2%	9.7%
on sub-samples	RMSE	0.166674	0.048038	0.150943	0.014060
of the model	MAE	0.145566	0.040314	0.13760	0.012375
	MAPE	121.7106	37.32195	5941.033	12.69810
	Theil	0.826713	0.191456	0.883610	0.067614

Notes: Data at 1952 constant prices. RMSE = root mean square error; MAE = mean absolute error; MAPE = mean absolute percentage error; Theil = Theil inequality coefficient.

and therefore also includes financial capital. This turns out to be consistent with reality, as the Summer of the year 2015 was marked in China, as we know, by a financial crisis, whose turbulence caused the Shanghai Stock Exchange index to drop by almost 50 percent from its high point (at 5,178 on June 12, 2015) to a low point (at 2,638 on January 27, 2016). And, if we consider both the Shanghai and Shenzhen stock exchanges, the total losses suffered reached 25.690 trillion yuan over one year (from June 12, 2015 to June 12, 2016 exactly), i.e., the approximate equivalent of the GDP of Germany.

Such a devaluation of financial capital has, in turn, weighed very heavily on the growth rate of the total capital profit rate, a fact which is consistent with our negative forecasts. Although it was not possible for us to pinpoint the precise sector in which this crisis was to break out – and, for sure, although we are aware that the real economy is much more sophisticated than is a

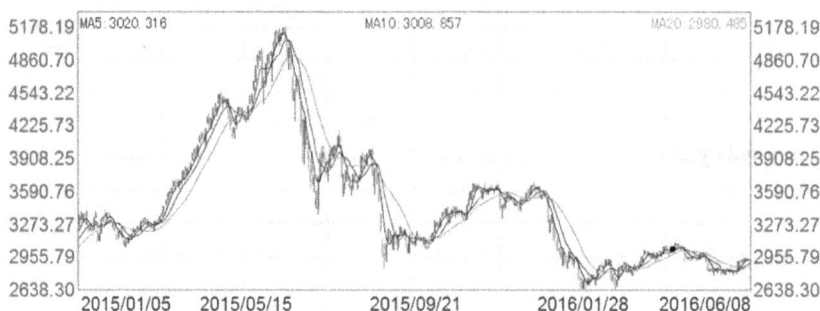

GRAPH 8.41   Shanghai stock exchange market index during the 2015–2016 Chinese financial crisis

quadrivariate model –, the results obtained thanks to our modeling for 2015 (that is to say, one year beyond the sample considered) using data from years prior to this date prove to be rather convincing. So also are the predictions concerning the GDP growth rate: GY is forecast at 6.6 percent in 2015 at constant prices on the full sample (from 1952 to 2014), when the NBS data put it at 6.9 percent the same year, always at constant prices.

This confirms that although the condition $c_{2,4} = 0$ is not acquired, SVARs tested on the full sample actually provide more information than do those tested on sub-samples. Such forecasts lead to the idea that the local financial crisis that hit China in mid-2015 may have been endogenous – marked by negative forecast values of the variable r_t – and caused by factors whose aggregation had operated over the long period.

In the end, we can conclude that, in the econometric modeling that we propose, the short-term a priori restrictions' hypotheses imposed to analyze the structure of the Chinese economy are difficult to validate – as the arguments in favor of these constraints are weak for the first two periods (1952–1977 and 1977–1992), which are close in economic terms, whereas they are almost all verified for the third period (1993–2014), which has more clearly distinct features –, and those of the long term are validated fully only on the 1993–2014 sub-sample. Therefore, the results of our tests encourage us to distinguish – at least – three periods in China's economic trajectory:

1)   1952–1977: The Soviet-type planned economy is characterized by large fluctuations (whose origin is often political) and by a rate of profit with movements synchronous with the other macroscopic variables and whose growth rate does not yet constitute the main determinant of the dynamics of investment, capital accumulation, and production.

2)   1978–1992: This is a time of transition, during which the complex economic structure cannot be described easily. Nevertheless, the amplitude of the cycles diminishes, and the variations in GDP growth precede those in the profit rate. If the reforms were launched from 1978, the nature of the system should still be interpreted as falling under a planned economy, with "the market in complement" – according to Deng Xiaoping's formula, "Socialism can also have the market economy as a mode of existence."

3)   From 1993 to the present: in the wake of the 1993 tax reform, it is the period of a market economy "with Chinese colors," with "planning in complement." The political sphere plays a decreasingly decisive role in economic fluctuations, which are themselves smaller. Unlike the preceding period, changes in GDP growth now follow those in profit rate. The gradual integration of the P.R. of China into globalization reduces the amplitude of its economic cycles, thanks to the shock absorbers that constitute the external markets (which absorb the Chinese surpluses of capital and labour, thus helping to resolve internal contradictions), but induces at the same time a new vulnerability by accentuating the risks of imported crises.

Conclusion

All of the original statistical databases that we have presented in this book could obviously be enriched by adding other variables related to the commercial (international trade), monetary (exchange rate) or financial (indebtedness) dimensions, especially. However, in the meantime, it constitutes a solid and precious base for the deepening of the quantitative and qualitative study of the innumerable relations characterizing the productive sphere – which in economic reality is found to be inextricably imbricated, interwoven in a network of commercial, monetary and financial interactions, and even more so in the world economy. As a matter of fact, for the community of scientific researchers, the opportunities for using these new time series are multiple, to be deployed in very diverse and broad fields of analysis.

At the end of this book, we would like to learn from this work a fact, extremely simple and singularly striking; so simple and striking that it is very often forgotten, oddly enough. How regrettable it would be, in passing, if this omission were only an ideological reaction to this other fact that the Communist Party of China continues to exercise leadership today over all the country's strategic decisions, with unparalleled success in terms of economic growth and of multidimensional development that the whole world has witnessed for decades. The fact that we allow ourselves here to emphasize, or to recall, is that the extraordinarily strong growth of the Chinese GDP turns out to be a phenomenon which did not begin with the reforms promoted in 1978, but goes back to well before the death of President Mao Zedong himself even to begin from the earliest days of the revolutionary People's Republic. While it is true that this economic growth accelerated from the 1980s–to the point of placing China, at that time, and despite its relatively low level of per capita income, far ahead of other so-called "socialists" countries during this same decade –, it would still be necessary to recognize that the growth of the net material product (ancestor of the GDP) had already been very high during the ten years which preceded the decision to "reform" the economy in order to open it up to the world system.

According to data provided by the World Bank,[1] expressed at constant prices (1980 base) and in ten-year averages, China's economic growth rate reached 6.8 percent between 1970 and 1979. If we look at the GDP official series published by the National Bureau of Statistics (NBS) of China in its *China Statistical Yearbooks*, a quality and reliable source, from its creation (in 1952) to the present day (2015), expressed at constant prices (in 1952 base), we observe that the

---

1   Marer, Arvay, O'Connor, Schrenk and Swanson (1992), for The World Bank.

Chinese GDP growth rate, which was on average 8.3 percent per year between 1952 and 2015, was, by sub-periods, 6.3 percent between 1952 and 1978 – which is fast – and 9.9 percent from 1979 to 2015 – which is very fast. If we put in brackets the first years from 1952 to 1962 (between the completion of the unification of the continental territory and the very disturbed period of the break with the Soviet Union), this is an average annual GDP growth rate of 8.2 percent which was recorded for China from 1963 to 1978 – reflecting a very rapid growth, even if this period includes the Cultural Revolution.

What about the accumulation of capital? If we take a closer look at our new time series of physical capital stocks for China over the long period (from 1952 to 2015),[2] we can find that the average growth rates of the capital stock that we have called "productive" (including all equipment, machines, tools, industrial installations, but not residential buildings and the value of their lands) were very similar over the two sub-periods 1952–1978 and 1979–2015, that is: 9.7 percent for the first sub-period and 10.9 percent for the second one. By now retaining an enlarged productive physical capital stock, also including inventories, we see that the average rhythm of accumulation of this broad capital stock was slightly higher during the sub-period 1952–1978 (10.41 percent) than during the sub-period 1979–2015 (10.39 percent). And if we select an even larger physical capital, also integrating built-up lands for residential use – components which are not directly productive –, the growth rate of this very extended capital stock was still rapid over the sub-period 1952–1978, i.e., on average 9.1 percent, against 10.9 percent from 1979 to 2015. It is therefore established that the effort to accumulate capital is not a recent phenomenon, but that it was decided and continuously planned by the Chinese leaders and authorities over the past six decades. And it is this prolonged effort of accumulation – made possible in particular by transfers of surplus from rural to urban areas – which explains the in-depth industrialization and, to a large extent, the very high GDP growth rate of China.

Other important factors have of course played a positive role in this exceptional dynamism. This is particularly the case with the massive investments performed in education and research. It appears from the long time series (1949–2015)[3] related to the levels of educational resources of the Chinese population that we have constructed that the average growth rates of the stock of total "human capital" were extremely close over the sub-period 1949–1978

---

2 After having written this book, we have updated our physical capital stock databases and extending them to 2015.

3 The series of "human capital" stocks could subsequently be extended until 2015. The same applies to those of R&D flows.

(4.19 percent) and the sub-period 1979–2015 (4.22 percent). And if we consider a "productive" educational stock, by performing the calculations on the basis of the active population, and no longer total population, then the average growth rate of this stock of educational resources was this time 5.07 percent from 1949 to 1978 and 3.55 percent from 1979 to 2015, that is to say, higher over the sub-period preceding the reforms of 1978. Therefore, investment in the educational sector must be analyzed as a process operating on the long term. Consequent and massive from the first years of the People's Republic, it aimed at the democratization of education – in parallel with a generalized access to the public health system and the extension of infrastructures to the whole territory. This is indeed one of the central pillars of the long-term development strategy pursued by the Chinese revolutionary government, which has decisively contributed to the strength and dynamism of the current economy.

Quid about research-and-development (R&D) expenses? If China did not enter the international accounting system for R&D activities until the year 1986, this does not mean that this country only started investing in them from that date; this just means that before 1986 it is impossible to have access to some homogeneous data on the subject. Indeed, the chronological series of R&D expenditure that we were able to reconstruct by going back further in the past (1949–2015) show that the average growth rates of this expenditure are of the order of +14.5 percent per year over the period. But it should be observed that the average rhythm of increase in R&D spending was markedly stronger from 1949 to 1978 than over the following sub-period, i.e., 1979–2015. Obviously, the technological levels of the early years and of today are completely different and, moreover, the public research system had to be built from zero – partly explaining the very rapid growth of R&D spending during the first years. Nevertheless, it should be understood that the efforts made by China in terms of R&D were far from being negligible at the very beginning of the revolution and that they too must be analyzed as a strategy patiently implemented and having bore its fruits in the long period. In other words, China, whose level of scientific and technological development no longer has anything to envy of the most advanced capitalist industrialized countries today, has not started to promote its R&D activities with its recent integration into globalization, but a long time before; in fact, as soon as the victory of the communist revolution in 1949, although the nature of these activities has become considerably more sophisticated in recent years.

In short, what we are saying is that the revolution's development strategy laid the conditions and foundations for the country's current success – in a system which remains that of a "socialist market economy" – and that this success is part of the continuity of the past, more than in contradiction with it.

Appendices

∵

Appendices to Chapter 1

A.1.1 Procedure Used to Determine the Initial Capital Stock and the Capital-Output Ratio

The values of the initial capital stock and the capital-output ratio associated to it can be calculated through an iterative procedure whose method is – partly – inspired by Nehru and Dhareshwar (1993). It consists in the following three steps:

Step 1. We set an initial capital $K_0^{(0)}$, no matter its value, and get an estimation of a first series of capital stock $\left\{ K_0^{(0)}, K_1^{(0)} ..., K_T^{(0)} \right\}$ with the permanent inventory method (PIM). This is how we get an average proportion of I_t/K_t, such as:

$$\alpha_0 = \frac{1}{T}\sum_{t=0}^{T} I_t / K_t^{(0)}$$

Step 2. We use this average proportion α_0 in order to calculate a second value of initial capital stock $K_0^{(1)}$ and get another estimation of the capital stock series $\left\{ K_0^{(1)}, K_1^{(1)} ..., K_T^{(1)} \right\}$, as well as a new average proportion of I_t/K_t:

$$\alpha_1 = \frac{1}{T}\sum_{t=0}^{T} I_t / K_t^{(1)}$$

Step 3. We repeat this procedure by iterations until we get a α_N (or $K_0^{(N)}$) which is unchanged.

It is possible to use such a procedure because the proportion I_t/K_t is convergent when $t \to \infty$.

As a matter of fact, from the PIM definition, we know that:

$$K_t = \sum_{\tau=0}^{\infty} d_\tau I_{t-\tau}$$

With a geometric declining of the age-efficiency of capital goods, we have:

$$d_\tau = (1 - \sigma)^\tau$$

where $\sigma > 0$.

Then:

$$I_t = (1+g)^t I_o$$

where g is the average growth rate of investment (supposed to be strictly positive).

As a consequence, with $0 < \sigma < 1$ and $g > 0$:

$$\frac{I_t}{K_t} = \frac{(1+g)^t I_o}{\sum_{\tau=0}^{\infty} d_\tau I_{t-\tau}} = \frac{(1+g)^t I_o}{\sum_{\tau=0}^{\infty} (1-\sigma)^\tau (1+g)^{t-\tau} I_o} = \frac{1}{\sum_{\tau=0}^{\infty} \left(\frac{1-\sigma}{1+g}\right)^\tau}$$

So:

$$0 < \frac{1-\sigma}{1+g} < 1$$

and:

$$\sum_{\tau=0}^{\infty} \left(\frac{1-\sigma}{1+g}\right)^\tau \to \frac{1}{1 - \frac{1-\sigma}{1+g}}$$

It comes that

$$\frac{I_t}{K_t} = \frac{g+\sigma}{1+g}$$

is convergent.

Or, strictly speaking:

$$g = g_t = \lim_{t_o \to -\infty} \frac{1}{t-t_o+1} \sum_{\tau=t_o}^{t} \Delta \log I_\tau$$

by supposing that g_t satisfies ergodicity properties, which allow us to use time averages.

Compared to Harberger (1978) or Nehru and Dhareshwar (1993), our method does not need the recourse to the highly controversial "steady state" hypothesis, according to which the economy would be at the stationary state from a particular year. With their method, we would have to assume that China was at its steady state in 1952 – which is obviously counterfactual. Harberger (1978) used a 3-year average economic growth rate; Nehru-Dhareshwar (1993) the average growth rate between 1950 and 1973; and Caselli (2005) the average growth rate until 1970.

In the framework mobilised by these authors, g_Y is the economic growth, with:

$$K_0 = I_0/(g_Y + \sigma)$$

In ours, taking into account the average growth rate of investment, we only need a sample of investment series to obtain g. To perform our iterations, we use the investment series over 60 years, with an implicit hypothesis that China's economy will tend to the steady state when t → ∞. Fundamentally, this procedure does not depend on preexisting historical data, but only on series of flows of depreciated investment. Our program simulated for 10,000 iterations converges, after few iterations, towards the value of an initial total capital found to be K_0= 1,018.5; that is to say, a capital-output ratio of 1.5 for the base run 1952.

A.1.2   Results of the Unit Root Tests for Price Series

TABLE A.1.2.1   Results of the unit root tests for P_C and P_S according to the information criteria

	Criteria	Models	Lags	Statistics	Critical values	Stationarity
ADF Test	AIC	Trend	7	−3.333062	*at 1 percent level:*	No
$H_0 : P_C$	SIC	Trend	7	−3.333062	−4.467895	No
has a	HQ	Trend	7	−3.333062	*at 5 percent level:*	No
unit root	Modified AIC	Trend	2	−3.868219	−3.644963	No
	Modified SIC	Trend	2	−3.868219	*and at 10 percent*	No
	Modified HQ	Trend	2	−3.868219	*level:* −3.261452	No
ERS Test	AIC	Trend	5	−4.523001	*at 1 percent level:*	Yes
$H_0 : P_C$	SIC	Trend	5	−4.523001	−3.770000	Yes
has a unit	HQ	Trend	5	−4.523001	*at 5 percent level:*	Yes
root	Modified AIC	Trend	0	−1.996714	−3.190000	No
	Modified SIC	Trend	0	−1.996714	*and at 10 percent*	No
	Modified HQ	Trend	0	−1.996714	*level:* −2.890000	No

TABLE A.1.2.1   Results of the unit root tests for P_C and P_S according to the information criteria (*cont.*)

	Criteria	Models	Lags	Statistics	Critical values	Stationarity
KPSS Test	AIC	Trend	5	0.493707	*at 1 percent level:*	No
$H_0 : P_C$	SIC	Trend	5	0.493707	−3.770000	No
has not a	HQ	Trend	5	0.493707	*at 5 percent level:*	No
unit root	Modified AIC	Trend	0	0.819755	−3.190000	No
	Modified SIC	Trend	0	0.819755	*and at 10 percent*	No
	Modified HQ	Trend	0	0.819755	*level:* −2.890000	No
PP Test	AIC	Constant	5	−4.367265	*at 1 percent level:*	Yes
$H_0 : P_C$	SIC	Constant	0	−1.863733	−3.752946	No
has a unit	HQ	Constant	5	−4.367265	*at 5 percent level:*	Yes
root	Modified AIC	Constant	8	−1.767226	−2.998064	No
	Modified SIC	Constant	8	−1.767226	*and at 10 percent*	No
	Modified HQ	Constant	8	−1.767226	*level:* −2.638752	No

TABLE A.1.2.2   Unit root tests for P_C (with a truncation parameter of 2)

	Models	Test statistics	Critical value at 1 percent	Critical value at 5 percent	Critical value at 10 percent	Stationarity
ADF	Trend	−3.868219	−4.467895	−3.644963	−3.261452	No
ERS	Trend	−2.280488	−3.770000	−3.190000	−2.890000	No
PP	Intercept	−1.923615	−3.752946	−2.998064	−2.638752	No
KPSS	Trend	0.213466	0.216000	0.146000	0.119000	No
ERS (PO)	Trend	8.153188	4.220000	5.720000	6.770000	No

TABLE A.1.2.3   Ng-Perron (NG) test critical values

		MZa	MZt	MSB	MPT
Asymptotic critical values	1 percent	−23.8000	−3.42000	0.14300	4.03000
	5 percent	−17.3000	−2.91000	0.16800	5.48000
	10 percent	−14.2000	−2.62000	0.18500	6.67000

TABLE A.1.2.4   Unit root tests for DP_C (with a truncation parameter of 2)

	Models	Comparison of the test statistics (and critical values)	Stationarity
ADF	None	$-2.612867 > -3.6449635$ (5 percent)	No
ERS	Trend	$-2.258079 > -3.1900000$ (5 percent)	No
PP	None	$-1.868275 > -2.998064$ (5 percent)	No
KPSS	Constant	$1.209340 > 0.146000$ (5 percent)	No
ERS (PO)	Trend	$24.55721 > 5.720000$ (5 percent)	No
Ng-Perron	Trend	$\{-3.38874; -1.29443; 0.38198; 26.7459\}$ (*)	No

Note: (*) Values superior to the corresponding critical values.

TABLE A.1.2.5   Unit root tests for $D2P_C$ (with a truncation parameter of 2)

	Models	Comparison of the test statistics (and critical values)	Stationarity
ADF	None	$-3.434618 < -3.261452$ (10 percent)	Yes
ERS	Constant	$-2.741595 < -1.960171$ (5 percent); -2.692358 (1 percent)	Yes
PP	Constant	$-5.905146 < -3.012363$ (5 percent); -3.788030 (1 percent)	Yes
KPSS	Constant	$0.031569 < 0.463$ (5 percent); 0.347 (10 percent); 0.739 (1 percent)	Yes
ERS (PO)	Constant	$2.328865 < 2.97$ (5 percent); 3.91 (10 percent)	Yes
Ng-Perron	Trend	$\{-14.7984; -2.72004; 0.18381; 6.15835\}$ (**)	Yes

Note: (**) = Respectively inferior to the critical values at 10 percent $\{-14.2000; -2.62000; 0.18500; 6.67000\}$.

TABLE A.1.2.6   Unit root tests for P_S (with a truncation parameter of 2)

	Models	Comparison of the test statistics (and critical values)	Stationarity
ADF	Trend	−4.462184 > −3.6449635 (1 percent)	No
ERS	Trend	−2.321128 > −3.19(5 percent); −2.89 (10 percent)	No
PP	Constant	−2.102704 > −2.998064 (5 percent); −2.638752 (10 percent)	No
KPSS	Trend	0.232288 > 0.146 (5 percent); 0.216 (10 percent)	No
ERS (PO)	Trend	9.042192 > 5.72 (5 percent); 6.77 (1 percent)	No
Ng-Perron	Trend	{−10.9734; 2.33028; 0.21236; 8.36175} (***)	Yes

Note: (***) = Values superior to the corresponding critical values.

TABLE A.1.2.7   Unit root tests for DP_S (with a truncation parameter of 2)

	Models	Comparison of the test statistics (and critical values)	Stationarity
ADF	None	−3.095380 < −2.685718 (1 percent)	Yes
ERS	Trend	−2.411599 > −3.19 (5 percent); −2.89 (10 percent)	No
PP	None	−2.602289 > −2.674290 (1 percent)	No
KPSS	Constant	1.584383 > 0.463 (5 percent); 0.739 (1 percent)	No
ERS (PO)	Trend	34.62528 > 5.72 (5 percent); 6.77 (1 percent)	No
Ng-Perron	Trend	{−2.46895; −1.10924; 0.44928; 36.8327} (****)	Yes

Note: (****) = Values superior to the corresponding critical values.

TABLE A.1.2.8   Unit root tests for $D2P_S$ (with a truncation parameter of 2)

	Models	Comparison of the test statistics (and critical values)	Stationarity
ADF	None	−3.083689 < −1.960171 (5 percent); −2.692358 (1 percent)	Yes
ERS	Constant	−2.396546 < −1.960171 (5 percent)	Yes
PP	None	−6.216319 < −1.958088 (5 percent); −2.679735 (1 percent)	Yes
KPSS	Constant	0.078957 < 0.463 (5 percent); 0.347 (10 percent)	Yes
ERS (PO)	Trend	6.213172 > 3.910000 (10 percent)	No
Ng-Perron	Trend	{−1.43700; −0.84727; 0.58961; 17.0401} (*****)	No

Note: (*****) = Respectively inferior to the critical values at 10 percent {−5.70000; −1.62000; 0.27500; 4.45000}.

TABLE A.1.2.9   Unit root tests for the four price indices (with a truncation parameter of 3)

Price indices		ADF	ERS	PP	KPSS	Stationarity
P_{FBCS}	Level	Trend −1.73	Trend −1.19	Trend −1.95	Trend 8.51	No
	D	None −2.04	Trend −2.63	Trend −5.82*	Trend 0.60	No
	D2	None −6.01	Constant −4.90	None −11.03	Constant 0.01	Yes
P_{FBCFS}	Level	Trend −1.42	Trend −0.91	Trend −1.80	Trend 11.13	No
	D	None −2.21	Constant −1.90	Trend −7.34	Trend 0.19	No
	D2	None −7.57	Constant −7.00	None −18.21	Constant 0.03	Yes
P_{FBCC}	Level	None 1.74	Trend −0.94	Trend −1.936	Trend 4.29	No
	D	None −1.69	Constant −2.17	None −2.12	Trend 0.11*	No
	D2	None −4.10	Constant −3.82	None −23.44	Constant 0.01	Yes
P_{FBCFC}	Level	None 1.68	Trend −0.99	Trend −2.08	Trend 3.74	No
	D	None −1.49	Constant −1.92	None −1.78	Trend 0.15	No
	D2	None −3.75	Constant −3.59	None −9.31	Constant 0.02	Yes

Notes: 1st column of each test = the valid model; 2nd column of each test = value of the corresponding statistical test.

TABLE A.1.2.10   OLS Estimates of GDP growth rate (G_Y) and its explicative factors (capital G_{KP} and labour G_L) for China between 1952 and 2014: dependent variable G_Y

	Coefficient	Std. Error	t-Statistic	Prob.
D_1	0.118987	0.019623	6.063611	0.0000
G_{KP}	0.628570	0.055403	11.34547	0.0000
G_L	0.878810	0.174957	5.023021	0.0000
R^2	0.670247	Mean dependent variable		0.077586
R^2 adjusted	0.658677	S.D. dependent variable		0.079677
S.E. of regression	0.046549	Akaike info criterion		−3.247902
Sum squared resid	0.123510	Schwarz criterion		−3.143185
Log likelihood	100.4371	Hannan-Quinn criterion		−3.206941
Durbin-Watson stat	2.027518	Points: 60		

A.1.3   Complementary Statistical Database on Inventories and Built-Up Lands for Residential Use in China from 1952 to 2014

TABLE A.1.3.1   Series of inventories and built-up lands for residential use: China, 1952–2014 (*in hundreds of millions of 1952 constant yuans*)

Years	Inventories V	Built-up lands for residential use T
1952	73.00	322.25
1953	151.09	353.21
1954	224.99	377.16
1955	286.03	389.84
1956	311.00	418.60
1957	386.19	441.38
1958	460.02	449.76
1959	619.49	471.42
1960	679.33	498.36
1961	678.14	488.41
1962	628.69	468.20
1963	625.25	459.79

TABLE A.1.3.1   Series of inventories and built-up lands for residential use: China (*cont.*)

Years	Inventories V	Built-up lands for residential use T
1964	631.11	466.06
1965	697.97	476.80
1966	810.96	491.18
1967	865.17	490.95
1968	955.19	486.49
1969	981.96	503.07
1970	1,138.10	518.14
1971	1,303.92	544.31
1972	1,409.46	571.60
1973	1,584.80	605.15
1974	1,693.80	640.65
1975	1,789.68	681.38
1976	1,824.23	717.99
1977	1,921.37	760.42
1978	2,138.73	828.96
1979	2,339.45	950.17
1980	2,484.63	1,102.78
1981	2,630.86	1,279.44
1982	2,754.88	1,512.67
1983	2,895.67	1,774.14
1984	3,076.58	2,045.46
1985	3,572.30	2,410.08
1986	4,026.41	2,784.49
1987	4,299.69	3,206.86
1988	4,711.18	3,648.19
1989	5,539.85	4,080.84
1990	6,240.94	4,433.58
1991	6,786.25	4,839.05
1992	7,085.66	5,267.90
1993	7,539.14	5,870.77
1994	8,066.49	6,687.00
1995	8,851.34	7,658.90
1996	9,567.25	8,645.46
1997	10,168.61	9,590.27

TABLE A.1.3.1   Series of inventories and built-up lands for residential use: China (*cont.*)

Years	Inventories V	Built-up lands for residential use T
1998	10,440.87	10,761.58
1999	10,501.54	12,051.51
2000	10,224.76	13,384.94
2001	10,281.54	14,829.58
2002	10,335.01	16,471.05
2003	10,557.81	18,324.08
2004	11,193.91	20,568.55
2005	11,728.63	23,076.98
2006	12,579.09	26,306.99
2007	13,950.31	30,647.92
2008	16,169.68	35,973.88
2009	17,626.77	42,098.66
2010	19,679.02	49,579.39
2011	22,827.04	59,140.95
2012	25,966.61	69,651.26
2013	29,288.48	81,697.89
2014	32,749.46	93,737.34

Note: The stock of the inventories in 1951 (one year before the base run) is supposed to be zero.

A.1.4   Complementary Statistical Database on Price Indices in China from 1952 to 2014

TABLE A.1.4.1   Price index series for gross capital formation and gross fixed capital formation: China, 1952–2014 (*base 100 in 1952*)

Years	Price index: gross capital formation $P_{FBC\,C}$	Price index: gross fixed capital formation $P_{FBCF\,C}$
1952	100	100
1953	99.321	98.807
1954	99.747	98.199

TABLE A.1.4.1   Price index series for gross capital formation and gross fixed capital (*cont.*)

Years	Price index: gross capital formation $P_{FBC\,C}$	Price index: gross fixed capital formation $P_{FBCF\,C}$
1955	95.947	94.003
1956	92.545	93.737
1957	92.007	89.745
1958	92.032	90.057
1959	97.656	97.596
1960	97.882	97.282
1961	97.203	95.507
1962	106.896	102.541
1963	111.074	107.490
1964	108.323	105.276
1965	102.019	101.790
1966	100.467	99.820
1967	98.635	100.154
1968	94.330	96.723
1969	93.228	94.494
1970	93.165	94.477
1971	93.780	95.490
1972	94.632	96.698
1973	94.507	96.793
1974	94.867	96.917
1975	96.020	98.105
1976	96.117	98.756
1977	97.349	100.230
1978	97.635	100.782
1979	101.053	102.964
1980	103.329	106.071
1981	106.170	109.486
1982	108.706	112.050
1983	111.653	114.781
1984	115.799	119.437
1985	123.984	128.004
1986	131.504	136.224
1987	139.774	143.344

TABLE A.1.4.1   Price index series for gross capital formation and gross fixed capital (*cont.*)

Years	Price index: gross capital formation $P_{FBC\,C}$	Price index: gross fixed capital formation $P_{FBCF\,C}$
1988	158.893	162.766
1989	173.721	176.639
1990	184.160	186.221
1991	198.332	202.014
1992	225.030	228.282
1993	281.244	285.493
1994	311.639	314.995
1995	336.082	333.901
1996	349.433	346.993
1997	348.453	352.793
1998	346.102	352.872
1999	348.854	351.392
2000	349.999	355.121
2001	351.063	356.561
2002	351.896	357.401
2003	359.872	365.433
2004	381.798	388.180
2005	389.988	397.362
2006	398.231	405.173
2007	402.515	410.037
2008	410.061	418.828
2009	419.379	427.169
2010	428.298	437.460
2011	435.108	449.175
2012	428.867	445.427
2013	430.842	448.345
2014	434.535	452.860

A.1.5   Statistical Data Sources

TABLE A.1.5.1   Data sources of the different types of investment and capital

Data source	Provincial SNA 2008 data	National SNA 2008 data		Investment in fixed assets
Data length	Since 2008	Since 1952		Since 1981
Types of investment or capital	Residential buildings	Built-up lands		Construction and installations
	Non-residential buildings	Others	Productive capital without land nor inventories (K_{Pe})	
	Machinery and equipment			Equipment and instruments
	Mineral exploration costs			Others
	Computer software			
	Land improvement expenditure	Agricultural land		
	Change in inventories	Inventories		

Appendices to Chapter 2

A.2.1 Complementary Statistical Database on Average Educational Levels Attained in China from 1949 to 2014

TABLE A.2.1.1 Time series of average educational levels attained by the population: China, 1949–2014 (*in years*)

Years	Educational level attained: index of productive human capital	Educational level attained: index of total human capital
1949	–	1.661363
1950	–	1.611056
1951	–	1.581098
1952	2.532596	1.553235
1953	2.479319	1.504484
1954	2.452926	1.505148
1955	2.442273	1.495671
1956	2.426741	1.504550
1957	2.420376	1.512890
1958	2.359017	1.539072
1959	2.553392	1.636246
1960	2.632492	1.767387
1961	2.740858	1.855566
1962	2.779589	1.881102
1963	2.765289	1.892675
1964	2.706208	1.883980
1965	2.685954	1.923337
1966	2.721460	1.942105
1967	2.787132	1.981926
1968	2.938847	2.101528
1969	2.942521	2.183032
1970	2.985328	2.284227
1971	3.007605	2.381435
1972	3.149004	2.516283
1973	3.301206	2.653580
1974	3.437825	2.808581

TABLE A.2.1.1   Time series of average educational levels attained by the population (*cont.*)

Years	Educational level attained: index of productive human capital	Educational level attained: index of total human capital
1975	3.575545	2.989263
1976	3.732683	3.224951
1977	3.967561	3.498719
1978	4.287547	3.751490
1979	4.618052	3.989364
1980	4.797477	4.154964
1981	5.010104	4.305844
1982	5.143608	4.471453
1983	5.272499	4.539877
1984	5.334295	4.670815
1985	5.421198	4.778870
1986	5.545608	4.899813
1987	5.666801	4.949181
1988	5.774639	5.194605
1989	5.917318	5.335863
1990	5.263244	5.339319
1991	5.404380	5.372887
1992	5.537248	5.470019
1993	5.665122	5.553464
1994	5.788621	5.447086
1995	5.925871	5.735072
1996	6.042241	5.808936
1997	6.180096	6.030021
1998	6.339149	6.127943
1999	6.502474	6.215343
2000	6.680101	6.628803
2001	6.864249	6.796719
2002	7.082126	6.875601
2003	7.333028	7.095361
2004	7.606782	7.282976
2005	7.929189	7.115449
2006	8.279690	7.330895
2007	8.406950	7.554750
2008	8.526371	7.674433

TABLE A.2.1.1   Time series of average educational levels attained by the population (*cont.*)

Years	Educational level attained: index of productive human capital	Educational level attained: index of total human capital
2009	8.648644	7.815117
2010	9.050352	8.244960
2011	9.581349	8.290434
2012	9.664047	8.402824
2013	9.726813	8.513552
2014	9.856383	8.507623

TABLE A.2.1.2   Time series of educational levels achieved by schooling cycle for total population in the base years: China, 1964, 1990 and 1993–2014 (*in years*)

Base years	Primary	First cycle of secondary	Second cycle of secondary	High school and university
1964	3.590	8.308	10.376	14.609
1990	4.140	8.136	11.806	13.742
1993	4.500	8.328	11.171	13.873
1994	4.440	8.336	11.154	14.244
1995	4.401	8.341	11.229	13.976
1996	4.393	8.332	11.266	14.095
1997	4.426	8.339	11.286	14.061
1998	4.449	8.349	11.295	14.125
1999	4.430	8.349	11.273	14.123
2000	4.435	8.308	11.347	14.023
2001	4.612	8.442	11.311	14.024
2002	4.739	8.378	11.288	13.983
2003	4.840	8.402	11.321	14.002
2004	4.931	8.547	11.325	14.063
2005	4.867	8.660	11.189	14.076
2006	4.852	8.722	11.195	14.118
2007	4.903	8.800	11.319	14.309
2008	4.920	8.805	11.426	14.501

TABLE A.2.1.2   Time series of educational levels achieved by schooling cycle (*cont.*)

Base years	Primary	First cycle of secondary	Second cycle of secondary	High school and university
2009	4.970	8.810	11.466	14.611
2010	4.942	8.759	11.878	14.560
2011	4.994	8.812	11.609	14.615
2012	5.024	8.812	11.622	14.688
2013	5.043	8.811	11.632	14.727
2014	5.036	8.806	11.640	14.802

TABLE A.2.1.3   Series of average educational levels attained by the graduates: China, 1949–2014 (*in years*)

Years	Average educational level attained by the graduates of primary schools	Average educational level attained by the graduates of secondary schools	Average educational level attained by the graduates of high schools
1949	6.000	9.000	12.000
1950	6.000	9.000	12.000
1951	6.000	9.000	12.000
1952	5.000	9.000	12.000
1953	5.000	9.000	12.000
1954	6.000	9.000	12.000
1955	6.000	8.000	12.000
1956	6.000	8.000	12.000
1957	6.000	9.000	12.000
1958	5.850	8.813	10.813
1959	5.850	8.813	10.813
1960	5.850	8.813	11.813
1961	6.000	8.850	11.813
1962	6.000	8.850	11.813
1963	6.000	8.850	11.813
1964	6.000	9.000	11.850
1965	6.000	9.000	11.850
1966	5.000	8.000	11.000

TABLE A.2.1.3   Series of average educational levels attained by the graduates (*cont.*)

Years	Average educational level attained by the graduates of primary schools	Average educational level attained by the graduates of secondary schools	Average educational level attained by the graduates of high schools
1967	5.000	8.000	11.000
1968	5.000	8.000	10.000
1969	5.000	7.000	10.000
1970	5.000	7.000	10.000
1971	5.000	7.000	9.000
1972	5.000	7.000	9.000
1973	5.000	7.000	9.000
1974	5.000	7.176	9.003
1975	5.010	7.155	9.003
1976	5.009	7.148	9.181
1977	5.007	7.161	9.159
1978	5.001	7.345	9.149
1979	5.000	7.777	9.163
1980	5.000	7.980	9.359
1981	5.000	7.981	9.822
1982	5.003	7.988	10.076
1983	5.030	8.000	9.981
1984	5.143	8.000	10.758
1985	5.232	8.003	10.966
1986	5.290	8.030	10.962
1987	5.398	8.143	10.980
1988	5.432	8.232	10.993
1989	5.510	8.290	11.025
1990	5.557	8.398	11.139
1991	5.576	8.432	11.232
1992	5.597	8.510	11.290
1993	5.589	8.557	11.398
1994	5.598	8.576	11.432
1995	5.610	8.597	11.510
1996	5.619	8.589	11.557
1997	5.666	8.598	11.576
1998	5.685	8.610	11.597

TABLE A.2.1.3   Series of average educational levels attained by the graduates (*cont.*)

Years	Average educational level attained by the graduates of primary schools	Average educational level attained by the graduates of secondary schools	Average educational level attained by the graduates of high schools
1999	5.619	8.619	11.589
2000	5.641	8.666	11.598
2001	5.773	8.685	11.610
2002	5.883	8.619	11.619
2003	5.933	8.641	11.666
2004	6.000	8.773	11.685
2005	6.000	8.883	11.619
2006	6.000	8.933	11.641
2007	6.000	9.000	11.773
2008	6.000	9.000	11.883
2009	6.000	9.000	11.933
2010	6.000	9.000	12.000
2011	6.000	9.000	12.000
2012	6.000	9.000	12.000
2013	6.000	9.000	12.000
2014	6.000	9.000	12.000

A.2.2   Complementary Statistical Database on Schooling Durations in China from 1949 to 2014

TABLE A.2.2.1   Series of the average durations of the educational cycles: China, 1949–2014 (*in years*)

Years	Average duration of primary education	Average duration of secondary education	Average duration of high-school education
1949	6.000	3.000	3.000
1950	6.000	3.000	3.000
1951	6.000		3.000
1952	5.000	3.000	3.000

TABLE A.2.2.1   Series of the average durations of the educational cycles (*cont.*)

Years	Average duration of primary education	Average duration of secondary education	Average duration of high-school education
1953	5.000	3.000	3.000
1954	6.000	3.000	3.000
1955	6.000	3.000	3.000
1956	6.000	3.000	3.000
1957	6.000	3.000	3.000
1958	5.850	2.813	2.813
1959	5.850	2.813	2.813
1960	5.850	2.813	2.813
1961	6.000	3.000	3.000
1962	6.000	3.000	3.000
1963	6.000	3.000	3.000
1964	6.000	3.000	3.000
1965	6.000	3.000	3.000
1966	5.000	2.000	2.000
1967	5.000	2.000	2.000
1968	5.000	2.000	2.000
1969	5.000	2.000	2.000
1970	5.000	2.000	2.000
1971	5.000	2.000	2.000
1972	5.000	2.000	2.000
1973	5.000	2.000	2.000
1974	5.000	2.176	2.003
1975	5.010	2.155	2.003
1976	5.009	2.148	2.006
1977	5.007	2.161	2.004
1978	5.001	2.335	2.001
1979	5.000	2.768	2.002
1980	5.000	2.973	2.014
1981	5.000	2.980	2.045
1982	5.003	2.988	2.096
1983	5.030	3.000	2.000

TABLE A.2.2.1　Series of the average durations of the educational cycles (*cont.*)

Years	Average duration of primary education	Average duration of secondary education	Average duration of high-school education
1984	5.143	3.000	2.777
1985	5.232	3.000	2.978
1986	5.290	3.000	2.962
1987	5.398	3.000	2.980
1988	5.432	3.000	2.989
1989	5.510	3.000	2.994
1990	5.557	3.000	2.996
1991	5.576	3.000	3.000
1992	5.597	3.000	3.000
1993	5.589	3.000	3.000
1994	5.598	3.000	3.000
1995	5.610	3.000	3.000
1996	5.619	3.000	3.000
1997	5.666	3.000	3.000
1998	5.685	3.000	3.000
1999	5.619	3.000	3.000
2000	5.641	3.000	3.000
2001	5.773	3.000	3.000
2002	5.883	3.000	3.000
2003	5.933	3.000	3.000
2004	6.000	3.000	3.000
2005	6.000	3.000	3.000
2006	6.000	3.000	3.000
2007	6.000	3.000	3.000
2008	6.000	3.000	3.000
2009	6.000	3.000	3.000
2010	6.000	3.000	3.000
2011	6.000	3.000	3.000
2012	6.000	3.000	3.000
2013	6.000	3.000	3.000
2014	6.000	3.000	3.000

A.2.3   Complementary Statistical Database on the New Increases
         in Human Capital in China from 1949 to 2014

TABLE A.2.3.1   Series of new increases in the total human capital stock: China, 1949–2014
                 (*in years × 10,000 persons*)

Year	Increase in total human capital (mid-year)	Increase in total human capital (at the end of the year)
1949	1,071.83	1,061.11
1950	1,134.95	1,126.86
1951	1,495.07	1,480.96
1952	1,464.46	1,448.43
1953	2,711.42	2,685.15
1954	3,418.48	3,389.85
1955	3,720.03	3,675.15
1956	4,532.37	4,501.86
1957	5,426.30	5,391.12
1958	9,624.46	9,554.34
1959	8,360.16	8,287.37
1960	7,509.38	7,453.39
1961	6,700.38	6,642.03
1962	6,140.47	6,074.26
1963	5,429.61	5,378.10
1964	5,859.25	5,816.62
1965	6,869.65	6,802.62
1966	6,537.45	6,509.25
1967	6,729.18	6,709.25
1968	12,565.76	12,534.92
1969	10,723.40	10,693.76
1970	13,469.20	13,405.56
1971	13,745.33	13,705.75
1972	16,426.60	16,361.91
1973	18,019.81	17,952.75
1974	19,265.02	19,205.31
1975	22,856.53	22,740.76
1976	27,737.35	27,656.36
1977	31,624.18	31,513.52

TABLE A.2.3.1   Series of new increases in the total human capital stock (*cont.*)

Year	Increase in total human capital (mid-year)	Increase in total human capital (at the end of the year)
1978	31,843.40	31,736.41
1979	31,432.70	31,332.28
1980	25,583.06	25,483.84
1981	26,342.38	26,256.30
1982	23,963.15	23,857.18
1983	21,786.92	21,705.80
1984	21,969.64	21,908.26
1985	23,107.61	22,959.02
1986	24,228.68	24,146.03
1987	25,818.73	25,728.75
1988	25,909.20	25,833.85
1989	25,603.62	25,543.14
1990	25,884.24	25,716.65
1991	26,035.25	25,954.82
1992	26,425.52	26,338.89
1993	26,681.81	26,594.43
1994	27,138.32	27,051.13
1995	28,736.38	28,642.84
1996	29,439.09	29,342.06
1997	31,624.42	31,525.22
1998	34,290.20	34,183.17
1999	35,731.78	35,620.88
2000	37,403.05	37,291.09
2001	38,949.63	38,832.77
2002	41,050.26	40,919.00
2003	43,444.68	43,309.20
2004	45,938.60	45,798.20
2005	48,708.67	48,556.94
2006	50,194.12	50,054.72
2007	51,601.35	51,449.68
2008	52,893.25	52,735.94
2009	52,683.07	52,533.62
2010	52,635.78	52,480.28

TABLE A.2.3.1   Series of new increases in the total human capital stock (*cont.*)

Year	Increase in total human capital (mid-year)	Increase in total human capital (at the end of the year)
2011	52,597.69	52,436.02
2012	52,302.50	52,139.05
2013	51,374.24	51,219.54
2014	49,360.56	49,360.56

Note: The amortization rate used is M_t^{6+} for the calculation at the end of the year.

TABLE A.2.3.2   Series of new increases in the productive human capital stock: China, 1949–2014 (*in years × 10,000 persons*)

Years	Increase in productive human capital (mid-year)	Increase in productive human capital (at the end of the year)
1949	684.23	677.39
1950	665.15	659.16
1951	795.47	788.71
1952	719.46	714.06
1953	1,243.92	1,234.86
1954	1,423.48	1,412.35
1955	1,782.63	1,769.47
1956	2,101.77	2,087.14
1957	2,438.30	2,422.02
1958	6,077.60	6,034.33
1959	5,158.45	5,115.88
1960	3,215.48	3,170.46
1961	3,215.58	3,187.78
1962	2,786.47	2,768.83
1963	2,568.81	2,552.68
1964	2,454.85	2,437.43
1965	2,864.05	2,846.88
1966	4,971.55	4,944.51
1967	5,622.48	5,593.91
1968	8,804.86	8,761.25
1969	4,872.10	4,849.32

TABLE A.2.3.2   Series of new increases in the productive human capital stock *(cont.)*

Years	Increase in productive human capital (mid-year)	Increase in productive human capital (at the end of the year)
1970	5,914.03	5,887.95
1971	5,323.65	5,298.82
1972	6,838.10	6,805.18
1973	9,160.81	9,119.11
1974	8,656.86	8,615.94
1975	9,252.80	9,209.36
1976	9,839.55	9,792.37
1977	12,657.12	12,599.33
1978	17,359.64	17,284.03
1979	18,920.74	18,836.18
1980	15,582.29	15,510.90
1981	17,802.97	17,720.64
1982	16,111.95	16,033.95
1983	14,399.43	14,323.13
1984	14,812.85	14,737.98
1985	15,951.16	15,870.62
1986	16,816.95	16,732.54
1987	17,819.41	17,725.28
1988	17,838.31	17,745.94
1989	17,315.12	17,216.44
1990	16,991.25	16,900.17
1991	16,759.08	16,672.43
1992	16,654.60	16,555.92
1993	16,806.68	16,702.82
1994	16,662.58	16,562.07
1995	17,732.02	17,624.14
1996	18,572.04	18,452.68
1997	20,517.57	20,382.13
1998	22,251.79	22,101.78
1999	22,730.57	22,575.34
2000	23,755.49	23,594.38
2001	25,112.69	24,936.04
2002	27,213.51	27,003.24
2003	29,990.26	29,758.29

TABLE A.2.3.2   Series of new increases in the productive human capital stock (*cont.*)

Years	Increase in productive human capital (mid-year)	Increase in productive human capital (at the end of the year)
2004	33,127.40	32,862.11
2005	36,591.81	36,290.28
2006	38,623.12	38,316.05
2007	40,380.32	40,030.36
2008	41,703.54	41,348.85
2009	41,851.88	41,514.22
2010	42,197.96	41,867.63
2011	42,620.86	42,298.59
2012	42,452.90	42,051.12
2013	41,887.89	41,495.44
2014	40,500.79	40,082.84

Note: The amortization rate used is σ_t for the calculation at the end of the year.

A.2.4   Chinese Literature on Human Capital in China

TABLE A.2.4.1   Some studies by Chinese authors on the effects of human capital in China

Method used	Authors	Period	Level	Elasticity
Kendrick *et al.*	Zhang (2000)	1953–1995	National	0.15
	Qian (2004)	1995–2001	National and provincial	–
	Qiao and Shen (2015)	1978–2011	National	–
Jorgenson – Fraumeni	Zhu (2007)	1990–2004	35 large cities	–
Mulligan – Martin	Li *et al.* (2010), or CUFE database	1985–2007	National	–
Barro – Lee	Cai and Wang (1999)	1982–1997	National	0.555
	Cai and Du (2003)	1949–1982	National	–
	Li (2001)	1949–2000	National	–
		1964–1995	Provincial	–
	Yue and Liu (2006)	1996–2003	Provincial	–

TABLE A.2.4.1   Some studies by Chinese authors on the effects of human capital in China (*cont.*)

Method used	Authors	Period	Level	Elasticity
	Wang (2002)	1990–2010	Values predicted by ARMA	0.306*
	Bai (2012)	1952–2008	National and provincial	–
	Jiao and Jiao (2010)	1978–2007	National	–
	Yang (2006)	1952–2006	National	–
	Yang *et al.* (2006)	1985–2000	Provincial	0.41 and 0.72**
	Wang *et al.* (2009)	1952–2008	National	from 0.66 to 0.83
	Yao and Lin (2006)	PWT data		0.21

Notes: (*) The elasticity of human capital is 0.306 at the national level, but 0.436 for the secondary sector and even 0.740 for the tertiary sector. (**) The elasticity of education is 0.72 in a Solowian model, while that of education and health is 0.41 in an endogenous growth model.

A.2.5   Chinese Educational System Reforms

TABLE A.2.5.1   Main dates of educational reforms in the People's Republic of China

Date	Regulations or Events	Comments
1922	*Renxu* Education System	Primary education consists of two levels: four years for the 1st cycle and two years for the 2nd one
1951 (1 October)	Decision of the Reform of the Education System by the Council of State	1) Primary education is a "coherent five-year system," and 2) the durations of colleges and universities are reduced from 4–6 to 3–5 years.
1953 (26 December)	The five-year primary school system is canceled. The duration of primary education is again extended to six years.	

TABLE A.2.5.1   Main dates of educational reforms in the People's Republic of China (*cont.*)

Date	Regulations or Events	Comments
1958	Educational reforms decided within the framework of the movement of the Great Leap Forward	Experiences of large-scale reforms: five-year primary school; five-year middle school; primary-middle school of seven, nine or ten years, or 9 + 2 years (1st and 2nd cycles); four-year middle secondary school, 4 + 2, 3 + 2 or 2 + 2 (1st and 2nd cycles), etc.
1959 (24 May)	Provisions concerning the Experimental Reforms of Education by the Council of State	Experiments in reforming the education system are put on hold
1960 (8 April)	Report *Education must be reformed* for the 2nd Session of the Second National People's Congress	The experiences of reforms resumed. Until September 1960, for data on 27 provinces, 14.8 per cent of primary schools and 18.7 per cent of secondary schools participated.
January 1961– May 1966	Before the Cultural Revolution	Some schools participated in the experiments as part of the Great Leap Forward
1966–1976	Cultural Revolution	The durations of education are reduced. Until 1973, 14 provinces were at nine years (five for primary, four for secondary); seven provinces at 10 years (5 + 5 or 6 + 4); nine at nine years in rural areas and 10 in urban ones; Tibet is at five or six years in primary and three in lower secondary.
After 1976	Economic reforms	The durations gradually meet the standards
1989	The numbers of graduated from six-year primary school exceeded that from five-year primary school.	
From 2004 to the present	All primary schools in China have a six-year curriculum, with the exception of Shanghai (a region where the system is five years in primary and four in lower secondary)	

A.2.6   Reforms in the Legal Ages of Retirement

TABLE A.2.6.1   Changes in the legal ages of retirement in China from 1951 to the present day
(*in years*)

Time	Executives		Workers		Legislation and	Implementation
	men	women	men	women	regulations in force	(and changes)
1951	60	50	60	50	*"Labour Insurance Regulations"*	26 February 1951 (26 January 1953)
1955	60	55	60	50	*"State Council Temporary Measures on State Organs' Retirement"*	1 January 1956
1958	60	55	60	55	*"State Council Temporary Measures on Workers and Staff's Retirement"*	9 February 1958
since 1978	60	55	60	50	*"State Council Temporary Measures on Providing for Old, Weak, Sick and Handicapped Cadres"* *"State Council Temporary Measures on Workers Retirement: Resignation"*	2 June 1978

Note: Exceptions exist for certain professions with special status. Examples: i) if the retirement age for provincial government executives is fixed at 65, there is no specific restriction on that of senior executives (at national levels); ii) since March 2015, the retirement age for female managers in national administrations has increased to 60 years.

A.2.7   Alternative Database on China's Human Capital Using Kendrick *et al.* (1976)'s Method

According to Kendrick (1979)'s method, human capital is the accumulated and depreciated expenditures in education to improve labour's quality. Human capital narrowly defined refers to education only, while human capital boardly defined also includes expenses in health. The latter are difficult to calculate in China, because of lacking data. We determine total expenses in education as the sum of budgetary education expenditure by the State, funds for private schools, social donation and fund raising, business income of schools, and

other educational funds. Data come from the NBS online database and from
China Compendium of Statistics 1949–2008 that provide "investment series." As
Kendrick's method is the PIM, we need the initial human capital and depreciation rate. The initial capital is obtained by the iterative method proposed in
Chapter 3. So we estimate two series of human capital *à la* Kendrick: the first
one with a constant depreciation rate at 5 percent and the second one with a
dynamic depreciation rate, i.e., the mortality rate of total population. We use
the consumer price index (CPI) as price index.

TABLE A.2.7.1   Series of total educational expenditures calculated using Kendrick *et al.*
(1976)'s method: China, 1952–2012 (*1952 constant prices, 100 million yuans*)

Years	Total educational expenditures
1952	11.03
1953	18.32
1954	18.74
1955	17.78
1956	24.84
1957	25.54
1958	23.60
1959	30.70
1960	41.60
1961	25.48
1962	20.52
1963	23.45
1964	28.59
1965	29.79
1966	34.13
1967	31.28
1968	23.27
1969	22.66
1970	23.09
1971	28.26
1972	32.97
1973	36.34
1974	42.37
1975	43.99
1976	47.17
1977	47.91

TABLE A.2.7.1 Series of total educational expenditures calculated using Kendrick (*cont.*)

Years	Total educational expenditures
1978	59.85
1979	72.90
1980	83.10
1981	87.21
1982	95.82
1983	105.97
1984	120.23
1985	137.94
1986	156.87
1987	156.42
1988	159.77
1989	156.55
1990	242.79
1991	260.49
1992	290.18
1993	309.27
1994	350.04
1995	377.07
1996	419.43
1997	456.59
1998	536.15
1999	617.51
2000	706.89
2001	845.78
2002	1,007.47
2003	1,127.82
2004	1,266.33
2005	1,445.96
2006	1,660.90
2007	1,961.48
2008	2,210.91
2009	2,533.89
2010	2,907.65
2011	3,366.13
2012	3,806.81

TABLE A.2.7.2   Series of human capital (with a 5 percent depreciation rate) calculated
using Kendrick *et al.* (1976)'s method: China, 1952–2012 (*1952 constant prices,*
100 million yuans)

Years	Human capital (with a 5 percent depreciation rate) (*1952 constant prices, 100 million yuans*)	Growth rate of this human capital (*in percentages*)
1952	82.16	–
1953	96.37	0.1729
1954	110.29	0.1445
1955	122.55	0.1112
1956	141.26	0.1527
1957	159.74	0.1308
1958	175.35	0.0978
1959	197.28	0.1251
1960	229.01	0.1609
1961	243.05	0.0613
1962	251.42	0.0344
1963	262.30	0.0433
1964	277.77	0.0590
1965	293.67	0.0573
1966	313.12	0.0662
1967	328.74	0.0499
1968	335.58	0.0208
1969	341.46	0.0175
1970	347.48	0.0176
1971	358.37	0.0313
1972	373.41	0.0420
1973	391.08	0.0473
1974	413.90	0.0583
1975	437.19	0.0563
1976	462.50	0.0579
1977	487.29	0.0536
1978	522.77	0.0728
1979	569.53	0.0895
1980	624.15	0.0959
1981	680.15	0.0897
1982	741.96	0.0909
1983	810.83	0.0928

TABLE A.2.7.2   Series of human capital (with a 5 percent depreciation rate) (*cont.*)

Years	Human capital (with a 5 percent depreciation rate) (*1952 constant prices, 100 million yuans*)	Growth rate of this human capital (*in percentages*)
1984	890.52	0.0983
1985	983.93	0.1049
1986	1,091.61	0.1094
1987	1,193.44	0.0933
1988	1,293.54	0.0839
1989	1,385.41	0.0710
1990	1,558.93	0.1252
1991	1,741.47	0.1171
1992	1,944.57	0.1167
1993	2,156.62	0.1090
1994	2,398.83	0.1123
1995	2,655.96	0.1072
1996	2,942.59	0.1079
1997	3,252.06	0.1052
1998	3,625.60	0.1149
1999	4,061.83	0.1203
2000	4,565.62	0.1240
2001	5,183.12	0.1353
2002	5,931.44	0.1444
2003	6,762.68	0.1401
2004	7,690.88	0.1373
2005	8,752.30	0.1380
2006	9,975.58	0.1398
2007	11,438.28	0.1466
2008	13,077.28	0.1433
2009	14,957.31	0.1438
2010	17,117.09	0.1444
2011	19,627.37	0.1467
2012	22,452.80	0.1440

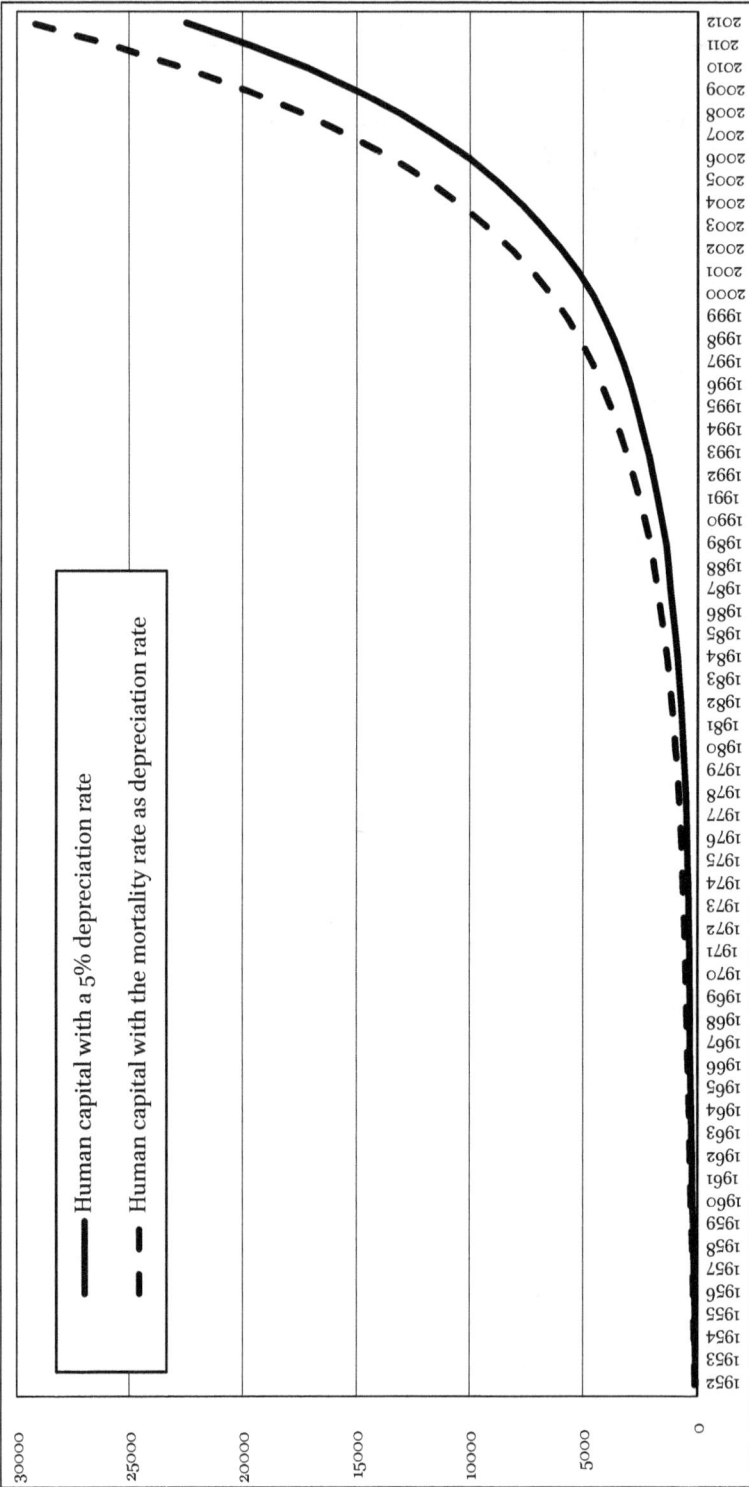

GRAPH A.2.7.1 Human capital in China calculated with the total educational expenditures: levels *(constant prices of 1952, in 100 million yuans)*

Legend:
— Human capital with a 5% depreciation rate
- - - Human capital with the mortality rate as depreciation rate

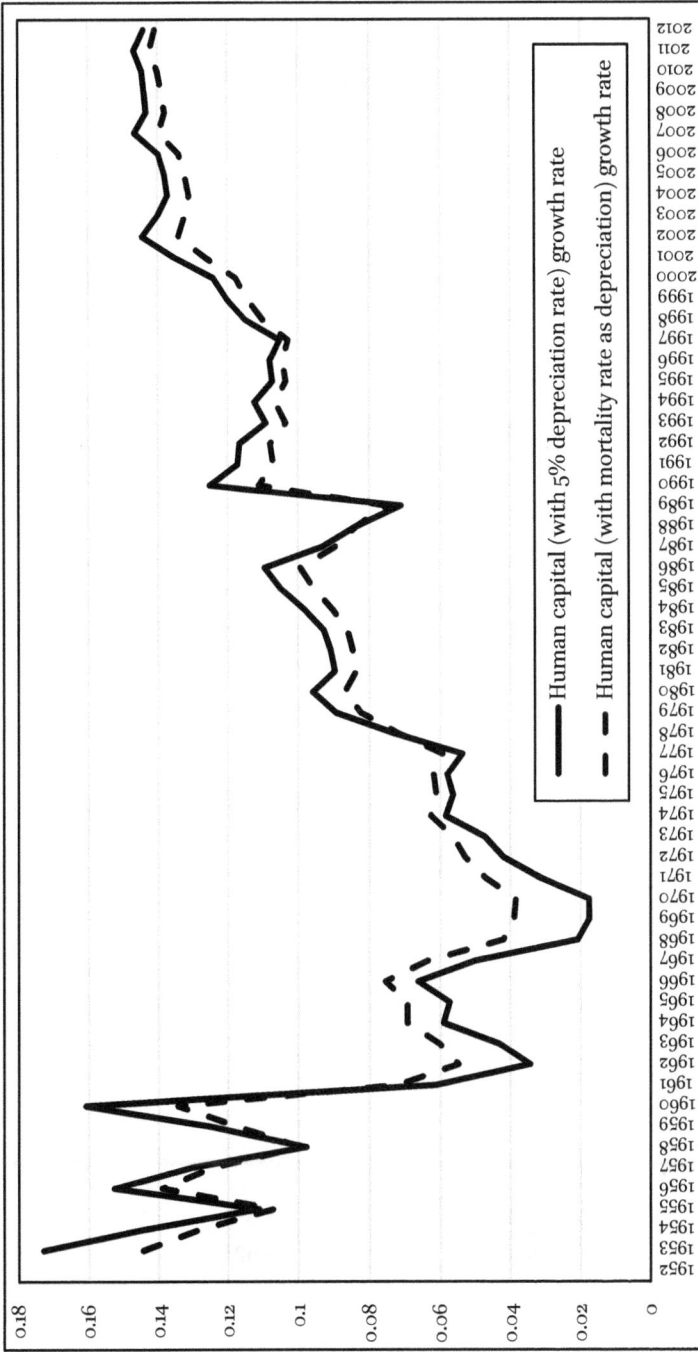

GRAPH A.2.7.2 Human capital in China calculated with the total educational expenditures: growth rates (*in percentages*)

TABLE A.2.7.3   Series of human capital (with the mortality rate as depreciation rate)
calculated using Kendrick *et al.* (1976)'s method: China, 1952–2012
(*1952 constant prices, 100 million yuans*)

Years	Human capital (with the mortality rate as depreciation rate) (*1952 constant prices, 100 million yuans*)	Growth rate of this human capital (*in percentages*)
1952	115.57	–
1953	132.27	0.1445
1954	149.27	0.1285
1955	165.21	0.1068
1956	188.17	0.1390
1957	211.68	0.1249
1958	232.74	0.0995
1959	260.04	0.1173
1960	295.02	0.1345
1961	316.28	0.0721
1962	333.61	0.0548
1963	353.69	0.0602
1964	378.19	0.0693
1965	404.39	0.0693
1966	434.94	0.0756
1967	462.53	0.0634
1968	481.99	0.0421
1969	500.76	0.0390
1970	520.03	0.0385
1971	544.47	0.0470
1972	573.28	0.0529
1973	605.55	0.0563
1974	643.46	0.0626
1975	682.71	0.0610
1976	724.90	0.0618
1977	767.80	0.0592
1978	822.85	0.0717
1979	890.64	0.0824
1980	968.09	0.0870
1981	1,049.14	0.0837

TABLE A.2.7.3   Series of human capital (with the mortality rate as depreciation rate) *(cont.)*

Years	Human capital (with the mortality rate as depreciation rate) *(1952 constant prices, 100 million yuans)*	Growth rate of this human capital *(in percentages)*
1982	1,138.03	0.0847
1983	1,236.15	0.0862
1984	1,347.95	0.0904
1985	1,476.75	0.0956
1986	1,623.49	0.0994
1987	1,769.00	0.0896
1988	1,917.02	0.0837
1989	2,061.03	0.0751
1990	2,290.07	0.1111
1991	2,535.21	0.1070
1992	2,808.56	0.1078
1993	3,099.19	0.1035
1994	3,429.11	0.1065
1995	3,783.65	0.1034
1996	4,178.26	0.1043
1997	4,607.66	0.1028
1998	5,113.86	0.1099
1999	5,698.33	0.1143
2000	6,368.46	0.1176
2001	7,173.29	0.1264
2002	8,134.78	0.1340
2003	9,210.53	0.1322
2004	10,417.73	0.1311
2005	11,795.88	0.1323
2006	13,376.44	0.1340
2007	15,245.23	0.1397
2008	17,348.51	0.1380
2009	19,759.57	0.1390
2010	22,526.73	0.1400
2011	25,732.02	0.1423
2012	29,354.84	0.1408

Appendices to Chapter 3

A.3.1 Complementary Statistical Database on R&D Expenditures in China from 1953 and 2014

TABLE A.3.1.1 Second series of R&D expenditures: China, 1953–2014 (*in hundreds of millions of 1952 constant yuans*)

Years	R&D Expenditures	Years	R&D Expenditures
1952	n.-a.	1984	62.959
1953	0.533	1985	62.388
1954	1.145	1986	63.604
1955	1.993	1987	63.121
1956	4.898	1988	63.782
1957	4.777	1989	56.596
1958	10.373	1990	62.371
1959	17.620	1991	73.708
1960	30.351	1992	85.064
1961	15.070	1993	94.980
1962	10.227	1994	86.785
1963	14.732	1995	70.012
1964	19.950	1996	74.990
1965	22.605	1997	91.826
1966	21.103	1998	100.195
1967	13.004	1999	125.180
1968	12.526	2000	164.488
1969	20.237	2001	190.122
1970	25.105	2002	236.725
1971	31.606	2003	279.695
1972	30.220	2004	343.803
1973	28.927	2005	420.790
1974	28.776	2006	508.170
1975	33.343	2007	599.073
1976	32.369	2008	703.800
1977	33.309	2009	890.878
1978	42.176	2010	1,049.773
1979	48.746	2011	1,225.071

TABLE A.3.1.1 Second series of R&D expenditures: China, 1953–2014 *(cont.)*

Years	R&D Expenditures	Years	R&D Expenditures
1980	47.019	2012	1,415.514
1981	43.735	2013	1,587.049
1982	45.460	2014	1,709.471
1983	53.996		

Notes: This series of R&D differs from the previous one (built in Chapter 3) by the fact that before the year 1986, the expenses correspond to those of Science & Technology. "n.-a." = non-available.

A.3.2   Data Sources on R&D Expenditures: China, 1953–2014

TABLE A.3.2.1 Data sources on R&D expenditures: China, 1953–2014

Period	Data sources
1953–1970	*55 Years Statistics Compilation of New China*
1971–1985	*55 Years Statistics Compilation of New China* and *China Statistical Yearbook 1988*
1986–1988	*40 Years Statistics of China's Science and Technology 1949–1989*
1989–1994	*"China Statistical Yearbook on Science and Technology"* (each year)
1995–2013	NBS online database

Note: The Chinese Academy of Science and Technology for Development, belonging to the Ministry of Science and Technology, also provides these same R&D data since 1987.

Appendix to Chapter 4

A.4.1 Complementary Statistical Database on Rural and Urban Gini Coefficients in China from 1978 and 1999

TABLE A.4.1.1 Rural and Urban Gini Coefficients: China, 1978–1999

Years	Rural Gini coefficient	Urban Gini coefficient
1978	0.21	0.16
1979	n.-a.	n.-a.
1980	0.24	0.16
1981	0.24	0.15
1982	0.23	0.15
1983	0.25	0.15
1984	0.24	0.16
1985	0.23	0.19
1986	0.30	0.19
1987	0.30	0.20
1988	0.30	0.23
1989	0.31	0.23
1990	0.31	0.23
1991	0.31	0.24
1992	0.31	0.25
1993	0.33	0.27
1994	0.32	0.30
1995	0.34	0.28
1996	0.32	0.28
1997	0.33	0.29
1998	0.34	0.30
1999	0.34	0.31

Note: "n.-a." = non-available.

Appendices to Chapter 5

A.5.1 Mathematical Reminders on Theoretical Neoclassical Modeling

A.5.1.1 *Neoclassical Modeling of Growth*
A.5.1.1.1 The Solowian Model
The production function F is at convexity in technology, that is, F is concave:

$$Y = F(K, L) = K^\alpha L^{1-\alpha}$$

where α, the elasticity of output with respect to capital, is such that: $0 < \alpha < 1$.

This function is homogeneous of degree one, with a share-exhausting income (Euler theorem) and a zero-profit *à la* Walras. It verifies the properties of continuity, derivability at order two, concavity and limit behaviours of the marginal productivities (Inada conditions):

$$f'(k) > 0$$
$$f''(k) > 0$$
$$\lim_{k \to +\infty} f'(k) \to 0$$
$$\lim_{k \to 0} f'(k) \to +\infty$$
$$f(0) = 0$$

where the variables are expressed *per capita*, such as: $y = Y/L = f(k)$, with: $k = K/L$.

Capital accumulation takes the form of a differencial equation of first order, non-linear, at constant coefficients (of Bernoulli type):

$$\dot{k} = sy - nk$$

For all s, it exists a single value of capital k^*, which is a stationary solution of:

$$\frac{\dot{k}}{k} = sk^{\alpha-1} - n = 0$$

According to the "Golden Rule" of accumulation, consumption is maximum when the interest rate is equal to the active population growth rate, that is to say as:

$$f'(k) = n$$

A.5.1.1.2   The AK Model

The production function, at single factor and at constant returns to scale, is written:

$$Y = A\,K$$

where K is a composite capital and A its apparent productivity, considered to be an exogenous constant.

If capital accumulation is given by:

$$\dot{K} = I = A\,K - C = s\,Y$$

then, the growth rate of the economy is equal to:

$$g = \frac{\dot{K}}{K} = s\,A$$

The resolution of the model consists in maximizing the following utility function:

$$U\left(c\right) = \int_{o}^{\infty} \frac{c^{1-\sigma}}{1-\sigma}\ e^{-\rho t}\ dt$$

where σ is the intertemporal elasticity of substitution and ρ the rate of preference for the present.

The optimization program allows us to obtain the growth rate of the economy:

$$g = \frac{\dot{c}}{c} \equiv \frac{\dot{k}}{k} = \frac{A - \rho}{\sigma}$$

This equation *à la* Keynes-Ramsey allows the equalization of the rate of return of investment for the enterprise (A) and of the rate of return of consumption for the household $(g\sigma + \rho)$. The growth rate g is determined by the marginal productivity of capital (A) and by the rate of savings, the latter being itself linked to σ and to ρ. The solution is not yet a level, but a growth rate – which is finally found to be endogeneized.

A.5.1.1.3   Canonical Models of Endogenous Growth

A.5.1.1.3.1   *Romer (1986)*

The technology used by the firms is supposed to be at constant returns to scale on private capital and labour, but at increasing returns to scale over the whole factors, including collective knowledge:

$$Y = K^{\beta} L^{1-\beta} x^{\gamma} = \left(N K_i\right)^{\beta} \left(N L_i\right)^{1-\beta} \left(\sum_{i=1}^{N} K_i\right)^{\gamma}$$

for a constant number of firms (N), and with $\beta < 1$ and $\gamma > 1$.

By maximizing the social utility function under constraint, we can write the growth rate of consumption *per capita* in competitive equilibrium (g_e) as the difference between the interest rate and the rate of psychological discount of the agents divided by the constant intertemporal elasticity of substitution:

$$g_e = \frac{\dot{c}}{c} = \frac{\beta \, k^{\beta+\gamma-1} \, L^{\gamma} - \rho}{\sigma}$$

where the expression $\beta \, k^{\beta+\gamma-1} L^{\gamma}$ represents the interest rate.

Thus, the model's resolution gives three configurations:

i)   if $\beta + \gamma < 1$, then the steady state growth rate is zero;

ii)   if $\beta + \gamma = 1$, then the growth is endogeneized (*à la* AK, with $L = A$);

iii)   if $\beta + \gamma > 1$, the growth is explosive and the model diverges.

When the planner integrates the externality, the growth rate at the social optimum (g_o) can be written as:

$$g_o = \frac{\left(\beta + \gamma\right) \, k^{\beta+\gamma-1} \, L^{\gamma} - \rho}{\sigma}$$

As the externality separates the two equilibria, finally we have: $g_o > g_e$.

A.5.1.1.3.2   *Romer (1990)*

The R&D sector, operating with dynamic increasing returns, uses human capital (H_A), as well as knowledge available at a determined moment (A) and accumuled according to the following equation:

$$\frac{\dot{A}}{A} = \delta \, H_A$$

The linearity in the process of knowledge accumulation involves that the growth rate of A is not cancelled when A tends to infinity.

The technology of the firms producing the final output is given by a production function at constant returns to scale, thanks to human capital (H_Y), non-skilled labour and a physical capital taking the form of a *continuum* of intermediary capital goods:

$$Y = H_Y^\alpha \ L^\beta \int_0^A x(i)^{1-\alpha-\beta} \ di$$

If we consider an equilibrium that is symmetrical with respect to the intermediary goods $x_i = \bar{x}$, it comes:

$$Y = H_Y^\alpha \ L^\beta \ A x^{-1-\alpha-\beta}$$

Decentralized non Pareto-optimal equilibrium and optimal equilibrium are such that: $g_e < g_o$. In other words, we get:

$$g_e = \frac{\delta H - \Phi \rho}{\Phi \sigma + 1} < g_o = \frac{\delta H - \Xi \rho}{\Xi \sigma + (1-\Xi)}$$

with

$$\Phi = \frac{\alpha}{(1-\alpha-\beta)(\alpha+\beta)}$$

and

$$\Xi = \frac{\alpha}{(\alpha+b)}$$

A.5.1.1.3.3 *Lucas (1988)*

The macroeconomic production function can be written as following:

$$Y = A K^\beta \left(u h L\right)^{1-\beta} h_\alpha^\psi$$

where u and (1-u) are the fractions of time that the agents allocate respectively to production and to their training, h being the efficiency of labour and L the number of individuals. The term (uhL) represents the stock of human capital. The externality Ψ is associated to human capital, whose average level is h_a.

The individual human capital is accumulated according to the following training process:

$$\frac{\dot{h}}{h} = \Phi(1-u)$$

where the proportionality constant Φ is a parameter of efficiency.

In the long run, the growth rate of the centralized equilibrium is superior to that of the decentralized equilibrium:

$$g_e = \frac{1-\beta+\Psi}{1-\beta}(g_h)_e < g_o = \frac{1-\beta+\Psi}{1-\beta}(g_h)_o$$

because

$$g_e = \left[\frac{1-\beta+\Psi}{1-\beta}\right]\left[\frac{(\phi-\rho)(1-\beta)}{\sigma(1-\beta+\psi)-\psi}\right] < g_o = \left[\frac{1-\beta+\psi}{1-\beta}\right]\left(\frac{q\frac{(1-\beta)\rho}{1-\beta+\psi}}{\sigma}\right)$$

where the expressions $(g_h)_e$ and $(g_h)_o$ correspond to the growth rates of human capital at the two respective equilibria.

Without externality (that is to say, if $\Psi = 0$), the growth rates of final output and of human capital coincide, as in the AK-type model.

A.5.1.1.3.4 *Barro (1990)*
The production function, at constant returns to scale, incorporates two factors, private capital *per capita* (k_p) and total productive public spending (d), so that:

$$y = A\,k^{1-\alpha}\,d^\alpha$$

A being a technological parameter, with $\alpha < 1$.

Goods provided by the state are financed by a tax at constant rate τ:

$$d = \tau y$$

The similarity between the Barro model and the AK one becomes clear when the production function is written as:

$$y = A^{\frac{1}{1-\alpha}} \, \tau^{\frac{\alpha}{1-\alpha}} \, k$$

where the constance of the expression $(A\tau^\alpha)^{1/1-\alpha}$ impedes the cancellation of the marginal productivity of capital.

Consequently, the externality of public spending involves the under-optimality of the decentralized equilibrium, that is:

$$g_e = \frac{(1-\alpha)\,A^{\frac{1}{1-\alpha}}\,(1-\tau)\,\tau^{\frac{\alpha}{1-\alpha}} - \rho}{\sigma} \; < \; g_o = \frac{A^{\frac{1}{1-\alpha}}\,(1-\tau)\,\tau^{\frac{\alpha}{1-\alpha}} - \rho}{\sigma}$$

Finally, the optimal level of public expenditure, which maximizes the growth rate in the long period, is reached if and only if:

$$\frac{D}{Y} = \tau = \alpha$$

A.5.1.2 *A Solowian Model of Endogenous Growth*
A.5.1.2.1   The Model
The model integrates two types of public expenditures: 1) those of consumption, as an argument of the social utility function; and 2) those of education and of infrastructure, incrementing the capital stocks, as inputs of the macroeconomic production function. Within such a framework with four factors (plus a fifth one which is an exogenous technical progress), the engine of endogenous growth corresponds to an accumulation of human capital in a public educational sector.

The production function of the final good is of Cobb-Douglas type. Here, it allows capital-labor substitutability and combines two C.E.S. functions (one for capital K, and the other one for labour L). Both of these C.E.S. functions are bi-factorial and symmetrical. With constant returns to scale on all factors (reproducible and non-reproducible), this macroscopic production function is written as follows:

$$Y = \left(\mu_P \, K_P^{\sigma_K - 1 / \sigma_K} + \mu_G \, K_G^{\sigma_K - 1 / \sigma_K} \right)^{\alpha \left(\phi_K \frac{\sigma_K}{\sigma_K - 1} \right)}$$

$$\cdot \left(\Lambda^{\sigma_L - 1 / \sigma_L} \left[\mu_N \, N_Y^{\sigma_L - 1 / \sigma_L} + \mu_S \, S_Y^{\sigma_L - 1 / \sigma_L} \right] \right)^{(1-\alpha)\left(\phi_L \frac{\sigma_L}{\sigma_L - 1} \right)}$$

where $\phi_K = \phi_L = 1$, $0 < \alpha < 1$, $\sigma_K < 1$, $\sigma_L > 1$, $\mu_N + \mu_S = 1$, $\mu_P + \mu_G = 1$ K_P and K_G being private and public capital stocks respectively, S_Y and N_Y skilled and unskilled labour (that is, human capital and simple labour) allocated to production, and Λ a Harrod-neutral technical progress.

The C.I.E.S. utility function U to be maximized over an infinite horizon and in discrete time is:

$$Max \, U_t = \sum_{t=0}^{+\infty} \frac{N_t \left[\left(\frac{C_t}{N_t} \right)^{\beta} \left(\frac{G_{Ct}}{N_t} \right)^{1-\beta} \right]^{1-\sigma} - 1}{1-\sigma} \cdot \frac{1}{(1+\rho)^t}$$

under the constraint of assets:

$$Z_{t+1} - Z_t = r \, Z_t + R_t - C_t$$

with $\sigma > 0$, $\sigma \neq 1$, $0 < \beta < 1$. N is the number of agents, C and G_C the private and public components of consumption, R the current income, Z the stock of assets, r the interest rate on these assets, σ the intertemporal elasticity of substitution, and ρ the rate of time preference.

The resolution of this intertemporal optimization program consists in using the following Hamiltonian $\mathcal{H}$:

$$\mathcal{H} = \frac{N_t \left[\left(\frac{C_t}{N_t} \right)^{\beta} \left(\frac{G_{Ct}}{N_t} \right)^{1-\beta} \right]^{1-\sigma} - 1}{1-\sigma} + \lambda_{t+1} \left(r \, Z_t + R_t - C_t \right)$$

λ being the associated multiplier.

At the optimum, $\mathcal{H}$ verifies

$$\frac{\partial \mathcal{H}}{\partial C_t} = 0$$

Then, this becomes

$$\frac{C_t}{C_{t-1}} = \left[\frac{1}{1+\rho}\left(\frac{\lambda_{t-1}}{\lambda_t}\right)\left(\frac{N_t}{N_{t-1}}\right)^{1-\beta(1-\sigma)}\left(\frac{\dfrac{G_{Ct}}{N_t}}{\dfrac{G_{Ct-1}}{N_{t-1}}}\right)^{(1-\beta)(1-\sigma)}\right]^{\frac{1}{1-\beta(1-\sigma)}}$$

Since we have:

$$\frac{\lambda_{t+1}}{\lambda_t} = \frac{\lambda_t}{\lambda_{t-1}} = 1 + r_t$$

the growth rate of consumption – which corresponds to that of output at the steady state – can finally be written as:

$$\frac{C_t}{C_{t-1}} = (1+n_t)\left[\left(\frac{1+r_t}{1+\rho}\right)\left(\frac{\dfrac{G_{Ct}}{N_t}}{\dfrac{G_{Ct-1}}{N_{t-1}}}\right)^{(1-\beta)(1-\sigma)}\right]^{\frac{1}{1-\beta(1-\sigma)}}$$

with

$$r_t = (1+\tau_T)\frac{\partial Y_t}{\partial K_{Pt}} - \delta_{KP}$$

where: $n_t = N_t/N_{t-1}$ and τ_T is the total taxation rate.

This expression represents the solution of the intertemporal optimization program of the agents, who maximize in time their social welfare ("Keynes-Ramsey rule"). Thus, the state can have an influence on the interest rate r, that is to say, in this neoclassical universe, on the profitability of private physical capital.

Human capital S is increased by an investment I_E considered as the output of the public education sector:

$$I_E = \xi_E\left(\mu_N N_E^{\theta_L} + \mu_S S_E^{\theta_L}\right)^{1/\theta_L}$$

where

$$S_t = S_{t-1}(1 - \delta_S) + I_{E\,t-1}$$

with

$$S = S_Y + S_E$$

and

$$\tau_{E\,t}\,Y_t = \omega_{S\,t}\,S_{E\,t} + \omega_{N\,t}\,N_{E\,t}$$

ζ_E being an efficiency parameter, δ_S a depreciation rate, τ_E the tax which finances the wages w_S and w_N paid to skilled workers (S_E) and to unskilled workers (N_E) allocated to education.

The dynamics of the private and public capital stocks are given by:

$$K_{P\,t+1} = K_{P\,t}\,(1 - \delta_{K_P}) + I_t$$

and

$$K_{G\,t+1} = K_{G\,t}\left(1 - \delta_{K_G}\right) + G_{I\,t}$$

where $\tau_{I\,t} = {}^{G_{I\,t}}\!\big/\!{}_{Y_t}$ finances infrastructure.

The "national accounting" equilibrium of the economy is:

$$I_t = (1 - \tau_C - \tau_E - \tau_I)\,Y_t - C_t$$

Finally, the factorial contributions to GDP growth can be approximated by the following fomula:

$$\frac{\dot{Y}}{Y} = \left[\mu_P\left(\frac{K_P}{K}\right)^{\sigma_K - 1/\sigma_K}\left(\frac{\dot{K}_P}{K_P}\right) + \mu_G\left(\frac{K_G}{K}\right)^{\sigma_K - 1/\sigma_K}\left(\frac{\dot{K}_G}{K_G}\right)\right]^{\alpha}$$
$$+ \left[\mu_N\left(\frac{N}{L}\right)^{\sigma_L - 1/\sigma_L}\left(\frac{\dot{N}}{N}\right) + \mu_S\left(\frac{S}{L}\right)^{\sigma_L - 1/\sigma_L}\left(\frac{\dot{S}}{S}\right)\right]^{1-\alpha} + \left(\frac{\dot{\Lambda}}{\Lambda}\right)^{1-\alpha}$$

By working on the steady state associated to this latest equation, we can understand that, if the accumulation rhythm of S can exceed the (demographic) growth rate of N, and if the parameter σ_L is less than unity, then the term $(S/N)^{(\sigma L - 1)/\sigma L}$ will tend to zero when S takes an infinitely high value – along with the ratio S/N. Similarly, if the elasticity of substitution between skilled labour and unskilled labour, σ_L, is supposed to be superior to one, but if N grows faster than S at the same time, then it comes that the expression $(S/N)^{(\sigma L - 1)/\sigma L}$ will also converge toward zero when S tends to infinity – and S/N tends to zero. So, we perceive what pressure will be put here on the hypothesis of complementarity between public capital and private capital (with an assumed value of σ_K less than unity) for determining the long-run growth rate of the aggregate total capital.

As a consequence, endogenous growth will appear under the following three *sine qua non* conditions:

i)   skilled labour and unskilled labour must be substitutable in order to alleviate the constraint of non-reproducibility of simple labour and thus to avoid, within the composite labour function, the third Inada condition (that is, the vanishing towards zero of the limit of marginal productivity of capital when the latter tends to infinity);

ii)   human capital growth rate must exceed the Solowian "natural" (demographic and technological) growth rate so that it can determine the growth rate of aggregate labour in the long run, and therefore to allow a convergence of the production function towards a functional form with constant returns to scale on accumulable capital stocks only;

iii) the rate of time preference must be inferior to the interest rate in the long period.

Mathematically, these three conditions can be written as:

i) $\sigma_L > 1$

ii) $I_E \big/ S > n + g_\Lambda$

iii) $\rho < r$

A.5.1.2.2   About the "Aggregation" Problem and the So-Called "Microfoundations" of the Model

In a neoclassical universe, the standard utility function u of the representative agent is traditionally written:

$$u\,(c_t) = \int_0^\infty \frac{(c_t)^{1-\sigma} - 1}{1-\sigma}\; e^{-\rho t}\; dt$$

In our model, this expression becomes:

$$u_t = u\left[\Gamma\left(\frac{C_t}{N_t}\right)\left(\frac{G_{Ct}}{N_t}\right)\right] = \frac{\left[\left(\frac{C_t}{N_t}\right)^\beta\left(\frac{G_{Ct}}{N_t}\right)^{1-\beta}\right]^{1-\sigma} - 1}{1-\sigma}$$

In these circumstances, the "aggregated" utility function U proceeds from the N-times duplication of the single agent:

$$U_t = N_t\, u_t = \frac{N_t\left[\left(\frac{C_t}{N_t}\right)^\beta\left(\frac{G_{Ct}}{N_t}\right)^{1-\beta}\right]^{1-\sigma} - 1}{1-\sigma}$$

A.5.1.2.3 About the Equilibria on the Markets of Production Factors

The conditions of the equilibria on the markets of production factors operate in perfect competition. If the effects of human capital occupy a central place in this model, the financing of public expenditures involves recognizing that the production of the final good is subject to a tax rate (τ_T), interpreted here as a distortion which perturbates the pricing system and the allocation of resources. This tax reduces the marginal productivity of private capital (that is to say, its rate of return), and negatively affects the dynamics of private investment.

The developed form of the macroeconomic production function allows us to determine the interest rate r, as:

$$r_t = (1-\tau_T)\frac{\partial Y_t}{\partial K_{Pt}} - \delta_{KP} = (1-\tau_T)\left(\frac{\alpha\, \mu_P\, Y_t\, K_{Pt}^{\theta_K - 1}}{\mu_P\, K_{Pt}^{Q_K} + \mu_G\, K_{Gt}^{\theta_K}}\right) - \delta_{KP}$$

with an elasticity of substitution between the stocks of private capital (K_P) and public capital (K_G) equal to:

$$\sigma_K = \frac{1}{1-\theta_K}$$

The wages of the skilled and unskilled components of the labour factor, respectively ω_S and ω_N, are (neo)classically given by the equalization of the factorial incomes at their marginal productivities.

In perfect competition, the wage of simple labour is:

$$\omega_N = \frac{\partial Y_t}{\partial N_Y} = \frac{(1-\alpha)\,\mu_N\,Y\,N_Y^{\theta_L-1}}{\mu_N\,N_Y^{\theta_L} + \mu_S\,S_Y^{\theta_L}}$$

Similarly, the wage of skilled labour is:

$$\omega_S = \frac{\partial Y_t}{\partial S_Y} = \frac{(1-\alpha)\,\mu_S\,Y\,S_Y^{\theta_L-1}}{\mu_N\,N_Y^{\theta_L} + \mu_S\,S_Y^{\theta_L}}$$

where θ_L is linked to the elasticity of substitution between skilled labour (S) and unskilled labour (N) by:

$$\sigma_L = 1/{1-\theta_L}$$

Consequently, the relative remuneration for this labour factor is such that:

$$\frac{\omega_S}{\omega_N} = \left(\frac{\mu_S}{\mu_N}\right)\left(\frac{S_Y}{N_Y}\right)^{\theta_L-1}$$

which is influenced by the degree of substitutability between N and S, with θ_L constant and independent from N_Y and S_Y.

The elasticity of substitution depends exclusively on the point of the iso-quante which characterizes a couple of factors N_Y and S_Y. The more σ_L is high, the less ω_S/ω_N varies in function of the ratio S_Y/N_Y, and the more there are opportunities of substitution for wide ranges of values of S_Y/N_Y.

This becomes:

$$\mu_S = \frac{\left[\left(\frac{\omega_S}{\omega_N}\right)\left(\frac{S_Y}{N_Y}\right)^{1-\theta_L}\right]}{\left[1+\left(\frac{\omega_S}{\omega_N}\right)\left(\frac{S_Y}{N_Y}\right)^{1-\theta_L}\right]}$$

With $\mu_N = 1 - \mu_S$.

In perfect competition, the wage rates equalize themselves between the two sectors, that of private production of the final good, and that of public formation of human capital, both of them using the same technology. As a consequence, the ratios between skilled labour and non-skilled labour equalize intersectorially, in a way that it verified the following equality:

$$\frac{S_Y}{N_Y} = \frac{S_E}{N_E} = \frac{S}{N}$$

From which we deduce:

$$\frac{\omega_S S}{\omega_N N} = \eta \left(\frac{S}{N}\right)^{\left(\sigma_L - 1 / \sigma_L\right)}$$

with η, a parameter of scale, such as:

$$\eta = \left(\frac{\mu_S}{\mu_N}\right)^{-\sigma_L} > 0$$

By assuming full employment as a postulate, and if the components of labour factor are substitutable, then the share of human capital wage (ω_S S) in total labour income (ω_S S $+\omega_S$ N) increases along with the proportion of human capital (S) in total labour (L). The relationship between the stocks of skilled labour employed in the public (education) and private (production) sectors is obtained by combining the equations for the use of resources in the educational sector and those related to factorial remunerations of human capital.

Thus, we can write:

$$\frac{\omega_S S_E}{Y} = \frac{\tau_E}{1 + \left(\dfrac{\omega_N}{\omega_S}\right)\left(\dfrac{N}{S}\right)}$$

In the same way, we obtain:

$$\frac{\omega_S S_Y}{Y} = \frac{\mu_S(1-\alpha)}{\mu_N\left(\dfrac{N}{S}\right)^{\theta_L} + \mu_S}$$

Therefore, it comes the ratio of the stocks of human capital respectively allocated to the sectors of human capital formation and of the production of the final output:

$$\frac{S_E}{S_Y} = \frac{\left(\tau_E \left[\mu_N \left(\dfrac{N}{S} \right)^{\theta_L} + \mu_S \right] \right)}{\left[\mu_S \left(1 - \alpha \right) \left(1 + \dfrac{\omega_N}{\omega_S} \dfrac{N}{S} \right) \right]}$$

Finally, the state's decisions to invest in education, translated into choices of fiscal allocations (more particularly through the variations of the term τ_E in our simulations), propel the engine of endogenous growth.

However, the problem remains that in this framework, the public educational sector itself has to be submitted to the rules of a market economy.

For more details about the mathematical and algorithmical structure of this model, see: Herrera (1998, 2010).

A.5.2   Unit Root Tests Applied to the Different Variables of the Estimated Models

Unit root tests were performed on all the variables used in our estimates. As is known, their results depend on the size of the sample, but also and above all on the choice of the truncation setting of the parameter number of lags of the autocorrelation function. According to the three formulas of the selected criteria (Schwert [1989], Newey and West [1994], Lardic and Mignon [2002]), the value obtained here is 3. Therefore, we fix the number of lags at 3 in a first stage. As the use of the Schwert (1989) criteria also suggests a different number of lags (10 precisely), we set in a second step – in the event that the first one would not be successful –:

$$L_{maxi} = \max \left\{ T^{\frac{1}{4}} \quad int \left[4 \left(\frac{T}{100} \right)^{\frac{1}{4}} \right] \quad l_{12} = int \left[12 \left(\frac{T}{100} \right)^{\frac{1}{4}} \right] \quad l = int \left[4 \left(\frac{T}{100} \right)^{\frac{2}{9}} \right] \right\}$$

So we use the maximum lag $L_{maxi} = 10$ in the unit root tests, then the information criteria (AIC SIC HQ and their modified forms) to determine the optimum
lag L_{opti}. Critical values shown in the following tables come from: MacKinnon
(1996) for the augmented Dickey-Fuller tes VAR Granger causality / Block exogeneity Wa ts (ADF), Elliott-Rothenberg-Stock (ERS [DF-GLS]) and Phillips-
Perron (PP); *Table 1* in Kwiatkowski-Phillips-Schmidt-Shin (1992) for the KPSS
tests; Table 1 in Elliott-Rothenberg-Stock (1996) for the ERS tests – optimal
point –; and Table 1 in Ng-Perron (2001) for NP the tests.

TABLE A.5.2.1   Verification of the stationarity of gY

Tests	Criteria and lags	Models	Test statistics and critical values	Stationarity
ADF	Fixed at 3	Trend	$-5.651646 < -3.492149$ (5 percent)	Stationary
ERS	Fixed at 3	Trend	$-3.802547 < -3.177200$ (5 percent)	Stationary
PP	Fixed at 3	Constant	$-4.906111 < -2.911730$ (5 percent)	Stationary
KPSS	Fixed at 3	Trend	$0.017122 < 0.146000$ (5 percent)	Stationary
ERS-PO	Fixed at 3	Trend	$1.949668 < 5.704000$ (5 percent)	Stationary
NP	Fixed at 3	Trend	$\{-49.6494; -4.98154; 0.10033; 1.83986\}$ $< \{-17.3; -2.91; 0.168; 5.48\}$ (5 percent)	Stationary

Note: With Spectral GLS detrended-AR as a method for estimating the PP and KPSS tests.

TABLE A.5.2.2   Verification of the stationarity of gK_{Pe}

Tests	Criteria and lags	Models	Test statistics and critical values	Stationarity
ADF	AIC SIC HQ 2	Constant	$-4.247029 < -2.913549$ (5 percent)	Stationary
ERS	Fixed at 3	Trend	$-2.881809 < -2.872000$ (10 percent)	Stationary

TABLE A.5.2.2   Verification of the stationarity of gK_{Pe} (*cont.*)

Tests	Criteria and lags	Models	Test statistics and critical values	Stationarity
PP	Fixed at 3	Constant	−2.968648 < −2.911730 (5 percent)	Stationary
KPSS	AIC 2	Constant	0.145053 < 0.146000 (5 percent)	Stationary
ERS-PO	Fixed at 3	Trend	6.214140 < 6.774000 (10 percent)	Stationary
NP	Fixed at 3	Trend	{−6.00936; −1.62669; 0.27069; 4.41187} < {−5.7; −1.62; 0.275; 4.45} (10 percent)	Stationary

TABLE A.5.2.3   Verification of the stationarity of gK_{Pl}

Tests	Criteria and lags	Models	Test statistics and critical values	Stationarity
ADF	SIC 0	Constant	−2.772817 < −2.593551 (10 percent)	Stationary
ERS	Fixed at 3	Constant	−1.906751 < −1.613062 (10 percent)	Stationary
PP	SIC 0	Constant	−2.803811 < −2.593551 (10 percent)	Stationary
KPSS	Fixed at 3	Constant	0.180918 < 0.463000 (5 percent)	Stationary
ERS-PO	Fixed at 3	Constant	3.848106 < 3.962000 (10 percent)	Stationary
NP	Fixed at 3	Trend	{−7.14784; −1.88529; 0.26376; 3.44657} < {−5.7; −1.62; 0.275; 4.45} (10 percent)	Stationary

TABLE A.5.2.4   Verification of the stationarity of gK_F

Tests	Criteria and lags	Models	Test statistics and critical values	Stationarity
ADF	AIC 6 SIC and HQ 1	Trend	For a lag of 6: −5.633805 < −3.496960 (5 percent) For a lag of 1: −4.016539 < −3.489228 (5 percent)	Stationary
ERS	Fixed at 3	Trend	−3.048851 < −2.872000 (10 percent)	Stationary
PP	AIC SIC HQ 2 modified HQ 4	Constant	For a lag of 2: 4.819035 < −2.911730 (5 percent) For a lag of 4: 3.861121 < −2.911730 (5 percent)	Stationary
KPSS	AIC SIC HQ 2 modified AIC SIC HQ	Trend Constant	For a lag of 2: 0.083551 < 0.146000 (5 percent) For a lag of 4: 0.059806 < 0.146000 (5 percent)	Stationary
ERS-PO	Fixed at 3	Trend	5.574630 < 5.704000 (5 percent)	Stationary
NP	Fixed at 3	Trend	{−16.5149; −2.86897; 0.17372; 5.54577} < {−5.7; −1.62; 0.275; 4.45} (10 percent)	Stationary

TABLE A.5.2.5   Verification of the stationarity of gK_T

Tests	Criteria and lags	Models	Test statistics and critical values	Stationarity
ADF	AIC SIC HQ 1	Trend	−4.976285 < −3.489228 (5 percent)	Stationary
ERS	Fixed at 3	Constant	−1.935007 < −1.613062 (10 percent)	Stationary
PP	SIC HQ 0	Constant	−2.683883 < −2.593551 (10 percent)	Stationary
KPSS	Fixed at 3	Trend	0.810268 > 0.216000 (1 percent)	Non-stationary

TABLE A.5.2.5   Verification of the stationarity of gK_T (cont.)

Tests	Criteria and lags	Models	Test statistics and critical values	Stationarity
ERS-PO	Fixed at 3	Constant	2.622232 < 2.998000 (5 percent)	Stationary
NP	Fixed at 3	Constant	{−7.92287; −1.95897; 0.24726; 3.21084} < {−5.7; −1.62; 0.275; 4.45} (10 percent)	Stationary

Note: As the R^2 of the KPSS test regression is zero, the result "gK_T is non-stationary" is not accepted.

TABLE A.5.2.6   Verification of the stationarity of gL

Tests	Criteria and lags	Models	Test statistics and critical values	Stationarity
ADF	Fixed at 3	Constant	−3.161359 < −2.914517 (5 percent)	Stationary
ERS	Fixed at 3	Trend	−3.784782 < −3.170800 (5 percent)	Stationary
PP	Fixed at 3	Constant	−6.565217 < −2.911730 (5 percent)	Stationary
KPSS	Fixed at 3	Trend	0.083131 < 0.146000 (5 percent)	Stationary
ERS-PO	Fixed at 3	Constant	1.870849 < 5.704000 (5 percent)	Stationary
NP	Fixed at 3	Constant	{−46.1065; −4.79988; 0.10410; 1.98405} < {−5.7; −1.62; 0.275; 4.45} (5 percent)	Stationary

TABLE A.5.2.7 Verification of the stationarity of gH_P

Tests	Criteria and lags	Models	Test statistics and critical values	Stationarity
ADF	AIC SIC HQ 0	Constant	$-3.513657 < -2.911730$ (5 percent)	Stationary
ERS	AIC SIC HQ 0	Constant	$-2.397496 < -1.946447$ (5 percent)	Stationary
PP	Fixed at 3	Constant	$-2.955642 < -2.911730$ (5 percent)	Stationary
KPSS	Fixed at 3	Constant	$2.143550 > 0.739000$ (1 percent)	Non-stationary
ERS-PO	AIC SIC HQ 0	Constant	$3.446020 < 3.962000$ (10 percent)	Stationary
NP	AIC 0	Constant	$\{-9.46486; -2.16371; 0.22860; 2.63460\}$ $< \{-5.7; -1.62; 0.275; 4.45\}$ (5 percent)	Stationary

Note: As the R^2 of the KPSS test regression is zero, the result "gH_P is non-stationary" is not accepted.

TABLE A.5.2.8 Verification of the stationarity of gH_T

Tests	Criteria and lags	Models	Test statistics and critical values	Stationarity
ADF	SIC 4	Trend	$-3.218534 < -3.175693$ (10 percent)	Stationary
ERS	AIC HQ 4 SIC 1	Constant	For a lag of 4: $-1.983160 < -1.613062$ (10 percent) For a lag of 1: $-1.907675 < -1.613181$ (10 percent)	Stationary
PP	Fixed at 3	Trend	$-3.726356 < -3.487845$ (5 percent)	Stationary
KPSS	Fixed at 3	Constant	$1.380493 > 0.146000$ (5 percent)	Non-stationary
ERS-PO	SIC HQ 4	Trend	$5.045172 < 5.704000$ (5 percent)	Stationary

TABLE A.5.2.8   Verification of the stationarity of gH_T (*cont.*)

Tests	Criteria and lags	Models	Test statistics and critical values	Stationarity
NP	SIC HQ 4	Trend	$\{-21.8727; -3.28658; 0.15026;$ $4.29048\}$ $< \{-17.3000; -2.91000; 0.16800;$ $5.48000\}$ (5 percent)	Non-stationary

Note: The modified SIC criterion gives 6 lags and the SIC HQ 2, all the tests concluding with the stationarity.

TABLE A.5.2.9   Verification of the stationarity of gH_{Is}

Tests	Criteria and lags	Models	Test statistics and critical values	Stationarity
ADF	Fixed at 3	Trend	$-3.748953 < -3{,}492149$ (5 percent)	Stationary
ERS	Fixed at 3	Constant	$-2.173918 < -1{,}946764$ (5 percent)	Stationary
PP	Fixed at 3	Trend	$-7.546324 < -3{,}487845$ (5 percent)	Stationary
KPSS	Fixed at 3	Trend	$0.476555 > 0{,}216000$ (1 percent)	Non-stationary
ERS-PO	Fixed at 3	Trend	$3.685824 < 5{,}704000$ (10 percent)	Stationary
NP	Fixed at 3	Constant	$\{-8.87490; -2.08310;$ $0.23472; 2.85178\}$ $< \{-8.10000; -1.98000;$ $0.23300; 3.17000\}$ (5 percent)	Stationary

TABLE A.5.2.10 Verification of the stationarity of $gR\&D_1$

Tests	Criteria and lags	Models	Test statistics and critical values	Stationarity
ADF	Fixed at 3	None	−2.599472 < −1.946878 (5 percent)	Stationary
ERS	Fixed at 3	Constant	−3.480046 < −3.164400 (5 percent)	Non-stationary
PP	Fixed at 3	Constant	−6.867736 < −2.912631 (5 percent)	Stationary
KPSS	Fixed at 3	Constant	2.302908 > 0.739000 (1 percent)	Non-stationary
ERS-PO	SIC 9	Constant	1.331171 < 2.995200 (5 percent)	Stationary
NP	SIC 1	Constant	{−10.9047; 2.30726; 0.21158; 2.35629} < {−8.1; −1.98; 0.233; 3.17} (5 percent)	Stationary

Notes: 1) As the R^2 of the KPSS test regression is zero, the result "$gR\&D_1$ is non-stationary" is not accepted.
2) The numbers of lags vary according to the different criteria used for the ERS-OP and NP tests, but most of them favor stationarity, which led us to use the method of the Default AR Spectral OLS.
3) The information criteria give high lags for the ERS tests, tending rather to conclude with non-stationarity. If the number of lags is fixed at 2 (the Lardic and Mignon criteria yield 2.77), then the ERS tests reveal stationarity (with −3.251121 < −3.170800 [5 percent]).

TABLE A.5.2.11 Verification of the stationarity of $gR\&D_2$

Tests	Criteria and lags	Models	Test statistics and critical values	Stationarity
ADF	Fixed at 3	None	−2.610026 < −1.946878 (5 percent)	Stationary
ERS	SIC 0	Trend	−3.480046 < −3.164400 (5 percent)	Stationary
PP	Fixed at 3	Constant	−11.03722 < −2.912631 (5 percent)	Stationary
KPSS	Fixed at 3	Constant	3.401799 > 0.739000 (1 percent)	Non-stationary

TABLE A.5.2.11 Verification of the stationarity of $gR\&D_2$ (cont.)

Tests	Criteria and lags	Models	Test statistics and critical values	Stationarity
ERS-PO	AIC 2	Trend	4.001652 < 5.705600 (5 percent)	Stationary
NP	SIC 0	Trend	$\{-15.1640; -2.72796; 0.17990; 6.16183\}$ < $\{-14.2; -2.62; 0.185; 6.67\}$ (10 percent)	Stationary

Notes: 1) As the R^2 of the KPSS test regression is zero, the result "$gR\&D_2$ is non-stationary" is not accepted.
2) However, as some tests reject stationarity (in GLS-detrended AR), we also use the Bartlett-Kernel method whose results finally lean in the direction of stationarity for the KPSS tests.

A.5.3   Some Comments on Econometric Tests of Total Factor Productivity (TFP)

To study technical progress, we can choose between two ways: 1) the total factor productivity (TFP) growth rate, or 2) an indicator representative of research-and-development (R&D).

Let us begin by measuring TFP. In Chapter 5, Table 5.4 shows the empirical results of 16 linear regressions, using a Solowian theoretical framework which incorporates various labour and capital inputs (according to combinations presented Table 5.3). As a consequence, we can obtain at least 16 different TFPs, determined in function of these factor combinations. If we use as TFP the Solowian residual – or an alternative indicator, more particularly the Törnqvist quantity index[1] – assuming a Hick-neutral technical progress, the basic equation will be:

$$\dot{A}/_A = \dot{Y}/_Y - \alpha_K \dot{K}/_K - \beta_L \dot{L}/_L$$

where A is the Solowian residual, K the physical capital input (i.e., productive capital in the narrow sense noted K_{Pe}, productive capital in the broad sense

---

1   Törnqvist (1981).

K_{Pl}, fixed capital K_F, or total capital K_T),[2] and L the labour input (that is, the number of employed persons, productive human capital H_P, total human capital H_T, or intermediate human capital H_I).[3]

Calculating capital and labour elasticities α_K and β_L corresponds to a process based on two main assumptions.

The first hypothesis consists in supposing constant returns to scale on the productive factors, or: $\alpha_K + \beta_l = 1$.

For our previous 16 Solowian regressions (indicated by numbers in square brackets going from [9] to [24] in Table 5.3), Wald tests show that this first hypothesis is valid when we use as a labour input the variable of productive human capital H_P or that of intermediate human capital H_I. Nevertheless, if we use simple labour, that is to say, the number of employed persons, we get increasing returns to scale, while returns to scale are decreasing if total human capital H_T is chosen as a labour factor (Table A.5.3.1).

TABLE A.5.3.1   Wald tests for returns to scale

Returns to scale	Number of regression in the classification (Table 5.3)
$\alpha_k + \beta_l < 1$	[11]; [15]; [19]; [23]
$\alpha_k + \beta_l = 1$	[10]; [12]; [14]; [16]; [18]; [20]; [22]; [24]
$\alpha_k + \beta_l > 1$	[9]; [13]; [17]; [21]

Due to the birth control policy which has long been applied in China, population growth is limited and the labour supply growth rate is much lower than the output one. So, if we mobilize simple labour in the production function, the elasticity of labour β_L (representing the share of GDP earned by the labour factor with an assumption of perfect competition), as well as the coefficient of labour in the linear regression will be high, then increasing returns to scale will appear. On the contrary, if we choose total human capital H_T as labour input, we get decreasing returns to scale, because this factor includes population aged over 6–15 and also the retired – most of them being however "non-productive."

---

2   We suggest not to use the physical capital stocks K_F or K_T in the production function, because both of them contain "non-productive" components.

3   As total human capital includes "non-productive" or inactive population aged under 16, it is better not to use it as labour input.

Besides, the presence of increasing returns to scale associated with simple labour could suggest that an indicator such as the Törnqvist quantity index may not be appropriate to calculate TFP, due to the fact that, in this case, the factor L is usually represented by simple labour and contains an implicit hypothesis of constant returns to scale.[4]

The second assumption is that of perfect competition on the factor as well as commodity markets. In this context, the enterprises maximize their profit in such a way that the profitabilities of inputs are equal to the values of their marginal outputs. Consequently, on a perfect competition market, the unobserved elasticities α_K and β_L respectively become the observable shares of GDP, s_K and s_L, which are earned by the two factors capital and labour:

$$s_K = p_K K \big/ pY$$

and

$$s_L = p_L L \big/ pY$$

with, at the equilibrium, p the output price level, and p_K and p_L the prices of capital and labour respectively:

$$p_K = p \partial Y \big/ \partial K$$

and

$$p_L = p \partial Y \big/ \partial L$$

which can be regarded as the interest rate, r_K, and wages, w_L.

The distribution shares of input factors could also be written as:

$$s_K = \frac{\partial Y}{\partial K} \frac{K}{Y}$$

4　See, for example, Inklaar and Timmer (2013) used the PWT database simple labour. See also: Feenstra, Inklaar and Timmer (2015).

and

$$s_L = \frac{\partial Y}{\partial L} \frac{L}{Y}$$

In other terms, we have:

$$s_K = \left. r_K K \middle/ pY \right.$$

and

$$s_L = \left. w_L L \middle/ pY \right.$$

In this context, we have different options available to calculate α_k and β_l according to the selected assumptions.

Case 1: If we consider that both the first and the second assumptions are valid, the formula to calculate the factor elasticities should be:

$$\alpha_K = \left. r_K K \middle/ r_K K + w_L L \right.$$

and

$$\beta_L = \left. w_L L \middle/ r_K K + w_L L \right.$$

Case 2: If we argue that China's economy does not function in perfect competition, the second hypothesis does not hold, and we only accept the first hypothesis. Then the equation for capital elasticity α_K would be:

$$\alpha_K = \frac{\partial y}{\partial k} \frac{k}{y}$$

where y corresponds to *per capita* output, $y = Y/L$, and k is *per capita* capital, $k = K/L$, respectively.

Case 3: If we can observe that the first hypothesis is not respected either in some configurations (for example, when we use the variables of simple labour or total human capital as a labour input), we have to calculate the factor elasticities according to the original definitions. As the specific form of production function is unknown (here, we do not assume that it is a Cobb-Douglas function, but only a function satisfying the Inada conditions), the terms of partial differentials are unknown, and we use the differences as approximations:

$$\alpha_K = \frac{\partial Y}{\partial K} \frac{K}{Y} \approx \frac{AY}{AK} \frac{K}{Y}$$

and

$$\beta_L = \frac{\partial Y}{\partial L} \frac{L}{Y} \approx \frac{AY}{AL} \frac{L}{Y}$$

To begin with, let us consider Case 3, that is to say, that of Solow residuals without any constraint. We first calculate w_{KPe}, w_{KPl}, w_{KF}, w_{KT} and w_L, w_{HP}, w_{HT}, w_{HI}, respectively, then get the TFPs corresponding to our 16 regressions.

TABLE A.5.3.2 Average elasticities of input factors without restriction

	Mean
w_{KPe}	0.686549
w_{KPl}	0.994089
w_{KF}	0.064151
w_{KT}	0.921681
w_L	7.838600
w_{HP}	2.212890
w_{HI}	2.076013
w_{HT}	1.187591

TABLE A.5.3.3   Average growth rates of TFPs according the 16 Solowian regressions

TFP	Elasticities	Average growth rate
TFP [9]	w_{KPe}, w_L	−0.070682
TFP [10]	w_{KPe}, w_{HP}	−0.071291
TFP [11]	w_{KPe}, w_{HT}	−0.071237
TFP [12]	w_{KPe}, w_{HI}	−0.071596
TFP [13]	w_{KPl}, w_L	−0.070692
TFP [14]	w_{KPl}, w_{HP}	−0.071301
TFP [15]	w_{KPl}, w_{HT}	−0.071247
TFP [16]	w_{KPl}, w_{HI}	−0.071606
TFP [17]	w_{KF}, w_L	−0.070623
TFP [18]	w_{KF}, w_{HP}	−0.071231
TFP [19]	w_{KF}, w_{HT}	−0.071178
TFP [20]	w_{KF}, w_{HI}	−0.071537
TFP [21]	w_{KT}, w_L	−0.070641
TFP [22]	w_{KT}, w_{HP}	−0.071249
TFP [23]	w_{KT}, w_{HT}	−0.071195
TFP [24]	w_{KT}, w_{HI}	−0.071554

As we can see, the TFP growth rates without any constraint are negative and around −7 percent (Table A.5.3.3). The influences of institutional changes on output (especially negative ones, such as three difficult years in the early 1960s, the Cultural Revolution which began in 1966, and the political unrest in 1989) are included in the TFP according to the Solowian residual definitions. However, the usual TFPs only excluded the contributions of capital and labour, which still include such influences of negative institutional changes. As a consequence, we see that the growth rate of the non-constrained TFPs in average are negative.

A method to improve the calculation of the TFPs consists in defining a new concept of the latter, by excluding the effects of institutional changes, that is, a productivity corresponding to the "real" technical progress, as follows:

$$\dot{A}/_A = \dot{Y}/_Y - \alpha_k \dot{K}/_K - \beta_l \dot{L}/_L - \widehat{\alpha_d} D$$

where D is the dummy of political-institutional changes (see Chapter 5), which respectively takes the values +1 or −1 if a significant institutional change happens and is positive or negative, and o if it is inexistent; $\widehat{\alpha_d}$ being the elasticity of the political-institutional change variable to output, approximated by the OLS estimator.

Using this new definition, we get a "real" technical progress excluding the institutional changes:

TABLE A.5.3.4   Average elasticity of input factors without restriction

Real TFP	Elasticity	Mean
TFP [9]	$w_{KPe}, w_L, 0.118987$	−0.068699
TFP [10]	$w_{KPe}, w_{HP}, 0.117659$	−0.069330
TFP [11]	$w_{KPe}, w_{HT}, 0.115308$	−0.069315
TFP [12]	$w_{KPe}, w_{HI}, 0.120679$	−0.069584
TFP [13]	$w_{KPl}, w_L, 0.118850$	−0.068712
TFP [14]	$w_{KPl}, w_{HP}, 0.118036$	−0.069333
TFP [15]	$w_{KPl}, w_{HT}, 0.115739$	−0.069318
TFP [16]	$w_{KPl}, w_{HI}, 0.120640$	−0.069595
TFP [17]	$w_{KF}, w_L, 0.117048$	−0.068673
TFP [18]	$w_{KF}, w_{HP}, 0.114836$	−0.069317
TFP [19]	$w_{KF}, w_{HT}, 0.112852$	−0.069297
TFP [20]	$w_{KF}, w_{HI}, 0.118473$	−0.069562
TFP [21]	$w_{KT}, w_L, 0.117250$	−0.068687
TFP [22]	$w_{KT}, w_{HP}, 0.115546$	−0.069323
TFP [23]	$w_{KT}, w_{HT}, 0.113437$	−0.069304
TFP [24]	$w_{KT}, w_{HI}, 0.118628$	−0.069577

Now let us move to Case 2 and assume that the first hypothesis (constant returns to scale) is valid. According to the Wald tests, without TFP, the constant returns to scale are recorded for models using productive human capital and intermediate human capital. For those with simple labour and total human capital (even though we have emphasized in the body of our development that we prefer not to recommend the use of such input factors), we have to build a post-estimation test after having got the TFPs in order to verify if the constant returns to scale hypothesis is valid or not after the introduction of the TFP terms.

Under this hypothesis, two methods at least are possible to calculate the elasticities of capital and TFPs:

1) we introduce the hypothesis of constant returns to scale at the last step of the TFP calculation, that is, we directly use the capital elasticity in Table A.5.3.2, then we get the labour elasticity as unity minus the capital elasticity (Method 1); or

2) we introduce the constant returns to scale hypothesis at the very beginning, that is, we transform the production function into its *per capita* form, in order to use the Inada condition of homogeneity of the production function (Method 2), as follows:

$$\dot{A}/A = \dot{y}/y - \alpha_k \dot{k}/k$$

These two methods give different results (Table A.5.3.5). The first one does not really introduce the hypothesis, except when the production function is at constant returns to scale exactly and the two methods are equivalent rigorously. However, as already pointed out, when we use simple labour as input factor, the production function exhibits increasing returns to scale. So the capital coefficient calculated with Method 2 is seriously underestimated. For a symmetrical reason, as the production function is at decreasing returns to scale for total human capital, the capital coefficient calculated by the second method will be overestimated.

After having introduced the hypothesis of constant returns to scale, the TFPs calculated by Method 2 seem to be consistent with the literature. Example: using simple labour as a labour input, the average TFP growth rate is about 2.3 percent, close to that got by Chow and Li (2003). With productive human capital, the average TFP growth rate is about 4.6 percent. If we add the population growth rate (1 to 2 percent) plus a 5 percent depreciation rate, we get a long-term economic growth rate of 10 percent, recalling the "golden rule." But when moving back to "augmented Solowian models," estimated under the first hypothesis, the TFPs appear to be non-significant (Table A.5.3.6).[5]

---

5 If we use "real" TFPs – linear combinations of TFP and dummy which contain the information in question –, we have no need to use the dummy anymore because this new TFP has already considered the institutional changes.

TABLE A.5.3.5   Average growth rates of TFPs under an assumption of constant returns to scale

Capital elasticity	Mean	TFP	Average growth rate of TFP	Augmented TFP	Elasticity	Average growth rate of TFP
			Simple labour as labour input			
w_{KPe}	-2.630462	TFP [9]	0.023631	TFP [9]	$w_{KPe}\, w_L$ 0.118987	0.025614
w_{KPl}	-3.146507	TFP [13]	0.023668	TFP [13]	$w_{KPl}\, w_L$ 0.118850	0.025649
w_{KF}	2.296574	TFP [17]	0.023646	TFP [17]	$w_{KF}\, w_L$ 0.117048	0.025597
w_{KT}	-0.094220	TFP [21]	0.023673	TFP [21]	$w_{KT}\, w_L$ 0.117250	0.025627
			Productive human capital as labour input			
w_{KPe}	1.669600	TFP [10]	0.046483	TFP [10]	$w_{KPe}\, w_L$ 0.115308	0.048444
w_{KPl}	-1.744363	TFP [14]	0.046444	TFP [14]	$w_{KPl}\, w_L$ 0.118036	0.048411
w_{KF}	-1.292383	TFP [18]	0.046484	TFP [18]	$w_{KF}\, w_L$ 0.114836	0.048398
w_{KT}	2.367989	TFP [22]	0.046458	TFP [22]	$w_{KT}\, w_L$ 0.115546	0.048384

TABLE A.5.3.5   Average growth rates of TFPs under an assumption of constant returns to scale (*cont.*)

Capital elasticity	Mean	TFP	Average growth rate of TFP	Augmented TFP	Elasticity	Average growth rate of TFP
			Total human capital as labour input			
w_{KPe}	4.371352	TFP [11]	0.049860	TFP [11]	$w_{KPe}\, w_L$ 0.117659	0.051821
w_{KPl}	1.124522	TFP [15]	0.049829	TFP [15]	$w_{KPl}\, w_L$ 0.115739	0.051758
w_{KF}	1.245862	TFP [19]	0.049802	TFP [19]	$w_{KF}\, w_L$ 0.112852	0.051683
w_{KT}	23.01203	TFP [23]	0.049790	TFP [23]	$w_{KT}\, w_L$ 0.118628	0.051767
			Intermediate human capital as labour input			
w_{KPe}	1.266492	TFP [12]	0.055098	TFP [12]	$w_{KPe}\, w_L$ 0.120679	0.057109
w_{KPl}	51.15039	TFP [16]	0.055098	TFP [16]	$w_{KPl}\, w_L$ 0.120640	0.057109
w_{KF}	-4.792879	TFP [20]	0.055029	TFP [20]	$w_{KF}\, w_L$ 0.118473	0.057004
w_{KT}	1.550984	TFP [24]	0.055045	TFP [24]	$w_{KT}\, w_L$ 0.118628	0.057022

Note: The first differences are used to approximate the first-order partial differentials.

TABLE A.5.3.6   Regressions of augmented Solowian models under an assumption of constant returns to scale

	D	Capital per labour	Growth rate of TFP	R^2	Autocorrelation	Heteroscedasticity	Correction
[9]	0.118672 (5.832274)	0.652764 (10.74081)	0.261065 (1.337967)	0.640409	No	Yes	Yes
[10]	0.115339 (4.812125)	0.710297 (9.389488)	-0.157289 (0.410600)	0.597327	No	Yes	Yes
[11]	0.111991 (4.687062)	0.818137 (11.21741)	-0.314247 (-1.756634)	0.600026	No	Yes	Yes
[12]	0.118432 (5.322993)	0.656521 (6.949718)	-0.117120 (-1.046855)	0.610633	No	Yes	Yes
[13]	0.118372 (8.642681)	0.661703 (8.977617)	0.215698 (1.268630)	0.633697	No	Yes	Yes
[14]	0.116057 (5.533018)	0.694971 (7.082562)	-0.124053 (-0.662292)	0.602733	No	Yes	Yes
[15]	0.112803 (5.464187)	0.807309 (8.240703)	-0.293522 (-1.731589)	0.601953	No	Yes	Yes
[16]	0.118527 (5.991694)	0.662433 (6.187561)	-0.117904 (-1.157664)	0.612621	No	Yes	Yes
[17]	0.116775 (5.973366)	0.691955 (15.02440)	0.296642 (1.726290)	0.668538	No	Yes	Yes
[18]	0.112464 (4.898881)	0.790352 (9.106673)	-0.174248 (-0.958735)	0.622469	No	Yes	Yes

TABLE A.5.3.6 Regressions of augmented Solowian models under an assumption of constant returns to scale (*cont.*)

	D	Capital per labour	Growth rate of TFP	R^2	Autocorrelation	Heteroscedasticity	Correction
[19]	0.110028 (4.821258)	0.859449 (10.68721)	−0.267409 (−1.651088)	0.626598	No	Yes	Yes
[20]	0.116573 (5.406839)	0.699247 (8.995286)	−0.082646 (−0.797159)	0.637145	No	Yes	Yes
[21]	0.116818 (6.491370)	0.697989 (12.18572)	0.248863 (1.561743)	0.662242	No	Yes	Yes
[22]	0.113420 (5.492795)	0.775814 (8.172679)	−0.155141 (−0.862760)	0.626439	No	Yes	Yes
[23]	0.112803 (5.464187)	0.807309 (8.240703)	−0.293522 (−1.731589)	0.601953	No	Yes	Yes
[24]	0.118527 (5.991694)	0.662433 (6.187561)	−0.117904 (−1.157664)	0.612621	No	Yes	Yes

Notes: 1) Here t-statistics are between parentheses.
2) The last column mentions whether a correction *à la* Newey-West for heteroscedasticity was needed or not.

From our empirical results, we can see that the TFP variable is statistically non-significant, except for some equations (for example, those using total physical capital) in which it is weakly significant. This suggests that the TFP would not be the main engine of China's economic growth. This conclusion is consistent with that underlined by Su and Xu (1999).

We need another definition of technical progress.

We might argue that the implicit Hicks-neutrality hypothesis used in this calculation may not hold in reality. As a matter of fact, the examination of Kaldor's "stylized facts" to verify the nature of China's technical progress give quite complicated behaviors: increasing ratio K/Y, increasing GDP per capita, increasing per capita capital, but decreasing interest rate. Technical progress in China looks like a mixed-type one, rather than any simple neutrality (Hicks, Solow, and Harrod), so that a single Solowian residual equation is insufficient to filter out all the variables. Therefore, additional assumptions are needed.

Moreover, it should be observed that the productive human capital indicator defined by educational attainment corresponds to some kind of Harrod-type technical progress. Thus, a better solution would be to redirect our researches towards alternative technical progress indicators, such as R&D. This is precisely one of the key reasons why we decided to orientate our theoretical frameworks towards models with endogenous technical progress.

A.5.4   Causality Tests between Dependent and Explicative Variables

TABLE A.5.4.1   Results of the Pairwise Granger causality tests

Lag = 2	gK_{Pe}	gK_{Pl}	gK_F	gK_T	gL	gH_P	gH_T	gH_I	$gR\&D_1$	$gR\&D_2$
gY	0.1955	0.6603	0.0112	0.2145	0.0944	0.5306	0.9109	0.3036	0.0039	0.0032
Inverse	0.0036	0.0036	0.0023	0.0481	0.7473	0.2693	0.0443	0.0779	0.0022	0.0021
Lag = 3	gK_{Pe}	gK_{Pl}	gK_F	gK_T	gL	gH_P	gH_T	gH_I	$gR\&D_1$	$gR\&D_2$
gY	0.1418	0.8497	0.0099	0.4328	0.0616	0.7103	0.6899	0.4420	0.0403	0.0279
Inverse	0.0276	0.0241	0.0176	0.1019	0.0483	0.2170	0.0372	0.0328	0.0023	0.0012

TABLE A.5.4.1   Results of the Pairwise Granger causality tests (*cont.*)

Lag = 4	gK_{Pe}	gK_{Pl}	gK_F	gK_T	gL	gH_P	gH_T	gH_I	$gR\&D_1$	$gR\&D_2$
gY	0.5230	0.3577	0.0779	0.1628	0.0651	0.3442	0.7893	0.3279	0.0389	0.0093
Inverse	0.0021	0.0005	0.0033	0.0055	0.0953	0.0692	0.0810	0.0846	0.0058	0.0006

Note: For each lag, the first line gives the Pairwise Granger causality test *p-values* with a null hypothesis that g_Y does not Granger-cause the explicative variable. The second line corresponds to the reverse relation: the explicative variable does not Granger-cause g_Y. The value of the first line is expected to be high to indicate that the explicative variable is not endogenous, while that of the second line is expected to be low, because it might be a statistically significant explicative variable. It is to be noted that there is small significant feedback effect between economic growth and technical progress.

The results of these causality tests are sensitive to the choice of the lag, and they are even better as it increases. We also test the causality within VAR models, using the following strategy to fit the models:

i)   we guess an initial lag of 3 with the truncation criterions, according to the size of the sample, and fit a VAR model with dummy as exogenous variable;

ii)   we use the information criterions to choose an optimal maximum lag (with the maximum set at 5, corresponding to a five-year plan); and

iii) we apply the VAR Lag Exclusion Wald Tests with a maximum lag (given by the information criterions) in order to determine the final significant lags, and keep the model with significant joint lags.

Finally, we built a VAR for each regression equation, all variables being included. Here, the results of VARs 1 to 8 are the same as above.

As we can observe in the tests for models [26], [28], [30] and [32], technical progress seems to be weakly endogenous, whereas all the other explicative variables are found to be exogenous.

TABLE A.5.4.2   VAR Granger causality / Block exogeneity Wald tests

Endogenous variables	Exogenous variables	Truncation criterions	LR	FPE	AIC	SIC	HQ	Lag Exclusion Wald Tests	X doesn't Granger cause Y	Y doesn't Granger cause X
gY, gK_{Pe}	D	3	5	5	5	5	5	1	0.0001	0.2970
gY, gK_{Pl}	D	3	4	4	4	1	4	2	0.0002	0.9181
gY, gK_F	D	3	5	5	5	2	5	1	0.0000	0.2043
gY, gK_T	D	3	4	4	4	1	1	2	0.0000	0.5542
gY, gL	D	3	4	5	5	1	1	1	0.0056	0.5009
gY, gH_P	D	3	4	4	4	1	1	1	0.0000	0.6284
gY, gH_T	D	3	1	4	4	1	1	1	0.0002	0.0787
gY, gH_I	D	3	2	2	4	2	2	2	0.0002	0.3404
$gY, gR\&D_1$	D	3	5	5	5	1	5	1	0.1002	0.5421
$gY, gR\&D_2$	D	3	4	4	4	1	4	1	0.1346	0.0750

Notes: 1) LR: sequential modified likelihood ratio test statistics (at 5% level); FPE: final prediction error; AIC: Akaike information criterion; SIC: Schwarz information criterion; HQ: Hannan-Quinn information criterion;

2) D = dummy variables; C = constant; X = explicative variables; Y = dependent variable (gY).

3) The last two columns are the *p-values* of VAR Granger causality / Block exogeneity Wald tests. The structures of VAR are consistent with the regression models. Consequently, the technical progress is no longer endogenous. The results are exactly as expected: all the explicative variables are not endogenous.

TABLE A.5.4.3   VAR Granger causality / Block exogeneity Wald tests for each regression

	Endogenous variables	LR	FPE	AIC	SIC	HQ	Lag Exclusion Wald Tests	Final lag	Explicative variables do not Granger-cause Y	Excluded variables do not Granger-cause dependent variable
[9]	gY, gK_{Pe}, gL	5	5	5	1	5	1	1	0.0000	0.1566 (gK_{Pe}); 0.1732 (gL)
[10]	gY, gK_{Pe}, gH_P	5	5	5	1	5	1	1	0.0000	0.2721 (gK_{Pe}); 0.4317 (gH_P)
[11]	gY, gK_{Pe}, gH_T	5	5	5	1	4	1	1	0.0001	0.4778 (gK_{Pe}); 0.0295 (gH_T)
[12]	gY, gK_{Pe}, gH_I	5	5	5	1	2	1	1	0.0001	0.4819 (gK_{Pl}); 0.0518 (gH_I)
[13]	gY, gK_{Pl}, gL	4	4	4	1	1	2	2	0.0004	0.3645 (gK_{Pl}); 0.4502 (gL)
[14]	gY, gK_{Pl}, gH_P	4	5	5	1	1	2	2	0.0001	0.7439 (gK_{Pl}); 0.2006 (gH_P)
[15]	gY, gK_{Pl}, gH_T	4	4	4	1	1	1	1	0.0000	0.2243 (gK_{Pl}); 0.0289 (gH_T)
[16]	gY, gK_{Pl}, gH_I	4	4	4	1	2	2	2	0.0001	0.7778 (gK_{Pl}); 0.4938 (gH_I)
[17]	gY, gK_F, gL	5	5	5	1	2	1	1	0.0000	0.1014 (gK_F); 0.0714 (gL)
[18]	gY, gK_F, gH_P	5	5	5	1	5	1	1	0.0000	0.0957 (gK_F); 0.3599 (gH_P)
[19]	gY, gK_F, gH_T	4	4	4	1	2	1	1	0.0000	0.3036 (gK_F); 0.0581 (gH_T)
[20]	gY, gK_F, gH_I	5	5	5	1	2	1	1	0.0000	0.2917 (gK_F); 0.0271 (gH_I)
[21]	gY, gK_T, gL	4	1	1	1	1	2	2	0.0001	0.2618 (gK_T); 0.3782 (gL)
[22]	gY, gK_T, gH_P	3	4	5	1	1	2	2	0.0000	0.3923 (gK_T); 0.0843 (gH_P)
[23]	gY, gK_T, gH_T	4	4	4	1	1	1	1	0.0000	0.1052 (gK_T); 0.0500 (gH_T)
[24]	gY, gK_T, gH_I	3	4	4	1	1	2	2	0.0001	0.6087 (gK_T); 0.5032 (gH_I)
[25]	$gY, gK_{Pe}, gH_P, gR\&D_1$	5	5	5	1	1	1	1	0.0000	0.4399 (gK_{Pe}); 0.3038 (gH_P); 0.0251 ($gR\&D_1$)
[26]	$gY, gK_{Pl}, gH_P, gR\&D_1$	5	5	5	1	5	5	1	0.0000	0.1426 (gK_{Pl}); 0.2479 (gH_P); 0.0028 ($gR\&D_1$)

TABLE A.5.4.3   VAR Granger causality / Block exogeneity Wald tests for each regression (*cont.*)

Endogenous variables	LR	FPE	AIC	SIC	HQ	Lag Exclusion Wald Tests	Final lag	Explicative variables do not Granger-cause Y	Excluded variables do not Granger-cause dependent variable
[27] $gY, gK_F, gH_P, gR\&D_1$	5	5	5	1	1	1	1	0.0000	0.1615 (gK_F); 0.3274 (gH_P); 0.0300 ($gR\&D_1$)
[28] $gY, gK_T, gH_P, gR\&D_1$	5	5	5	1	5	5	1	0.0000	0.0492 (gK_T); 0.3055 (gH_P); 0.0082 ($gR\&D_1$)
[29] $gY, gK_{Pe}, gH_P, gR\&D_2$	5	5	5	1	1	1	1	0.0000	0.3010 (gK_{Pe}); 0.5002 (gH_P); 0.0438 ($gR\&D_2$)
[30] $gY, gK_{Pt}, gH_P, gR\&D_2$	5	5	5	1	1	2	2	0.0000	0.0045 (gK_{Pt}); 0.2990 (gH_P); 0.0000 ($gR\&D_2$)
[31] $gY, gK_F, gH_P, gR\&D_2$	3	5	5	1	1	1	1	0.0000	0.0915 (gK_F); 0.4778 (gH_P); 0.0635 ($gR\&D_2$)
[32] $gY, gK_T, gH_P, gR\&D_2$	5	3	5	1	1	2	2	0.0000	0.0061 (gK_T); 0.1660 (gH_P); 0.0000 ($gR\&D_2$)

Notes: Dependent variables are indicated between parentheses. If the Lag exclusion Wald tests tend to reserve lags as maximum as possible, the optimal lag might exceed the possible maximum lag for a small sample. But too many lags will introduce too numerous coefficients in the VAR models. As a consequence, the number of observations might be not enough to estimate so many parameters. From the previous tests, we see that the Lag exclusion Wald tests generally give consistent results with those of SIC. So, if the Lag exclusion Wald rests reserve all lags, then we adopt SIC.

TABLE A.5.4.4 Some details of VAR Granger causality / Block exogeneity Wald tests

	Dependent variable	Excluded variable	The excluded variable does not Granger-cause the dependent one
[26]	$gR\&D_1$	gY	0.0500
		gK_{Pl}	0.0272
		gH_P	0.5900
[28]	$gR\&D_1$	gY	0.0591
		gK_T	0.0890
		gH_P	0.3760
[30]	$gR\&D_2$	gY	0.0000
		gK_{Pl}	0.0000
		gH_P	0.2270
[32]	gK_T	gY	0.0585
		gH_P	0.4253
		$gR\&D_2$	0.0010
	$gR\&D_2$	gY	0.0000
		gK_T	0.0000
		gH_P	0.7704

Appendices to Chapter 6

A.6.1   Results of the Unit Root Tests for the Selected Variables

TABLE A.6.1.1   Results of the unit root tests for the ratio K/Y and its first difference

Tests		Lags and criterions	Models	Statistics of tests and critical values	Stationarity
ADF	Level	o modified AIC, SIC, HQ	Trend	−2.842638 > −3.492149 (5 percent)	Non-stationary
	First difference	10 AIC	Constant	−4.493974 < −3.492149 (5 percent)	Stationary
ERS	Level	2 AIC, SIC, HQ	Trend	−2.998089 > −3.164400 (5 percent)	Non-stationary
	First difference	1 AIC, SIC, HQ	Constant	−6.167994 < −3.164400 (5 percent)	Stationary
PP	Level	2 AIC, SIC, HQ	Trend	−3.625520 > −4.118444 (1 percent)	Non-stationary
	First difference	1 AIC, SIC, HQ	None	−5.995174 < −1.946447 (5 percent)	Stationary
KPSS	Level	2 AIC, SIC, HQ	Trend	0.343452 > 0.146000 (5 percent)	Non-stationary
	First difference	3 AIC	Constant	0.004932 < 0.463000 (5 percent)	Stationary
ERS-PO	Level	o modified AIC, SIC, HQ	Trend	10.38294 > 5.704000 (5 percent)	Non-stationary
	First difference	1 SIC, HQ	Constant	0.462519 < 2.998000 (5 percent)	Stationary

TABLE A.6.1.1   Results of the unit root tests for the ratio K/Y and its first difference (*cont.*)

Tests		Lags and criterions	Models	Statistics of tests and critical values	Stationarity
NP	Level	2 SIC, AIC, SIC, HQ	Trend	{−18.5174; −3.04278; 0.16432; 4.92121} > {−23.8000; −3.42000; 0.14300; 4.03000} (1 percent)	Non-stationary
	First difference	3 SIC	Constant	{−85.2498; −6.51326; 0.07640; 0.318701} < {−8.10000; −1.98000; 0.2330; 3.17000} (5 percent)	Stationary

Note: The PP and KPSS tests are estimated in Spectral GLS-detrended AR to use a fixed truncation parameter.

TABLE A.6.1.2   Results of unit root tests for the ratio s_l/g and its first difference

Tests		Lags and criterions	Models	Statistics of the tests and critical values	Stationarity
ADF	Level	7 modified AIC, SIC, HQ	None	−0.553456 > −3.492149 (5 percent)	Non-stationary
	First difference	6 AIC, HQ, 1 SIC (−8.096)	None	−8.115098 < −1.947248 (5 percent)	Stationary
ERS	Level	8 modified AIC, SIC (model constant), HQ	Trend	−1.944014 > −3.492149 (5 percent)	Non-stationary
	First difference	0 modified AIC, SIC, HQ	Trend	−12.01813 < −3.164400 (5 percent)	Stationary
PP	Level	0 modified AIC, SIC, HQ	Constant	−7.157595 < −3.492149 (5 percent)	Stationary
KPSS	Level	8 modified AIC, SIC, HQ	Constant	4.985143 > 0.463000 (5 percent)	Non-stationary
	First difference	9 modified AIC, SIC, HQ	Constant	4.306462 > 0.463000 (5 percent)	Stationary

TABLE A.6.1.2　Results of unit root tests for the ratio s_l/g and its first difference *(cont.)*

Tests		Lags and criterions	Models	Statistics of the tests and critical values	Stationarity
ERS-PO	Level	8 modified AIC, HQ	Trend	31.92552 > 5.704000 (5 percent)	Non-stationary
	First difference	0 AIC	Constant	0.861565 < 2.998000 (5 percent)	Stationary
NP	Level	8 modified AIC, HQ	Trend	{−2.42030; −1.09672; 0.45313; 37.5081} > {−17.3000; −2.91000; 0.16800; 5.48000} (5 percent)	Non-stationary
	First difference	1 SIC, HQ	Trend	{−31.9449; −3.99380; 0.12502; 2.86825} < {−17.3000; −2.91000; 0.16800; 5.48000} (5 percent)	Stationary

Note: PP tests indicates that $s_l/g \sim I(0)$ and KPSS tests that $s_l/g \sim I(2)$ at least, but all other tests that $s_l/g \sim I(1)$.

TABLE A.6.1.3　Unit root tests in moving average (5 years) of s_l/g and its first difference

Tests		Lags and criterions	Models	Statistics of tests and critical values	Stationarity
ADF	Level	0 modified AIC, SIC, HQ	Trend	−3.176335 > −3.493692 (5 percent)	Non-stationary
	First difference	10 AIC, 0 SIC (−6.195244), 4 HQ (−7.141228)	None	−3.430766 < −1.948495 (5 percent)	Stationary
ERS	Level	9 AIC {−3.56 > −3.77 (1 percent)}; 1 SIC, HQ	Trend	−3.008917 > −3.177200 (5 percent)	Non-stationary
	First difference	10 AIC, 0 SIC (−6.191609), 4 HQ (−7.182789)	Constant	−3.544307 < −1.948495 (5 percent)	Stationary

TABLE A.6.1.3   Unit root tests in moving average (5 years) of s_l / g and its first difference (*cont.*)

Tests		Lags and criterions	Models	Statistics of tests and critical values	Stationarity
PP	Level	5 AIC, 0 SIC {−1.989571 > −2.607686 (1 percent)}, 1 HQ (−2.353158)	None	−1.483446 > −1.946878 (5 percent)	Non-stationary
	First difference	10 AIC, 0 SIC (−6.195244), 4 HQ (−6.553179)	None	−23.28402 < −1.946447 (5 percent)	Stationary
KPSS	Level	0 modified AIC, SIC, HQ	Trend	0.426371 > 0.146000 (5 percent)	Non-stationary
	First difference	0 modified AIC, SIC, HQ	Constant	0.102408 < 0.463000 (5 percent)	Stationary
ERS-PO	Level	9 AIC, HQ; 1 SIC (7.385567)	Trend	40.289570 > 5.704000 (5 percent)	Non-stationary
	First difference	0 modified AIC, SIC, HQ	Constant	0.910050 < 2.998000 (5 percent)	Stationary
NP	Level	1 SIC, HQ	Trend	{−15.9925; −2.82123; 0.17641; 5.73742} > {−17.3000; −2.91000; 0.16800; 5.48000} (5 percent)	Non-stationary
	First difference	0 modified AIC, SIC, HQ	Constant	{−85.2498; −6.51326; 0.07640; 0.318701} < {−27.2910; −3.69049; 0.13523; 0.90903} (5 percent)	Stationary

TABLE A.6.1.4   Unit root tests in moving average (7 years) of s_l/g and its first difference

Tests		Lags and criterions	Models	Statistics of tests and critical values	Stationarity
ADF	Level	0 modified AIC, SIC, HQ	Trend	−3.453658 > −3.493692 (5 percent)	Non-stationary
	First difference	0 AIC, SIC, HQ	None	−8.057235 < −1.948495 (5 percent)	Stationary
ERS	Level	0 AIC, SIC, HQ	Trend	−2.272326 > −3.180400 (5 percent)	Non-stationary
	First difference	7 AIC, SIC, HQ	Constant	−0.261449 > −1.948495 (5 percent)	Non-stationary
PP	Level	0 AIC, SIC, HQ	Trend	−3.516188 > −4.140858 (1 percent)	Non-stationary
	First difference	0 AIC, SIC, HQ	None	−8.057235 < −1.946447 (5 percent)	Stationary
KPSS	Level	0 AIC, SIC, HQ	Trend	0.921497 > 0.146000 (5 percent)	Non-stationary
	First difference	2 SIC	Constant	0.519222 < 0.739000 (1 percent)	Stationary
ERS-PO	Level	0 AIC, SIC, HQ	Trend	18.41997 > 5.704000 (5 percent)	Non-stationary
	First difference	0 AIC, SIC, HQ	Constant	7.566758 > 2.998000 (5 percent)	Non-stationary
NP	Level	0 AIC, SIC, HQ	Trend	{−7.31149; −1.90973; 0.26120; 12.4674} > {−17.3000; −2.91000; 0.16800; 5.48000} (5 percent)	Non-stationary
	First difference	7 AIC, 2 SIC, HQ (−2.26022; −0.96250; 0.42584; 10.1238)	Constant	{0.07910; 0.08653; 1.09387; 66.7986} > {−27.2910; −3.69049; 0.13523; 0.90903} (5 percent)	Non-stationary

TABLE A.6.1.5   Unit root tests in moving average (10 years) of s_l / g and its first difference

Tests		Lags and criterions	Models	Statistics of tests and critical values	Stationarity
ADF	Level	10 AIC, 0 SIC, HQ {−0.629332 > −1.947520 (5 percent) (none)}	Constant	−3.453658 > −3.605593 (1 percent)	Non-stationary
	First difference	9 AIC, 0 SIC, HQ (−6.321679)	None	−2.394787 < −1.948495 (5 percent)	Stationary
ERS	Level	10 AIC, 0 SIC, HQ (−2.129396)	Trend	−2.064532 > −3.180400 (5 percent)	Non-stationary
	First difference	9 AIC, 0 SIC, HQ (−6.343354)	Constant	−2.467597 < −1.948495 (5 percent)	Stationary
PP	Level	10 AIC, 0 SIC, HQ (−0.629332)	None	−0.140463 > −1.947520 (1 percent)	Non-stationary
	First difference	9 AIC, 0 SIC, HQ (−6.321679)	None	−19.05976 < −1.946447 (5 percent)	Stationary
KPSS	Level	0 SIC, HQ	Trend	1.611819 > 0.146000 (5 percent)	Non-stationary
	First difference	9 AIC, 0 SIC, HQ (0.062901)	Constant	0.009623 < 0.463000 (5 percent)	Stationary
ERS-PO	Level	0 SIC, HQ	Trend	11.31461 > 5.718400 (5 percent)	Non-stationary
	First difference	9 AIC, 0 SIC, HQ (0.977323)	Constant	0.444232 < 2.970000 (5 percent)	Stationary
NP	Level	0 SIC, HQ	Trend	{−7.82152; −1.96352; 0.25104; 11.6869} > {−17.3000; −2.91000; 0.16800; 5.48000} (5 percent)	Non-stationary
	First difference	0 SIC, HQ	Constant	{−27.0540; −3.67617; 0.13588; 0.91123} < {−8.10000; −1.98000; 0.23300; 3.17000} (5 percent)	Stationary

TABLE A.6.1.6   Unit root tests in moving average (15 years) of s_l/g and its first difference

Tests	Lags and criterions		Models	Statistics of tests and critical values	Stationarity
ADF	Level	○ AIC, SIC, HQ	None	−0.028875 > −1.948313 (5 percent)	Non-stationary
	First difference	○ AIC, SIC, HQ	None	−6.871520 < −1.948495 (5 percent)	Stationary
ERS	Level	○ AIC, SIC, HQ	Trend	−1.900002 > −3.180400 (5 percent)	Non-stationary
	First difference	○ AIC, SIC, HQ	Constant	−5.414951 < −1.948495 (5 percent)	Stationary
PP	Level	○ AIC, SIC, HQ	None	−0.028875 > −1.948313 (5 percent)	Non-stationary
	First difference	○ AIC, SIC, HQ	None	−6.871520 < −1.946447 (5 percent)	Stationary
KPSS	Level	○ AIC, SIC, HQ	Trend	2.296261 > 0.146000 (5 percent)	Non-stationary
	First difference	○ AIC, SIC, HQ	Constant	0.068903 < 0.463000 (5 percent)	Stationary
ERS-PO	Level	○ AIC, SIC, HQ	Trend	13.50218 > 5.718400 (5 percent)	Non-stationary
	First difference	○ AIC, SIC, HQ	Constant	0.444232 < 2.970000 (5 percent)	Stationary
NP	Level	○ AIC, SIC, HQ	Trend	{−6.48895; −1.76957; 0.27270; 14.0480} > {−17.3000; −2.91000; 0.16800; 5.48000} (5 percent)	Non-stationary
	First difference	○ AIC, SIC, HQ	Constant	{−18.5210; −3.03395; 0.16381; 1.35598} < {−8.10000; −1.98000; 0.23300; 3.17000} (5 percent)	Stationary

TABLE A.6.1.7   Unit root tests in moving average (20 years) of s_I / g and its first difference

Tests	Lags and criterions		Models	Statistics of tests and critical values	Stationarity
ADF	Level	o AIC, SIC, HQ	None	0.371972 > −1.948313 (5 percent)	Non-stationary
	First difference	o AIC, SIC, HQ	None	−5.387667 < −1.948495 (5 percent)	Stationary
ERS	Level	o AIC, SIC, HQ	Trend	−2.031831 > −3.180400 (5 percent)	Non-stationary
	First difference	o AIC, SIC, HQ	Constant	−5.479711 < −1.948495 (5 percent)	Stationary
PP	Level	o AIC, SIC, HQ	None	0.371972 > −1.948313 (5 percent)	Non-stationary
	First difference	o AIC, SIC, HQ	None	−5.387667 < −1.946447 (5 percent)	Stationary
KPSS	Level	o AIC, SIC, HQ	Trend	1.519928 > 0.146000 (5 percent)	Non-stationary
	First difference	o AIC, SIC, HQ	Constant	0.081285 < 0.463000 (5 percent)	Stationary
ERS-PO	Level	o AIC, SIC, HQ	Trend	13.18748 > 5.718400 (5 percent)	Non-stationary
	First difference	o AIC, SIC, HQ	Constant	1.226366 < 2.970000 (5 percent)	Stationary
NP	Level	o AIC, SIC, HQ	Trend	{−6.83286; −1.83621; 0.26873; 13.3469} > {−17.3000; −2.91000; 0.16800; 5.48000} (5 percent)	Non-stationary
	First difference	o AIC, SIC, HQ	Constant	{−21.2154; −3.25639; 0.15349; 1.15675} < {−8.10000; −1.98000; 0.23300; 3.17000} (5 percent)	Stationary

TABLE A.6.1.8   Unit root tests in moving average (25 years) of s_1/g and its first difference

Tests		Lags and criterions	Models	Statistics of tests and critical values	Stationarity
ADF	Level	0 AIC, SIC, HQ	None	0.599695 > −1.948313 (5 percent)	Non-stationary
	First difference	5 AIC, HQ, 0 SIC (−5.634825) (none)	Trend	−4.664124 < −1.948495 (5 percent)	Stationary
ERS	Level	0 AIC, SIC, HQ	Trend	−1.800094 > −3.180400 (5 percent)	Non-stationary
	First difference	3 AIC, HQ, 0 SIC (−5.826299)	Constant	−4.041863 < −1.948495 (5 percent)	Stationary
PP	Level	0 AIC, SIC, HQ	None	0.599695 > −1.948313 (5 percent)	Non-stationary
	First difference	8 AIC, 0 SIC (−5.634825) 3 HQ (−74.93186)	None	−7.958524 < −1.946447 (5 percent)	Stationary
KPSS	Level	0 AIC, SIC, HQ	Trend	1.680445 > 0.146000 (5 percent)	Non-stationary
	First difference	3 AIC, HQ 0 SIC (0.114576)	Constant	0.007777 < 0.463000 (5 percent)	Stationary
ERS-PO	Level	6 AIC, HQ 0 SIC (15.01703)	Trend	115.5049 > 5.718400 (5 percent)	Non-stationary
	First difference	3 AIC, HQ, 0 SIC (1.360799)	Constant	0.092445 < 2.970000 (5 percent)	Stationary
NP	Level	0 AIC, SIC, HQ	Trend	{−5.83277; −1.64161; 0.28145; 15.5071} > {−17.3000; −2.91000; 0.16800; 5.48000} (5 percent)	Non-stationary
	First difference	3 AIC, HQ, 0 SIC (−18.3762; −3.03111; 0.16495; 1.33354)	Constant	{−347.162; −13.1750; 0.03795; 0.07059} < {−8.10000; −1.98000; 0.23300; 3.17000} (5 percent)	Stationary

TABLE A.6.1.9   Unit root tests in moving average (30 years) of s_l / g and its first difference

Tests	Lags and criterions	Models	Statistics of tests and critical values	Stationarity
ADF	Level	o AIC, SIC, HQ	None	0.482501 > −4.127338 (1 percent)	Non-stationary
	First difference	o AIC, SIC, HQ	None	−5.987276 < −1.948495 (5 percent)	Stationary
ERS	Level	o AIC, SIC, HQ	Trend	−1.899149 > −3.180400 (5 percent)	Non-stationary
	First difference	o AIC, SIC, HQ	Constant	−6.140835 <−1.948495 (5 percent)	Stationary
PP	Level	o AIC, SIC, HQ	None	0.482501 > −1.948313 (5 percent)	Non-stationary
	First difference	o AIC, SIC, HQ	None	−5.987276 < −1.946447 (5 percent)	Stationary
KPSS	Level	o AIC, SIC, HQ	Trend	0.842365 > 0.146000 (5 percent)	Non-stationary
	First difference	o AIC, SIC, HQ	Constant	0.094751 < 0.463000 (5 percent)	Stationary
ERS-PO	Level	o AIC, SIC, HQ	Trend	14.13701 > 5.718400 (5 percent)	Non-stationary
	First difference	o AIC, SIC, HQ	Constant	1.615170 < 2.970000 (5 percent)	Stationary
NP	Level	o AIC, SIC, HQ	Trend	{−6.13965; −1.68656; 0.27470; 14.7826} > {−17.3000; −2.91000; 0.16800; 5.48000} (5 percent)	Non-stationary
	First difference	o AIC, SIC, HQ	Constant	{−15.6278; −2.79527; 0.17887; 1.56795} < {−8.10000; −1.98000; 0.23300; 3.17000} (5 percent)	Stationary

TABLE A.6.1.10 Unit root tests for the series with HP filter of s_l / g and its first difference

Tests		Lags and criterions	Models	Statistics of tests and critical values	Stationarity
ADF	Level	2 modified AIC, SIC, HQ	Trend	−3.542906 > −1.948313 (5 percent)	Non-stationary
	First difference	7 AIC, 2 SIC (−3.125308), 5 HQ (−4.404825)	None	−3.770759 < −1.948495 (5 percent)	Stationary
ERS	Level	2 modified AIC, SIC, HQ	Trend	−1.799482 > −3.180400 (5 percent)	Non-stationary
	First difference	2 AIC, SIC, HQ	Constant	−1.344437 > −1.948495 (5 percent)	Non-stationary
PP	Level	3 AIC, SIC, HQ	Trend	−3.389429 > −3.487845 (5 percent)	Non-stationary
	First difference	7 AIC, SIC, HQ	None	−17.40960 < −1.946447 (5 percent)	Stationary
KPSS	Level	3 AIC, SIC, HQ	Trend	0.782160 > 0.146000 (5 percent)	Non-stationary
	First difference	7 AIC, SIC, HQ	Trend	2.06 E-06 < 0.463000 (5 percent)	Stationary
ERS-PO	Level	3 AIC, SIC, HQ	Trend	26.35647 > 5.718400 (5 percent)	Non-stationary
	First difference	7 AIC, SIC, HQ	Constant	1.40 E-05 < 5.705600 (5 percent)	Stationary
NP	Level	3 AIC, SIC, HQ	Trend	{−7.62609; −1.93277; 0.25344; 11.9960} > {−17.3000; −2.91000; 0.16800; 5.48000} (5 percent)	Non-stationary
	First difference	5 AIC, SIC, HQ	Trend	{−24.3423; −3.48591; 0.14320; 3.76043} < {−8.10000; −1.98000; 0.23300; 3.17000} (5 percent)	Stationary

TABLE A.6.1.11 Summary of unit root test results

Series	Comments
K/Y	$K/Y \sim I(1)$, with trend.
s_1/g	Looking at the graph and correlogram, the series of s_1/g seemed to be non-stationary. The unit root tests allow us to conclude: $s_1/g \sim I(1)$ The existence of strong fluctuations leads to the use of moving averages in order to represent the long-term trend.
$MM_5 \, s_1/g$	All tests indicate that $MM_5 \, s_1/g \sim I(1)$ and suggest that the moving average represents the trend.
$MM_7 \, s_1/g$	ERS and NP tests indicate that $MM_7 \, s_1/g$ is at least $I(2)$, but all other tests show that the series is $I(1)$. From the graph and correlogram, we conclude that $MM_7 \, s_1/g \sim I(1)$, because the functions of autocorrelation and partial autocorrelation of the first difference of MM_7 s_1/g are within the confidence interval.
$MM_{10} \, s_1/g$	The tests lead to convergent results, indicating that $MM_{10} \, s_1/g \sim I(1)$. SIC and HQ tests give a lag of 0 in all sets, while AIC gives lags of 9 or 10.
$MM_{15} \, s_1/g$	The tests and criterions all give identical results, which show that $MM_{15} \, s_1/g \sim I(1)$.
$MM_{20} \, s_1/g$	The test results are similar: $MM_{20} \, s_1/g \sim I(1)$. However, the critical values of some tests (ERS and ERS-PO), calculated for 50 observations, may not be appropriate on a sample size of 40 points. The profiles of the graph and correlogram lead us to conclude that MM_{20} $s_1/g \sim I(1)$.
$MM_{25} \, s_1/g$	The tests and criterions all give similar results: $MM_{25} \, s_1/g \sim I(1)$. However, the critical values of certain tests (ERS and ERS-PO), calculated for 50 points, may be inappropriate on a sample of 35 observations. In view of the graph and correlogram, we conclude that: $MM_{25} \, s_1/g \sim I(1)$.
$MM_{30} \, s_1/g$	Tests and criterions give similar results: $MM_{30} \, s_1/g \sim I(1)$. However, the critical values of certain tests (ERS and ERS-PO), calculated for 50 observations, can be unsatisfactory on a sample of 35 points. In view of the graph and correlogram, we conclude that $MM_{30} \, s_1/g \sim I(1)$, while remaining careful.
$Filter_{HP} \, s_1/g$	All tests indicate that the s_1/g series with HP filter is $I(1)$ – except the ESR test which suggests it is $I(2)$. Under these conditions, we conclude that $s_1/g \sim I(1)$.

TABLE A.6.1.11　Summary of unit root test results (*cont.*)

Series	Comments
Conclusion	All the series considered are $I(1)$. The higher the number of years taken into account in the moving average (and the more fluctuations are therefore attenuated), the more the information criterions lead to clear and consistent results. As a consequence, we can test the cointegration relationships.

A.6.2　Results of Tests with Smoothing through Moving Averages: China, 1952–2012

TABLE A.6.2.1　Results of tests according to the univariate approach *à la* Engle-Granger with smoothing through moving average for s / g_R and β

	Level	5 years	7 years	10 years	15 years	20 years	25 years	30 years
$c(1)$								
Wald Test	0.86191	0.81812	0.80357	0.80357	0.81090	0.81421	0.79775	0.79576
p-value (Fisher)	0.5781	0.1118	0.0207	0.0067	0.0010	0.0000	0.0000	0.0000
p-value (Chi²)	0.5760	0.1060	0.0171	0.0047	0.0004	0.0000	0.0000	0.0000
t-statistics ([−1.68, 1.68]	−0.5592	−1.6163	−2.3854	−2.8303	−3.5189	−4.7419	−6.3827	−7.4208
at 10% Gauss.)								
Scale coefficient	$c(1)=1$	$c(1)=1$	$c(1)<1$	$c(1)<1$	$c(1)<1$	$c(1)<1$	$c(1)<1$	$c(1)<1$
ADF Test	−7.20785	−3.75474	−3.64981	−5.70419	−1.84345	−1.91795	−1.71583	−1.78651
Lags	0	9	0	9	0	0	4	0
Models	None	None	Trend	Constant	None	None	None	None
Criterion	AIC	AIC	AIC	AIC	AIC	AIC	AIC	AIC
Critical values at 1% (*)	−3.37*	−3.17**	−3.37*	−3.17**	−3.37*	−3.37*	−3.17**	−3.37*
or 5% (**)								
Relationship of cointegration	Yes	Yes	Yes	Yes	No	No	No	No
Sample size	60	56	54	51	46	41	35	31

Note: The first horizontal block gives the results of the Wald test and the scale coefficient; the second block, those of the ADF test for the cointegration relationship.

TABLE A.6.2.2   Results of tests according to the multivariate approach à la Johansen with smoothing through moving averages for s / g_R and β

	Level	5 years	7 years	10 years	15 years	20 years	25 years	30 years
Lags	3	3	2	1	1	1	1	1
Criterions	LR FPE AIC HQ	LR FPE AIC SIC HQ	SIC	LR SIC HQ	LR SIC HQ	LR SIC HQ	SIC	SIC
Dummy	With	Without	Without	Without	Without	Without	Without	Without
p-value (Jarque-Bera test)	0.0206	0.0315	0.5967	0.2627	0.2627	0.3525	0.2736	0.3541
Trace test	1	1	1	0	0	0	0	0
Max-Eig test	1	1	1	0	0	0	0	0
Cointegration	Yes	Yes	Yes	No	No	No	No	No

Notes: The criterions indicated are: LR = sequential modified LR test statistic; FPE = final prediction error; AIC = Akaike information criterion; SC = Schwarz information criterion; and HQ = Hannan-Quinn information criterion. The critical values are those of MacKinnon-Haug-Michelis, used at 5 percent. The p-value is that of a Jarque-Bera test performed with Doornik-Hansen Orthogonalization.

A.6.3   Database Related to Piketty's "Laws": China, 1952–2012

TABLE A.6.3.1   Stock of general capital à la Piketty, implicit rate of return of this capital and corresponding coefficient of capital

Years	General capital stock	Rate of return on general capital	General capital coefficient
1952	1,024.9	0.3043	1.5094
1953	1,156.7	0.3113	1.4754
1954	1,307.2	0.2832	1.6218
1955	1,452.9	0.2694	1.7048
1956	1,633.3	0.2710	1.6950
1957	1,828.9	0.2450	1.8745
1958	2,175.5	0.2549	1.8022
1959	2,667.0	0.2282	2.0130
1960	3,075.4	0.1954	2.3513
1961	3,153.0	0.1375	3.3397
1962	3,108.3	0.1267	3.6254
1963	3,140.7	0.1431	3.2100
1964	3,255.7	0.1689	2.7202
1965	3,491.8	0.1879	2.4443

TABLE A.6.3.1   Stock of general capital *à la* Piketty, implicit rate of return of this capital (*cont.*)

Years	General capital stock	Rate of return on general capital	General capital coefficient
1966	3,828.3	0.1892	2.4272
1967	4,004.8	0.1730	2.6557
1968	4,198.8	0.1602	2.8677
1969	4,445.3	0.1685	2.7260
1970	4,940.0	0.1762	2.6074
1971	5,485.1	0.1710	2.6855
1972	5,961.3	0.1632	2.8147
1973	6,518.9	0.1610	2.8522
1974	7,090.0	0.1509	3.0447
1975	7,727.2	0.1481	3.1005
1976	8,243.8	0.1360	3.3760
1977	8,831.0	0.1345	3.4143
1978	9,648.3	0.1386	3.3147
1979	10,491.8	0.1394	3.2960
1980	11,357.0	0.1340	3.4276
1981	12,170.2	0.1312	3.5000
1982	13,056.9	0.1308	3.5115
1983	14,058.9	0.1338	3.4334
1984	15,310.0	0.1448	3.1718
1985	17,010.4	0.1489	3.0858
1986	18,893.3	0.1431	3.2099
1987	20,869.6	0.1417	3.2426
1988	23,052.9	0.1347	3.4093
1989	25,168.0	0.1185	3.8773
1990	27,293.0	0.1167	3.9376
1991	29,673.3	0.1209	3.7980
1992	32,147.3	0.1295	3.5468
1993	35,611.7	0.1334	3.4428
1994	40,500.5	0.1290	3.5612
1995	45,621.0	0.1216	3.7776
1996	51,278.1	0.1171	3.9210
1997	57,025.7	0.1141	4.0271
1998	62,491.7	0.1116	4.1163
1999	68,089.3	0.1107	4.1497

TABLE A.6.3.1   Stock of general capital *à la* Piketty, implicit rate of return of this capital (*cont.*)

Years	General capital stock	Rate of return on general capital	General capital coefficient
2000	73,813.6	0.1126	4.0779
2001	81,080.2	0.1123	4.0906
2002	90,011.5	0.1124	4.0881
2003	101,566.5	0.1115	4.1195
2004	116,082.5	0.1109	4.1420
2005	131,590.2	0.1107	4.1509
2006	149,819.1	0.1127	4.0754
2007	172,731.8	0.1153	3.9823
2008	198,047.3	0.1127	4.0753
2009	230,146.5	0.1057	4.3440
2010	265,238.3	0.1048	4.3829
2011	302,334.6	0.1028	4.4703
2012	342,809.8	0.0981	4.6804

Notes: The general capital stock, at 1952 constant prices, is measured in hundreds of millions of yuans (or in *yì*, that is, 10^8). The implicit rate of return on this capital is calculated using an elasticity of the product with respect to general capital *à la* Piketty of 0.45.

TABLE A.6.3.2   National income growth rate and ratio of savings rate to national income growth rate

Years	National Income Growth Rate	Ratio Savings Rate / National Income Growth Rate
1952	n.-a.	n.-a.
1953	0.1547	1.4093
1954	0.0281	8.4940
1955	0.0574	3.6109
1956	0.1307	1.9071
1957	0.0125	18.8336
1958	0.2372	1.4679
1959	0.0976	4.3997
1960	−0.0129	−27.9599
1961	−0.2782	−0.6651

TABLE A.6.3.2   National income growth rate and ratio of savings rate to national income (*cont.*)

Years	National Income Growth Rate	Ratio Savings Rate / National Income Growth Rate
1962	−0.0918	−1.5637
1963	0.1412	1.2705
1964	0.2233	1.1610
1965	0.1936	1.6800
1966	0.1041	3.1884
1967	−0.0439	−6.4512
1968	−0.0291	−9.1675
1969	0.1137	2.6508
1970	0.1619	2.1894
1971	0.0780	4.6159
1972	0.0369	9.4768
1973	0.0792	4.5378
1974	0.0188	18.8167
1975	0.0703	5.3175
1976	−0.0202	−16.5786
1977	0.0592	6.0992
1978	0.1254	3.0835
1979	0.0936	3.8904
1980	0.0409	8.4739
1981	0.0494	6.6679
1982	0.0693	4.7517
1983	0.1012	3.1777
1984	0.1788	1.8981
1985	0.1420	2.4341
1986	0.0678	5.1086
1987	0.0935	3.9327
1988	0.0506	7.4101
1989	−0.0401	−8.8439
1990	0.0678	5.3359
1991	0.1272	2.9789
1992	0.1601	2.4990
1993	0.1412	2.9206
1994	0.0995	4.1699
1995	0.0619	6.4273

TABLE A.6.3.2   National income growth rate and ratio of savings rate to national income (*cont.*)

Years	National Income Growth Rate	Ratio Savings Rate / National Income Growth Rate
1996	0.0829	4.6895
1997	0.0828	4.7624
1998	0.0721	5.3136
1999	0.0808	4.4930
2000	0.1032	3.4260
2001	0.0950	3.8796
2002	0.1109	3.4343
2003	0.1200	3.4498
2004	0.1367	3.2430
2005	0.1312	3.4275
2006	0.1596	2.9518
2007	0.1799	2.7355
2008	0.1204	4.1945
2009	0.0902	5.5265
2010	0.1423	3.5849
2011	0.1176	4.2210
2012	0.0830	5.9065

Note: "n.-a." = non-available.

Appendices to Chapter 7

A.7.1 Complementary Statistical Database on the Industrial Capital Stocks in China from 1952 to 2014

TABLE A.7.1.1 Micro- and macroeconomic series of industrial capital stocks: China, 1952–2014 (*in hundreds of millions of yuans, 1952 constant prices*)

Years	Initial values of fixed assets K_{AO}	Total value of fixed assets K_{AT}	*Stricto sensu* capital $K_{Pe\,(I)}$	*Lato sensu* capital $K_{Pl\,(I)}$
1952	107.300	71.100	113.646	126.957
1953	128.473	86.588	132.819	163.948
1954	166.722	115.893	155.091	205.257
1955	199.277	139.140	167.243	229.829
1956	245.718	176.454	207.357	279.455
1957	297.808	217.376	263.757	366.708
1958	405.727	308.804	421.914	576.852
1959	532.586	417.078	621.013	866.964
1960	673.157	533.703	781.348	1,062.807
1961	759.748	591.132	601.486	808.190
1962	735.295	567.375	585.795	770.169
1963	747.970	567.640	629.520	822.574
1964	829.741	622.952	708.301	917.440
1965	950.605	710.748	760.725	991.897
1966	1,041.141	771.101	903.819	1,196.464
1967	1,114.103	809.750	838.496	1,114.367
1968	1,211.812	872.895	803.341	1,083.528
1969	1,296.931	921.721	983.221	1,311.736
1970	1,467.608	1,037.619	1,251.270	1,686.244
1971	1,674.776	1,203.672	1,442.901	1,961.331
1972	1,846.308	1,327.245	1,619.701	2,194.697
1973	2,034.664	1,461.268	1,766.389	2,413.724
1974	2,210.578	1,574.316	1,908.747	2,591.347
1975	2,410.124	1,703.917	2,263.630	3,036.812
1976	2,624.818	1,843.896	2,428.288	3,206.583
1977	2,828.387	1,973.109	2,734.244	3,589.982

TABLE A.7.1.1   Micro- and macroeconomic series of industrial capital stocks (*cont.*)

Years	Initial values of fixed assets K_{AO}	Total value of fixed assets K_{AT}	*Stricto sensu* capital $K_{Pe\ (I)}$	*Lato sensu* capital $K_{Pl\ (I)}$
1978	3,561.860	2,165.714	3,028.473	3,997.135
1979	3,764.166	2,221.410	3,209.372	4,253.197
1980	4,000.826	2,290.265	3,513.955	4,638.821
1981	4,244.834	2,391.830	3,547.691	4,680.282
1982	4,532.105	2,529.856	3,637.901	4,783.880
1983	4,835.878	2,682.051	3,814.808	4,998.221
1984	5,108.879	2,705.114	4,016.987	5,233.116
1985	5,553.841	3,759.587	4,346.779	5,744.347
1986	6,023.689	4,119.151	4,826.923	6,421.127
1987	6,552.186	4,540.750	5,269.982	6,951.553
1988	6,697.069	4,670.000	5,857.292	7,714.247
1989	7,180.445	5,037.744	6,103.626	8,257.965
1990	7,813.844	5,505.479	6,230.638	8,570.844
1991	8,650.287	6,060.395	6,771.309	9,347.031
1992	8,871.327	6,273.975	7,729.648	10,513.879
1993	9,180.052	7,635.822	9,250.405	12,402.703
1994	10,730.842	7,771.550	10,493.428	13,880.276
1995	13,386.258	9,211.488	12,034.331	15,819.778
1996	14,888.875	10,627.496	13,695.783	17,833.101
1997	17,095.481	12,041.169	15,391.362	19,803.337
1998	18,732.052	13,206.835	16,562.156	20,934.276
1999	20,595.198	14,717.765	18,118.860	22,473.519
2000	22,470.454	16,990.777	20,152.811	24,411.121
2001	24,580.541	18,077.679	21,926.956	26,127.428
2002	26,680.607	19,290.523	24,237.911	28,412.732
2003	29,331.870	20,996.596	28,204.736	32,577.299
2004	32,939.410	24,158.612	32,207.952	36,868.050
2005	36,704.600	27,167.962	37,308.417	42,298.027
2006	42,400.036	31,436.532	42,706.353	48,101.417
2007	49,374.386	36,446.299	47,566.145	53,429.380
2008	59,833.301	43,698.837	54,445.784	61,214.836
2009	66,417.490	49,443.465	60,829.439	67,921.557
2010	78,179.153	55,591.677	70,861.167	78,832.498
2011	88,733.538	58,192.033	80,857.266	89,992.452

TABLE A.7.1.1   Micro- and macroeconomic series of industrial capital stocks (*cont.*)

Years	Initial values of fixed assets K_{AO}	Total value of fixed assets K_{AT}	*Stricto sensu* capital $K_{Pe\,(I)}$	*Lato sensu* capital $K_{Pl\,(I)}$
2012	101,307.418	66,209.522	89,441.292	99,385.376
2013	115,913.556	73,398.420	97,733.525	108,426.101
2014	129,761.692	81,877.888	105,896.939	117,389.290

Notes: K_{AO} = initial value of the fixed assets of the industrial enterprises at the microeconomic level;

K_{AT} = total (or net) value of the fixed assets of the industrial enterprises at the microeconomic level;

$K_{Pe\,(I)}$ = stock of narrowly-defined productive capital of the industrial sector at the macroeconomic level (without inventories);

$K_{Pl\,(I)}$ = stock of broadly-defined productive capital of the industrial sector at the macroeconomic level (with inventories).

A.7.2   Complementary Statistical Database on the Construction of Industrial Profit Rates in China from 1952 to 2014

TABLE A.7.2.1   Workers' (direct and indirect) income and taxes in China from 1952 to 2014 (*in hundreds of millions of current yuans*)

Years	Workers' direct income	Indirect income or welfare expenses	Total taxes (excluding personal income taxes)
1952	102.92	2.05	97.69
1953	121.21	2.57	113.86
1954	120.02	2.78	124.03
1955	135.01	3.05	119.23
1956	190.45	4.46	131.93
1957	214.42	5.22	141.37
1958	235.89	5.84	172.91
1959	280.85	7.26	188.36
1960	299.99	7.99	182.81
1961	264.02	6.51	122.75
1962	236.33	5.68	120.73
1963	237.20	5.93	130.07

TABLE A.7.2.1 Workers' (direct and indirect) income and taxes in China (*cont.*)

Years	Workers' direct income	Indirect income or welfare expenses	Total taxes (excluding personal income taxes)
1964	259.92	6.50	149.61
1965	297.88	7.05	169.98
1966	328.25	7.49	186.91
1967	312.31	7.84	166.58
1968	338.66	7.92	162.12
1969	344.54	8.11	197.29
1970	368.87	8.40	235.63
1971	372.21	9.16	262.17
1972	413.44	10.29	265.39
1973	490.71	10.77	291.82
1974	583.33	11.01	299.30
1975	624.20	11.50	333.16
1976	643.53	12.10	336.44
1977	822.18	12.40	376.03
1978	1,378.15	62.28	414.09
1979	1,569.30	83.97	420.88
1980	1,617.56	99.29	416.18
1981	1,750.62	110.01	447.32
1982	1,904.35	125.68	487.34
1983	2,092.10	145.06	529.32
1984	2,578.36	171.29	629.46
1985	2,903.07	199.10	1,240.26
1986	3,104.99	205.61	1,190.83
1987	3,346.44	208.40	1,135.21
1988	3,495.02	188.49	1,066.84
1989	3,338.55	165.42	1,028.88
1990	3,692.81	197.93	1,031.25
1991	4,066.92	227.11	1,055.88
1992	4,538.10	289.19	1,092.94
1993	5,150.83	337.72	1,227.97
1994	5,782.61	377.40	1,188.39
1995	6,364.39	415.00	1,185.99
1996	6,867.96	463.49	1,245.28
1997	7,395.98	521.98	1,438.19

TABLE A.7.2.1   Workers' (direct and indirect) income and taxes in China (*cont.*)

Years	Workers' direct income	Indirect income or welfare expenses	Total taxes (excluding personal income taxes)
1998	7,953.85	600.31	1,622.45
1999	8,436.92	755.00	1,893.43
2000	9,082.75	869.55	2,189.45
2001	9,879.47	988.35	2,609.05
2002	10,857.85	1,236.03	3,019.57
2003	11,716.78	1,424.98	3,378.82
2004	12,078.88	1,553.53	3,921.53
2005	13,907.60	1,808.86	4,583.00
2006	15,901.38	1,935.40	5,474.21
2007	18,547.65	2,284.27	6,851.98
2008	22,442.86	2,706.97	7,699.91
2009	24,740.82	3,238.24	8,532.78
2010	27,353.51	3,737.11	10,162.95
2011	30,683.26	4,484.52	11,801.45
2012	33,471.73	5,336.30	13,029.42
2013	36,130.24	6,048.36	13,932.42
2014	38,855.27	6,815.83	14,683.63

A.7.3   Statistical Database on Industrial Profit Rates in China from 1952 to 2014

TABLE A.7.3.1   Microeconomic industrial profit rates: China, 1952–2014 (*in percentages*)

Year	r_1	r_2	r_3	r_4
1952	28.239	20.597	42.616	31.083
1953	30.642	21.787	45.465	32.326
1954	30.127	21.768	43.339	31.315
1955	29.446	21.810	42.172	31.236
1956	27.880	19.965	38.824	27.802
1957	28.869	20.730	39.550	28.400

TABLE A.7.3.1   Microeconomic industrial profit rates: China, 1952–2014 *(in percentages)* *(cont.)*

Year	r_1	r_2	r_3	r_4
1958	55.249	40.145	72.590	52.745
1959	58.777	41.973	75.055	53.597
1960	53.908	39.475	67.994	49.789
1961	19.323	11.036	24.835	14.184
1962	15.204	8.232	19.703	10.668
1963	19.632	12.494	25.868	16.463
1964	24.622	16.455	32.795	21.918
1965	29.016	20.035	38.808	26.796
1966	34.273	23.862	46.276	32.219
1967	22.131	13.650	30.450	18.781
1968	17.934	10.139	24.897	14.076
1969	26.574	16.732	37.391	23.542
1970	32.721	21.597	46.281	30.547
1971	31.810	20.610	44.259	28.677
1972	29.098	18.767	40.478	26.107
1973	27.646	17.947	38.494	24.989
1974	22.722	13.881	31.905	19.491
1975	23.697	14.618	33.519	20.677
1976	19.997	11.748	28.466	16.724
1977	21.530	12.886	30.862	18.472
1978	17.234	15.134	34.344	21.774
1979	17.201	15.570	35.611	22.853
1980	16.739	15.650	36.269	23.296
1981	14.184	13.667	33.457	20.525
1982	12.753	12.509	31.646	18.883
1983	13.949	12.688	31.353	19.078
1984	14.162	12.975	32.737	19.620
1985	13.491	8.913	19.930	13.166
1986	11.079	7.618	16.201	11.140
1987	10.973	7.960	15.834	11.486
1988	11.182	8.938	16.036	12.817
1989	8.019	6.363	11.430	9.070

TABLE A.7.3.1   Microeconomic industrial profit rates: China, 1952–2014 (*in percentages*) (*cont.*)

Year	r_1	r_2	r_3	r_4
1990	3.892	2.728	5.523	3.872
1991	3.747	2.785	5.348	3.976
1992	4.871	4.199	6.887	5.937
1993	6.207	5.801	7.462	6.974
1994	5.373	3.550	7.419	4.901
1995	3.634	1.946	5.281	2.828
1996	2.864	1.283	4.012	1.798
1997	2.859	1.525	4.059	2.165
1998	2.249	1.102	3.190	1.562
1999	3.185	2.295	4.456	3.212
2000	5.586	4.616	7.388	6.105
2001	5.485	4.458	7.458	6.062
2002	6.161	4.989	8.521	6.900
2003	7.898	6.540	11.034	9.136
2004	9.486	7.814	12.933	10.654
2005	10.341	8.534	13.971	11.530
2006	11.551	9.663	15.580	13.032
2007	13.664	11.563	18.511	15.665
2008	12.457	10.570	17.056	14.472
2009	12.401	10.656	16.658	14.314
2010	15.843	13.755	22.281	19.344
2011	15.902	13.714	24.248	20.912
2012	14.249	12.253	21.803	18.749
2013	13.692	11.795	21.623	18.626
2014	12.087	10.333	19.156	16.376

Notes: r_1 = nominal profit rate before taxes for the industrial enterprises at the microeconomic level;

r_2 = nominal profit rate after taxes for the industrial enterprises at the microeconomic level;

r_3 = real profit rate before taxes for the industrial enterprises at the microeconomic level;

r_4 = real profit rate after taxes for the industrial enterprises at the microeconomic level.

TABLE A.7.3.2   Macroeconomic industrial profit rates: China, 1952–2014 (*in percentages*)

Year	r_5	r_6	r_7	r_8
1952	89.547	59.621	80.158	53.370
1953	99.619	61.673	80.704	49.963
1954	94.236	58.636	71.204	44.305
1955	89.327	55.714	65.002	40.542
1956	81.068	49.595	60.153	36.800
1957	73.005	44.899	52.510	32.294
1958	74.226	50.355	54.289	36.830
1959	65.051	46.447	46.597	33.271
1960	52.428	37.746	38.544	27.750
1961	34.122	22.167	25.395	16.497
1962	30.182	18.678	22.957	14.207
1963	34.407	22.524	26.332	17.238
1964	41.834	28.994	32.297	22.385
1965	48.034	33.757	36.840	25.890
1966	49.054	35.313	37.056	26.676
1967	43.190	30.314	32.498	22.810
1968	39.678	27.141	29.418	20.123
1969	42.749	29.111	32.043	21.821
1970	46.047	32.744	34.169	24.297
1971	44.789	31.356	32.950	23.068
1972	41.981	29.478	30.982	21.755
1973	41.877	29.913	30.646	21.891
1974	38.780	27.648	28.565	20.365
1975	37.782	27.075	28.163	20.182
1976	33.411	23.344	25.301	17.678
1977	33.504	23.566	25.518	17.948
1978	35.448	25.448	26.858	19.281
1979	35.701	26.055	26.939	19.660
1980	33.860	25.152	25.649	19.053
1981	33.492	24.582	25.387	18.633
1982	33.729	24.279	25.649	18.463
1983	35.091	25.440	26.782	19.417
1984	38.194	28.035	29.318	21.520
1985	40.539	24.159	30.676	18.281
1986	39.182	24.957	29.454	18.761
1987	38.956	26.887	29.533	20.383

TABLE A.7.3.2   Macroeconomic industrial profit rates: China, 1952–2014 (*in percentages*) (*cont.*)

Year	r_5	r_6	r_7	r_8
1988	37.361	27.638	28.368	20.985
1989	34.159	25.551	25.248	18.885
1990	34.002	25.613	24.718	18.619
1991	36.132	28.395	26.175	20.570
1992	38.323	31.489	28.174	23.151
1993	38.963	33.411	29.060	24.919
1994	38.032	33.272	28.752	25.153
1995	36.450	32.292	27.728	24.565
1996	35.126	31.158	26.977	23.929
1997	34.364	30.273	26.708	23.529
1998	33.597	29.448	26.580	23.298
1999	32.881	28.673	26.510	23.117
2000	32.918	28.317	27.176	23.377
2001	32.706	26.273	27.448	22.049
2002	32.426	25.663	27.662	21.892
2003	32.087	25.243	27.781	21.855
2004	32.164	24.848	28.099	21.707
2005	32.320	25.954	28.507	22.892
2006	32.858	25.307	29.172	22.469
2007	34.115	26.227	30.371	23.349
2008	33.157	26.750	29.491	23.792
2009	31.091	23.661	27.845	21.190
2010	30.900	24.612	27.775	22.123
2011	29.931	23.629	26.892	21.230
2012	27.857	20.575	25.070	18.517
2013	25.516	18.900	23.000	17.037
2014	24.113	17.839	21.752	16.093

Notes: r_5 = narrowly-defined capital profit rate before taxes for the industrial sector at the macroeconomic level;

r_6 = narrowly-defined capital profit rate after taxes for the industrial sector at the macroeconomic level;

r_7 = broadly-defined capital profit rate before taxes for the industrial sector at the macroeconomic level;

r_8 = broadly-defined capital profit rate after taxes for the industrial sector at the macroeconomic level.

TABLE A.7.3.3   An example of decomposition into trend and cycles for a profit rate of productive capital with inventories: China, 1952–2014 (*in percentages*)

Year	Profit rate	Cycles	Trend
1952	0.594528	−0.016063	0.610591
1953	0.593275	0.019084	0.574190
1954	0.533895	−0.001324	0.535219
1955	0.498032	0.003871	0.494161
1956	0.453636	0.002349	0.451288
1957	0.383564	−0.023926	0.407491
1958	0.403384	0.039355	0.364036
1959	0.342020	0.023657	0.318363
1960	0.283371	0.009167	0.274204
1961	0.187749	−0.051333	0.239081
1962	0.171631	−0.050347	0.221978
1963	0.207019	−0.016650	0.223669
1964	0.255574	0.018704	0.236870
1965	0.287366	0.035731	0.251635
1966	0.287416	0.026406	0.261010
1967	0.266683	0.002924	0.263759
1968	0.235878	−0.026989	0.262867
1969	0.252464	−0.009329	0.261793
1970	0.267406	0.007734	0.259672
1971	0.263268	0.009119	0.254149
1972	0.246452	0.002344	0.244108
1973	0.233211	0.003322	0.229889
1974	0.204797	−0.007411	0.212209
1975	0.199373	0.007058	0.192315
1976	0.178143	0.007874	0.170269
1977	0.155421	0.008157	0.147263
1978	0.103052	−0.022696	0.125749
1979	0.099364	−0.010118	0.109482
1980	0.098998	0.000410	0.098588
1981	0.092392	0.000819	0.091574
1982	0.088849	0.001840	0.087009
1983	0.091261	0.007663	0.083598
1984	0.089569	0.009231	0.080338
1985	0.065099	−0.012351	0.077451

TABLE A.7.3.3   An example of decomposition into trend and cycles for a profit rate *(cont.)*

Year	Profit rate	Cycles	Trend
1986	0.071111	−0.005526	0.076637
1987	0.082409	0.004787	0.077622
1988	0.087044	0.007801	0.079243
1989	0.078796	−0.002312	0.081108
1990	0.074022	−0.010047	0.084069
1991	0.084379	−0.004232	0.088611
1992	0.099201	0.005591	0.093610
1993	0.103629	0.006363	0.097265
1994	0.102936	0.004265	0.098671
1995	0.097908	−3.05E-05	0.097939
1996	0.095878	1.45E-05	0.095863
1997	0.092032	−0.001203	0.093235
1998	0.089235	−0.001610	0.090845
1999	0.086949	−0.002344	0.089293
2000	0.089859	0.000939	0.088920
2001	0.088527	−0.001168	0.089695
2002	0.086562	−0.005170	0.091733
2003	0.090625	−0.004341	0.094966
2004	0.104085	0.005589	0.098495
2005	0.102134	0.001404	0.100730
2006	0.105159	0.004187	0.100972
2007	0.106169	0.007421	0.098748
2008	0.090653	−0.003604	0.094257
2009	0.083419	−0.005462	0.088881
2010	0.085003	0.001573	0.083429
2011	0.079624	0.001788	0.077836
2012	0.069547	−0.002739	0.072285
2013	0.063614	−0.003636	0.067249
2014	0.066189	0.003427	0.062762

Appendix to Chapter 8

A.8.1   Gross Domestic Product Growth Rate in China from 1952 to 2015

TABLE A.8.1.1   Values of gY (in real terms): China, 1952–2015 (*in percentages*)

Year	GDP growth rate	Year	GDP growth rate
1952	n.-a.	1984	15.2
1953	15.6	1985	13.4
1954	4.3	1986	8.9
1955	6.9	1987	11.7
1956	15.0	1988	11.2
1957	5.1	1989	4.2
1958	21.3	1990	3.9
1959	9.0	1991	9.3
1960	8.0	1992	14.2
1961	−16.2	1993	13.9
1962	−5.7	1994	13.0
1963	10.3	1995	11.0
1964	18.2	1996	9.9
1965	17.0	1997	9.2
1966	10.7	1998	7.8
1967	−5.7	1999	7.7
1968	−4.1	2000	8.5
1969	16.9	2001	8.3
1970	19.3	2002	9.1
1971	7.1	2003	10.0
1972	3.8	2004	10.1
1973	7.8	2005	11.4
1974	2.3	2006	12.7
1975	8.7	2007	14.2
1976	−1.6	2008	9.7
1977	7.6	2009	9.4
1978	11.7	2010	10.6
1979	7.6	2011	9.6
1980	7.8	2012	7.9
1981	5.1	2013	7.8

TABLE A.8.1.1   Values of gY (in real terms): China, 1952–2015 (*in percentages*) (*cont.*)

Year	GDP growth rate	Year	GDP growth rate
1982	9.0	2014	7.4
1983	10.8	2015	7.0

SOURCE: NBS (VARIOUS YEARS).

Archives: On the Nature of the Chinese Economic System

1   Marxist Debates on China[1]

China's ruling class admits that the capitalist private sector plays a very important role in the country's economy. However, it claims that this sector is one of the many components of a mixed economy, in which the public sector and the power of the state must be strengthened. Based on their speeches, many Chinese leaders seem to argue that China is currently in a "primary phase of socialism," an essential step toward developing the necessary productive forces for full-fledged socialism. Are such statements accurate? Do they deserve to be taken seriously? Put another way: Is Chinese socialism over? We do not think so.

Yet in debates among Marxist thinkers, most of them say that the Chinese economy is now capitalist. David Harvey, for example, believes that since the 1978 reforms, a "neoliberalism with Chinese characteristics" has arisen, in which a particular type of market economy has increasingly incorporated neoliberal elements yet operated under strictly authoritarian centralized control. Meanwhile, Giovanni Arrighi mobilizes a progressive rereading of Adam Smith, arguing that the Chinese elite use "the market as a tool of government" to explain the success of China's economy. Leo Panitch and Sam Gindin understand China's integration into the circuits of the world economy less as an opportunity to reorient global capitalism, and more as China playing a complementary role, formerly held by Japan, in providing the United States with the capital flow needed to maintain its global hegemony. Hence, Panitch and Gindin argue, there is a trend toward the liberalization of financial markets in China, a weakening of capital controls, and an undermining of the Chinese Communist Party's (CCP) power bases.[2]

There are, however, other Marxists – rare, but no less important – who continue to defend the idea that, although the system currently operational in

---

1   With the kind agreement of the journal, we reproduce here an article cosigned by the two authors of this book with Tony Andréani and published in *Monthly Review* (n° 70, n° 5, pp. 32–43, October 2018, New York).

2   David Harvey, *A Brief History of Neoliberalism* (New York: Oxford University Press, 2005). Giovanni Arrighi, *Adam Smith in Beijing* (London: Verso, 2009). Leo Panitch and Sam Gindin, "The Integration of China into Global Capitalism," *International Critical Thought* 3, no. 2 (2013): 146–158.

China could be absorbed into a form of state capitalism, there is also a wide range of other possible paths it could take.[3] In this article, we will push this idea further, arguing that the Chinese system today still contains some key components of socialism and is compatible with a market, or market-based, socialism that is clearly distinct from capitalism.

2   Characteristics of Chinese Market Socialism

For Marx, capitalism implies a pronounced separation between producing value through labour, and owning the means of production. In this schema, the owners of capital do not work in production. This is the case in current Western financial capitalism, where management is delegated to managers and corporate profit takes the form of shareholder value. However, under this criteria, small Chinese enterprises, of which there are many, are more akin to family or craft production than to the capitalist mode of production in the strictest sense. Additionally, the maximization of profit for the owners – the fundamental logic of capitalism – is not observed in China's large state-owned enterprises (SOEs), as evidenced by the weakness, if not non-existence, of dividends paid to the state, which are more like a tax on capital. The capital-labor separation is often very relative: it is limited in public enterprises, which prevents them from being rigorously considered a form of state capitalism, and even more so in the so-called collective economy, where workers participate in the ownership of capital, and even have full ownership of their workplace, such as in cooperatives and the popular communes. Of course, even in these collective production units, workers remain more or less separated from management, but this whole non-state economy cannot be forgotten or placed under the banner of "capitalism."

Our understanding of the Chinese system as market socialism, or socialism with a market, is based on the following ten pillars, largely foreign to capitalism:

1.   The persistence of powerful and modernized planning, which takes various modalities and mobilizes different tools according to the sectors concerned.
2.   A form of political democracy that makes possible the collective choices that underpin this planning.

---

3   Some examples of such Marxists and their work: Wen Tiejun, "Centenary reflections on the 'three dimensional problem' of rural China," *Inter-Asia Cultural Studies* 2, no. 2 (2001): 287–295. Samir Amin, "China 2013," *Monthly Review* 64, no. 10 (March 2013): 14–33.

3. Very extensive public services, which condition political, social, and economic citizenship and, as such, are off the market or weakly marketable.
4. Public ownership of land and natural resources – state-owned at the national level and collective at the local level – thereby guaranteeing farmers access to land.
5. Diverse forms of ownership suitable to the socialization of productive forces: (1) SOEs, provided that they differ from capitalist firms, particularly with regard to the participation of workers in management, (2) small individual private property, and (3) socialized property. In addition, there is capitalist property, which was maintained and even at times encouraged during the long socialist transition in order to stimulate activity and make effective other forms of property.
6. A general policy consisting of increasing labour income relative to other sources of income.
7. The promotion of social justice from a more egalitarian perspective.
8. The preservation of nature, considered to be inseparable from social progress, as a goal of development in order to maximize wealth.
9. Economic relations between states based on a win-win principle, that is, systematically seeking mutual benefits.
10. Political relations between states based on the pursuit of peace and more equitable relationships.

These points are the subject of fierce debate, both in China and abroad, analysis of which must be deepened without prejudice or preconceptions. Despite the criticisms, these ten pillars give us a framework through which to better understand China's economic system as market socialism.[4]

3 Public Enterprises, Public Services, and Planning

In China, the justification for public enterprises is threefold: they can distribute more to their employees; the state is free to define the method of management, particularly in terms of salaries; and such enterprises can be easily put at the service of state projects. In a rather socialist fashion, the state allocates dividends from a special support fund for SOEs, which also benefit from credit and interest rate advantages.

---

4 Tony Andréani and Rémy Herrera, "Which Economic Model for China?" *International Critical Thought* 5, no. 1 (2015): 111–125.

Part of the strength of these SOEs comes from the fact that they are not managed like Western private companies, which are listed on the stock exchange and oriented toward maximizing shareholder value with dividend distribution, stock valorization, and high returns on investment by pressuring subcontractors. If Chinese public entities operated in such a way, it would be to the detriment of the local industrial fabric, which is obviously not the case. We would then be dealing with a savage form of "state capitalism," as is often claimed, and there could be no dynamic economic growth. Most Chinese SOEs are, or have become, profitable because the principle that guides them is not the enrichment of shareholders, but productive investment and service rendered to customers. It does not matter if their profits are lower than those of their Western competitors; they serve in part to stimulate the rest of the economy.

One of the specificities of these public companies is to pay relatively little – around 10 percent – in dividends to the state shareholder. Today, many foreign experts advocate increasing these dividends and the Securities Regulatory Commission sometimes seems to lean in this direction. Inspired by Western capitalist practices, this orientation is not the right fit for China's public companies, which would be deprived of their advantages and, even though they would still be under state control, would increasingly cater to private shareholders, as is the case for Western firms that, in turn, most often depend on the portfolio strategies of the world's leading financial oligopolies. Instead, it would be better for the Chinese state to introduce a tax on capital in the form of rent for the provision of property, and profitable companies could retain a larger share of the profits for investment, as well as research and development.

China's SOEs should not be managed like private companies. "Chinese-style market socialism" is based on maintaining a strong public sector that has a strategic role in the economy. There is every reason to believe that this is one of the essential explanations for the performance of the Chinese economy. This is probably also related to the size of SOEs: giants that benefit from economies of scale that reduce costs at all levels, and provide a myriad of small and medium production units with inexpensive inputs that ensure competitive manufacturing conditions in the markets.

A laudable characteristic of Chinese public enterprises is the limited but real participation of personnel in the management of units through representatives on the supervisory board and in the workers' congress. The shareholder logic would run counter to such participation – a participation that must be strengthened. Another advantage is that these SOEs can more easily meet planning objectives. This is not a question of imposing political tasks that would reduce their autonomy and weigh on their results, but it is to say that by controlling the appointment and management of leaders, public authorities on which many companies depend have the means to ensure that they act appropriately in public services as well as in the market sectors that planning can help guide, such as through subsidies and taxation.

In China, social services, such as education, health care, and pensions, are wholly or mostly controlled by the state, namely, the central government or, more often, local governments. Such services do not provide goods marketed by the private sector, but rather social goods necessary for individuals to be thriving political, social, and economic subjects – who are in good health, have access to employment, enjoy public transportation, are educated, and so on. However, public services are considered strategic goods in that they provide essential inputs for the rest of the economy: energy, infrastructure, basic materials, and even banking and research. While the private sector is considered complementary or stimulating, the state favors the public sector in the exercise of competition. The broad conception of these "strategic" public services is one of the greatest strengths of the Chinese economy. Hence, through the adoption of this coherent strategy of development focused on large public services, what is at stake here is also the defense of national sovereignty.

A remarkable feature of China's political and economic system is its powerful planning, which continues today despite changes in objectives and instruments over recent decades. The speeches given before the National People's Congress every year indicate whether the quantified objectives set out in the Five-Year Plan have been achieved, as is often the case, and which ones to reach in the year to come. This planning, which looks to a future in a world marked by uncertainty, is the expression of collective choices and a general will. It is the crystallization of a common national destiny and the means for people to become its master in all spheres of life, from consumption to housing. These choices are made by the CCP for citizens, with the principle of consultation increasingly posited as a necessity. This strong strategic planning, with modernized techniques adapted to the needs of the present, by means such as subsidized rates, price controls, and public orders, is one of the distinctive features of a socialist system.

Nevertheless, today we are obviously far from the egalitarian ideal of socialism. China remains a country with immense social inequality. The line on equality was suspended to accelerate growth (hence the motto "enrich yourselves"), and then taken up again with the recent promotion of social justice themes. The exaltation of "socialist morality" by CCP leaders can lead to skepticism when we know about the consumerism, desire for luxury, and even corruption that exists in China. We must not, however, take lightly that the Chinese state is consistently opposed to this moral degradation. There is a continuation of the ideals of socialism – not just of a social justice restricted to limited redistribution of income, that employs notions of fairness to justify inequality, or exploits representative democracy effectively to eradicate the participation of people. It is in the public sector that the state has the means to reduce these inequalities through the participation of workers in management and the role of public enterprises as "social engines." This is yet another argument in favor of strengthening the public sector.

4   Controlling the Banking System and Financial Markets

Many economists consider the current Chinese financial system to be obsolete and call for its modernization, that is, its incorporation into the extended financial markets that they believe are necessary for growth.[5] Financial sector reforms have been accelerating since 2005 and have taken the form of opening up the capital of state-owned banks and the creation of new stock exchanges. These reforms have followed those previously taken by SOEs, which were empowered and given increasing autonomy with regard to following the Five-Year Plan; transformed into joint stock companies; and encouraged to adopt market-management criteria, to draw on the methods of market finance, and to develop partnerships with foreign investors. Thus, the initial public offerings of the largest banks – Bank of China, Industrial and Commercial Bank of China, and China Construction Bank – were preceded by the entry of foreign institutions into their capital structures, such as Goldman Sachs, UBS, and Bank of America, respectively, in order to facilitate the learning of corporate governance. Nevertheless, the financing system of the Chinese economy is still based on banking intermediation, even if it tends to move away from it rather quickly, on the political authorities' grounds that there must be a balance struck between financial markets and bank credits.

We must be careful not to confuse modernization in this sphere with the adoption of capitalist methods. It is far from clear that a choice in favor of market finance has been made, seeing as interventions into the financial system by monetary authorities remain massive and the pragmatism of their approach is perceptible. The Chinese public authorities are experiencing both advances

---

5   Frederic Mishkin, *Economics of Money, Banking, and Financial Markets*, 9th ed. (Boston: Pearson, 2010).

and setbacks in the context of a deeper, but contradictory, integration of the country into globalization. This was particularly true during each phase of the economic slowdown after 2008, marked by a stimulation of bank credits to correct the disorders of finance. At the turn of the 1990s, following the crisis of 1990–91, banks that had engaged in adventurous operations, such as insurance and real estate, had already been banned from doing so between 1992 and 1995, even though they have since been allowed to conduct operations combining bank credits and financial markets. More recently, after 2008, as observed previously, China's authorities were forced to firmly limit the destabilizing social impact of the global crisis by changing the existing institutional framework, acquiring powerful control instruments, and consolidating their development strategy.

Chinese political leaders know the benefits of banking intermediation and are aware of the serious malfunctioning of financial markets, regularly calling for the reform of the world monetary and financial order. They prefer to keep much of the banking system under state control by striving to improve its functioning, are reluctant to abandon the "universal banking" model, and are moving toward mixed operations, but carried out in specialized subsidiaries, separate from the rest of the public holding company, and placed under the watchful eye of the Banking Regulatory Commission.

Furthermore, despite reforms, interest rates are still largely administered. For the interest rates that have been liberalized, the supply of credit is strongly controlled by the central bank, notably through reserve requirements. The easing of some constraints imposed on banks to fix rates on deposits should not cause us to forget that, historically, monetary authorities have willingly reduced the remuneration on deposits to a minimum (under the inflation rate) and this has not altered the national savings rate, which still remains very high.

One of the specificities and strengths of the Chinese economy is the voluntarist twist in factor prices. The government was right not to let the market "freely" fix the price, so as to control the supply of credit, which is difficult to manage but vital for the economy. State authorities with a macroscopic view of the risks are the only ones able to guide the economy according to a plan. As administered interest rates do not allow for timely adjustments between household savings and the economy's financing needs, the preferred rate regime is a semi-administered one, with upper limits for credit supply and lower limits for the remuneration of savings. Thus, in the debate on interest rates, we lean toward maintaining some degree of control.

The expansion of the private sphere logically implies a rise in the stock market. Nevertheless, the latter should remain limited. Whereas the stock market can be useful for the private sector, public enterprises must, on the contrary, rely on it less and less as they increase their self-financing capacities and provide the funds available to the state for carrying out capital increases. For the time being, the opening of the equity market to international investors is restricted to allegedly qualified players. The authorities, who are rightly suspicious of speculative movements, have so far prohibited foreign firms from issuing shares in yuans in the domestic market. To release these brakes, particularly to advance toward full convertibility of the yuan and its supposed advantages, would involve submitting to the powerful financial oligopolies, especially U.S. ones. The use of the stock market should remain as limited as possible and should not lead to aligning with the shareholder value model. China's savings are plentiful enough to be mobilized through domestic institutional investors, which can be subject to limits of profitability.

5   A Coherent Domestic Development Strategy

A feature often emphasized in describing the success of the Chinese economy is the boom in its exports of goods and services since the early 1990s, especially in the year 2000. It is hastily concluded that these exports drive the country's growth. This is to forget that the strategy of development – one of the "secrets" of China's performance in the world market – is conceived and applied with regularity and pragmatism by Chinese leaders. This strategy is focused on a more domestically oriented model and the maintenance of very powerful state sectors such as energy, transportation, telecommunications, raw materials, semi-finished products, construction, and the banking system.

The vast majority of entrepreneurs in China's manufacturing sector are primarily interested in domestic outlets for their products. It is especially the rise in internal demand, stimulated by a sharp increase in household consumption and very active state capital expenditure – particularly infrastructure – which guides their optimistic investment programs. Thanks to the progress of increasingly well-controlled national technological innovation operating in all fields, including space, robotics, and telecommunications, the productive scheme of the country has evolved from "made in China" to made *by* China.

The accelerated pace of labour productivity gains is helping support the rapid growth in industrial real wages, while the rise in Chinese labour costs relative to other competing countries in the global South is not detrimental to competition. Exports play a supporting role, as does foreign direct investment, since over half of exports come from foreign firms based in China. This makes it possible to understand that in 2011, for example, the negative net contribution of exports to Gross Domestic Product (GDP) growth (−5.8 percent) did not hinder the dynamism of the latter (close to +10.0 percent), nor even slow the rise in profit margins. The GDP growth forecast for 2018 is 6.7 percent (against an inflation rate of 1.5 percent), with contributions estimated at 4.5 percent for consumption, 2.0 percent for investment, and only 0.2 percent for exports.

It is often said that the success of Chinese exports would be due to the very low cost of labour. This is a largely insubstantial assessment: labour costs represent only a small proportion of sales prices (5 to 10 percent on average), and do not compensate for the transportation costs to importing countries, even though Chinese wages tend to grow faster than those of competitors in the global South. China's export success is largely due to the lower costs for inputs, such as energy and basic materials, provided by SOEs. Admittedly, Chinese wages are significantly lower than in the global North, but much higher than the alleged "miserable" wages.

In response to the 2008 crisis, whose effects were felt some years later in China, the state's anti-crisis policies aimed at correcting imbalances in the economy, particularly through massive expansion in public infrastructure, including in rural areas; promotion of new mid-sized urban poles in the inner parts of the country; and the adoption of measures favorable to the agricultural population.[6] The net income of rural households thus increased, in real terms and per capita, considerably faster than those in urban areas. Thus the share devoted to consumption in the national income increases relative to that of investment. Investment in services to households and enterprises is also progressing. In addition, the financing of real estate, including the credit system, is more controlled.

6   The Destiny of the Yuan

The rise of China's exports of goods and services, coupled with the exports of capital, such as in the refunding of the U.S. Treasury and the restructuring of European sovereign debts, crystallizes another point of tension.[7] One often reads in the West that the undervaluing of the Chinese currency, the renminbi, whose basic unit is the yuan, is the starting point for the bilateral trade deficits

6 Erebus Wong and Jade Tsui Sit, "Rethinking 'Rural China', Unthinking Modernisation," in Rémy Herrera and Kin Chi Lau, eds., *The Struggle for Food Sovereignty*, (London: Pluto, 2015), 83–108.

7 Alexandra Stevenson, "More UK Equities for China …?" *Financial Times*, June 3, 2011.

with most Western countries, starting with the United States.[8] Pressure from Washington for the appreciation of the renminbi vis-à-vis the dollar is met with resistance in Beijing, but has resulted in several reassessments, the most recent ones being in July 2005 and April 2012. Between the summer of 2005 – when China decided to stop linking its currency to the dollar – and the spring of 2012, the value of the renminbi appreciated, in real terms, by 32 percent against the dollar.[9] Nevertheless, the idea persisted that the already cheap products exported by China would be made more competitive by an artificially depreciated currency.

The "fair value" of currencies, articulated by commercial policy decisions, is extremely contentious. However, among the criteria available, the ratio of the current account balance to GDP is most widely used by the U.S. administration. This makes it so the benchmark used to define the "equilibrium" exchange rate is a ratio of the current account surplus or deficit to GDP of ±3 or 4 percent. Applying this measure to China, marked by the weight of bilateral trade with the United States, we see that the Chinese ratio fell from 10.6 percent in 2007 to 2.8 percent in 2011. The undervaluation of the renminbi is, therefore, not obvious when one refers to the standard most often employed by the United States. This does not prevent the United States, despite the serious imbalances that characterize its economy, from having a continued "currency war," with the depreciation of the dollar in the foreign exchange market, to impose terms of capitulation on Beijing. One of the effects of this is to devalue China's foreign exchange reserves that are mostly held in dollar-denominated assets.[10]

Internationalization of the renminbi, especially to transform it into a global reserve currency, would require the adoption of very strict conditions: opening of the capital account as well as flexibility of the exchange rate; integrating Chinese financial markets into the capitalist world system; applying macroeconomic policies to fight against inflation and limit public debt aimed at gaining the confidence of the financial markets; and having an economy of critical size to justify this ambition of internationalizing the currency. The first two conditions are essential requirements, but the last two are not, as they have not always been respected by Western countries with currencies used as international reserves.

The critical size has clearly been attained: the economic weight of China ranks second, behind the United States, in the world for GDP, and ranks between

---

8   See the U.S. Congressional Research Service reports, http://fas.org.
9   See the Annual Economic Reports by the Bank for International Settlements, http://bis.org.
10   Martin Wolf, "Why America is Going to Win the Global Currency Battle," *Financial Times*, October 12, 2010.

the United States and the eurozone for exports. The criterion on macro policies also seems to be fulfilled, as the adoption of anti-inflationary measures, public accounts control, and renminbi price control have yielded favorable results in recent years. If inflationary pressure remains a danger, the price stability index is better in China than in other BRICS countries. Public debt is contained at lower levels than in most Western countries themselves. The indices of variability of the national currency also show a less volatile renminbi than the real, the rupee, the ruble, and the rand. Nevertheless, regarding the opening of the capital account and further integration of Chinese financial markets into the global system, it must be recognized that despite the adoption of market mechanisms for monetary policy, easing some regulations related to the capital account and the determination of the renminbi, the Chinese monetary authorities continue to have powerful tools of control. Similarly, the renminbi is used to a limited extent in the over-the-counter derivatives market and is still concentrated on conventional hedging instruments, such as forwards.[11]

The internationalization of the currency would bring benefits to China, starting with a right to seigniorage, which is clear in the case of the United States. Nevertheless, such an orientation would mean an injurious submission to globally dominant high finance and a relative loss of control over monetary policy. How would China succeed in taking advantage of an internationalized renminbi without paying a heavy price, and would it mean renouncing the full exercise of its national sovereignty and a reduction in the autonomy of its development strategy? Today, domestic pressures strongly favor financial market liberalization, but are still dampened by the reassuring, rather credible, official discourses about the control of the reform process. These pressures are particularly troubling compounded with the recommendations made by International Monetary Fund experts and Western leaders that China take the path of neoliberalism. Chinese leaders, generally nuanced and cautious, are perfectly aware of the dangers that an internationalized renminbi implies for the future of market socialism. Let us hope that they will be able to resist neoliberalism. In the meantime, they are strengthening numerous partnerships with countries to the south and the east, particularly within the Shanghai group, and are reopening a new silk route to loosen the grip of aggressive U.S. encirclement.

---

11   Rémy Herrera, "A Marxist Interpretation of the Current Crisis," *World Review of Political Economy* 5, no. 2 (2014): 128–148.

7   Conclusion

The evolving relationships between, on the one hand, the ruling CCP and the social bloc on which it relies – the middle-class beneficiaries of growth, but also private entrepreneurs – and, on the other hand, the masses of workers and peasants, opens up prospects for large-scale confrontation, as well as divergent trajectories and economic structures.[12] One question, however, still remains: How can the ruling elites, whose legitimacy is reinforced by the positive spin-offs generated by growth, succeed in renewing the conditions of China's success story without relying on an internal change in favor of the popular classes – workers and peasants – and on a reorientation of the national project toward social policies? Would the elites' choice of a clear capitalist path – which would lead to a disruption of the country's internal and external balance and a loss of control in the face of growing contradictions – not guarantee the failure of the strategy adopted until now? What will be the geoeconomic stance and geopolitical military perspective of the United States faced with the continued rise of China? The future of China remains largely indeterminate not only because of its own dynamics, but also because the financial oligopolies of the global North seem to increasingly want to enter into conflict, despite their close interdependence. Even in the face of U.S. hegemony, China's current economic system still contains elements of socialism, as well as the potential for its reactivation. Moreover, it also contains possibilities for transforming the global economic and political order into a multipolar world.

---

12   Samir Amin, preface to Rémy Herrera, *Avances revolucionarios en América Latina* (Quito: FEDAEPS, 2012).

Bibliography

Articles and Books Co-authored by Rémy Herrera and Zhiming Long on China

(Publications are classified indifferently of the order of the authors' names and identifiable by their date and index given in square brackets.)

In English

[2016a]: "Building Original Series of Physical Capital Stocks for China's Economy: Methodological Problems, Proposals of Solutions and a New Database (from 1952 to 2015)," *China Economic Review*, vol. 40, n° 9, pp. 33–53, Columbus, OH.

[2017a]: "Capital Accumulation, Profit Rates and Cycles in China's Economy from 1952 to 2014," *Journal of Innovation Economics and Management*, vol. 2, n° 23, p. 226 et s., Brussels.

[2018a]: "The Laws of Capital in the Twenty-First Century in China. Piketty in Beijing," *China Economic Review*, vol. 50, n° 3, pp. 153–174, Columbus, OH.

[2018b]: "Some Considerations on China's Long Run Economic Growth: 1952–2015 – From the Analysis of Factor Contributions to that of the Profit Rate," *Structural Change and Economic Development*, vol. 44, n° 3, pp. 14–22, March, New York.

[2018c]: "On the Nature of the Chinese Economic System," (with Tony Andréani), *Monthly Review*, n° 70, n° 5, pp. 32–43, October, New York.

[2018d]: "The Enigma of China's Economic Growth," *Monthly Review*, vol. 70, n° 7, pp. 52–62, December, New York.

[2020a]: "Explaining Economic Growth in China – New Time Series and Econometric Tests of Various Models," (with Weinan Ding), *Journal of Innovation Economics and Management*, vol. 3, n° 33, pp. 195–228, Brussels.

[2020b]: "U.S.-China Trade War: Real 'Thief' Finally Unmasked?," (with Zhixuan Feng and Bangxi Li), *Monthly Review*, vol. 72, n° 5, pp. 32–43, New York.

[2020c]: "Spurious OLS Estimators of Detrending Method by Adding a Linear Trend in Difference-Stationary Processes – A Mathematical Proof and its Verification by Simulation," *Mathematics*, vol. 8, n° 1931, pp. 2–19, Basel.

[2020d]: "Study on the Evolution of China's Economic Structure Between 1952 and 2014 – An Analysis of the Role of Profit Rate by Impulse Response Functions," *Research in Political Economy*, vol. 36, pp. 95–119, New York and London.

[2020e]: "Turning One's Loss into a Win? The U.S.-China Trade War in Perspective," (with Zhixuan Feng and Bangxi Li), *mimeo*, currently under evaluation by a U.S. peer-review.

[2021a]: "Is China Transforming the World?," (with Tony Andréani), *Monthly Review*, vol. 73, n° 3, pp. 21–30, New York.

In Spanish

[2016b]: "Construcción de series de stocks de capital físico para la economía china. Problemas metodológicos, propuestas de soluciones y nueva base de datos," *Ekotemas – Revista Cubana de Ciencias Económicas*, vol. 2, n° 3, September–December, Havana.

[2017b]: "Elementos de reflexión sobre el crecimiento económico de China en el largo plazo:1952–2014," *Temas de Economía Mundial – Revista del Centro de Investigaciones de la Economía Mundial* (CIEM), época II, n° 32, pp. 63–81, September, Havana.

[2017c]: "Las Leyes del Capital en el Siglo XXI de Piketty en China," *Economía y Desarrollo*, año XLVIII, vol. 158, n° 2, pp. 6–21, July–December, Havana.

[2018e]: "Una Contribución a la explicación del crecimiento económico en China – Nuevas series temporales y pruebas econométricas de varios modelos," *Cuadernos de Economía – Spanish Journal of Economics and Finance*, vol. 41, n° 115, pp. 1–18, January–April, London.

[2018f]: "Acumulación de capital y ciclos en la economía china. Reflexiones basadas en las tasas de ganancias industriales (1952–2014)," *Revista de Economía Critica*, n° 25, pp. 3–25, primer semestre, Madrid.

[2019a]: "Emigma del crecimiento chino," *Politica Internacional – Revista del Instituto Superior de Relaciones Internacionales* (ISRI), n° 1, pp. 26–33, January–March, Havana.

[2020f]: "Sobre la Naturaleza del Sistema económico chino," in M. Bruckman (ed.), collective book, to be published, La Paz.

[2020g]: "Estudio de los cambios en la estructura de la economía china entre 1952 y 2014 – Un Análisis del papel de la tasa de ganancia por funciones de respuestas impulsionales," *mimeo*, currently under evaluation by a Cuban peer-review.

[2020h]: "Guerra comercial China-Estados Unidos: el verdadero 'ladrón' finalmente desenmascarado?," (with Zhixuan Feng and Bangxi Li), *Politica Internacional – Revista del Instituto Superior de Relaciones Internacionales* (ISRI), n° 8, pp. 103–110, October–December, Havana.

[2020i]: *¿Es China capitalista?*, Barcelona: El Viejo Topo.

[2021b]: "¿El que pierde gana? La guerre comercial sino-estadounidense en perspectiva," (with Zhixuan Feng and Bangxi Li), *El Trimestre Económico*, vol. LXXXVIII (4), n° 352, October–December, Mexico.

In French

[2018g]: "Piketty à Pékin. Les Lois du Capital au XXIᵉ siècle à l'épreuve de la Chine," *Revue d'Économie politique*, vol. 128, n° 1, pp. 59–108, January–February, Paris.

[2018h]: "Une Nouvelle Base de données de stocks de capital physique pour la Chine (1952–2016)," *Innovations – Revue d'Économie et de Management de l'Innovation*, n° 57, 2018/3, pp. 189–214, Brussels.

[2018i]: "Sur la Nature du système économique chinois," (with Tony Andréani), *Recherches internationales*, n° 112, pp. 9–23, January–March, Paris.

[2018j]: "L'Énigme de la croissance économique chinoise," *La Pensée*, n° 396, pp. 121–131, October–December, Paris.

[2018k]: "Estimations économétriques de modèles de croissance pour la Chine," *Mondes en développement*, vol. 46, 2018/4, n° 184, pp. 119–136, Brussels.

[2019b]: "Réflexions sur la croissance économique chinoise sur le long terme : 1952–2014. Pour un passage de l'étude de la contribution des facteurs à l'analyse marxiste du taux de profit," *Actuel Marx*, vol. 2019/2, n° 66, pp. 171–192, Paris.

[2019c]: *La Chine est-elle capitaliste ?*, 196 pp., Paris: Éditions Critiques.

[2020j]: "Construction de séries de stocks de capital humain pour la Chine de 1949 à 2014," *Revue économique*, vol. 71, n° 1, pp. 163–193, Paris.

[2020k]: "Guerre commerciale sino-étasunienne : le vrai 'voleur' enfin démasqué ?," (with Zhixuan Feng and Bangxi Li), *Recherches internationales*, n° 119, pp. 29–40, January–March, Paris.

[2020l]: *Dynamique de l'économie chinoise – Croissance, cycles et crises de 1949 à nos jours*, Éditions Critiques, April, Paris.

[2020m]: "Comprendre la croissance économique chinoise," *Revue marocaine de Sciences politiques et sociales*, October issue, www.sciencepo.ma, Casablanca.

[2020n]: "Étude des évolutions de la structure de l'économie chinoise entre 1952 et 2014 : analyse du role du taux de profit avec fonctions de réponses impulsionnelles," *mimeo*, currently under revision in a European peer-review.

[2020o]: "À Qui perd gagne ? La guerre commerciale sino-étasunienne en perspective," (with Zhixuan Feng and Bangxi Li), *mimeo*, currently under revision in a French peer-review.

[2021c]: "À Propos de la croissance économique chinoise," in M. Vivas and J.-P. Page (eds.), *La Chine sans œillères*, pp. 141–148, Paris: Éditions Delga.

[2021d]: "Accumulation du capital et cycles de l'économie chinoise de 1952 à 2014 : deux méthodes d'analyse par les taux de profit industriels," accepted by *Revue française de socio-économie*, to be published.

[2021e]: "La Chine (vue de France), une inconnue ? Sur les contradictions, la dialectique, la morale et le socialisme," (with Tony Andréani), accepted by *Revue de Philosophie économique*, to be published, Paris.

In Portuguese

[2017d]: "Sobre o crescimento econômico chinês no longo período: 1952–2014 – Para uma passagem da análise da contribuição dos fatores até a da taxa de lucro," *Argumentum – Universidade Federal de Espírito Santo*, vol. 9, n° 1, pp. 180–196, January–April, Vitória.

[2018l]: "The Enigma of China's Economic Growth," *Pesquisa e Debate – Revista da Pontifícia Universidade Católica de São Paulo*, vol. 29, n° 1 (53), pp. 8–22, São Paulo.

[2019d]: "Acumulação de capital e os ciclos da economía chinesa de 1952 a 2014 – Dois métodos de análise através das taxas de lucro das indústrias," *Revista da Sociedade de Economia Politica*, n° 52, pp. 155–177, Rio de Janeiro.

[2019e]: *A China é capitalista?*, 152 pp., Página a página, Lisbon.

[2020p]: "Guerra comercial Chinês-EUA: o real 'ladrão' finalmente desmascarado?," (with Zhixuan Feng and Bangxi Li), *Revista Pesquisa & Debate*, n° 2020-2, pp. 3–13.

[2020q]: "Quem perde ganha? Guerre comercial China-Estados Unidos em perspectiva," (with Zhixuan Feng and Bangxi Li), *mimeo*, currently under revision in a peer-review.

In Italian

[2020r]: *La Cina è capitalista?*, 152 pp., Bari: Edizioni Marx Ventuno, August.

[2020s]: "Guerra commerciale USA-Cina: il vero 'ladro' finalmente smascherato?," (with Zhixuan Feng and Bangxi Li), *Materialismo Storico – Rivista di filosofia, storia e scienze umane*, vol. 8, n° 1, pp. 2–14, Rome.

In Greek

[2018m]: "Προβλήρματισμοι σχετικά με τη μακροχρονια οικονομική ανάπτυξη της Κίνας (1952–2014): Για τη μετάβαση από τη μελέτη της συμβολής των συντελεστών στη μαρξιστική ανάλυση του ποσοστούπ κέρδους," *Θέσεις* (Theseis), n° 142, pp. 101–127, January–March, Athens.

[2020t]: "Εμπορικός πόλεμος Κίνας-ΗΠΑ: ο πραγματικός « κλέφτης » τελικά αποκάλυψε?," (with Zhixuan Feng and Bangxi Li), *Τετράδια μαρξιαμού* (Notebooks of Marxism), to be published, Athens.

In Chinese

[2020u]: "论中国经济体系的性质 (lùn zhōngguó jīngjì tǐxì dì xìngzhì)," 政治经济学季刊 (*zhèngzhì jīngjì xué jìkān, Quarterly Review of Political Economics*), (with Tony Andréani), vol. 3, n° 3, pp. 41–52, 政治经济学与当代问题 (zhèngzhì jīngjì xué yǔ dāngdài wèntí), Beijing.

[2021f]: "中美贸易摩擦：真正的 "盗贼" 终于摘下面具？ (zhōng měi màoyì mócā: zhēnzhèng de "dàozéi" zhōngyú zhāi xià miànjù?)," 政治经济学季刊 (*zhèngzhì*

jīngjì xué jìkān, Quarterly Review of Political Economics), (with Zhixuan Feng and Bangxi Li), vol. 3, n° 1, pp. 29–38, 政治经济学与当代问题 (zhèngzhì jīngjì xué yǔ dāngdài wèntí), Beijing.

[2021g]: "'21世纪资本论' 在中国：皮凯蒂的资本定律在中国成立吗？(21 shìjì zīběn lùn' zài zhōngguó: Pí kǎi dì de zīběn dìnglǜ zài zhōngguó chénglì ma)," 政治经济学报 (*zhèngzhì jīngjì xuébào, Review of Political Economics*), vol. 21, n° 4, pp. 94–116, Tsinghua University, Beijing.

[2021h]: "一人所得即为另一人所失吗？对中美贸易摩擦的透视 (yīrén suǒdé jí wèi lìng yīrén suǒ shī ma? Duì zhōng měi màoyì mócā de tòushì)," 政治经济学报 (*zhèngzhì jīngjì xuébào, Review of Political Economics*), (with Zhixuan Feng and Bangxi Li), to be published, Tsinghua University, Beijing.

[2022a]: *Public Budgets and Economic Growth: Modelization and Econometrics – Part 1*, Beijing: China's Social Sciences Academic Press, to be published (in Chinese).

[2022b]: *Public Budgets and Economic Growth: Modelization and Econometrics – Part 2*, Beijing: China's Social Sciences Academic Press, to be published (in Chinese).

Bibliographical References of Interest on the Subject

Aghion P. and P. Howitt (1998), *Endogenous Growth Theory*, Cambridge, MA: The MIT Press.

Aglietta M. and G. Bai (2012), *La Voie chinoise : Capitalisme et empire*, Paris: Odile Jacob.

Aglietta M. and F. Lemoine (2010), "La nouvelle Frontière de l'économie chinoise," *in* CEPII (ed.), *L'Économie mondiale 2011*, pp. 32–49, Paris: La Découverte.

Amin S. and R. Herrera (2000), "Le Sud dans le système mondial en transformation," *Cahier de la Maison des Sciences économiques*, CNRS – Université de Paris 1 Panthéon-Sorbonne, n° 77, Paris.

Amin S. and R. Herrera (2005), "Towards a Revival of the Solidarity Between the Peoples of the South?," *Inter Asia Culture Studies*, vol. 6, n° 4, pp. 546–556, London.

Amin S. (1981), *L'Avenir du maoïsme*, Éditions de Minuit, Paris.

Amin S. (2005), "China, Market Socialism, and U.S. Hegemony," *Fernand Braudel Center Review*, vol. 28, n° 3, pp. 259–279.

Amin S. (ed.) (2008), *Les Luttes paysannes et ouvrières face aux défis du XXIᵉ siècle*, Paris: Les Indes savantes.

Amin S. (2010), "Prefacio," in R. Herrera, *Avances revolucionarios en América Latina*, Quito: Fundación de Estudios, Acción y Participación Social (FEDAEPS).

Amin S. (2013), "China 2013," *Monthly Review*, vol. 64, n° 10.

Andréani T. and R. Herrera (2013a), "Système financier et socialisme de marché 'à la chinoise'," *La Pensée*, n° 373, pp. 65–76 (published in Chinese in *Marxism and Reality* [Beijing], n° 2–2013, pp. 22–28).

Andréani T. and R. Herrera (2013b), "Un Modèle social-démocrate pour la Chine ?," in P. Theuret (ed.), *La Chine et le monde : développement et socialisme*, pp. 208–241, September, Paris: Le Temps des Cerises.

Andréani T. and R. Herrera (2014a), "Quel Modèle économique pour la Chine ? Analyse critique sur *La Voie chinoise* de Michel Aglietta et Guo Bai," *Marché & Organisations*, n° 21, pp. 163–183.

Andréani T. and R. Herrera (2014b), "Financial System and 'Chinese Style Market Socialism'," in R. Herrera, W. Dierckxsens and P. Nakatani (ed.), *Beyond the Systemic Crisis and Capital-Led Chaos – Theoretical and Applied Studies*, pp. 223–235, July, Brussels and Berlin: P.I.E. Peter Lang.

Andréani T. and R. Herrera (2014c), "Quel Modèle économique pour la Chine ? Analyse critique sur *La Voie chinoise*," *Marché & Organisations*, n° 21, pp. 163–183, Paris.

Andréani T. and R. Herrera (2015a), "Which Economic Model for China?," *International Critical Thought – A Journal of the China's Academy of Social Sciences*, vol. 5, n° 1, pp. 111–125, London and Beijing.

Andréani T. and R. Herrera (2015b), "Un Modelo socialdemócrata para China? Comentarios críticos sobre el libro 'La Vía China'," *Revista Herramienta*, web n° 16, February, Buenos Aires.

Andréani T. and R. Herrera (2015c), "Thomas Piketty : 'réguler' le capitalisme ?," *La Pensée*, n° 381, pp. 105–117, Paris.

Andréani T. and R. Herrera (2016), "Que modelo econômico para a China?," *Marx e o Marxismo – Revista do NIEP da Universidade Federal Fluminense*, vol. 4, n° 6, pp. 13–34, Rio de Janeiro.

Andréani T. (2001), *Le Socialisme est (a)venir*, vol. 1, Éditions Syllepse, Paris.

Andréani T. (2004), *Le Socialisme est (a)venir*, vol. 2, Éditions Syllepse, Paris.

Andréani T. (2018), *Le "Modèle" chinois et nous*, Paris: L'Harmattan.

Ansley C.F. and R. Kohn (1985), "Estimation, Filtering, and Smoothing in State Space Models with Incompletely Specified Initial Conditions," *The Annals of Statistics*, vol. 13, n° 4, pp. 1286–1316.

Arrighi G. (2009), *Adam Smith in Beijing – Lineages of the Twenty-First Century*, London: Verso.

Atkinson A.B., T. Piketty and E. Saez (2011), "Top Incomes in the Long Run of History," in Atkinson A.B. and T. Piketty (eds.), *Top Incomes: A Global Perspective*, pp. 664–759, New York: Oxford University Press.

Bai C.-E., C.-T. Hsieh and Y. Qian (2006), "The Return to Capital in China," *Brookings Papers on Economic Activity*, Economic Studies Program, vol. 37, n° 2, pp. 61–102.

Bairoch P. (1999), *Mythes et paradoxes de l'histoire économique*, Paris: La Découverte.

Barro R.J. and J.W. Lee (1993), "International Comparisons of Educational Attainment," *Journal of Monetary Economics*, vol. 32, n° 3, pp. 363–394.

Barro R.J. and J.W. Lee (2018), *Educational Attainment Dataset*, available on Barro-Lee's website: www.barrolee.com.

Baxter M. and R.G. King (1995), "Measuring Business Cycles: Approximate Band-Pass Filters for Economic Time Series," *NBER Working Paper Series*, n° 5022, Cambridge, MA.

Belsley D.A., E. Kuh and R.E. Welsch (1980), *Regression Diagnostics: Identifying Influential Data and Sources of Collinearity*, New York: John Wiley and Sons.

Bettelheim C., J. Charrière and H. Marchisio (1972), *La Construction du socialisme en Chine*, Paris: François Maspéro.

Beveridge S. and C.R. Nelson (1981), "A New Approach to Decomposition of Economic Time Series into Permanent and Transitory Components with Particular Attention to Measurement of the 'Business Cycle'," *Journal of Monetary Economics*, vol. 7, n° 2, pp. 151–174.

Blanchard O.J. (2006), "Discussion of 'The Return to Capital in China' by Chong-En Bai, Chang-Tai Hsieh, Yingyi Qian and Zhenjie Qian," *mimeo*, available on: http://economics.mit.edu/files/679.

Blanchard O.J. and P.A. Diamond (1990), "The Beveridge Curve," *NBER Working Paper*, n° R1405.

Blanchard O.J. and D. Quah (1989), "The Dynamic Effects of Aggregate Demand and Supply Disturbances," *American Economic Review*, vol. 79, n° 4, pp. 655–673.

Box G.E. and D.R. Cox (1964), "An Analysis of Transformations," *Journal of the Royal Statistical Society*, Series B (Methodological), vol. 26, n° 2, pp. 211–252.

Box G.E. and G. Jenkins (1976), *Time Series Analysis: Forecasting and Control*, San Francisco: Holden-Day.

Breusch T.S. (1978), *Testing for Autocorrelation in Dynamic Linear Models*, Australian Economic Papers, n° 17, pp. 334–355.

Breusch T.S. and A. Pagan (1979), "A Simple Test for Heteroscedasticity and Random Coefficient Variation," *Econometrica*, vol. 47, n° 5, pp. 1287–1294.

Cai F. (1999), *Sustainability of China's Economic Growth*, Economic Science Press: Beijing.

Cai F. and Y. Du (2003), "Destructive Effects of Cultural Revolution on Physical and Human Capital," *China Economic Quarterly*, vol. 2, n° 4, pp. 795–806 (in Chinese).

Casanova A. and R. Herrera (2015) (eds.), *Penser les crises*, 150 pp., August, Paris: Le Temps des Cerises.

Centre Tricontinental (2001), *Socialisme et marché : Chine, Vietnam, Cuba*, Pairs: L'Harmattan.

Centre Tricontinental (2005), *Le Miracle chinois vu de l'intérieur – Points de vue d'auteurs chinois*, Paris: Syllepse.

CEIC (various years), *China Premium Database – Macroeconomic, Industry and Financial time-Series Databases for Global Emerging and developed Markets*, Beijing: CEIC Data Company.

Chan K.H., J.C. Hayya and J.K. Ord (1977), "A Note on Trend Removal Methods: The Case of Polynomial Regression Versus Variate Differencing," *Econometrica*, vol. 45, n° 3, pp. 737–744.

Chaumet J.-M. and T. Pouch (2017), *La Chine au risque de la dépendance alimentaire*, Rennes: Presses Universitaires de Rennes.

Chen K., H. Wang, Y. Zheng, G.H. Jefferson and T.G. Rawski (1988), "Productivity Change in Chinese Industry: 1953–1985," *Journal of Comparative Economics*, vol. 12, n° 4, pp. 570–591.

Cheung S.N.-S. (1998), "The Curse of Democracy as an Instrument of Reform in Collapsed Communist Economies," *Contemporary Economic Policy*, vol. 16, n° 2, pp. 247–249.

Chi T. (1949), *Histoire de la Chine et de la civilisation chinoise*, Paris: Payot.

Cholesky A.-L. (1910), "Manuscrit de 1910," *Bulletin de la société des amis de la bibliothèque de l'École polytechnique*, n° 39, December.

Chow G.C. (1993), "Capital Formation and Economic Growth in China," *Quarterly Journal of Economics*, vol. 108, n° 3, pp. 809–842.

Chow G.C. and K.W. Li (2002), "China's Economic Growth: 1952–2010," *Economic Development* and *Cultural Change*, vol. 51, n° 1, pp. 247–256.

Christiano L.J. and T.J. Fitzgerald (1999), "The Band Pass Filter," *NBER Working Paper Series*, n° 7257, Cambridge, MA.

Clark P.K. (1987), "The Cyclical Component of U.S. Economic Activity," *Quarterly Journal of Economics*, vol. 102, n° 4, pp. 797–814.

Cohen D. and Leker L. [2014], "Health and Education: Another Look with the Proper Data," *CEPR Discussion Papers*, n° 9940, Centre for Economic Policy Research.

Cohen D. and Soto M. [2007], "Growth and Human Capital: Good Data, Good Results," *Journal of Economic Growth*, vol. 12, n° 1, pp. 51–76.

Crédit suisse (2012), *China Market Strategy*, February, Geneva.

De Jong P. and J. Penzer (1998), "Diagnostic Shocks in Time Series," *Journal of the American Statistical Association*, vol. 93, n° 442, pp. 796–806.

De la Fuente A. and R. Doménech (2006), "Human Capital in Growth Regressions: How Much Difference Does Data Quality Make?," *Journal of the European Economic Association*, vol. 4, n° 1, pp. 1–36.

De la Fuente A. and R. Doménech (2015), "Educational Attainment in the OECD, 1960–2010. Updated Series and a Comparison with Other Sources," *Economics of Education Review*, n° 48 (Suppl C), pp. 56–74.

DeJong D.N., J.C. Nankervis, N.E. Savin and C.H. Whiteman (1992), "The Power Problems of Unit Root Test in Time Series with Autoregressive Errors," *Journal of Econometrics*, vol. 53, n° 1–3, pp. 323–343.

Delaunay J.-C. (2018), *Les trajectoires chinoises de modernisation et de développement*, Paris: Éditions Delga.

DeLong J.B. and L.H. Summers (1991), "Equipment Investment and Economic Growth," *Quarterly Journal of Economics*, vol. 106, n° 2, pp. 445–502.

Delozier B. and D. Hochraich (2006), "L'Investissement en Chine est-il excessif?," *Économie & Prévision*, vol. 173, n° 2, pp. 155–162.

Dessus S. and R. Herrera (1999), "Capital public et croissance: une étude en économétrie de panel," *Revue économique*, vol. 50, n° 1, pp. 113–126.

Dessus S. and R. Herrera (2000), "Public Capital and Growth: A Panel Data Assessment," *Economic Development and Cultural Change*, vol. 48, n° 2, pp. 407–418.

Dickey D.A. and W.A. Fuller (1979), "Distribution of the Estimators for Autoregressive Time Series with a Unit Root," *Journal of the American Statistical Association*, vol. 74, n° 366, pp. 427–431.

Ding S. and J. Knight (2009), "Can the Augmented Solow Model Explain China's Remarkable Economic Growth? A Cross-Country Panel Data Analysis," *Journal of Comparative Economics*, vol. 37, n° 3, pp. 432–452.

Dufour J.-F. (2012), *Made by China – Les Secrets d'une conquête industrielle*, Paris: Dunod.

Elliott G., T.J. Rothenberg and J.H. Stock (1996), "Efficient Tests for an Autoregressive Unit Root," *Econometrica*, vol. 64, n° 4, pp. 813–836.

Enders W. (1995), *Applied Econometric – Time Series*, New York: John Wiley & Sons.

Engle R.F. and C.W.J. Granger (1987), "Co-integration and Error Correction: Representation, Estimation, and Testing," *Econometrica*, vol. 55, n° 2, pp. 251–276.

Evans G.W. (1989), "Output and Unemployment Dynamics in the United States: 1950–1985," *Journal of Applied Econometrics*, vol. 4, n° 3, pp. 213–237.

Feenstra R., R. Inklaar and M.P. Timmer (2015), "The New Generation of the Penn World Table," *American Economic Review*, vol. 105, n° 10, pp. 3150–3182.

Feuerwerker A. (1977), *Economic Trends in the Republic of China: 1912–1949*, Ann Arbor: Michigan Papers in Chinese Studies.

Financial Times (2011), "More UK equities for China?," June 3.

Findley D.F., B.C. Monsell, W.R. Bell, M.C. Otto and B.-C. Chen (1998), "New Capabilities and Methods of the X-12-ARIMA Seasonal-Adjustment Program," *Journal of Business and Economic Statistics*, vol. 16, n° 2, pp. 27–152.

Fine B. (2000), "Endogenous Growth Theory: A Critical Assessment," *Cambridge Journal of Economics*, vol. 24, n° 2, pp. 245–265.

Florens J.-P. and M. Mouchart (1985), "Conditioning in Dynamic Models," *Journal of Time-Series Analysis*, vol. 53, n° 1, pp. 15–35.

Fraumeni B. (1997), "The Measurement of Depreciation in the U.S. National Income and Product Accounts," available on: https://www.bea.gov/scb/account_articles/national/0797fr/maintext.htm.

Gazier, B. and R. Herrera (2003), "Active Labor Market Policies in the Republic of Korea and Europe," in K. Marshall and O. Butzbach (eds.), *New Social Policy Agendas for Europe and Asia*, pp. 405–417, The World Bank, Washington, DC.

Ge J. (2012), "The Estimation of China's Infrastructure Capital Stock," *Economic Research Journal*, vol. 47, n° 4, pp. 4–14 (in Chinese).

Giannini C. (1992), *Topics in Structural VAR Econometrics*, Berlin: Springer.

Godfrey L.G. (1978a), "Testing Against General Autoregressive and Moving Average Error Models when the Regressors Include Lagged Dependent Variables," *Econometrics*, n° 46, pp. 1293–1301.

Godfrey L.G. (1978b), "Testing for Multiplicative Heteroskedasticity," *Journal of Econometrics*, vol. 8, n° 2, pp. 227–236.

Goldsmith R.W. (1951), "A Perpetual Inventory of National Wealth," Conference on Research in Income and Wealth, *Studies in Income and Wealth*, National Bureau of Economic Research, vol. 14, pp. 5–73.

Government of India (various years), *First Five-Year Plan (1951–56)*, India's Five Year Plans Complete Documents, New Delhi: Planning Commission.

Gramlich E.M. (1944), "Infrastructures Investment: A Review Essay," *Journal of Economic Literature*, vol. 32, n° 9, pp. 1176–1196.

Granger C.W.J. (1969), "Investigating Causal Relations by Econometric Models and Cross Spectral Methods," *Econometrica*, vol. 37, n° 3, pp. 424–438.

Granger C.W.J. and P. Newbold (1974), "Spurious Regressions in Econometrics," *Journal of Econometrics*, vol. 2, n° 2, pp. 111–120.

Green T. (1999), *Central Bank Gold Reserves: An Historical Perspective Since 1845*, London: World Gold Council.

Gu S. and B.-Å. Lundvall (2006), "China's Innovation System and the Move Towards Harmonious Growth and Endogenous Innovation," *Innovation, Management, Policy and Practice*, vol. 8, n° 1–2, pp. 1–26.

Guo Q. and J. Jia (2005), "Estimating Total Factor Productivity in China," *Economic Research Journal*, n° 6, pp. 51–60.

Hamermesh D.S. (1986), "The Demand for Labor in the Long Run," in O. Ashenfelter and R. Layard (eds.), *Handbook of Labor Economics*, pp. 429–471, Amsterdam: Elsevier.

Hamilton J.D. (1994), *Time Series Analysis*, Princeton: Princeton University Press.

Hao F. (2006), "Estimates of Provincial Capital Stock in China: 1952–2004," *Journal of Data Analysis*, vol. 6, n° 1, pp. 6–13.

Hao F., H.H. Hao and H.-Q. Zhao (2009), "Research on Benchmark Capital Stock of China," *Statistics & Information Forum*, vol. 2, pp. 7–13.

Harberger A. (1978), "Perspectives on Capital and Technology in Less-Developed Countries," in Artis L.J. and A.R. Nobay (eds.), *Contemporary Economic Analysis*, London: Croom Helm.

Harvey A.C. (1989), *Forecasting, Structural Time Series Models and the Kalman Filter*, Cambridge: Cambridge University Press.

Harvey D. (2005), *A Brief History of Neoliberalism*, New York: Oxford University Press.

He F., R. Chen and L. He (2003), "The Estimation and Correlation Analysis on Our Country's Cumulative Amount of Capital," *Economist*, n° 5, pp. 29–35 (in Chinese).

He J.H. (1992), "Estimation of Assets in China," *Journal of Quantitative and Technical Economics*, n° 8, pp. 24–27 (in Chinese).

Herrera R. and K.-C. Lau (2015), *The Struggle for Food Sovereignty – Alternative Development and the Renewal of Peasant Societies Today*, July, London: Pluto Press.

Herrera R. and K.-C. Lau (2018), "The Convergence of Peasant Struggles Worldwide," *Economic and Political Weekly*, vol. LIII, n° 11, pp. 42–49.

Herrera R. and K.-C. Lau (2020), "Agrarian Labour and the Peasantry in the Global South," *Palgrave's Encyclopedia of Imperialism and Antiimperialism*, New York: Palgrave Macmillan.

Herrera R. and P. Nakatani (2007), "What Rich Countries Owe Poor Ones," *Monthly Review*, vol. 59, n° 2, pp. 31–36, New York.

Herrera R. and P. Nakatani (2010), "Keynes (et Marx), la monnaie et la crise," *La Pensée*, n° 364, pp. 57–68.

Herrera R. and P. Nakatani (2013), "Keynes et la crise. Hier et aujourd'hui," *Actuel Marx*, n° 53, pp. 153–168.

Herrera R. (1997), "Productivités et externalités des dépenses publiques : une étude économétrique sur séries temporelles," *Économie & Prévision*, vol. 5, n° 131, pp. 145–153.

Herrera R. (1998a), "Dépenses publiques d'éducation et capital humain dans un modèle convexe de croissance endogène," *Revue économique*, vol. 49, n° 3, pp. 831–844.

Herrera R. (1998b), "Dépenses militaires : quels effets sur les finances publiques et la croissance économique ?," *Revue d'Économie politique*, vol. 108, n° 4, pp. 503–530.

Herrera R. (2000a), "Pour une Critique de la nouvelle théorie de la croissance néo-classique," *Cahier de la Maison des Sciences économiques*, University of Paris 1 Panthéon-Sorbonne, n° 75, Paris.

Herrera R. (2000b), "Por uma crítica da nova teoria neoclássica do crescimento," *Revista da Sociedade Brasileira de Economia Política*, n° 7, pp. 55–73.

Herrera R. (2000c), "Critique de l'économie 'apolitique'," *L'Homme et la Société*, n° 135, pp. 87–104.

Herrera R. (2001), "Y a-t-il une 'Pensée unique' en économie politique ?," *La Pensée*, n° 325, pp. 99–111.

Herrera R. (2003), "L'État contre le service public ?," *Actuel Marx*, n° 34, pp. 147–160.

Herrera R. (2004), "Good Governance *vs.* Good Government?," *Written Statement* du Centre Europe Tiers-Monde (CETIM, Center Europe – Third World), Human Rights Commission, United Nations Organisation, E/CN.4/2004/NGO/124, 60th session, July, Geneva.

Herrera R. (2006a), "The Hidden Face of Endogenous Growth Theory," *Review of Radical Political Economics*, vol. 38, n° 2, pp. 243–257.

Herrera R. (2006b), "The 'New' Development Economics: A Neoliberal *Con?*," *Monthly Review*, vol. 58, n° 1, pp. 38–50.

Herrera R. (2010a), *Dépenses publiques et croissance économique – Pour sortir de la science(-fiction) néo-classique*, 275 pp., January, Paris: L'Harmattan.

Herrera R. (2010b), *Un Autre Capitalisme n'est pas possible*, 202 pp., February, Paris: Syllepse.

Herrera R. (2010c), *Estado y crecimiento*, 185 pp., September, Madrid: Ediciones Maia.

Herrera R. (2011), "A Critique of Mainstream Growth Theory: Ways out of the Neoclassical Science(-Fiction) and Towards Marxism," *Research in Political Economy*, vol. 27, n° 1, pp. 3–64.

Herrera R. (2012), *Gastos públicos y crecimiento económico*, 375 pp., December, Caracas: Ediciones del Banco Central de Venezuela.

Herrera R. (2013a), "Neoclassical Economic Fiction and Neoliberal Political Reality," *International Critical Thought*, vol. 3, n° 1, pp. 98–107, London and Beijing.

Herrera R. (2013b), "Le Yuan et ses mystères," *Afrique Asie*, pp. 81–82, March, Paris.

Herrera R. (2014a), "A Marxist Interpretation of the Current Crisis," *World Review of Political Economy*, vol. 5, n° 2, pp. 128–148, Shanghai.

Herrera R. (2014b), "Some Problems (and Paradoxes) Related to the Internationalization of China's Economy," *in* R. Herrera, W. Dierckxsens and P. Nakatani (eds.), *Beyond the Systemic Crisis and Capital-Led Chaos*, pp. 237–251, July, Brussels and Berlin: P.I.E. Peter Lang.

Herrera R. (2015), "L'Économie chinoise est-elle 'en crise' ?," *Afrique Asie*, Afriam, pp. 16–20, February, Paris.

Herrera R. (2021a), "Guerre(s) et crise(s) globales : sur les relations systémiques," *Marché et organisation*, vol. 2, n° 41, pp. 139–155, Paris.

Herrera R. (2021b) (ed.), *Imperialism and Transitions to Socialism*, September, Bingley (U.K.): Emerald.

Herrera R. (2021c), *La Monnaie : du pouvoir de la finance à la souveraineté des peuples*, Geneva: Éditions du Centre Europe – Tiers-Monde (CETIM), to be published.

Hodrick R. and E. Prescott (1981), "Postwar U.S. Business Cycles: An Empirical Investigation," *Carnegie Mellon University Discussion Paper*, n° 451.

Holz C.A. (2006), "New Capital Estimates for China," *China Economic Review*, vol. 17, n° 2, pp. 142–185.

Hosking J. [1981], "Fractional differencing," *Biometrika*, vol. 68, n° 1, pp. 165–176.

Hu Z.F. and M.S. Khan (1997), "Why is China Growing so Fast?," *International Monetary Fund Staff Papers*, vol. 44, n° 1, pp. 103–131.

Huang Y., R.E. Ren and X. Liu (2002), "Capital Stock Estimates in Chinese Manufacturing by Perpetual Inventory Approach," *China Economic Quarterly*, vol. 1, n° 2, pp. 377–396 (in Chinese).

Hulten C.R. and F.C. Wycoff (1995), "Issues in the Measurement of Economic Depreciation," *Economic Inquiry*, vol. 24, n° 1, pp. 31–40.

Inklaar R. and M.P. Timmer (2013), "Capital, Labor and TFP in PWT8.0," Working Paper, Groningen Growth and Development Centre, University of Groningen, July. Available on: https://www.rug.nl/ggdc/productivity/pwt/related-research-papers/capital _labor_and_tfp_in_pwt8o.pdf.

International Monetary Fund (various years), *International Financial Statistics*, Washington, DC. I.M.F.

International Crisis Observatory (2019), *Le Capitalisme face à son déclin* (co-authors: W. Dierckxsens, A. Piqueras, R. Herrera, W. Formento and P. Nakatani), 167 pp., April, Paris: Éditions Critiques.

Jarque C.M. and A.K. Bera (1987), "A test for Normality of Observations and Regression Residuals," *International Statistical Review*, n° 55, pp. 163–172.

Jefferson G.H. (1990), "China's Iron and Steel Industry: Sources of Enterprise Efficiency and the Impact of Reform," *Journal of Development Economics*, vol. 33, n° 2, pp. 329–355.

Jefferson G.H., T.G. Rawski and Y. Zhang (2008), "Productivity Growth and Convergence Across China's Industrial Economy," *Journal of Chinese Economic and Business Studies*, vol. 6, n° 2, pp. 121–140.

Jefferson G.H., T.G. Rawski and Y. Zheng (1996), "Chinese Industrial Productivity: Trends, Measurement Issues, and Recent Developments," *Journal of Comparative Economics*, vol. 23, n° 2, pp. 146–180.

Johansen S. (1988), "Statistical Analysis of Cointegration Vectors," *Journal of Economic Dynamics and Control*, vol. 12, n° 2, pp. 231–254.

Jorgenson D. (1996), "Empirical Studies of Depreciation," *Economic Inquiry*, vol. 34, n° 1, pp. 24–42.

Jorgenson D. and B. Fraumeni (1989), "Investment in Education," *Educational Researcher*, vol. 18, n° 4, pp. 35–44.

Kadiyala K.R. and S. Karlsson (1997), "Numerical Methods for Estimation and Inference in Bayesian VAR-Models," *Journal of Applied Econometrics*, vol. 12, n° 2, pp. 99–132.

Kendrick J., Y. Lethem and J. Rowley (1976), "The Formation and Stocks of Total Capital," NBER, Columbia University Press, 256 pp.

Koop G. and D. Korobilis (2009), "Bayesian Multivariate Time Series Methods for Empirical Macroeconomics," *Rimini Centre for Economic Analysis Working Paper*, n° 47, September.

Kroeber A. (2016), *China's Economy: What Everyone Needs to Know*, New York: Oxford University Press.

Krusell P. and A. Smith (2015), "Is Piketty's 'Second Law of Capitalism' Fundamental?," *Journal of Political Economy*, vol. 123, n° 4, pp. 725–748.

Kwiatkowski D., P.C.B. Phillips, P. Schmidt and Y. Shin (1992), "Testing the Null Hypothesis of Stationarity Against the Alternative of a Unit Root," *Journal of Econometrics*, vol. 54, n° 1–3, pp. 159–178.

Lardic S. and V. Mignon (2002), *Économétrie des séries temporelles macroéconomiques et financières*, Paris: Economica.

Lau K.-C. and P. Huang (eds.) (2003), *China Reflected*, Hong Kong: Asian Regional Exchange for New Alternatives (ARENA) Editions.

Li Z.G. and G.X. Tang (2003), "The Capital Formation and the Capital Adjustment Model During the China's Transition," *Economic Research Journal*, n° 2, pp. 12–21 (in Chinese).

Lin C. (2006), *The Transformation of Chinese Socialism*, Durham: Duke University Press.

Lin J.Y., F. Cai and Z. Li (2001), *Le Miracle chinois, Stratégie de développement et réforme économique*, Paris: Economica.

Litterman R. (1986), "Forecasting with Bayesian Vector Autoregressions-Five Years of Experience," *Journal of Business and Economic Statistics*, vol. 4, n° 1, pp. 25–38.

Liu T.-C. and K.-C. Yeh (1965), *Economy of the Chinese Mainland: National Income and Economic Development: 1933–1959*, Princeton, NJ: Princeton University Press.

Liu T.-C. and K.-C. Yeh (1973), "Chinese and Other Asian Economies: A Quantitative Evaluation," *American Economic Review*, vol. 63, n° 2, pp. 215–233.

Long Z. (2013a), *Real equilibrium exchange rate of the Chinese currency – RMB and BEER approach*, Master 2 ("mémoire majeur") in International Economics, Macroeconomic Policies and Conjoncture, University of Paris Ouest Nanterre La Défense, Nanterre.

Long Z. (2013b), *Dynamic Factor Models: Application to Macroeconomic Short-Run Forecasting for GDP and inflation of China*, Master 2 ("mémoire mineur") in International Economics, Macroeconomic Policies and Conjoncture, University of Paris Ouest Nanterre La Défense, Nanterre.

Long Z. (2017), *Growth, Institutions, and "Socialist Transition with Chinese Characteristics"*, Ph.D. dissertation in Economics, University of Paris 1 Panthéon-Sorbonne, Paris.

Lütkepohl H. (1990), "Asymptotic Distributions of Impulse Response Functions and Forecast Error Variance Decompositions of Vector Autoregressive Models," *Review of Economics and Statistics*, vol. 72, n° 1, pp. 116–125.

Lütkepohl H. (1991), *Introduction to Multiple Time Series Analysis*, Berlin: Springer.

Lütkepohl H. and M. Krätzig (eds.) (2004), *Applied Time Series Econometrics*, Cambridge: Cambridge University Press.

MacKinnon, J.G. (1996), "Numerical Distribution Functions for Unit Root and Cointegration Tests," *Journal of Applied Econometrics*, vol. 11, n° 6, pp. 601–618.

Maddison A. (1994), *Standardised Estimates of Fixed Capital Stock*, Institute of Economic Research Memorandum n° 570, University of Groningen, available on: www.ggdc.net/publications/memorandum/gd9.pdf.

Maddison A. (1995), *Monitoring the World Economy: 1820–1992*, Development Centre Studies, Paris: Organisation for Economic Cooperation and Development.

Maddison A. (1997), *China Statistical Yearbook on Investment in Fixed Assets: 1950–1995*, Beijing: NBS.

Maddison A. (1998), *L'Économie chinoise – Une perspective historique*, Centre de Développement de l'OCDE, Paris.

Maddison A. (2006), "La Chine dans l'économie mondiale de 1300 à 2030," *Outre-Terre*, vol. 2, n° 15, p. 27.

Maddison A. (2007), *Data of Gross Domestic Product of China (1952–2004)*, Beijing: NBS.

Mao J. (2005), "Comparison and Refinement on the Studies of Estimating Capital Stock," *Henan Social Sciences*, n° 2, pp. 75–78 (in Chinese).

Marer P., J. Arvay, J. O'Connor, M. Schrenk and D. Swanson (eds.) (1992), *Historically Planned Economies – A Guide to the Data*, Washington, DC: The World Bank Publication.

Ministry of Finance of the P.R. of China (Ministry of Finance) (1999), *China Finance Yearbook 1999*, Beijing: Financial Magazine of China.

Mishkin F. (2010), *The Economics of Money Banking and Financial Markets*, Upper Saddle River: Pearson.

Morley J. (2002), "A State-Space Approach to Calculating the Beveridge-Nelson Decomposition," *Economics Letters*, vol. 75, n° 1, pp. 123–127.

Nakatani P. and R. Herrera (2008), "La Crise financière : racines, mécanismes, effets," *La Pensée*, n° 353, pp. 109–116.

Nakatani P. and R. Herrera (2009), "Critique des politiques anticrise orthodoxes," *La Pensée*, n° 360, pp. 31–42.

National Bureau of Statistics of China (NBS) (1984), *China Education Statistical Yearbook 1949–1981*, Beijing: China Publishing House.

National Bureau of Statistics of China (1988), *China Population Statistics Collection 1949–1985*, Department of Population Statistics and Department of Ministry of Public Security, Beijing: Chinese Financial & Economic Publishing House.

National Bureau of Statistics of China (1997), *China Statistical Yearbook on Investment in Fixed Assets: 1950–1995*, Beijing: NBS.

National Bureau of Statistics of China (2002), *China Statistical Yearbook on Investment in Fixed Assets: 1950–1995*, Beijing: NBS.

National Bureau of Statistics of China (2007), *Data of Gross Domestic Product of China (1952–2004)*, Beijing: NBS.

National Bureau of Statistics of China (various years), *China Statistical Yearbook*, Beijing: NBS.

National Bureau of Statistics of China (various years), *China Population / Population and Employment Statistics Yearbook*, Department of Population and Employement Statistics, Beijing: China Statistics Publisher.

Nehru V. and A. Dhareshwar (1993), "A New Database on Physical Capital Stock: Sources, Methodologies and Results," *Revista de Análisis Económico*, vol. 8, n° 1, pp. 37–59.

Nelson C.R. and H. Kang (1981), "Spurious Periodicity in Inappropriately Detrended Time Series," *Econometrica*, vol. 49, n° 3, pp. 741–751.

Nelson C.R. and C.I. Plosser (1982), "Trends and Random Walks in Macroeconomic Time Series: Some Evidence and Implication," *Journal of Monetary Economics*, vol. 10, n° 2, pp. 139–162.

Newey W.K. and K.D. West (1994), "Automatic Lag Selection in Covariance Matrix Estimation," *Review of Economic Studies*, vol. 61, n° 4, pp. 631–653.

Ng S. and P. Perron (1995), "Unit Root Tests in ARMA Models with Data-Dependent Methods for the Selection of Trucation Lag," *Journal of the American Statistical Association*, vol. 90, n° 429, pp. 268–281.

Ng S. and P. Perron (2001), "Lag Length Selection and the Construction of Unit Root Tests with Good Size and Power Lag," *Econometrica*, vol. 69, n° 6, pp. 1519–1554.

Organisation for Economic Cooperation and Development (1993), *Methods Used by OECD Countries to Measure Stocks of Fixed Capital, National Accounts: Sources and Methods*, Paris: OECD.

Organisation for Economic Cooperation and Development (2009), *Measuring Capital OECD Manual – Measurement of Capital Stocks, Consumption of Fixed Capital and Capital Services*, Statistics, Organisation for Economic Cooperation and Development, Paris (2nd édition on: https://www.oecd.org/std/productivity-stats/43734711.pdf).

Organisation for Economic Cooperation and Development (2015), *The Measurement of Scientific, Technological and Innovation Activities – Frascati Manual: Guidelines for Collecting and Reporting Data on Research and Experimental Development*, Paris: Organisation for Economic Cooperation and Development.

Panitch L. and S. Gindin (2013), "The Integration of China into Global Capitalism," *International Critical Thought*, vol. 3, n° 2, pp. 146–158.

Penn World Tables (PWT) (various years), https://ptw-sas.upenn.edu, for version 8.1: www.rug.nl/research/ggdc/data/ptw.

People's Bank of China (1992), *China Financial Statistics 1952–1991*, Beijing: Research and Statistics Department.

Perkins D.H. (1988), "Reforming China's Economic System," *Journal of Economic Literature*, vol. 26, n° 2, pp. 601–645.

Perkins D.H. and T.G. Rawski (2008), "Forecasting China's Economic Growth to 2025," *in* Brandt L. and T.G. Rawski (eds.), *China's Great Economic Transformation*, pp. 829–886, Cambridge: Cambridge University Press.

Pesaran M. and Y. Shin (1998), "Generalized Impulse Response Analysis in Linear Multivariate Models," *Economics Letters*, vol. 58, n° 1, pp. 17–29.

Phillips P.C.B. and P. Perron (1988), "Testing for a Unit Root in Time Series Regression," *Biomètrika*, vol. 75, n° 2, pp. 335–346.

Phillips, P.C.B. and S. Ouliaris (1990), "Asymptotic Properties of Residual Based Tests for Cointegration," *Econometrica*, vol. 85, n° 1, pp. 165–193.

Piketty T. (1995), "On the Long-Run Evolution of Inheritance: France 1820–2050," *Quarterly Journal of Economics*, vol. CXXVI, n° 3, pp. 1071–1131.

Piketty T. (2003), "Income Inequality in France, 1901–1998," *Journal of Political Economy*, vol. 111, n° 5, pp. 1004–1042.

Piketty T. (2013), *Le Capital au XXIe siècle*, Paris: Éditions du Seuil.

Piketty T., Y. Li and G. Zucman (2017), "Capital Accumulation, Private Property and Rising Inequality in China, 1978–2015," NBER Working Paper n° 23368, avril.

Piketty T. and N. Qian (2011), "Income Inequality and Progressive Income Taxation in China and India, 1986–2015," *in* Atkinson A.B. and T. Piketty (eds.), *Top Incomes: A Global Perspective*, pp. 40–75, New York: Oxford University Press.

Piketty T. and E. Saez (2003), "Income Inequality in the United States, 1913–1998," *Quarterly Journal of Economics*, vol. 118, n° 1, pp. 1–39.

Piketty T. and G. Zucman (2014), "Capital is Back: Wealth-Income Ratios in Rich Countries 1700–2010," *Quarterly Journal of Economics*, vol. 129, n° 3, pp. 1255–1310.

Prasad E. and L. Ye (2012), "The Renminbi's Role in the Global Monetary System," *Global Economy and Development at Brookings*, February.

Psacharopoulos G. (1994), "Returns to Investment in Education," *World Development*, vol. 22, n° 2, pp. 1325–1343.

Quah D. (1992), "The Relative Importance of Permanent and Transitory Components: Identifications and Some Theoretical Bounds," *Econometrica*, vol. 60, n° 1, pp. 107–118.

Ramey V.A. and K.D. West (1999), "Inventories," chapter 13, *Handbook of Macroeconomics*, vol. 1, part B, pp. 863–923, Amsterdam: Elsevier.

Ravn M.O. and H. Uhlig (2002), "On Adjusting the Hodrick-Prescott Filter for the Frequency of Observations," *Review of Economics and Statistics*, vol. 84, n° 2, pp. 371–376.

Runkle D.E. (1987), "Vector Autoregressions and Reality," *Journal of Business & Economic Statistics*, vol. 5, n° 4, pp. 437–442.

Salvadori N. (ed.) (2003), *The Theory of Economic Growth: A Classical Perspective*, Cheltenham: Edward Elgar.

Schwert G.W. (1989), "Tests for Unit Roots: A Monte Carlo Investigation," *Journal of Business & Economic Statistics*, vol. 7, n° 2, pp. 147–159.

Shan H. (2008), "Re-estimating the Aggregate Capital Stock K of China: 1952–2006," *Journal of Quantitative and Technical Economics*, n° 10, pp. 17–31 (in Chinese).

Shanghai Bureau of Statistics (various years), *Shanghai Statistical Database Yearbook*, Wang Zhixiong, Shanghai: China Statistics Press.

Sims C.A. (1980), "Macroeconomics and Reality," *Econometrica*, vol. 48, n° 1, pp. 1–48.

Sims C.A. (1981), "An Autoregressive Index Model for the US 1948–1975," *in* Kmenta J. and J.B. Ramsey (eds.), *Large-Scale Macro-Econometric Models*, pp. 283–327, Amsterdam: Elsevier.

Sims C.A. (1986), "Are Forecasting Models Usable for Policy Analysis," *Federal Reserve Bank of Mineapolis Quarterly Review*, n° 10, pp. 2–16.

Sims C.A. and T. Zha (1998), "Bayesian Methods for Dynamic Multivariate Models," *International Economic Review*, vol. 39, n° 4, pp. 949–968.

Sit T., E. Wong, K.-C. Lau and T. Wen (2021), "Land Revolution and Local Governance: Socialist Transformation in China," in R. Herrera (ed.), *Imperialism and Transitions to Socialism*, pp. 123–140, Bingley, U.K.: Emerald.

Solow R.M. (1988), "Growth Theory and After," *American Economic Review*, vol. 78, n° 3, pp. 307–317.

Song H., Z. Liu and P. Jiang (2001), "Analyzing the Determinants of China's Aggregate Investment in the Reform Period," *China Economic Review*, vol. 12, n° 2, pp. 227–242.

South-South Forum (2011), "China's Real Experience: Course of Industrialization; Eight Crises with Subsequent Soft Landing in 60 Years," *Mimeograph*, Lingnan University, Hong Kong.

Stock J.H. (1987), "Asymptotic Properties of Least Squares Estimators of Cointegrating Vectors," *Econometrica*, vol. 55, n° 5, pp. 1035–1056.

Su Y. and X. Xu (2002), "The Specification of China's Economic Growth Model: 1952–1998," *Economic Research Journal*, n° 11, pp. 3–11 (in Chinese).

Sun L.L. and R.E. Ren (2005), "Capital Input Measurement: a Survey," *China Economic Quarterly*, vol. 4, n° 4, p. 823 (in Chinese).

The Economist (2010), "The Dangers of a Rising China," December 4.

Törnqvist, L. (1981), *Collected scientific papers of Leo Törnqvist*, Research Institute of the Finnish Economy. Series A7, Helsinki.

UBS (2012), *China Economics – Outlook 2011*, UBS Investment Research, Hong Kong.

Wallerstein I. (2011), *The Modern World-System*, San Francisco: The University of California Press.

Wang J. (2002), "China's Economic Growth and Total Factor Productivity and Human Capital Needs," *Chinese Journal of Population Science*, 2, pp. 13–19.

Wang L. and A. Szirmai (2012), "Capital Inputs in the Chinese Economy: Estimates for the Total Economy, Industry and Manufacturing," *China Economic Review*, vol. 23, n° 1, pp. 81–104.

Wang X. and G. Fan (eds.) (2000), *The Sustainability of China's Economic Growth*, Beijing: Economic Sciences Press.

Wang Y.X. and Y. Wu (2003), "Preliminary Estimates of Fixed Capital Stock in China's State Economy," *Statistical Research*, n° 5, pp. 40–45 (in Chinese).

Ward M. (1976), *The Measurement of Capital – The Methodology of Capital Stock Estimates in OECD Countries*, Paris: Organisation for Economic Cooperation and Development.

Watson M.W. (1986), "Univariate Detrending Methods and Stochastic Trends," *Journal of Monetary Economics*, vol. 18, n° 1, pp. 49–75.

Watson M.W. (1994), "Vector Autoregression and Cointegration," *in* Engle R. and D. McFadden (eds.), *Handbook of Econometrics*, vol. IV, chap. 47, pp. 2843–2915, New York: Elsevier.

Weisskopf T.E. (1979), "Marxian Crisis Theory and the Rate of Profit in the Postwar U.S. Economy," *Cambridge Journal of Economics*, vol. 3, n° 4, pp. 341–378.

Wen T. (2001), "Centenary Reflections on the 'Three Dimensional Problem' of Rural China," *Inter-Asia Cultural Studies*, vol. 2, n° 2, pp. 287–295.

Wen T. (2009), *The 'San Nong' Problem and Institutional Transition*, Beijing: China Economic Press.

Wen T. (2021), *Ten Crises: The Political Economy of China's Development (1949–2020)*, New York: Palgrave Macmillan.

Wolff M. (2010), Tribune, *Financial Times*, October 12.

Wong E. and T. Sit (2012), "Rethinking 'Rural China', Unthinking Modernization," *in* R. Herrera and K.-C. Lau (eds.), *The Struggle for Food Sovereignty*, pp. 83–108, London: Pluto Press.

World Bank (The) (1993), *The East Asian Miracle*, New York: Oxford University Press.

World Bank (The) (1995), *India Country Economic Memorandum – Recent Economic Developments: Achievements and Challenges*, Washington, DC: The World Bank.

World Bank (The) (various years), *World Development Indicators*, Washington, DC: The World Bank.

Wu F.W. (1999), "Estimates of China's Agricultural Capital Stock," *Journal of Agrotechnical*, n° 6, pp. 34–38 (in Chinese).

Wu H.X. (1993), "The 'Real' Chinese Gross Domestic Product for the Pre-Reform Period: 1952–1977," *Review of Income and Wealth*, vol. 39, n° 1, pp. 63–87.

Wu H.X. *et al.* (2014), "China's Growth and Productivity Performance Debate Revisited – Accounting for China's Sources of Growth in 1949–2012," The Conference Board Economics Program Working Paper Series, n° 14–01, New York.

Xu Xianchun (1999), "Evaluation and Adjustments of China's Official GDP by the World Bank and Prof. Maddison," *Journal of Econometric Study of Northeast Asia*, vol. 1, n° 2, pp. 52–58.

Xu Xianchun (2004), "China's Gross Domestic Product Estimation," *China Economic Review*, vol. 15, n° 3, pp. 302–322.

Xu Xiang and A.S. Han (2018), "Will China Collapse: A Review, Assessment and Outlook," *Hoover Institution*, Economics Working Paper n° 18104, Stanford, CA.

Xue J. and W. Zheng (2007), "A Research on the Capital Calculation of 17 Industries of China," *Statistical Research*, vol. 7, pp. 10–14.

Ye Z.Y. (2010), "The Estimation of China's Provincial Capital Stock," *Statistical Research*, n° 12, pp. 65–71 (in Chinese).

Young A. (2000), "Gold into Base Metals: Productivity Growth in the People's Republic of China During the Reform Period," *National Bureau of Economic Research Working Papers*, n° 7856, Cambridge, MA.

Zhang Jun and Y. Zhang (2003), "Recalculating the Capital of China and a Review of Li and Tang's Article," *Economic Research Journal*, n° 7, pp. 35–43 (in Chinese).

Zhang Jun, S. Shi and S. Chen (2003), "Industrial Reform and Efficiency Change in China: Method, Data, Literatures and Present Results," *Economics Quarterly*, vol. 2, n° 1, pp. 1–38.

Zhang Jun, Wu G. and Zhang Ji (2004), "The Estimation of China's provincial capital stock: 1952–2000," *Economic Research Journal*, n° 10, pp. 35–44 (in Chinese).

Zhang Junk. (1991), "Systemic Analysis of Economic Efficiency During the 5th Five Year Plan," *Journal of Economic Research*, n° 4, pp. 8–17 (in Chinese).

Zhang L. (2009), "China's Policy Responses to the Global Financial Crisis: Efficacy and Risks," *German Development Institute*, September, Berlin.

Zheng J., A. Bigsten and A. Hu (2009), "Can China's growth be sustained? A Productivity Perspective," *World Development*, vol. 37, n° 4, pp. 874–888.

Index

Note: Page numbers followed by a *t* refer to tables.

www.ingramcontent.com/pod-product-compliance
Lightning Source LLC
Chambersburg PA
CBHW062129040426
42335CB00039B/1857